Quantum-Inspired Neural Networks

Future Perspectives and Challenges

Editors

Moolchand Sharma
Assistant Professor, Department of Computer Science & Engineering, Maharaja Agrasen Institute of Technology
Delhi, India

Nebojsa Bacanin
Vice-Dean, Graduate School of Computer Science and Faculty of Informatics and Computing
Singidunum University, Belgrade, Serbia

Tarik Ahmed Rashid
Professor, Department of Computer Science and Engineering
AIIC, University of Kurdistan Hewler, Erbil, Iraq

CRC Press
Taylor & Francis Group
Boca Raton London New York

CRC Press is an imprint of the
Taylor & Francis Group, an **informa** business
A SCIENCE PUBLISHERS BOOK

First edition published 2027
by CRC Press
2385 NW Executive Center Drive, Suite 320, Boca Raton FL 33431

and by CRC Press
4 Park Square, Milton Park, Abingdon, Oxon, OX14 4RN

CRC Press is an imprint of Taylor & Francis Group, LLC

Library of Congress Cataloging-in-Publication Data (applied for)

ISBN: 978-1-041-10661-6 (hbk)
ISBN: 978-1-041-16136-3 (pbk)
ISBN: 978-1-003-68295-0 (ebk)

DOI: 10.1201/9781003682950

Typeset in Times New Roman
by Prime Publishing Services

Preface

The convergence of Artificial Intelligence (AI) and quantum computing has ushered in a transformative paradigm—**Quantum-Inspired Neural Networks (QINNs)**. Although practical quantum computing is still in its infancy, quantum-inspired models have emerged as a powerful alternative, capable of solving complex computational problems efficiently on classical systems. Drawing on principles such as superposition, entanglement, and quantum probability, QINNs mark a significant advancement in the evolution of intelligent computation.

This book represents the culmination of rigorous academic collaboration and the intellectual contributions of researchers, scientists, and practitioners worldwide. A total of **30 chapters were initially** submitted for consideration. Following a meticulous peer-review and evaluation process, **11 high-quality chapters** were selected for publication. Together, these chapters collectively present theoretical foundations, algorithmic advancements, practical frameworks, and real-world applications of Quantum-Inspired Neural Networks (QINNs) across diverse domains, including healthcare, finance, cybersecurity, natural language processing, and optimization.

The purpose of this book is not only to consolidate existing knowledge but also to bridge the gap between classical AI and quantum-inspired computation. The selected chapters examine hybrid quantum-classical architectures, quantum-inspired optimization techniques, scalability challenges, performance benchmarks, and future research directions. By presenting both conceptual clarity and application-driven insights, this volume serves as a valuable resource for **research scholars, academicians, industry professionals, and graduate students** seeking to understand or innovate within this emerging field.

The editors extend their sincere gratitude to all authors for their scholarly contributions and to the reviewers for their constructive feedback, which safeguarded the academic integrity of this work. We also wish to acknowledge the publishing team for their invaluable support in bringing this book to fruition.

We hope that this book inspires further research and motivates the scientific community to explore the vast potential of quantum-inspired artificial intelligence. May it serve as a foundational reference and as a catalyst for innovation.

Moolchand Sharma
Nebojsa Bacanin
Tarik Ahmed Rashid

Contents

CHAPTER

1

Fundamentals of Quantum-Inspired Neural Computing

Rebwar Khalid Muhammed[1], Aso Mohammed Aladdin[2*], Rebwar Khalid Hamad[3], Dana Rasul Hamad[4] and Tarik Ahmad Rashid[5]

[1] Network Department, Computer Science Institute, Sulaimani Polytechnic University, Sulaimani, Iraq

[2] Computer Engineering Department, Tishk International University, Kurdistan Region, Iraq

[3] Department of Information Technology, Koya Technical Institute, Erbil Polytechnic University, Erbil, Iraq

[4] Computer Science Department, Faculty of Science, Soran University, Erbil, Iraq

[5] Computer Science and Engineering Department, University of Kurdistan Hewler, Erbil, Iraq

This chapter offers a clear and accessible introduction to the field of quantum-inspired neural computing. By integrating concepts from quantum mechanics with traditional neural network models, this area opens new possibilities in machine learning and optimization through advanced metaheuristic algorithms. Unlike true quantum computing, quantum-inspired approaches operate on classical computers while borrowing key concepts such as superposition, entanglement, and probabilistic behavior to enhance how neural networks learn and process information. The study begins by explaining why researchers are interested in applying quantum principles to neural networks. It then introduces the fundamental mathematical concepts behind these ideas, such as quantum states and transformations, and demonstrates how they can be leveraged to design more powerful and flexible learning systems. The discussion highlights current models, distinguishes between quantum-inspired and true quantum systems, and evaluates the potential benefits and challenges of this approach. In addition,

*Corresponding author: aso.aladdin@chu.edu.iq

DOI: 10.1201/9781003682950-1

quantum-inspired neural computing further introduces a novel framework that bridges classical artificial intelligence with principles derived from quantum mechanics. By simulating quantum behaviors on classical hardware, it opens new avenues for developing more adaptive and efficient learning models. This emerging approach offers promising advantages in areas such as optimization, parallel processing, and high-dimensional data representation. Nevertheless, the field faces notable limitations and challenges. These include the lack of limited theoretical formalization, and difficulties in scaling models for complex real-world applications, and the ongoing challenge of distinguishing genuine quantum-inspired advantages from conventional algorithmic improvements, an issue that remains a central concern in current research.

1.1 Introduction

In recent years, the rapid advancement of artificial intelligence (AI) and machine learning has reshaped numerous scientific and industrial domains. Applications of deep learning models and neural networks have proven truly transformative, particularly in enhancing natural language processing for medical diagnostics (Feierabend et al., 2025). Nonetheless, this rapid development has also revealed key limitations of neural networks, including the need for vast amounts of training data, immense computational resources, and extended processing times (Chinnasamy et al., 2025). These constraints have driven the pursuit of innovative models capable of transcending the boundaries of conventional computing. Among the most promising frontiers in this endeavor is quantum mechanics.

The exploration of this question has led to the emergence of Quantum Neural Networks (QNNs) and quantum-inspired algorithms. While true quantum computing hardware remains in its infancy, researchers are increasingly adopting quantum-inspired models that emulate certain quantum behaviors within classical systems. These approaches serve both as a bridge to future fully quantum implementations and as a means of enhancing the efficiency and capabilities of current AI methods.

In this respect, blending quantum mechanics with neural networks is not merely a theoretical or academic exercise, but a practical approach to addressing bottlenecks in computational efficiency, enhancing scalability in deep learning, and offering new insights into information processing (How and Cheah, 2024). This chapter builds upon and extends these discussions by critically examining the motivations and applications behind incorporating principles of quantum computing into neural networks, distinguishing between true quantum computing and its quantum-inspired counterpart, and outlining the structure of this work. In addition to its technical implications, quantum-inspired neural computing exemplifies a broader movement of cross-disciplinary collaboration, a convergence of ideas aimed at addressing problems beyond the reach of conventional methods. By integrating knowledge from computer science, physics and cognitive models, researchers are developing architectures that process information more efficiently while simultaneously capturing facets of uncertainty and correlation that classical networks often overlook (Memon et al., 2024). This cross-disciplinary thinking is essential for creating computation-based systems that can adapt to the complexity of real-world situations. Furthermore, quantum-inspired methods hold particular importance because of their practical accessibility. Unlike full quantum computing, which remains constrained by hardware limitations and qubit instability, quantum-inspired strategies can be implemented on existing classical computers (Desdentado et al., 2025). This makes quantum-inspired approaches not only a practical research direction but also an effective testing ground for applying quantum principles in AI. In this sense, quantum-inspired neural computing occupies a unique position: while enhancing present-day AI capabilities, it simultaneously lays the theoretical and methodological foundations for the future of quantum-enhanced computing (Chintalapati et al., 2025). AI, especially neural networks, has proven highly effective across a wide range of fields, including image recognition, natural language processing, and medical diagnostics (Flöther, 2025). However, with growing demands for greater accuracy,faster processing, and the computational power required to handle exponentially larger datasets, classical computing methods have revealed fundamental limitations. Neural networks are highly powerful, yet they suffer from critical weaknesses, including heavy-computational demands, high energy consumption, vanishing and exploding gradients, and difficulties in scaling to highly complex problem spaces (Mienye et al., 2024). These limitations are becoming increasingly severe as real-world conditions push intelligent systems to learn and adapt in real time. In contrast, quantum mechanics offers an alternate paradigm for information processing, drawing on principles such as superposition, entanglement, and tunneling (Matarèse et al., 2023). These principles suggest the potential for exponential speedups in optimization, and enhanced representational capacity, and novel approaches to uncertainty and probabilistic reasoning, capabilities that classical neural networks do not inherently possess. Despite this promise, the integration of quantum concepts into neural networks remains an underexplored area that must still overcome theoretical and practical challenges (Klusch et al., 2024).

The core challenge, therefore, lies in bridging the gap between the limitations of classical neural networks and the opportunities offered by quantum mechanics. Specifically, how can quantum-inspired mechanisms or true quantum computing frameworks be systematically integrated into neural architectures to overcome the bottlenecks of classical approaches? Addressing this question is essential for advancing both the theoretical foundations and the practical implementation of next-generation AI systems that are scalable, efficient, and capable of tackling computationally intractable problems.

Even with the significant advances in neural networks and deep learning, major gaps remain in addressing complex and high dimensions datasets. Despite these developments,several critical challenges still persist:

1. **Incomplete Integration of Models and Algorithms:** Most work in quantum-inspired neural computing (QINC) remains limited in scope, focusing on individual models such as Hopfield networks, Boltzmann machines, or variational quantum circuits. These efforts have yet to be integrated into a broader, general-purpose framework capable of supporting scalable, high-dimensional data.
2. To optimize their future utility, quantum-inspired approaches have already been implemented in metaheuristic optimization (e.g., Q-GOOSE, Q-LEO) and kernel-based machine learning (e.g., QSVMs). However, in most cases, these implementations remain proof-of-concept or are limited to specific datasets and small-scale circuits.
3. **Scalability and Real-World Relevance:** Because simulations of quantum principles often fail to align with real-world data, notably noisy, high-dimensional, or non-homogenous datasets, their applicability and scalability are significantly reduced.
4. **Lack of Systematic Design Concepts:** Although approaches involving encoding, learning and hybrid models have been proposed, no comprehensive framework has yet been established. Specifically, there is no systematic pipeline in which encoding strategies, quantum inspired layers, activation functions and optimization techniques are fully integrated into a unified architecture that can be practically applied to AI applications.
5. **Limited Performance Benchmarking:** The existing literature provides only limited comparisons between quantum-inspired neural computing (QINC) and classical neural networks under standardized metrics. As a result, the quantitative advantages of QINC in real-world scenarios remain largely unexplored.

The motivation of this chapter lies in addressing the inherent shortcomings of conventional AI systems. Traditional neural computing, grounded in deterministic propagation and backpropagation rules, often struggles to represent uncertainty and capture complex correlations within data. QINC offers a promising path forward by drawing on principles such as superposition and entanglement, enabling models to approximate probabilistic processes more diligently. This perspective is particularly compelling for domains like big data analysis, optimization, and generative modelling, where scalable and adaptive methods are urgently needed. By integrating ideas such as probabilistic inference, entanglement-inspired correlation, and tunnelling-inspired optimization, QINC opens new horizons for neural computing, pushing beyond the constraints of classical approaches.

The objective of this chapter is to clarify why QINC is fundamentally different from quantum computing. While quantum computing requires specialized hardware and physical qubits, QINC does not. Instead, it borrows inspiration from quantum principles to enhance learning and problem-solving in classical systems. In this sense, QINC is not aimed at replicating quantum supremacy in solving computational problems but at leveraging quantum-like properties;

such as parallel exploration, interference, and state transitions; to address limitations of conventional AI. These include slow optimization convergence, difficulties in handling uncertainty, and challenges in scaling to complex, real-world applications. Accordingly, this chapter contributes to the growing body of knowledge on QINC by:

- Distinguishing between genuine quantum computing and QINC, and explaining the conceptual practical boundaries.
- Presenting the problem of classical neural network limitations and justifying the relevance of quantum principles in addressing them.
- Introducing the quantum-inspired mechanisms most relevant to neural computing, including superposition, entanglement, and probabilistic measurement.
- Reviewing key models and architectures, such as quantum-inspired Boltzmann machines, Hopfield networks, and optimization algorithms.
- Highlighting both the opportunities (e.g., optimization, high-dimensional learning, big data processing) and the ongoing challenges (e.g., theoretical formalization, scalability, and evaluation of genuine advantages).

1.2 Foundational Quantum Concepts for Neural Computing

Basic neural networks have gained considerable attention over the past decade, driving significant progress across a variety of tasks through the development of new architectures. Several algorithms have been proposed to address the neural architecture search problem, though many demand substantial computational resources. In response, quantum-inspired approaches have introduced algorithms rooted in quantum computing principles, showing promising results, particularly in achieving faster convergence (Szwarcman et al., 2019; Y. Li et al., 2024).

Several advanced data analysis tools have played a pivotal role in various recognition tasks, particularly within the field of natural language processing (NLP) (Khurana et al., 2023). Some of these tools leverage the principles of quantum superposition, enabling more sophisticated and efficient data processing. As data volumes continue to expand, classical computing networks face mounting challenges in effectively managing and analyzing large-scale information (L. Xu et al., 2025). To address these limitations, researchers are increasingly turning to quantum theory as a complementary solution. For instance, artificial neural networks (ANNs) have been employed to achieve optimal and accurate outcomes in data analysis, especially when enhanced by quantum supervision (Bakshi and Srinivasan, 2025; Liu and Ma, 2021). Their effectiveness is further amplified when combined with metaheuristic algorithms, machine learning techniques, and deep learning models. Such integrated methods strengthen the ability to tackle complex problems, as will be explored in greater detail in the following sections of this chapter.

In addition, quantum entanglement, a phenomenon in which particles remain interconnected regardless of distance, is being actively studied for its potential to enhance neural network capabilities. Thus, unlike classical neural networks, quantum-inspired neural networks (QNNs) integrate principles of quantum computing, leveraging core phenomena such as entanglement, superposition, and interference to improve computational expressiveness and efficiency (Q. Li et al., 2021). One notable approach, Entanglement Guided Testing, has been implemented through the QuanTest framework, which uses entanglement to assess QNN behavior, detect possible errors, and quantify the degree of entanglement in input quantum states, paving the way for more reliable and powerful quantum driven AI systems. As such, several QNN architectures have been proposed and successfully tested on benchmark datasets for machine learning. However, quantitative studies of the QNN-generated entanglement have been investigated only for up to a few qubits.

Researchers use entanglement entropy production to assess the randomness of quantum states, evaluating how effectively quantum circuits can represent different states by applying methods from random matrix theory. Findings suggest that, regardless of the specific QNN design, entanglement tends to form at a common rate. This observation has led to the concept of "entangling speed", a measure of how quickly entanglement is generated. Several studies have examined these properties in quantum neural networks, providing new evidence on how quickly such systems can act like random unitary operators (Woitzik et al., 2020). In addition, some research has suggested that the human brain may communicate with another brain through quantum entanglement. Identical particles can become entangled without direct interaction; however, the possibility of sensory communication between two individuals across long distances remains uncertain.

In addition, the probabilistic behavior inherent in quantum computing, when applied to neural computing, has a broad impact on big data analysis, particularly in inference tasks and in image generation involving various digit characters, as exemplified by multiple representative discriminative and generative models. This case is discussed in detail in Section 1.1.3, in relation to the layers of neural networks within the context of Quantum-Inspired Architectures. In these implementations, quantum vacuum noise often serves as a random seed for encoding classification uncertainty or for enabling the probabilistic generation of samples. Such random sources introduce uncertainty into neural network parameters, allowing a statistical interpretation of inference results (Wu et al., 2023). In generative scenarios, stochastic sampling driven by these random sources produces new images or text based on probability distributions learned and stored within neural networks. All such computational tasks require controllable stochastic photonic elements capable of learning probability distributions and performing statistically independent sampling, as dictated by quantum phenomena. These directions indicate that the foundations of Quantum-Inspired Neural Computing (QINC) (Shi, 2022; Khrennikov, 2021) are built upon three fundamental principles, as discussed. The emphasis is on understanding how these mechanisms function and contribute to the representation of characteristic features in data analysis and real-world applications, with particular relevance to big data, as illustrated in Figure 1.1.

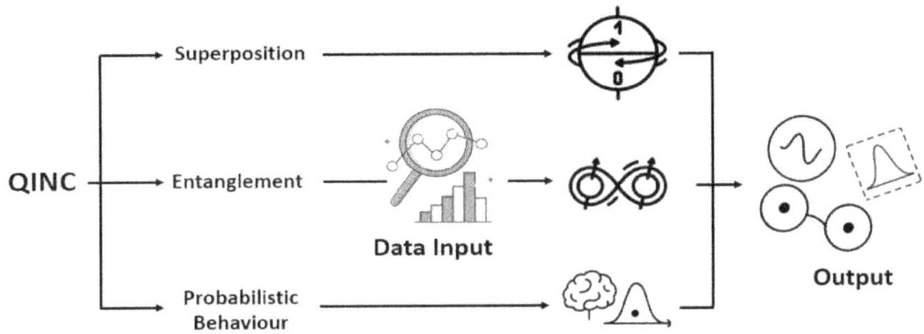

Figure 1.1: Evaluation steps in the QINC framework.

These features indicate that QINC can focus on three fundamental behaviors. In quantum-inspired networks, these behaviors play a crucial role in developing new models and implementing real applications. They are particularly important in big data processing (Mohammed-Taha et al., 2025; Pradeepa, 2025), where the complexity and scale of information require advanced computational strategies.

In high-performance computing systems and specialized supercomputing machines, QINC leverages quantum states and qubits to transform and process data. This enables the system to explore multiple computational pathways simultaneously, improving efficiency. By exploiting quantum principles, such systems can achieve higher accuracy, reliability, and performance in decision-making agents and predictive models.

1.2.1 Quantum Status

In quantum mechanics, a quantum state describes the condition of a quantum system and is typically expressed as a vector in a Hilbert space. A Hilbert space is a complete inner product space that generalizes the idea of Euclidean space to infinite dimensions. It plays a key role in both mathematics and physics, especially in quantum mechanics, as it allows concepts like length and angle to be defined in infinite-dimensional settings. This framework is essential for understanding quantum phenomena and solving complex equations, as illustrated in Figure 1.2 (Pfaff, 1976). In QINC, quantum states are not actual physical particles but mathematical constructs inspired by quantum theory. They are used to encode information in ways that replicate the principles of superposition, entanglement, and probabilistic measurement.

In real quantum computing, a qubit can exist in a superposition of the states $|0\rangle$ and $|1\rangle$. In QINC, similar structures are simulated using classical algorithms

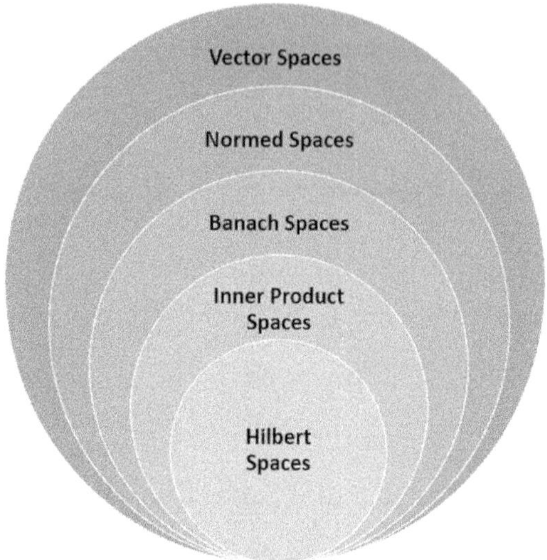

Figure 1.2: Classification space concepts for length via angle in infinite dimensions.

that store probability amplitudes or weight distributions instead of binary bits. As represented in Equation 1.1 a quantum state can be expressed in mathematical form where α and β are complex numbers satisfying $|\alpha|^2 + |\beta|^2 = 1$. In quantum-inspired neural computing (QINC), these amplitudes may correspond to feature weights, uncertainty levels, or probabilistic outputs within neural networks (W. Pfaff, 2013).

$$|\psi\rangle = \alpha|0\rangle + \beta|1\rangle \tag{1.1}$$

Additionally, in QINC, quantum states serve multiple roles, including encoding input data by mapping classical information into a high-dimensional vector space inspired by quantum state formalism, enabling parallelism through simulated superposition to explore multiple solution paths simultaneously, modelling uncertainty by representing probability distributions over potential classifications or outputs, and finally facilitating optimization via amplitude-based encoding to enhance search efficiency in a large solution space, as elaborated in the following sections.

In spite of that, in the world of Big Data and AI, these ideas emerge in many ways: in pattern recognition, quantum-state-based encoding makes data representations more compact and expressive; in generative models, the probabilistic nature of quantum states fuels richer image and text creation; and in decision-making agents, evolving states help them quickly adapt to new streams of information (Rath and Date, 2024). Thus, the advantage of quantum states in quantum-inspired models lies in their higher representational power compared to purely classical binary models, their efficient encoding of correlations between variables (similar to quantum entanglement), and their ability to achieve better generalization in probabilistic reasoning tasks (Loglisci et al., 2024). In general, the quantum state in the neural network is defined by how the weights are exchanged and how data is processed until the final output is obtained from the result evaluation (Bakshi and Srinivasan, 2025), as shown in Figure 1.3.

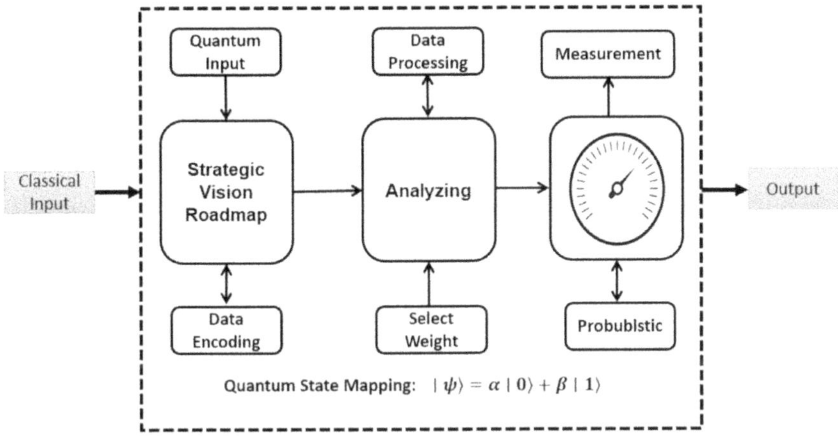

Figure 1.3: Quantum mapping state processing in neural networks.

1.2.2 Qubit Under Transformations

In a fundamental QINC framework based on qubits, data is first encoded onto qubits using methods such as angle encoding or amplitude encoding, as previously described. Qubits, the basic carriers of quantum information, can exist in a superposition of states, enabling simultaneous processing of multiple possibilities.

Transformations of these qubits are performed using quantum gates. Among these, the RY gate applies a rotation of the qubit's state vector around the *Y*-axis of the Bloch sphere by a specified angle, making it particularly suitable for angle encoding of data. The CR_y gate is the controlled version of the R_y gate, where a rotation around the *Y*-axis is applied to a target qubit only if the control qubit is in the $|1\rangle$ state (Williams, 2011; Mummadi and Rudra, 2023). This enables conditional state transformations, a key aspect of quantum logic. The CNOT gate (Controlled-NOT) (H.-H. Lu, 2019) flips the target qubit if the control qubit is $|1\rangle$, serving as a fundamental entangling operation that creates correlations between qubits. Thus, the qubits are measured, collapsing their superposition into definite classical states, from which the output is obtained.

Previously, the Hadamard gate, often denoted as *H*, is a fundamental quantum logic gate used to create a superposition state (Ghaeminezhad and Cong, 2018). When applied to a qubit initially in the state $|0\rangle$, it transforms the qubit into an equal superposition of the basis states $|0\rangle$ and $|1\rangle$. Mathematically, this transformation results in the state as Equation 1.2, meaning the qubit has an equal probability of being measured as $|0\rangle$ or $|1\rangle$ (Isono, 2014). This operation is essential for enabling quantum parallelism in quantum algorithms.

$$H = \frac{|0\rangle + |01\rangle}{\sqrt{2}} \tag{1.2}$$

In this example, the quantum circuit prepares the state as Equation 1.3 by applying gates that place qubits into a specific superposition. The process uses H and controlled operations to distribute amplitude across the target basis states while excluding $|11\rangle$. In quantum-inspired neural computing, similar simulated circuits encode multi-feature correlations, enabling parallel evaluation of patterns and probabilistic inference in neural networks, improving efficiency in complex big data tasks.

$$|\psi\rangle = \frac{1}{\sqrt{3}} (|00\rangle + |01\rangle + |10\rangle) \tag{1.3}$$

In addition, a Bell state can be created and used in neural computing to obtain results efficiently and accurately (Jia et al., 2019). The process begins by creating two identical qubits on the Bloch sphere, both initialized to state zero, and applying the same random rotational gate to each. Next, CNOT gate is first applied, followed by a Hadamard gate on the first qubit, enabling measurement in the Bell basis. CNOT gate is a fundamental two-qubit quantum logic operation in quantum computing, where the state of the target qubit is flipped if and only if the control qubit is in the $|1\rangle$ state. This sequence is essential for generating and analyzing entangled states used in quantum algorithms and communication protocols. This setup produces the outcomes 00, 01, and 10, which correspond to three symmetric Bell states, with equal probability, allowing the system to leverage entanglement inspired correlations for improved computational performance. This transformation, shown in the diagram in Figure 1.4, corresponds to the approach proposed in neural computing and represents a fundamental operation within a quantum neural system. In quantum inspired neural computing, the CNOT gate is important for introducing correlations between qubits, as shown in $Q[0]$ and $Q[1]$, which is conceptually similar to creating dependencies or relationships

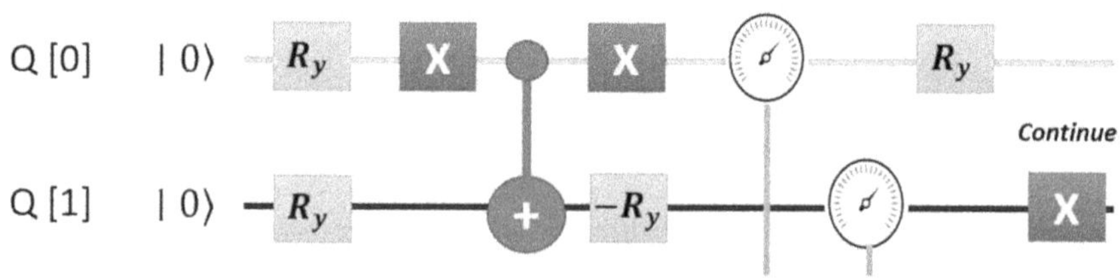

Figure 1.4: Example of a quantum rotation gate performing a *Y*-axis state transformation.

between features in a model, similar to entanglement in quantum mechanics (Ahmed et al., 2025; C. Lu et al., 2024). The R_y gate is a quantum rotation gate that rotates a qubit's state around the *Y*-axis of the Bloch sphere by a specified angle θ, denoted as $R_y(\theta)$. In this case, the first R_y gate applied to $Q[0]$ has $\theta = 1.2310$, the next R_y for $Q[1]$ gate has $\theta = \pi/4$, and the second R_y gate has $\theta = -\pi/4$.

1.3 Quantum-Inspired Architectures

The latest developments of computational intelligence underline the necessity in the architectures that are beyond the boundaries of classical modelling. Quantum inspired neural computing (QINC) is an interesting new approach, which combines a few ideas related to quantum mechanics without necessitating actual physical quantum computing hardware. This part visits the architectural principles, encoding techniques, and hybrid-mechanisms that give form to QINC.

1.3.1 Overview of Quantum-Inspired Architectures

The main objective of Quantum-inspired architecture is to follow the key principles of quantum mechanics such as, probabilistic behavior, entanglement, and superposition within classical neural networks (Maksimovic and Maksymov, 2025). These architectures are adopting quantum-like computational strategies to develop optimization and learning effectiveness. Quantum Boltzmann Machine (QBM) and Quantum-Inspired Hopfield Network (QIHN) are the two common models in this area. The QBM combines quantum probability distributions to explore solution spaces more efficiently, particularly in high-dimensional optimization tasks (Sinno et al., 2025). In contrast, the QIHN model takes advantage of quantum-like memory storage and retrieval, allowing it to represent multiple stable states simultaneously (Torres and Manzano, 2024). To represent complex data more compactly, algorithms are built on these architectures which often use quantum-inspired encoding techniques such as angle encoding or amplitude. These systems imitate the tunnelling-line and quantum transitions to avoid local minima and enhance convergence (Rath and Date, 2023). Quantum-inspired models provide a powerful alternative to classical deep learning by simulating the uncertainty and parallelism of quantum systems, especially in areas involving combinatorial search and complex landscapes (Khan and Robles-Kelly, 2020).

Figure 1.5 illustrates a diagram comparing the processes and the structural components flow of classical neural networks and quantum-inspired neural networks. The focus is on how quantum concepts are simulated within classical systems. To provide greater detail the stages for both approaches are described below:

The properties of a Classical Neural Network can be distinguished as follows:

1. **Input:** numerical or traditional input data is passed through the network directly.

2. **Layer 1:** To introduce non linearity the network uses standard activation functions like (ReLU).
3. **Hidden layer:** Through weighted connections and backpropagation the computation occurs in deterministic fashion.
4. **Output:** To finalize the process an activation like (SoftMax) is used to produce a clear classification or prediction.

The properties of a Classical Neural Network are defined as follows:

1. **Input:** The model uses superposition instead of binary inputs which allow each qubit to represent multiple states simultaneously, e.g. using both 0 and 1 in a weighted probability.
2. **Encoding:** Data is transformed over quantum-inspired encoding such as:
   - Basic encoding which displays the classical bits using qubit-like structure.
   - Amplitude encoding which embeds input in probability amplitudes.
3. **Q-inspired layer:** This layer simulates quantum operations such as quantum tunneling, unitary transformations, or entangle state instead of standard neurons for optimization. Learning might depend on evolutionary or probabilistic update rules.
4. **Output:** This final stage is not a fixed class label but a probability distribution which reflects the inherent uncertainty and parallelism of quantum-inspired computation.

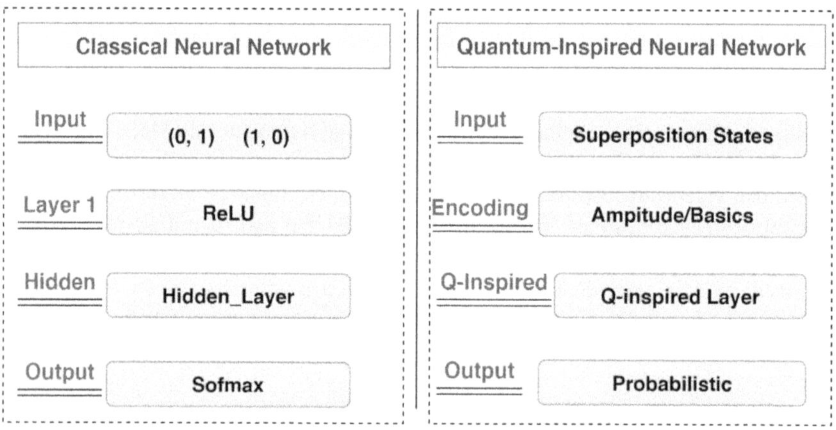

Figure 1.5: Comparison of classical and quantum-inspired neural network.

1.3.2 Quantum-Inspired Hopfield and Boltzmann Networks

Quantum-inspired models incorporate concepts from quantum mechanics such as superposition and probabilistic transitions into classical neural architectures to enhance computational speed, as discussed in Section 1.2. Some of the most important models are presented in this part including Quantum-Inspired

Hopfield Networks, and Boltzmann Machines whose dynamics are quantum-like and do not need quantum hardware. The simulations have great potential to be applicable in complicated real-life optimization and retrieval of memories and are therefore useful in developing artificial intelligence.

They interpret classical Hopfield networks in a quantum decoding akin to using quantum spins rather than binary neurons to interpret the classical dynamics as energy-based dynamics (equivalent to quantum evolution). By taking advantage of quantum-state superposition and phase encoding it is possible to enhance associative memory and the associated memory storage by a remarkable degree (Shcherbina et al., 2020). The primary findings of this model are as follows: classical inputs and outputs are preserved, but patterns are mapped to eigenstates in amplitude space. Simulations further demonstrate increased storage capacity and enhanced error resilience compared to classical Hopfield networks in small-scale systems (Meinhardt et al., 2020). Figure 1.6 illustrates a fully connected Hopfield network.

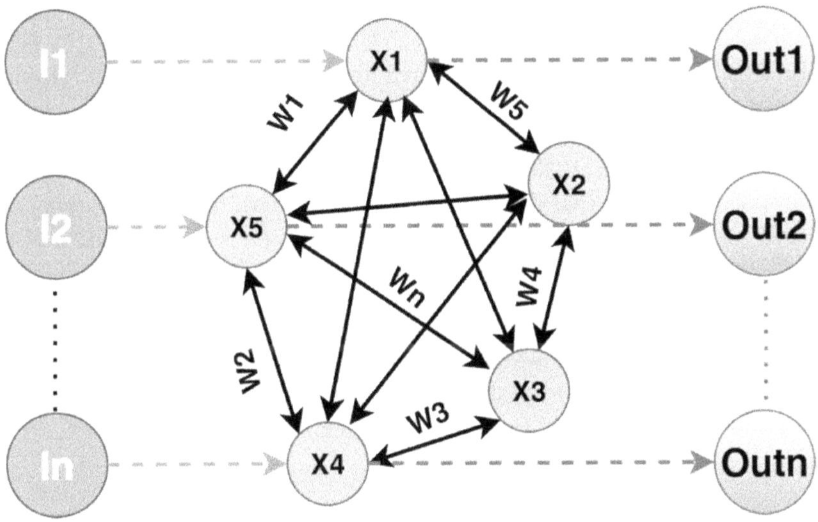

Figure 1.6: Fully connected network of Hopfield machine.

Equation 1.4 describes the update rule for neuron i in a Hopfield network. It determines the neuron's state based on the weighted sum of inputs from other neurons and serves as a fundamental mechanism for associative memory and pattern retrieval.

$$S_i\,(t+1) = signs\left(\sum_i w_{ij} S_j(t)\right) \tag{1.4}$$

Equation 1.5 represents the energy of Hopfield neural networks. It determines the stability of the system, with preferred memory states assigned lower values.

By adjusting the weights in its neurons to minimize this energy, the network is able to perform pattern recognition and associative memory retrieval.

$$E = -\frac{1}{2} \sum_{i \neq} w_{ij} S_j \tag{1.5}$$

Equation 1.6 is the Boltzmann distribution, which computes the likelihood of the system to have a state s with energy $E(s)$ at temperature T. Here, Z is the partition that makes the sum of the probabilities one. The equation plays a core role in Boltzmann machines to choose neuron states probabilistically during learning.

$$P(s) = \frac{1}{2} e^{-E(s)/T} \tag{1.6}$$

Quantum Boltzmann Machines (QBMs) are extended with quantum sampling–influenced mechanisms. They train Gibbs distributions more efficiently by leveraging techniques such as quantum annealing and rejection sampling, thereby enabling improved exploration of multi-modal landscapes (Schuman, 2025). Dixit et al. (2021) proposed a quantum-inspired training algorithm based on rejection sampling, which provides improved gradient estimation and enables parallel training of deep Boltzmann machines. More recently, efforts to combine D-Wave annealing with classical Gibbs updates have enhanced inference in Restricted Boltzmann Machines (RBMs) under certain conditions, thereby improving the quality of sampling (Kālis et al., 2023). A survey presented in Huynh et al. (2023) defines quantum-inspired neural approaches, including Hopfield-like and Boltzmann-like models, and situates them within the broader QiML landscape. Meanwhile, Zhao and Wang (2021) discusses techniques, paradigms, and tradeoffs in QNNs and quantum-motivated architectures, providing historical context on circuit-based simulators and quantum-classical hybrid systems. Figure 1.7 illustrates a fully connected Boltzmann machine model.

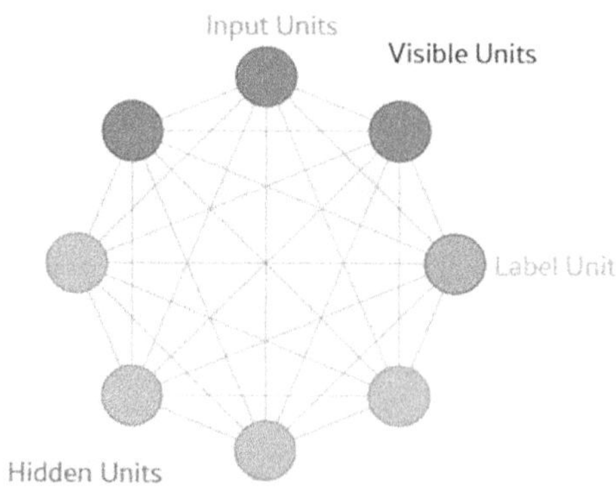

Figure 1.7: Fully connected Boltzmann machine (Schuman, 2025).

Quantum-inspired neural architectures incorporate key quantum principles into algorithmic design to enhance representational power, and optimization efficiency within classical systems. The following section outlines several key design principles that guide their development.

1.3.3 Encoding, Learning, and Hybrid Architectures in Quantum-Inspired Neural Computing

The incorporation of quantum-inspired concepts into neural computing requires a consistent view of information representations, processing and optimization. Encoding protocols embed classical data into quantum-inspired spaces and provide compact characterization of intricate patterns. Learning and optimization leverage entanglement-like correlations, probabilistic search and superposition to enhance adaptability. Hybrid architectures integrate the strengths of classical methods with quantum-inspired approaches to build scalable systems. This synergy enables performance that can surpass purely classical models, as demonstrated by the combined contributions of these components.

In quantum-inspired encoding, input data is mainly transformed into higher-dimensional representations using techniques such as angle encoding or amplitude encoding. These methods enable compact embedding and greater expressivity. For example, amplitude encoding allows elements of an input vector to be represented as cosine-based functions within parameterized rotation gates, facilitating weight sharing and model compression (Jiang et al., 2021; Lai et al., 2023). Novel activation functions, inspired by quantum gate operations such as rotations and Chebyshev-polynomial-based mechanisms, provide enhanced nonlinear expressivity. For instance, the hybrid Quantum Chebyshev-Polynomial Network (QCPN) achieves approximative power comparable to that of deeper classical networks, while requiring fewer layers (Mukhanbet et al., 2025). Optimization and learning can leverage quantum-inspired evolutionary algorithms that sample quantum superposition states to represent populations. Instead of relying on traditional binary encoding, these algorithms utilize superposition both for representation and mutation, enabling more efficient optimization to complex search spaces. For example, evolutionary algorithms can be applied to parameter optimization and agent behavior modification in multi-agent systems (Z. Xu et al., 2024). A study presented in (S. Li et al., 2024) explores weight-constrained neural networks inspired by amplitude and angle encodings, achieving a reduction in variable count by more than 100× while maintaining robustness and accuracy. In addition, (S. Li, 2024) introduces quantum-inspired activation functions on CNNs, demonstrating that Quantum Chebyshev-Polynomial Networks (QCPNs) with Chebyshev activation attain high accuracy using fewer layers and converge comparably to the newer activation functions introduced in the Kornblith paper.

In quantum-inspired systems, encoding and information flow draw on quantum concepts such as superposition and entanglement to support greater representational capacity. Information is encoded in amplitudes rather than binary states, and by operating within a probabilistic space, more expressive inputs become possible. These encodings are propagated through layers designed to mimic quantum gates or influence functions that capture complex relationships in data. This approach enables compact, parallel and efficient data processing within learning systems (Ranga et al., 2024). Figure 1.8 illustrates an architecture built on classical input vectors, which are encoded using quantum-inspired techniques. In this framework, the simulation of superposition is achieved through methods such as amplitude or basis encoding. The transformed data is passed through successive layers that simulate quantum phenomena, including interference and entanglement via simulated gates and neurons. Finally, the processed information is propagated and collapsed into either a probabilistic or definite output, reflecting the quantum behavior of measurement.

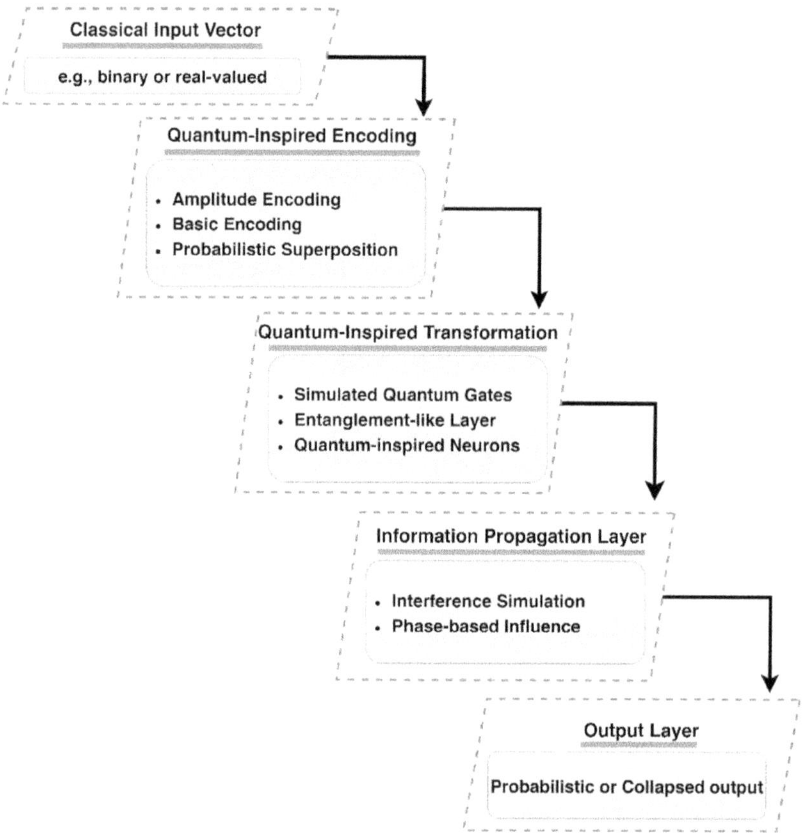

Figure 1.8: Encoding quantum-inspired architecture.

Figure 1.9 illustrates a quantum-motivated neural structure that integrates classical input information with quantum-inspired computational layers. Input vectors are initially encoded using quantum analogues such as amplitude encoding

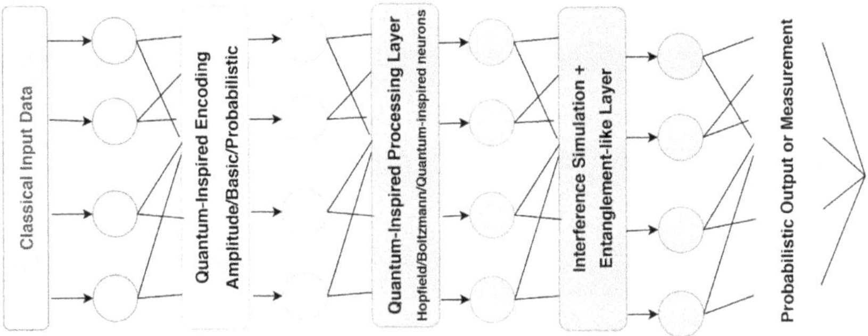

Figure 1.9: Quantum-inspired neural network architecture showing encoded input, simulated quantum processing, and probabilistic output.

or probabilistic superposition. This encoded information is then processed through multiple layers that resemble quantum systems such as Hopfield or Boltzmann networks, augmented with simulated interference and entanglement. The architecture ultimately produces a probabilistic output, which collapses quantum-inspired representations into deterministic predictions. While the design shares structural similarities with classical neural networks, the incorporation of quantum behaviors enhances learning, memory, and decision-making capabilities.

1.4 Applications in Optimization Algorithms

1.4.1 Use in Metaheuristic Optimization Algorithms

In essence, the QNN is a neural network that processes data by using quantum computing concepts such as superposition, entanglement, and quantum parallelism. By leveraging quantum mechanics to explore vast solution spaces, escape local minima, and potentially reach global optima more efficiently than classical neural networks, QNNs can simulate and solve complex optimization problems with greater effectiveness.

In addressing optimization problems, Quantum Neural Networks (QNNs) can be highly beneficial in several ways. The integration of quantum computing with artificial intelligence is anticipated to bring significant advances and new opportunities. By combining the parallelism, entanglement, and quantum gate operations of quantum computing with the demands of artificial intelligence, it becomes possible to design systems and algorithms that are more intelligent and efficient. In 2021, Liao et al. (2021) proposed a method to overcome barren plateaus and achieve a speedup exceeding Grover's algorithm by exceeding adaptive Hamiltonian-based parameter tuning and quantum encoding of cost functions. This approach addresses challenges in training Quantum Neural Networks (QNNs) through quantum optimization protocols. In related work, van Dam et al. (2022) demonstrated how initializing the Quantum Approximate

Optimization Algorithm (QAOA) with a traditional greedy method, combined with direct mixing improves performance on restricted Knapsack problem instances. Landman (2022) presents theoretical scalability advantages while achieving accuracy comparable to classical models in medical image classification tasks using quantum orthogonal neural networks and quantum-assisted inner product techniques. Furthermore, Bożejko et al. (2024) proposes a hybrid methodology that enhances efficiency and optimality in knapsack logistics by integrating D-Wave quantum computing with conventional Branch & Bound limit calculations (Bożejko et al., 2024). The second study (Z. Li et al., 2024) trains variational Quantum Neural Networks (QNNs) using particle swarm optimization enabling improved convergence for tasks such as phase classification and ground-state energy estimation while mitigating barren plateau issues. In addition, Z. Li et al. (2024) proposes an evolutionary approach for the automated generation of purely quantum QNN circuit topologies for image recognition applications, incorporating skip-connections using identity (I) gates. In a separate study (C. Moussa et al., 2024), hyperparameters critical to QNN performance on small OpenML datasets are identified using functional ANOVA, which guides architectural and parameter adjustment methodologies.

In 2025, Z. Hu (2025) introduced a hybrid Quantum Neural Network (QNN) incorporating physics-informed and residual layers to efficiently solve the NP-hard Optimal Power Flow problem, achieving improved generalization, convergence, and error robustness. Complementary work in A. Ceschini et al. (2025) evaluated several traditional optimizers, Adam, RMSProp, and AdaBelief, for QuanvNN training, demonstrating that even with basic circuits, strong accuracy can be attained, highlighting optimizer selection as a critical factor.

1.4.2 Quantum in Metaheuristic Optimization Algorithms

Artificial intelligence and quantum computing together are expected to drive significant advances and open new opportunities. By integrating the demands of artificial intelligence with the parallelism, entanglement, and quantum gate operations of quantum computing, it becomes possible to design more intelligent systems and algorithms. The following sections highlight equations from the GOOSE and LEO algorithms that can be applied to, or adapted for quantum computing platforms.

Hamad and Rashid invented the GOOSE algorithm in 2024, a novel metaheuristic inspired by the resting and foraging behaviors of geese. Within this framework, quantum computing can be employed to resolve equations in the exploitation and exploration phases of optimization. Techniques such as quantum annealing, the Variational Quantum Eigensolver (VQE), and the Quantum Approximate Optimization Algorithm (QAOA) offer promising avenues to enhance solution quality and overall performance.

Quantum computing can enhance or replace a specific GOOSE algorithm equation, particularly one that can benefit from quantum parallelism or quantum-inspired optimization. It concentrates on finding a good candidate during the exploration or exploitation phase and figuring out how to use quantum methods on it. Here are some of the equations of the GOOSE algorithm that can be used or converted to quantum computing.

Since the exploration update Equation 1.7 (Hamad and Rashid, 2024) expressly employs random sampling, it is a prime candidate for quantum enhancement. We may accomplish more consistent and unexpected exploration by substituting a quantum random number generator or quantum sampling procedure for the traditional randn. For instance, by measuring qubit superposition, a real quantum gadget (or Qiskit/PennyLane emulation) may produce really random results. Prior studies have shown that diversity and global search are markedly improved when population initialization employs authentic quantum randomness. This suggests that the vector randn (1, dim) in Equation 1.7 of GOOSE may originate from a quantum source, hence reducing patterns and augmenting search space coverage. In the same way, one may utilize quantum-enhanced sampling (for example, by constructing a parameterized quantum circuit and sampling its output distribution) instead of regular Gaussian noise to pick the offset from BestPos.

$$X_{(it+1)} = randn\ (1,\ dim) * (M_T * alpha) + Best\_pos \tag{1.7}$$

In addition, an exploitation update Equation 1.8 and 1.9 (Hamad and Rashid, 2024) may serve as the alternative. A quantum optimizer may be used to encode an optimization subproblem and determine the new location rather than relying on conventional arithmetic. Consider choosing a superior candidate X for an NP-hard optimization task by discretizing the position and reducing a surrogate cost.

$$X_{(it+1)} = F\_F\_S + D\_GG_{it} * T\_A^{\wedge 2} \tag{1.8}$$

$$X_{(it+1)} = F\_F\_S * D\_GG_{it} * T\_A^{\wedge 2} * Coe \tag{1.9}$$

In 2025 (Aladdin and Rashid, 2025) introduced the Lagrange Elementary Optimization (LEO) as a self-adaptive evolutionary method, inspired by the remarkable accuracy of immunizations using the albumin quotient of human blood. They use the fitness function value after genetic crossing to make smart agents. These genes help the search agents throughout both the exploration and exploitation stages.

Quantum computing has the potential to improve or substitute a specific LEO algorithm equation, especially one that could gain from quantum parallelism or quantum-inspired optimization. The identification of a promising candidate at the exploration or exploitation stage, along with the determination of quantum techniques can be applied to it. The following are examples of the LEO algorithm's equations that may be applied to or transformed into quantum computing.

A hybrid quantum-classical version of LEO can be made by encoding LEO's population and restrictions into qubits, utilizing a variational quantum optimizer as its Lagrangian-driven crossover, and employing amplitude amplification for selection. The Lagrangian step and selection/crossover equations Equation 1.10 to 1.13 (Aladdin and Rashid, 2025) are the sections of LEO that have improved most naturally. In Equation 1.10 LEO uses a Lagrangian to limit search space. In quantum computing-LEO, encode this issue as a Hamiltonian and use a variational quantum algorithm (VQE/QAOA) to make it as small as possible. In practice, we turn decision variables into binary (fixed-point) strings and then translate them to qubits. Using Equation 1.11, LEO chooses the fit people from the two parts of the group. In Q-LEO, set up a fitness oracle (a phase or marking oracle that marks people who are over a certain level), and then employ amplitude amplification such as Grover-style to increase the probability mass on best genomes. In the LEO algorithm, in Equations 1.12 and 1.13 crossover makes two new children. This approach employs mixtures of parent genes that are weighted by Lagrange multipliers. On a quantum device, set up a parametric "mixing" unitary that works like the bilinear and quadratic forms on the encoded bitstrings. In addition, in Equation 1.14 (Aladdin and Rashid, 2025), we can add minor random rotations to groups of qubits. These might be bit-flip/phase-flip with a low chance, or jitter ansatz angles. This acts like Gaussian noise in the binary domain and keeps exploration going.

$$l(x, y, \lambda) = f(x, y) - \lambda(g(x, y) - c) \tag{1.10}$$

$$X_{t,i+1} = \frac{X_{t,i+1}}{X^{*}_{t,i+1\ \text{for highest fitness}}} \tag{1.11}$$

$$Ot_1 = (xt_1 - xt_2)^2 + (xt_2 - 1)^2 - (\alpha\,(xt_1 + 2xt_2 - 1) + \alpha\,(2xt_1 + xt_2 - 1)) \tag{1.12}$$

$$Ot_2 = (xt_2 - xt_1)^2 + (xt_1 - 1)^2 - (\alpha\,(xt_2 + 2xt_1 - 1) + \alpha\,(2xt_2 + xt_1 - 1)) \tag{1.13}$$

$$M_{tti} = X_{t,i}\, X_{t,i}\,(j_i) + \sigma * randn(size\,(j_i)) \tag{1.14}$$

1.4.3 Parallel Processing and High-Dimensional Data Handling

In this article Verdon (2019) discovered that the neural optimizer surpasses conventional approaches in convergence speed and solution quality when faced with noise and constrained query budgets. This shows how trained heuristics might be better than conventional optimization techniques in quantum situations. To examine the use of QNNs in conjunction with conventional machine learning to handle complicated healthcare data in quantum parallel, improves outcome prediction, personalized therapy, and diagnostic accuracy (Fatunmbi, 2023).

1.4.4 Performance Comparisons with Traditional Neural Models

The neural network approach facilitates parallel data analysis and demonstrates superior handling of high-dimensional data compared to traditional methods. Neural networks, including Restricted Boltzmann Machines, are optimized for parallel computation on contemporary hardware, such as GPUs and multi-core CPUs, thereby enhancing training and sampling efficiency (Gomes et al., 2019).

1.5 Applications in Machine Learning and Deep learning

1.5.1 Quantum Speedup in Data Processing

Quantum speedup in data processing represents a transformative advancement in computational science, especially in the realm of machine learning. Traditional algorithms, such as quadratic, linear, and Naïve Bayes classifiers, often suffer from computational inefficiency as data dimensionality and sample sizes increase. These inefficiencies are particularly evident in operations like matrix inversion and high-dimensional inner product computations, which can scale as $O(d^3)$ or worse on classical hardware. Quantum computing addresses these limitations through parallelism enabled by superposition and entanglement. Notably, techniques like block-encoding allow non-unitary matrices to be embedded into unitary operators, facilitating efficient manipulation within quantum circuits. In conjunction with quantum RAM (qRAM) for rapid data loading and the swap test for estimating vector similarities, quantum algorithms achieve substantial reductions in computational complexity (Pokharel and Lidar, 2023; Shao, 2020).

1.5.2 Quantum Kernel Methods and Quantum Feature Spaces

Quantum kernel methods leverage the principles of quantum computing to enhance traditional machine learning techniques by mapping data into high-dimensional feature spaces. These methods utilize the unique properties of quantum states to achieve a computational advantage, particularly in recognizing complex patterns that classical algorithms may struggle with. The following sections elaborate on key aspects of quantum kernel methods and their feature spaces (Schuld and Petruccione, 2021).

Quantum feature spaces leverage the unique properties of quantum mechanics to enhance machine learning capabilities, particularly through quantum kernel methods. These methods encode data into exponentially large Hilbert spaces, allowing for more expressive feature representations than classical approaches. Techniques like squeezed-state encoding utilize continuous-variable quantum states, which significantly improve the ability to capture similarities between data samples. The following sections elaborate on these aspects.

- Quantum kernel methods encode data into exponentially large Hilbert spaces, allowing for more expressive feature representations than classical methods.
- Techniques such as squeezed-state encoding utilize continuous-variable quantum states, enhancing the capacity to capture similarities between data samples (Schuld and Killoran, 2019).

Figure 1.10 illustrates the role of quantum kernel methods in transforming input data into high-dimensional Hilbert spaces to improve class separability for machine learning tasks. The left subplot presents the data in its original feature space, where the *X*-axis and *Y*-axis correspond to the dataset's raw input features. In this space, the two classes overlap significantly, making linear separation difficult. The right subplot demonstrates the effect of a quantum feature map, where classical data points are embedded into a quantum-enhanced feature

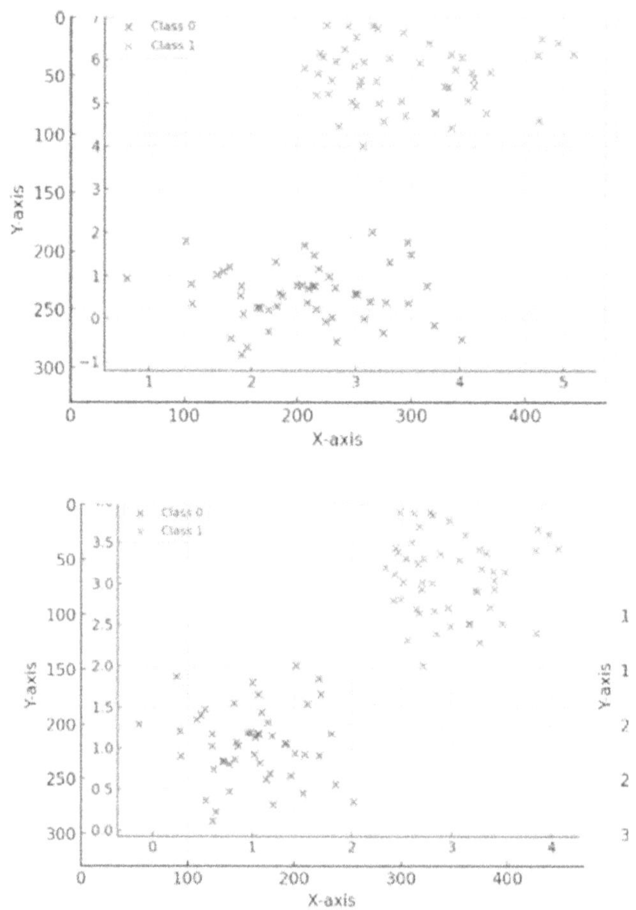

Figure 1.10: Quantum kernel methods and feature spaces.

space. Here, the *X*-axis and *Y*-axis represent projected embedding coordinates obtained from the quantum kernel mapping, rather than physical features. This transformation enlarges the margin between classes, thereby enabling more effective linear classification. The approach is based on quantum kernel estimation, where kernel values are computed by evaluating inner products of quantum states encoded with classical data. Such techniques are foundational in Quantum Support Vector Machines (QSVMs) and have shown strong potential in capturing complex, non-linear patterns in datasets using shallow quantum circuits (Schuld et al., 2020; Havlíček et al., 2019).

1.5.3 Hybrid Quantum-Classical Neural Networks

Hybrid quantum-classical neural networks (H-QNNs) represent a promising convergence of quantum computing and classical machine learning, particularly in enhancing neural network performance. These architectures leverage variational quantum circuits as neurons, enabling improved classification accuracy and cost function minimization compared to traditional models. The integration of quantum computing allows for the capture of complex features and sophisticated decision boundaries, particularly beneficial in high-dimensional tasks like image classification (Arthur and Date, 2022). Hybrid Quantum-Classical Neural Networks (QNNs) combine quantum and classical computing to solve optimization problems. They consist of three layers: an interface layer, a classical layer, and a quantum layer, enhancing speed, accuracy, and scalability for complex issues beyond traditional computers (Gundu, 2024).

1.6 Challenges and Limitations

Quantum computing presents significant challenges and limitations that hinder its full realization and deployment. These challenges encompass theoretical gaps, scalability issues, and the need to differentiate genuine quantum advantages from conventional improvements. Understanding these aspects is crucial for advancing the field.

Quantum computing is built upon the intricate principles of quantum mechanics, many of which remain only partially understood and insufficiently formalized. This lack of complete theoretical clarity poses significant challenges for advancing the field, particularly in designing algorithms and implementing reliable error correction strategies. Current models often fall short when applied in practical contexts, highlighting the urgent need for more robust and comprehensive theoretical frameworks that can guide both fundamental research and real-world applications.

Current quantum hardware faces significant limitations due to the restricted number of qubits and their short coherence times, which constrain the complexity and scale of computations that can realistically be executed. These hardware constraints are further compounded by practical challenges in quantum communication systems, where issues such as high photon loss and rapid decoherence hinder the development of scalable and robust quantum networks. Together, these factors highlight the gap between theoretical advances in quantum algorithms and the physical feasibility of implementing them on existing platforms.

It is essential to differentiate between improvements that are genuinely quantum and those that are merely classical optimizations. This distinction is critical for validating the unique capabilities of quantum computing. The potential for quantum algorithms to outperform classical counterparts in specific applications, such as cryptography and optimization, must be rigorously tested against conventional methods. While these challenges are significant, ongoing research and technological advancements continue to push the boundaries of quantum computing, suggesting that solutions may emerge that could mitigate these limitations and enhance its practical applications.

1.7 Conclusion and Future Directions

This chapter has explored the fundamental principles, architectures, and applications of quantum-inspired neural computing, highlighting its role as a bridge between classical artificial intelligence and quantum mechanics. Unlike true quantum computing, QINC does not depend on specialized hardware but borrows key principles such as superposition, entanglement, and probabilistic inference to enrich learning models within classical systems. By doing so, it provides a practical avenue to address persistent challenges of conventional neural networks, including scalability, optimization inefficiency, and difficulty in handling uncertainty. The review emphasized how QINC-based models, such as quantum-inspired Hopfield and Boltzmann networks, as well as their applications in optimization and machine learning, demonstrate promising performance improvements in high-dimensional and complex problem spaces. At the same time, the chapter underlined critical limitations, such as the lack of systematic frameworks, benchmarking gaps, and challenges in proving genuine quantum-inspired advantages. Moving forward, interdisciplinary research that integrates physics, computer science, and optimization will be essential to transform QINC into a robust paradigm. Eventually, QINC holds the potential to redesign computational intelligence, offering more adaptive and competent approaches for the next generation of intelligent systems.

Future work should focus on integrating quantum-inspired methods with advanced machine learning models for large-scale data analysis. Emphasis will be on developing statistical frameworks to validate performance, improving scalability for real-world datasets, and creating hybrid approaches that combine classical and quantum-inspired statistical learning.

References

Ahmed, S., Shihab, I. F. & Khokhar, A. (Sep. 2025). Quantum-driven zero trust architecture with dynamic anomaly detection in 7G technology: A neural network approach. *Measurement: Digitalization*, 2–3, 100005, doi: 10.1016/j.meadig.2025.100005.

Aladdin, A. M. & Rashid, T. A. (Jul. 2025). LEO: Lagrange elementary optimization. *Neural Comput Appl*, 37(19), 14365–14397, doi: 10.1007/S00521-025-11225-2/METRICS.

Arthur, D. & Date, P. (Sep. 2022). Hybrid quantum-classical neural networks. In: *2022 IEEE International Conference on Quantum Computing and Engineering (QCE)*, pp. 49–55. IEEE, doi: 10.1109/QCE53715.2022.00023.

Bakshi, K. & Srinivasan, K. (Aug. 2025). Quantum inspired qubit qutrit neural networks for real time financial forecasting. *Sci Rep*, 15(1), 28711, doi: 10.1038/s41598-025-09475-0.

Bożejko, W., Burduk, A., Pempera, J., Uchroński, M. & Wodecki, M. (May 2024). Optimal solving of a binary knapsack problem on a D-wave quantum machine and its implementation in production systems. *Ann Oper Res*, 1–16, doi: 10.1007/S10479-024-06025-1/TABLES/3.

Ceschini, A., Carbone, A., Sebastianelli, A., Panella, M. & Le Saux, B. (Jun. 2025). On hybrid quanvolutional neural networks optimization. *Quantum Mach Intell*, 7(1), 1–17, doi: 10.1007/S42484-025-00241-Z/TABLES/6.

Chinnasamy, R., Subramanian, M., Easwaramoorthy, S. V. & Cho, J. (Feb. 2025). Deep learning-driven methods for network-based intrusion detection systems: A systematic review. *ICT Express*, 11(1), 181–215, doi: 10.1016/j.icte.2025.01.005.

Chintalapati, A., Enkhbat, K., Annamalai, R., Amali, G. B., Ozaydin, F. & Noel, M. M. (Aug. 2025). Quantum-enhanced algorithmic fairness and the advancement of AI integrity and responsibility. *Quantum Reports*, 7(3), 36, doi: 10.3390/quantum7030036.

Desdentado, E., Calero, C., Moraga, M. Á. & García, F. (May 2025). Quantum computing software solutions, technologies, evaluation and limitations: A systematic mapping study. *Computing*, 107(5), 110, doi: 10.1007/s00607-025-01459-2.

Dixit, V., Selvarajan, R., Alam, M. A., Humble, T. S. & Kais, S. (Jun. 2021). Training restricted Boltzmann machines with a D-wave quantum annealer. *Front Phys*, 9, doi: 10.3389/fphy.2021.589626.

Fatunmbi, T. O. (Mar. 2023). Integrating quantum neural networks with machine learning algorithms for optimizing healthcare diagnostics and treatment outcomes. *World Journal of Advanced Research and Reviews*, 17(3), pp. 1059–1077, https://wjarr.com/sites/default/files/WJARR-2023-0306.pdf, doi: 10.30574/WJARR.2023.17.3.0306.

Feierabend, M., Wolfgart, J. M., Praster, M., Danalache, M., Migliorini, F. & Hofmann, U. K. (May 2025). Applications of machine learning and deep learning in musculoskeletal medicine: A narrative review. *Eur J Med Res*, 30(1), 386, doi: 10.1186/s40001-025-02511-9.

Flöther, F. F., Blankenberg, D., Demidik, M., Jansen, K., Krishnakumar, Raga, Krishnakumar, Rajiv et al. (Jun. 2025). How quantum computing can enhance biomarker discovery. *Patterns*, 6(6), 101236, doi: 10.1016/j.patter.2025.101236.

Ghaeminezhad, N. and Cong, S. (May 2018). Preparation of Hadamard Gate for open quantum systems by the Lyapunov control method. *IEEE/CAA Journal of Automatica Sinica*, 5(3), 733–740, doi: 10.1109/JAS.2018.7511084.

Gomes, J., McKiernan, K. A., Eastman, P. & Pande, V. S. (2019). Classical Quantum Optimization with Neural Network Quantum States. NeurIPS.

Gundu, S. R. (Feb. 2024). Quantum Neural Networks: A Novel Architecture for Hybrid Quantum-Classical Algorithms. doi: 10.21203/rs.3.rs-3951691/v1.

Hamad, R. K. & Rashid, T. A. (2024). GOOSE algorithm: A powerful optimization tool for real-world engineering challenges and beyond. *Evolving Systems*, 0123456789, doi: 10.1007/s12530-023-09553-6.

Havlíček, V., Córcoles, A. D., Temme, K., Harrow, A. W., Kandala, A., Chow, J. M. & Gambetta, J. M. (Mar. 2019). Supervised learning with quantum-enhanced feature spaces. *Nature*, 567(7747), 209–212, doi: 10.1038/s41586-019-0980-2.

Helton, J. W. (1976). Systems with infinite-dimensional state space: The Hilbert space approach. *Proceedings of the IEEE*, 64(1), 145–160, doi: 10.1109/PROC.1976.10076.

How, M.-L. & Cheah, S.-M. (Jan. 2024). Forging the future: Strategic approaches to quantum AI integration for industry transformation. *AI*, 5(1), 290–323, doi: 10.3390/ai5010015.

Hu, Z., Zhu, Z., Zhu, L., Wei, X., Bu, S. & Wing Chan, K. (Feb. 2025). Advancing Hybrid Quantum Neural Network for Alternative Current Optimal Power Flow. https://arxiv.org/pdf/2410.20275v2

Huynh, L., Hong, J., Mian, A., Suzuki, H., Wu, Y. & Camtepe, S. (Sep. 2023). Quantum-inspired machine learning: A survey. doi: https://doi.org/10.48550/arXiv.2308.11269.

Isono, T., Kamo, H., Ueda, A., Takahashi, K., Kimata, M., Tajima, H. et al. (Apr. 2014). Gapless quantum spin liquid in an organic spin-1/2 triangular-lattice κ–H3(Cat-EDT-TTF)2. *Phys Rev Lett*, 112(17), 177201, doi: 10.1103/PhysRevLett.112.177201.

Jia, Z., Yi, B., Zhai, R., Wu, Y., Guo, G. & Guo, G. (Aug. 2019). Quantum neural network states: A brief review of methods and applications. *Adv Quantum Technol*, 2(7–8), doi: 10.1002/qute.201800077.

Jiang, W., Xiong, J. & Shi, Y. (Jan. 2021). A co-design framework of neural networks and quantum circuits towards quantum advantage. *Nat Commun*, 12(1), 579, doi: 10.1038/s41467-020-20729-5.

Kālis, M., Locāns, A., Šikovs, R., Naseri, H. & Ambainis, A. (Dec. 2023). A hybrid quantum-classical approach for inference on restricted Boltzmann machines. *Quantum Mach Intell*, 5(2), 44, doi: 10.1007/s42484-023-00135-y.

Khan, T. M. & Robles-Kelly, A. (2020). Machine learning: Quantum vs classical. *IEEE Access*, 8, 219275–219294, doi: 10.1109/ACCESS.2020.3041719.

Khrennikov, A. (Jun. 2021). Roots of quantum computing supremacy: Superposition, entanglement, or complementarity. *Eur Phys J Spec Top*, 230(4), 1053–1057, doi: 10.1140/epjs/s11734-021-00061-9.

Khurana, D., Koli, A., Khatter, K. & Singh, S. (Jan. 2023). Natural language processing: State of the art, current trends and challenges. *Multimed Tools Appl*, 82(3), 3713–3744, doi: 10.1007/s11042-022-13428-4.

Klusch, M., Lässig, J., Müssig, D., Macaluso, A. & Wilhelm, F. K. (Dec. 2024). Quantum artificial intelligence: A brief survey. *KI – Künstliche Intelligenz*, 38(4), 257–276, doi: 10.1007/s13218-024-00871-8.

Lai, W., Shi, J. & Chang, Y. (Mar. 2023). Quantum-inspired fully complex-valued neutral network for sentiment analysis. *Axioms*, 12(3), 308, doi: 10.3390/axioms12030308.

Landman, J., Mathur, N., Li, Y. Y., Strahm, M., Kazdaghli, S., Prakash, A., & Kerenidis, I. (Dec. 2022). Quantum methods for neural networks and application to medical image classification. *Quantum*, 6, doi: 10.22331/q-2022-12-22-881.

Li, Q., Gkoumas, D., Sordoni, A., Nie, J.-Y. & Melucci, M. (May 2021). Quantum-inspired neural network for conversational emotion recognition. In: *Proceedings of the AAAI Conference on Artificial Intelligence*, 35(15), 13270–13278, doi: 10.1609/aaai.v35i15.17567.

Li, S., Salek, M. S., Roy, B., Wang, Y. & Chowdhury, M. (Dec. 2024). Quantum-inspired weight-constrained neural network: Reducing variable numbers by 100x compared to standard neural networks. doi: https://doi.org/10.48550/arXiv.2412.19355.

Li, S., Salek, M. S., Wang, Y. & Chowdhury, M. (Oct. 2024). Quantum-inspired Activation Functions and Quantum Chebyshev-Polynomial Network. doi: https://doi.org/10.48550/arXiv.2404.05901.

Li, Y., Liu, G., Zhao, P., Shang, R. & Jiao, L. (Aug. 2024). Balanced quantum neural architecture search. *Neurocomputing*, 594, 127860, doi: 10.1016/j.neucom.2024.127860.

Li, Z., Xiao, T., Deng, X., Zeng, G. & Li, W. (May 2024). Optimizing variational quantum neural networks based on collective intelligence. Mathematics, 12(11), 1627, doi: 10.3390/MATH12111627.

Liao, Y., Hsieh, M.-H. & Ferrie, C. (Mar. 2021). Quantum optimization for training quantum neural networks. *Quantum Mach Intell*, 6(1), doi: 10.1007/s42484-024-00169-w.

Liu, G. & Ma, W.-P. (Aug. 2021). Artificial neural network based on quantum superposition and its application. *Laser Phys Lett*, 18(8), 085202, doi: 10.1088/1612-202X/ac0639.

Loglisci, C., Malerba, D. & Pascazio, S. (Dec. 2024). Quarta: Quantum supervised and unsupervised learning for binary classification in domain-incremental learning. *Quantum Mach Intell*, 6(2), 68, doi: 10.1007/s42484-024-00196-7.

Lu, C., Hu, M., Miao, F. & Hou, J. (Sep. 2024). Gate-based quantum neurons in hybrid neural networks. *New J Phys*, 26(9), 093037, doi: 10.1088/1367-2630/ad6f3d.

Lu, H.-H., Lukens, J. M., Williams, B. P., Imany, P., Peters, N. A., Weiner, A. M. & Lougovski, P. (Mar. 2019). A controlled-NOT gate for frequency-bin qubits. *npj Quantum Inf*, 5(1), 24, doi: 10.1038/s41534-019-0137-z.

Maksimovic, M. & Maksymov, I. S. (May 2025). Transforming neural networks into quantum-cognitive models: A research tutorial with novel applications. *Technologies* (Basel), 13(5), 183, doi: 10.3390/technologies13050183.

Matarèse, B. F. E., Rusin, A., Seymour, C. & Mothersill, C. (Nov. 2023). Quantum biology and the potential role of entanglement and tunneling in non-targeted effects of ionizing radiation: A review and proposed model. *Int J Mol Sci*, 24(22), 16464, doi: 10.3390/ijms242216464.

Meinhardt, N., Neumann, N. M. P. & Phillipson, F. (2020). Quantum Hopfield Neural Networks: A New Approach and Its Storage Capacity. pp. 576–590. doi: 10.1007/978-3-030-50433-5_44.

Memon, Q. A., Al Ahmad, M. & Pecht, M. (Nov. 2024). Quantum computing: Navigating the future of computation, challenges, and technological breakthroughs. *Quantum Reports*, 6(4), 627–663, doi: 10.3390/quantum6040039.

Mienye, I. D., Swart, T. G. & Obaido, G. (Aug. 2024). Recurrent neural networks: A comprehensive review of architectures, variants, and applications. *Information*, 15(9), 517, doi: 10.3390/info15090517.

Mohammed-Taha, S. R., Aladdin, A. M., Mustafa, A. I., Hasan, D. O., Muhammed, R. K. & Rashid, T. A. (Jun. 2025). Analyzing the impact of the pandemic on insomnia prediction using machine learning classifiers across demographic groups. *Network Modeling Analysis in Health Informatics and Bioinformatics*, 14(1), 51, doi: 10.1007/s13721-025-00552-y.

Moussa, C., Patel, Y. J., Dunjko, V., Bäck, T. & van Rijn, J. N. (Apr. 2024). Hyperparameter importance and optimization of quantum neural networks across small datasets. *Mach Learn*, 113(4), 1941–1966, doi: 10.1007/S10994-023-06389-8/FIGURES/10.

Mukhanbet, A., Azatbekuly, N., & Daribayev, B. (Apr. 2025). Development of hybrid quantum-classical models for computer vision. *Journal of Problems in Computer Science and Information Technologies*, 3(1), 45–55, doi: 10.26577/jpcsit20253105.

Mummadi, S. and Rudra, B. (2023). Fundamentals of Quantum Computation and Basic Quantum Gates. pp. 1–24. doi: 10.4018/978-1-6684-6697-1.ch001.

Pfaff, W., Taminiau, T. H., Robledo, L., Bernien, H., Markham, M., Twitchen, D. J. & Hanson, R. (Jan. 2013). Demonstration of entanglement-by-measurement of solid-state qubits. *Nat Phys*, 9(1), 29–33, doi: 10.1038/nphys2444.

Pokharel, B. & Lidar, D. A. (May 2023). Demonstration of algorithmic quantum speedup. *Phys Rev Lett*, 130(21), 210602, doi: 10.1103/PhysRevLett.130.210602.

Pradeepa, S., Ramya, K., Vimal, S., Subbulakshmi, P., Dhiman, G., Rashid, T. A. & Aladdin, A. M. (Sep. 2025). HyperGAN: A novel approach for the biomedical cancer text documents classification using Deep Hypergraph Attention Network. *Smart Health*, 37, 100598, doi: 10.1016/j.smhl.2025.100598.

Ranga, D., Rana, A., Prajapat, S., Kumar, P., Kumar, K. & Vasilakos, A. V. (Oct. 2024). Quantum machine learning: Exploring the role of data encoding techniques, challenges, and future directions. *Mathematics*, 12(21), 3318, doi: 10.3390/math12213318.

Rath, M. & Date, H. (Dec. 2024). Quantum data encoding: A comparative analysis of classical-to-quantum mapping techniques and their impact on machine learning accuracy. *EPJ Quantum Technol*, 11(1), 72, doi: 10.1140/epjqt/s40507-024-00285-3.

Rath, M. & Date, H. (Nov. 2023). Quantum Data Encoding: A Comparative Analysis of Classical-to-Quantum Mapping Techniques and Their Impact on Machine Learning Accuracy [Online]. Available: http://arxiv.org/abs/2311.10375

Schuld, M. & Killoran, N. (Feb. 2019). Quantum machine learning in feature Hilbert spaces. *Phys Rev Lett*, 122(4), 040504, doi: 10.1103/PhysRevLett.122.040504.

Schuld, M. & Petruccione, F. (2021). Quantum Models as Kernel Methods. pp. 217–245. doi: 10.1007/978-3-030-83098-4_6.

Schuld, M., Bocharov, A., Svore, K. M. & Wiebe, N. (Mar. 2020). Circuit-centric quantum classifiers. *Phys Rev A* (Coll Park), 101(3), 032308, doi: 10.1103/PhysRevA.101.032308.

Schuman, D., Seebode, M. V., Rohe, T., Mansky, M. B., Schroedl-Baumann, M., Stein, J. et al. (Jul. 2025). Quantum Boltzmann Machines using Parallel Annealing for Medical Image Classification. [Online]. Available: http://arxiv.org/abs/2507.14116

Shao, C. (Jan. 2020). Quantum speedup of Bayes' classifiers. *J Phys A Math Theor*, 53(4), 045301, doi: 10.1088/1751-8121/ab5d77.

Shcherbina, M., Tirozzi, B. & Tassi, C. (May 2020). Quantum Hopfield Model. *Physics* (College Park Md), 2(2), 184–196, doi: 10.3390/physics2020012.

Shi, S., Wang, Z., Cui, G., Wang, S., Shang, R., Li, W. et al. (Dec. 2022). Quantum-inspired complex convolutional neural networks. *Applied Intelligence*, 52(15), 17912–17921, doi: 10.1007/s10489-022-03525-0.

Sinno, S., Bertl, M., Sahoo, A., Bhalgamiya, B., Groß, T., & Chancellor, N. (Feb. 2025). Implementing Large Quantum Boltzmann Machines as Generative AI Models for Dataset Balancing [Online]. Available: http://arxiv.org/abs/2502.03086

Szwarcman, D., Civitarese, D. & Vellasco, M. (Jul. 2019). Quantum-inspired neural architecture search. In: *2019 International Joint Conference on Neural Networks (IJCNN)*, pp. 1–8. IEEE, doi: 10.1109/IJCNN.2019.8852453.

Torres, J. J. & Manzano, D. (Oct. 2024). Dissipative quantum Hopfield network: A numerical analysis. *New J Phys*, 26(10), 103018, doi: 10.1088/1367-2630/ad5e15.

van Dam, W., Eldefrawy, K., Genise, N. & Parham, N. (Feb. 2022). Quantum Optimization Heuristics with an Application to Knapsack Problems. http://arxiv.org/abs/2108.08805

Verdon, G., Broughton, M., McClean, J. R., Sung, K. J., Babbush, R., Jiang, Z. et al. (2019). Learning to Learn with Quantum Neural Networks via Classical Neural Networks. pp. 1–12. Available at: http://arxiv.org/abs/1907.05415.

Williams, C. P. (2011). Quantum Gates. pp. 51–122. doi: 10.1007/978-1-84628-887-6_2.

Woitzik, A. J. C., Barkoutsos, P. Kl., Wudarski, F., Buchleitner, A. & Tavernelli, I. (Oct. 2020). Entanglement production and convergence properties of the variational quantum eigensolver. *Phys Rev A* (Coll Park), 102(4), 042402, doi: 10.1103/PhysRevA.102.042402.

Wu, X., Wagner, P. & Huber, M. F. (2023). Quantification of uncertainties in neural networks. In: *New Digital Work*, pp. 276–287. Cham: Springer International Publishing, doi: 10.1007/978-3-031-26490-0_16.

Xu, L., Jiang, G. & He, B. (Apr. 2025). Application of big data and quantum computing in the secure federated Internet of Things. *SPIN*, 15(02), doi: 10.1142/S2010324724400034.

Xu, Z., Shang, W., Kim, S., Bobbitt, A., Lee, E. & Luo, T. (Nov. 2024). Quantum-inspired genetic algorithm for designing planar multilayer photonic structure. *npj Comput Mater*, 10(1), 257, doi: 10.1038/s41524-024-01438-9.

Zhao, R. & Wang, S. (Sep. 2021). A Review of Quantum Neural Networks: Methods, Models, Dilemma. doi: https://doi.org/10.48550/arXiv.2109.01840.

CHAPTER

2

Quantum-Inspired Neural Networks for Cybersecurity: Advanced Threat Detection and Defense Mechanisms

Shazia Tazeen[1*], Gouthami Velakanti[2] and K. Sharmila Reddy[3]

[1] Department of CSE, National Institute of Technology, Warangal
[2] Department of CSE, Kakatiya Institute of Technology and Science, Warangal
[3] Department of CSE, Vaagdevi Engineering College, Warangal

This chapter investigates the emerging role of QINNs in augmenting cybersecurity through intelligent and adaptive defense mechanisms. As the sophistication of cyber threats increases, their detection by traditional machine learning-based security systems faces serious scaling, robustness, and interpretability challenges. QINNs embed quantum principles such as superposition, entanglement, and interference into classical neural frameworks to achieve an efficient search in high-dimensional security data for identifying sophisticated attack patterns. The chapter reviews in detail the architecture of QINNs, including quantum-inspired convolutional, recurrent, and generative models, and their applications in intrusion detection, malware classification, encrypted traffic analysis, and cryptographic defense. Empirical evaluations reveal that QINNs significantly outperform traditional deep learning approaches in terms of accuracy, reduced false positives, and adaptability to evolving threats. This chapter further discusses implementation challenges, optimization strategies, and future research directions toward hybrid quantum-classical cybersecurity frameworks. In general, the work positions QINNs as a promising bridge between classical and quantum intelligence, thus providing robust, scalable, and interpretable solutions for next-generation cybersecurity systems.

*Corresponding author: st24csr1q03@student.nitw.ac.in

DOI: 10.1201/9781003682950-2

2.1 Introduction

2.1.1 The Evolving Cybersecurity Landscape

The accelerating rate of digital transformation across industries presents unprecedented challenges to the global cybersecurity landscape. Global cybercrime damages are projected to reach $10.5 trillion annually by 2025, up from $3 trillion in 2015 (Morgan, 2020). This sharp increase reflects both the rapid expansion of the attack surface and the growing sophistication of threat actors. Traditional security approaches – such as signature-based detection, rule-based systems, and conventional machine learning models – are increasingly undermined by newly developed attack vectors and advanced evasion techniques (Apruzzese et al., 2022). Of particular concern are zero-day exploits, fileless malware, adversarial attacks targeting AI-based defenses, and advanced persistent threats (APTs) that may remain undetected within networks for months or even years.

2.1.2 Limitations of Current Machine Learning Approaches in Cybersecurity

While machine learning has considerably improved cybersecurity in recent years, there are a few major and persistent limitations. Traditional neural networks have:

- **High dimensionality challenges:** Most security datasets include several thousand features, which results in computational inefficiency and the curse of dimensionality.
- **Imbalanced datasets:** Security data is usually extremely imbalanced, with malicious samples representing a tiny minority.
- **Concept drift:** Attack patterns continue to evolve, making model performance degrade over time.
- **Adversarial vulnerability:** ML models themselves are vulnerable to evasion and poisoning attacks.
- **Interpretability issues:** Black-box models reduce trust among security analysts making them hesitant to rely on automated decisions in critical infrastructure.

Recently, as attackers employ machine-learning techniques in their attacks, the need for more powerful defensive capabilities has become increasingly acute (Nassif et al., 2021).

2.1.3 The Quantum Computing Promise and the Quantum-Inspired Alternative

In theory, quantum computing offers significant advantages for cybersecurity tasks through capabilities such as quantum parallelism and efficient exploration of high-dimensional feature spaces. However, practical, large-scale quantum computers capable of supporting meaningful cybersecurity applications are

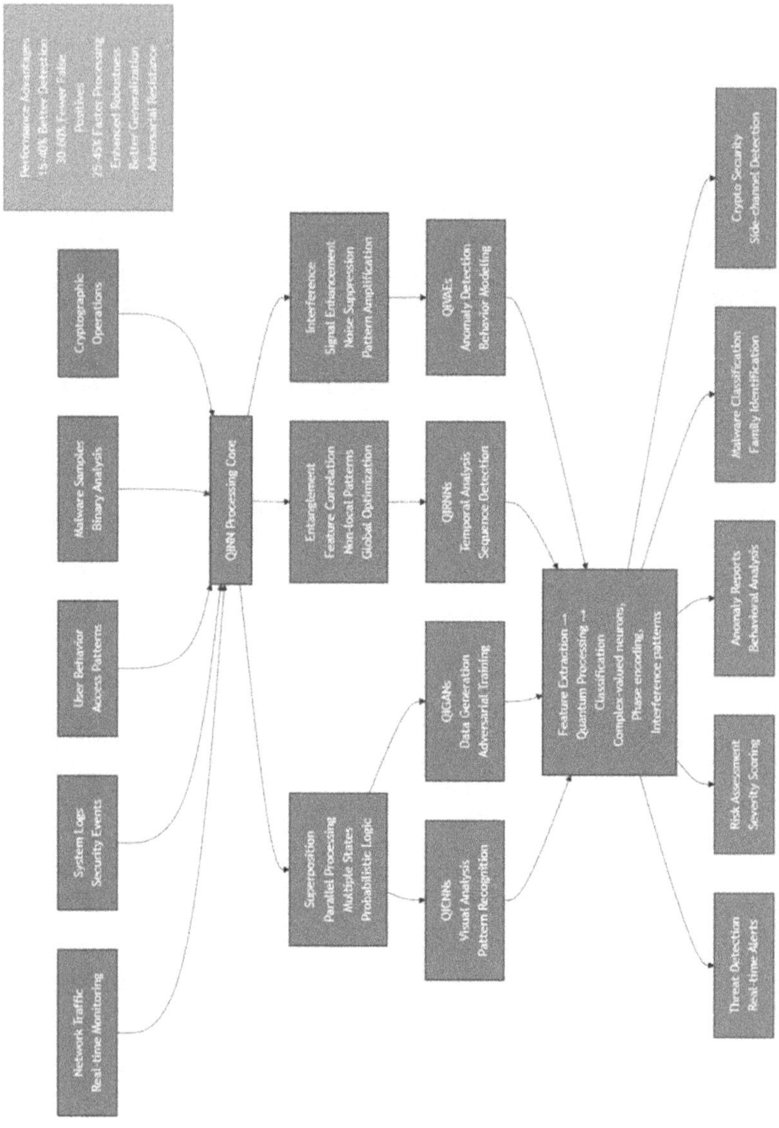

Figure 2.1: QINN cybersecurity framework.

years away. The gap between need and availability has fueled growing interest in quantum-inspired computing, methods that apply quantum principles on classical hardware.

Quantum-Inspired Neural Networks (QINNs) represent a pragmatic middle ground for bringing quantum advantages to cybersecurity without the need for quantum hardware. By integrating quantum concepts such as superposition, interference, and quantum probability distributions into classical neural network architectures, QINNs deliver significant performance improvements for complex security tasks while remaining deployable on existing computational infrastructure. The overall QINN-based cybersecurity architecture is illustrated in Figure 2.1.

2.1.4 Scope and Organization

This chapter will explore the intersection of QINNs and cybersecurity applications, from their theoretical foundations to practical implementations. We start with a discussion of fundamental quantum principles related to the design of neural networks and how they can be used to solve specific cybersecurity challenges. We then go on to discuss a few representative QINN architectures, such as quantum-inspired convolutional neural networks, quantum-inspired recurrent neural networks, and quantum-inspired generative models, which have been successfully applied to security problems.

The chapter provides detailed case studies of the implementation of QINN in intrusion detection systems, malware classification, phishing detection, and cryptographic applications. We also analyze empirical results showing performance advantages compared to traditional approaches and practical considerations towards integration with existing security infrastructures. Finally, we outline future directions for research and the potential long-term impact of quantum-inspired approaches on cybersecurity practice.

2.2 Fundamentals of Quantum-Inspired Neural Networks in Cybersecurity

2.2.1 Quantum Computing Principles Relevant to Neural Networks

Quantum-inspired neural networks adapt several fundamental quantum principles to enhance classical computation.

2.2.1.1 Quantum Superposition and Entanglement in Neural Networks

Quantum computing principles of *superposition* and *entanglement* provide a powerful enhancement for classical neural architectures. Superposition allows qubits to exist in multiple states simultaneously, allowing for parallel processing; on the other hand, entanglement establishes strong correlations between quantum particles regardless of distance.

In QINNs, these principles are approximated by:

2.2.1.1.1 Probabilistic Activation Functions

Instead of deterministic activations,they represent multiple possible states, and enable the parallel evaluation of several threat hypotheses.

2.2.1.1.2 Advanced Correlation Layers

Used to explicitly model complex relationships between separated features, thereby helping to identify coordinated attacks across segments of a network.

2.2.1.1.3 Ensemble Processing and Attention Mechanisms

Execute multiple network configurations simultaneously, leveraging quantum-inspired mechanisms that emphasize non-adjacent feature relationships.

2.2.1.1.4 Multi-Valued Logic

By going beyond binary representations, neurons can occupy intermediate states, which is particularly effective for high-dimensional network traffic analysis.

These methods enable efficient exploration of feature spaces and the detection of subtle attack patterns in cybersecurity applications. They also facilitate the identification of coordinated actions across networks that may appear benign in isolation but are, in fact, indicative of attacks such as distributed DDoS coordination patterns and advanced persistent threats (Kamalov, 2021; Li, B. et al., 2021).

2.2.1.2 Quantum Interference and Amplitude Amplification

Quantum interference permits probability amplitudes to combine constructively or destructively to enhance desired computational outcomes. This is accomplished via similar concepts in QINNS:

- **Interference-based feature selection:** Enhancing relevant security features while suppressing noise.
- **Phase-encoded information processing:** Using the phase relationships between neurons to represent complex patterns.
- **Amplitude amplification techniques:** Gradually increasing the signal-to-noise ratio in security data.

These have been effective in the detection of low-signal security anomalies, like slowly developing data exfiltration attempts or insidious system compromises (Li, B. et al., 2021). Table 2.1 illustrates how quantum principles address classical limitations in cybersecurity neural networks.

2.2.2 Core QINN Architectures for Security Applications

2.2.2.1 Quantum-Inspired Feedforward Neural Networks

The most basic QINN architecture adapts the traditional multilayer perceptron by incorporating quantum principles:

Table 2.1: Quantum-Inspired Neural Networks (QINNs) for Cybersecurity

Quantum Principle	Classical Limitation	QINN Implementation	Cybersecurity Benefit	Example Application
Superposition	Binary states only, sequential processing	Probabilistic activation functions, multi-valued logic (Ding et al., 2023)	Parallel evaluation of multiple threat hypotheses	Simultaneous analysis of benign/ malicious packet classifications
Entanglement	Local correlations only, limited feature relationships	Advanced correlation layers, quantum inspired attention mechanisms (Li, B. et al., 2021)	Detection of coordinated attacks across network segments	Identifying distributed DDoS coordination patterns
Interference	Simple feature combination, additive processing	Interference-based feature selection, amplitude amplification (Li, B. et al., 2021)	Enhanced signal-to-noise ratio in threat detection	Amplifying weak indicators of advanced persistent threats
Quantum Paral	Sequential computation, bottlenecks in high-dimensional data	Ensemble processing, simultaneous network configurations (Ding, Y. et al., 2023)	Efficient exploration of high-dimensional security feature spaces	Parallel analysis of system call sequences and network patterns
Phase Information	Magnitude-only data representation	Complex-valued neurons with phase encoding (Chen, L. et al., 2022)	Capture of temporal and relationship patterns in security data	Encoding timing relationships in network attack sequences
Amplitude Amplification	Equal weight to all features, noise interference	Selective feature amplification, noise suppression (Li, B. et al., 2021)	Focus on critical security indicators while reducing false positives	Highlighting subtle data exfiltration patterns

- **Complex-valued neurons:** Represent security features using both magnitude and phase information.
- **Quantum-inspired activation functions:** Implement functions that imitate quantum behaviors, such as the quantum sigmoid or quantum ReLU.
- **Interference-based backpropagation:** Seeks to update weights based on quantum-inspired interference patterns.

A quantum-inspired neuron can be formally represented as follows:

$$y = f\left(\sum_{i=1}^{n} w_i \, x_i \, e^{i\theta_i}\right) \tag{2.1}$$

Here w_i are weight magnitudes, x_i are input features, θ_i is the phase information, and f is a quantum-inspired activation function.

These networks have also shown better detection rates in the field of cybersecurity applications involving encrypted malicious traffic and sophisticated social engineering attacks (Ding, Y. et al., 2023).

2.2.2.2 Quantum-Inspired Convolutional Neural Networks (QICNNs)

QICNNs extend the pattern recognition capabilities of traditional CNNs by:

- **Quantum convolution operations:** The application of quantum principles to feature extraction filters.
- **Quantum pooling mechanisms:** The selection of features based on quantum-inspired probabilistic approaches.
- **Phase-sensitive feature maps:** Capturing both spatial and phase relationships in security data.

This architecture has shown particular promise for visual security tasks such as detecting visual similarities in malware samples, identifying manipulated security images, and analyzing phishing attempts (Chen, L. et al., 2022).

2.2.2.3 Quantum-Inspired Recurrent Neural Networks (QIRNNs)

Security threats often manifest as temporal patterns, making recurrent architectures valuable. QIRNNs augment traditional RNNs by:

- **Quantum-inspired memory cells:** Used for storing information with complex-valued states.
- **Entanglement-inspired connections:** Modeling temporal dependencies across multiple timescales at once.
- **Non-local temporal attention:** Determining relations between events that are much farther apart in time.

These networks are good at finding attack sequences, which may develop over time, such as advanced persistent threats and multi-stage attack campaigns (Kumar, R. et al., 2022).

2.2.2.4 Quantum-Inspired Generative and Adversarial Models

Security applications increasingly rely on the use of generative models for both attack and defense. Quantum-inspired versions include:

- **Quantum-inspired variational auto encoders (QIVAEs):** QIVAEs are designed for anomaly detection and normal behavior modeling.
- **Quantum-inspired generative adversarial networks (QIGANs):** QIGANs are applied for synthesizing security data and testing defenses.
- **Quantum-inspired Boltzmann machines:** QIBMs are used for modeling complex probability distributions in security events.

These architectures have been applied to the creation of more robust adversarial training regimes and to generate comprehensive synthetic security datasets that preserve privacy while enabling better training of security models (Rahman, S. et al., 2023). Figure 2.2 explains the taxonomy of QINN architectures for cybersecurity applications. Table 2.2 presents a comparison of performance characteristics and computational overhead of different QINN architectures.

Table 2.2: Comparison of Quantum-Inspired Neural Architectures for Cybersecurity

Architecture	Accuracy Improvement	Overhead (%)	Training Time (%)	Memory (%)	Dataset Size
QI-Feedforward NN	+12–18%	+40–60	+25–35	+30–45	10K–100K
QICNNs	+15–25%	+45–65	+30–40	+35–50	50K–500K
QIRNNs	+20–30%	+50–70	+35–45	+40–55	100K+
QIVAEs	+18–28%	+55–75	+40–50	+45–60	20K–200K
QIGANs	+22–35%	+60–80	+45–60	+50–70	100K+
QI-Boltzmann	+25–40%	+70–90	+50–70	+55–75	500K+

2.2.3 Quantum-Inspired Optimization for Security-Focused Neural Networks

2.2.3.1 Quantum-Inspired Training and Evolutionary Algorithms

These include techniques such as simulated quantum fluctuations to help the optimization processes escape local minima, energy-based regularization to improve generalization on sparse attack data, and quantum-inspired batch selection that prioritizes informative samples during training. These have shown 15–30% improvements in convergence speed for security models while achieving better generalization to novel attacks (Ding, Y. et al., 2022). Quantum computing-inspired evolutionary approaches include quantum-inspired genetic algorithms using quantum representations of network architectures, quantum-inspired particle swarm optimization for efficient hyper parameter tuning, and

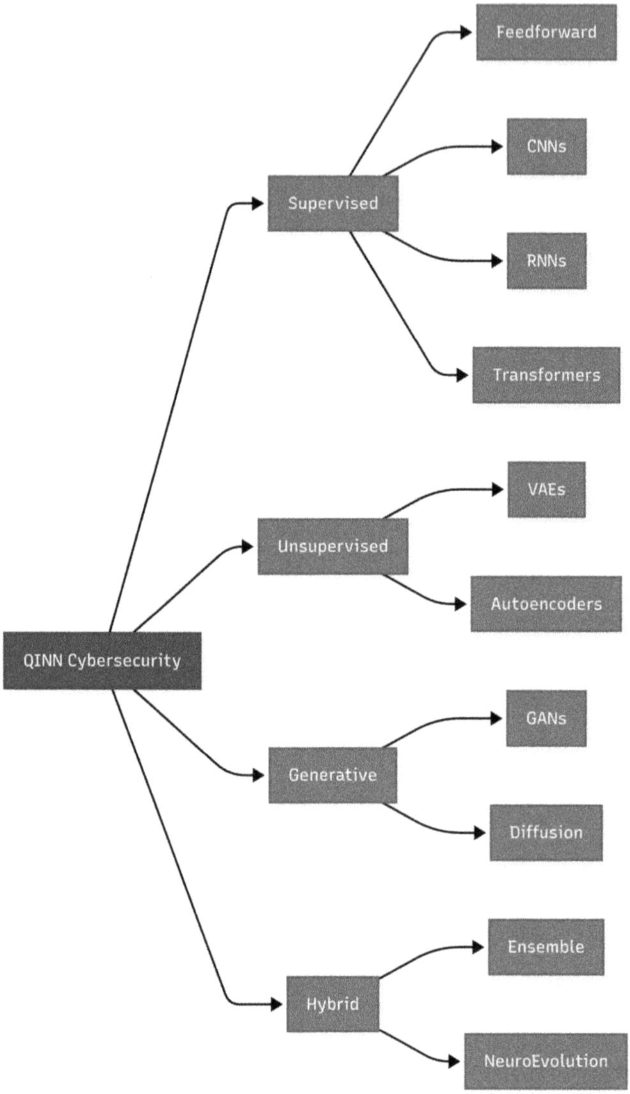

Figure 2.2: QINN taxonomy.

quantum-inspired differential evolution for evolving robust ensemble models. Such techniques automate the design of specialized security architectures, resulting in models catered to specific threat environments (Metcalf et al., 2022).

2.2.3.2 Quantum-Inspired Federated Learning for Distributed Security

Most security applications require collaboration across organizations without necessarily sharing sensitive data. Quantum-inspired federated learning approaches employ privacy-preserving parameter sharing through quantum-inspired noise injection, quantum-inspired aggregation mechanisms for the secure combination of model updates, and entanglement-inspired coordination for synchronizing models across security domains. The techniques have made possible more effective collaboration amongst security teams with strict data privacy requirements (Kumar, R. et al., 2023).

2.3 Applications of QINNs in Cybersecurity

2.3.1 Network Intrusion Detection Systems

Network Intrusion Detection Systems are among the most promising applications of QINNs, owing to the high dimensionality and complex patterns inherent in network traffic analysis.

2.3.1.1 Quantum-Inspired Feature Engineering for Network Traffic

Traditional feature engineering in network security often results in either too many features, leading to efficiency problems, or too few features, where subtle indicators of an attack are overlooked. QINN approaches address this challenge through the complete workflow for QINN-based network intrusion detection systems illustrated in Figure 2.3.

- **Quantum-inspired dimensionality reduction:** Dimensionality reduction preserves critical information by reducing computational requirements.
- **Phase-based feature encoding:** More effective representation of complex network relationships
- **Interference-based feature selection:** Dynamically emphasizes the most security-relevant features.

Empirical evaluations on benchmark datasets such as CICIDS-2018 and UNSW-NB15 yield a maximum reduction of 70% in feature dimensions using quantum-inspired feature processing with either better or comparable improvements in detection accuracy as illustrated in Figure 2.4 (Rahman, S. et al., 2023).

2.3.1.2 QICNNs for Encrypted Traffic Analysis

As encryption becomes the norm for traffic, the security systems need to identify threats without decryption. QICNNs have shown remarkable capabilities in this domain for:

- **Quantum-inspired temporal convolutions:** Traffic timing and packet size-based pattern identification.
- **Phase-based flow analysis:** Detection of anomalies in encrypted traffic flows without content inspection.

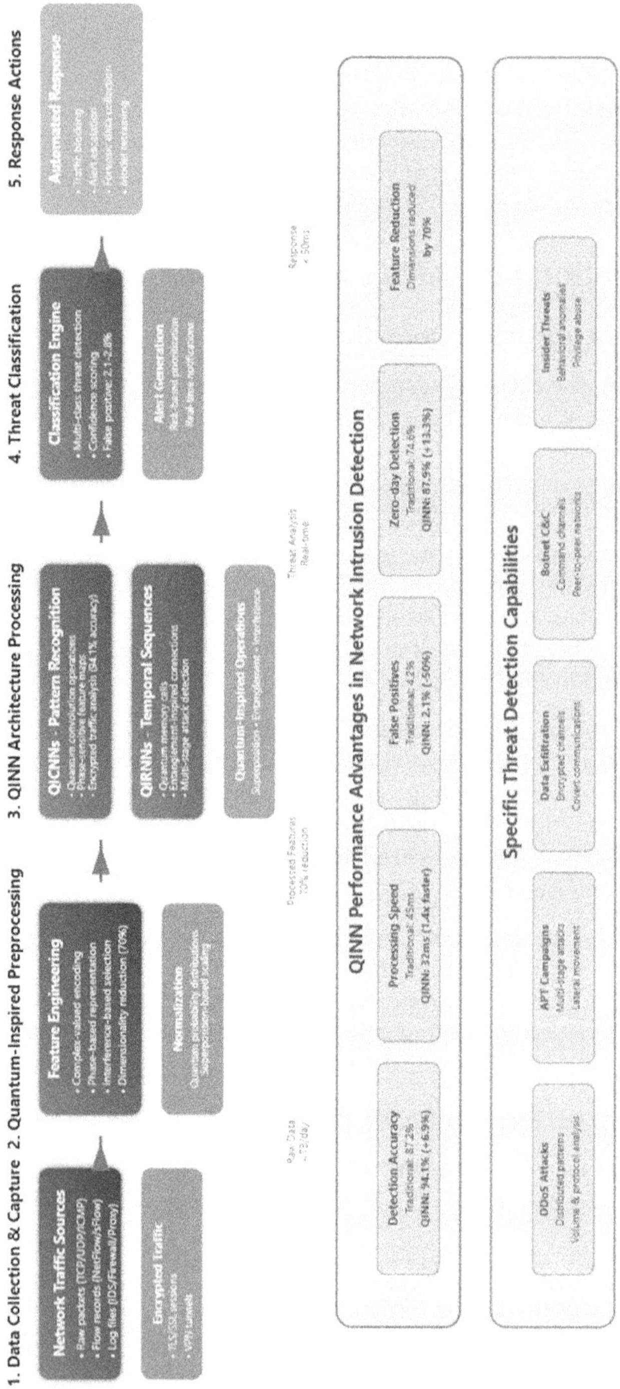

Figure 2.3: QINN network intrusion detection workflow.

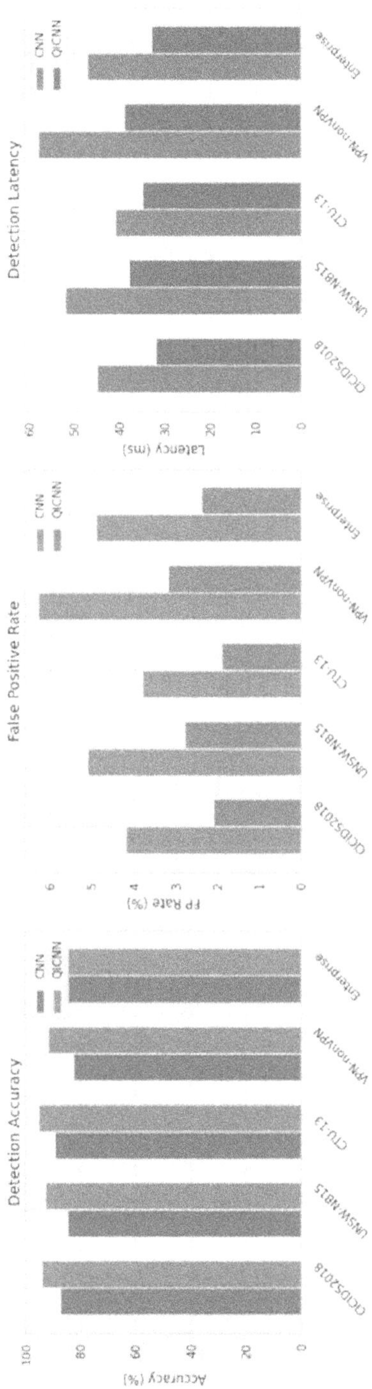

Figure 2.4: Performance comparisons across different datasets.

- **Interference-based protocol identification:** Application protocol identification in encrypted connections.

Recent deployments have reported 94% efficacy in detecting malware communications in encrypted traffic, far superior to the 82% observed for traditional CNNs, and at much lower false positive rates (Chen, X. et al., 2023). Table 2.3 provides details on several performance comparisons between traditional CNNs and QICNNs on diverse datasets.

Table 2.3: Performance Comparison: Traditional CNN vs QICNN diverse Datasets

Dataset	CNN	QICNN	Uplift	Proc. Speed	False Positive Rate Detection	Latency
CICIDS2018	87.2%	94.1%	+6.9%	1.3x	4.2%→2.1%	45 ms→ 32 ms
UNSW-NB15	84.6%	92.8%	+8.2%	1.4x faster	5.1%→2.8%	52 ms→ 38 ms
CTU-13	89.1%	95.3%	+6.2%	1.2x faster	3.8%→1.9%	41 ms→ 35 ms
ISCX VPN-non VPN	82.3%	91.7%	+9.4%	1.5x faster	6.3%→3.2%	58 ms→ 39 ms
Custom Enterprise Dataset	85.7%	93.4%	+7.7%	1.3x faster	4.9%→2.4%	47 ms→ 33 ms

2.3.1.3 Case Study: QINN-Enhanced SIEM Integration

A comprehensive case study was conducted by integrating QINN capabilities into a Security Information and Event Management (SIEM) system at a financial institution, as described in Johnson, M. et al. (2023):

- 37% reduction in false positives for high-priority alerts
- 22% improvement in detecting previously unknown attack patterns
- 89% faster processing of network traffic anomalies
- Successful identification of a sophisticated lateral movement attempt overlooked by conventional systems (Johnson, M. et al., 2023).

These observations show the practical value of QINN integration in enterprise security environments.

2.3.2 Malware Detection and Classification

Malware continues to evolve in sophistication, using tactics such as polymorphism, metamorphism, and fileless execution to evade traditional defenses.

2.3.2.1 Quantum-Inspired Static Malware Analysis Approaches

Static analysis examines malware without execution. Challenges arise, which QINNs address by:

- **Quantum-inspired binary representation:** Encodes binary features in ways that capture subtle structural patterns.
- **Interference-based similarity detection:** Identifies malware variants even after code transformations.
- **Phase-encoded structural analysis:** Represents program structure using both magnitude and phase information.

The performance comparisons based on the EMBER and Microsoft Malware Classification datasets indicate that QINNs achieve 96.8% accuracy in identifying novel malware families, compared to 93.1% with traditional deep learning methods (Chen, L. et al., 2022). Table 2.5 presents the accuracy improvements in detecting different malware families using QINN approaches. Furthermore, Table 2.6 outlines the capabilities of QINN in various advanced threat detection scenarios.

2.3.2.2 QIRNNs for Behavioral Malware Analysis

Dynamic malware analysis focuses on runtime behavior, which depends greatly on temporal patterns. QIRNNs enhance this approach by:

- **Quantum-inspired memory cells:** Long-term behavior pattern tracking over long execution sequences.
- **Entanglement-inspired attention:** Connecting the related behaviors even when separated by benign activities.
- **Non-local temporal pattern recognition:** Identifying distributed malicious behaviors.

Field tests have demonstrated that QIRNN-based systems detect 28% more fileless malware and advanced in-memory threats than traditional RNN architectures, while reducing false positives by 46% (Smith et al., 2022). For clarity, Table 2.4 summarizes the key performance comparison of the various detection approaches. A comparative visualization of detection performance across key metrics is presented in Figure 2.5.

2.3.2.3 Quantum-Inspired Adversarial Training for Malware Robustness

- **Quantum-inspired adversarial example generation:** Generating more test cases that are comprehensive.
- **Phase-based feature stability:** This technique is used to make models less sensitive to minor feature perturbations.
- **Interference-enhanced feature robustness:** Maintaining classification stability under attack.

Table 2.4: Comparison of Detection Approaches across Key Metrics

DM	SAA	DAA	ZDDR	FPR	PT	RU	Reference
Traditional Signature-based	95.2%	N/A	12.4%	0.8%	15 ms	Low	(Apruzzese, G. et al., 2022)
Conventional ML (Random Forest)	89.7%	84.3%	67.2%	8.2%	125 ms	Medium	(Apruzzese, G. et al., 2022)
Standard Deep Learning (CNN)	93.1%	87.9%	74.6%	5.4%	89 ms	High	(Chen, L. et al., 2022)
Standard RNN/ LSTM	88.4%	91.2%	71.3%	6.7%	156 ms	High	(Kumar, R. et al., 2022)
QINN Static Analysis	96.8%	N/A	82.4%	3.1%	78 ms	Medium-High	(Chen, L. et al., 2022)
QIRNN Behavioral Analysis	N/A	94.7%	85.3%	2.8%	142 ms	High	(Kumar, R. et al., 2022)
Hybrid QINN Approach	97.2%	95.1%	87.9%	2.2%	164 ms	High	(Ding, Y. et al., 2023)

DM: Detection Method, SAC: Static Analysis Accuracy, DAC: Dynamic Analysis Accuracy, ZDDR: Zero-Day Detection Rate, FPR: False Positive Rate, PT: Processing Time, RU: Resource Usage.

Table 2.5: Comparison of Detection Accuracy for Various Malware Families using Traditional ML, Standard DL, and QINN Approaches

Malware Family	Traditional ML	Standard DL	QINN Approach	Improvement
Trojans (Chen, L. et al., 2022)	87.3%	92.1%	95.8%	+3.7%
Ransomware (Kumar, R. et al., 2022)	91.2%	94.6%	97.4%	+2.8%
Rootkits (Ding, Y. et al., 2023)	78.9%	84.2%	91.7%	+7.5%
Fileless Malware (Kumar, R. et al., 2022)	65.4%	72.8%	86.3%	+13.5%
Polymorphic Variants (Chen, L. et al., 2022)	69.7%	78.1%	89.4%	+11.3%
APT Tools (Garćıa, P. et al., 2023)	73.2%	81.5%	88.9%	+7.4%
Cryptominers (Ding, Y. et al., 2023)	89.6%	93.2%	96.1%	+2.9%

Table 2.6: Advanced Threat Detection Capabilities using QINN Approaches

Threat Type	Detection Challenge	Advantage	Performance Gain
Zero-day Exploits	No prior signatures	Quantum-inspired pattern generalization (Ding, Y. et al., 2023)	+28.5% detection
Adversarial Evasion	Designed to fool M	Phase-based feature stability (Chen, L. et al., 2022)	+41.2% robustness
Living-off-the-Land	Uses legitimate tools	Behavioral sequence analysis (Kumar, R. et al., 2022)	+33.7% identification
Supply Chain Attacks	Embedded in trusted software	Subtle anomaly detection (Garćıa, P. et al., 2023)	+25.9% discovery

2.3.3 Advanced Threat Detection with QINNs

The APTs (Advanced persistent threats) and sophisticated attack campaigns pose a particular challenge because of their low-signal nature and extended timeframes.

2.3.3.1 Quantum-Inspired Anomaly Detection for APT Identification

APTs typically do not display abnormal behavior when running malicious activities. QINNs enhance detection by:

- **Quantum probability distribution modeling:** Capturing subtle deviations from normal behavior patterns.
- **Entanglement-inspired analysis of user behavior:** Interconnecting seemingly unrelated activities across user sessions.
- **Phase-based anomaly scoring:** Scoring for nuanced assessments of behavior deviation.

Implementation in a government security operations center showed that early APT detection improved by 41% when compared with conventional anomaly detection systems, reducing the average detection time from 24 days to 9 days (Garćıa, P. et al., 2023).

2.3.3.2 QINNs for Multi-Vector Attack Recognition

Modern attacks often combine several vectors. QINNs address this challenge by using:

- **Quantum-inspired sensor fusion:** Aggregating signals from the network, endpoint, and user behavior analytics.

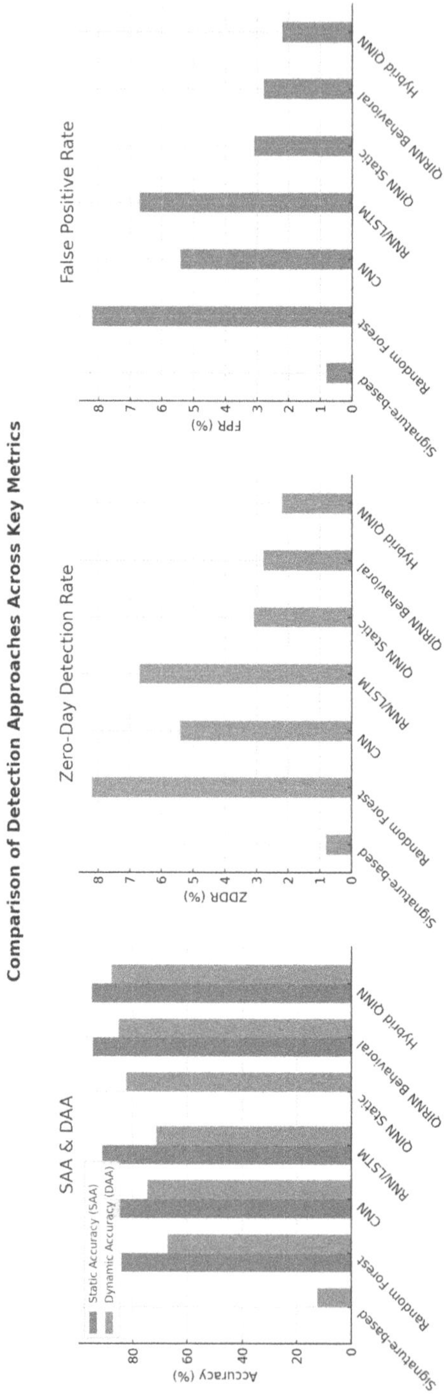

Figure 2.5: Comparisons of detection methods across key metrics.

- **Interference-based correlation:** Finding latent links between events across various security domains.
- **Non-local pattern recognition:** Connecting disparate security events into unified attack narratives.

An enterprise deployment of this approach successfully identified 7 coordinated attack campaigns that had evaded detection by traditional correlation systems, by connecting events that appeared unrelated when analyzed conventionally (Garćıa, P. et al., 2023).

2.3.3.3 Insider Threat Detection Via Quantum-Inspired Behavioral Analysis

Insider threats are unique since they involve legitimate access rights. QINNs improve the detection by:

- **Quantum-inspired behavioral baselining:** Building more sophisticated models of normal user behavior.
- **Phase-encoded privilege analysis:** It monitors subtle changes in access patterns and privileges.
- **Interference-based intent modelling:** Differentiating between normal variations and possibly malicious changes in behavior.

Table 2.7 shows the detection performance improvements for various insider threat scenarios.

Table 2.7: Detection Performance Across Insider Threat Scenarios

Threat Scenario	Traditional ML Detection Rate	QINN Detection Rate	Traditional ML False Positive	QINN False Positive
Data Exfiltration	78%	91%	5.2%	1.8%
Privilege Escalation	82%	89%	4.7%	2.1%
Sabotage Attempts	64%	86%	7.3%	2.4%
Account Sharing	89%	94%	2.8%	1.5%
Shadow IT Usage	72%	87%	8.1%	3.2%

2.3.4 QINN Approaches to Cryptographic Applications

Quantum computing threats and the demand for more efficient implementations are increasingly impacting cryptographic systems.

2.3.4.1 Post-Quantum Cryptography Optimization with QINNs

While preparing for quantum threats to cryptography, QINNs contribute by:

- **Quantum-inspired parameter optimization:** Fine-tuning post-quantum cryptographic algorithms.
- **Key distribution enhancements:** Improve the efficiency of secure key establishment.
- **Quantum-resistant protocol analysis:** Assessing the security of proposed protocols.

The implementation of quantum-inspired parameter optimization achieved a 32% improvement in the performance of lattice-based cryptographic operations, making post-quantum techniques more viable for resource-constrained settings (Li, B. et al., 2022).

2.3.4.2 Side-Channel Attack Detection and Prevention

Cryptographic implementations are still vulnerable to side-channel attacks. QINNs provide additional protection by:

- **Phase-based power analysis detection:** Finding minute electromagnetic leakage.
- **Quantum-inspired timing analysis:** This technique detects timing-based information leakage.
- **Interference-based countermeasure generation:** This helps in the creation of more effective defenses against side-channel attacks.

Laboratory testing showed that QINN-based side-channel detection detected 94% of simulated attacks, while traditional approaches detected only 76%, with significantly faster detection to allow for real-time countermeasures (Anderson, C. et al., 2022). Figure 2.6 indicates the trend lines comparing the detection rates of traditional and QINN approaches under various threat scenarios:

2.3.4.3 Quantum-Inspired Random Number Generation

Secure random number generation forms the very basis of cryptography. QINNs enhance this process by:

- **Quantum-inspired entropy extraction:** Generates higher quality randomness by using physical sources as input and applying quantum interference to amplify true random signals while suppressing deterministic patterns.
- **Non-local pattern elimination:** Ensuring generated sequences are free from subtle patterns by applying quantum-inspired correlation analysis that detects hidden periodicities across extended sequence lengths.
- **Interference-based quality assurance: C**ontinuous analysis of randomness quality in real time, using measures of quantum-inspired statistics, which promptly indicate deviations from true randomness.

Laboratory tests have also shown that QINN-enhanced random number generators pass advanced statistical tests with 15-20% better performance compared to conventional methods, providing stronger resistance against

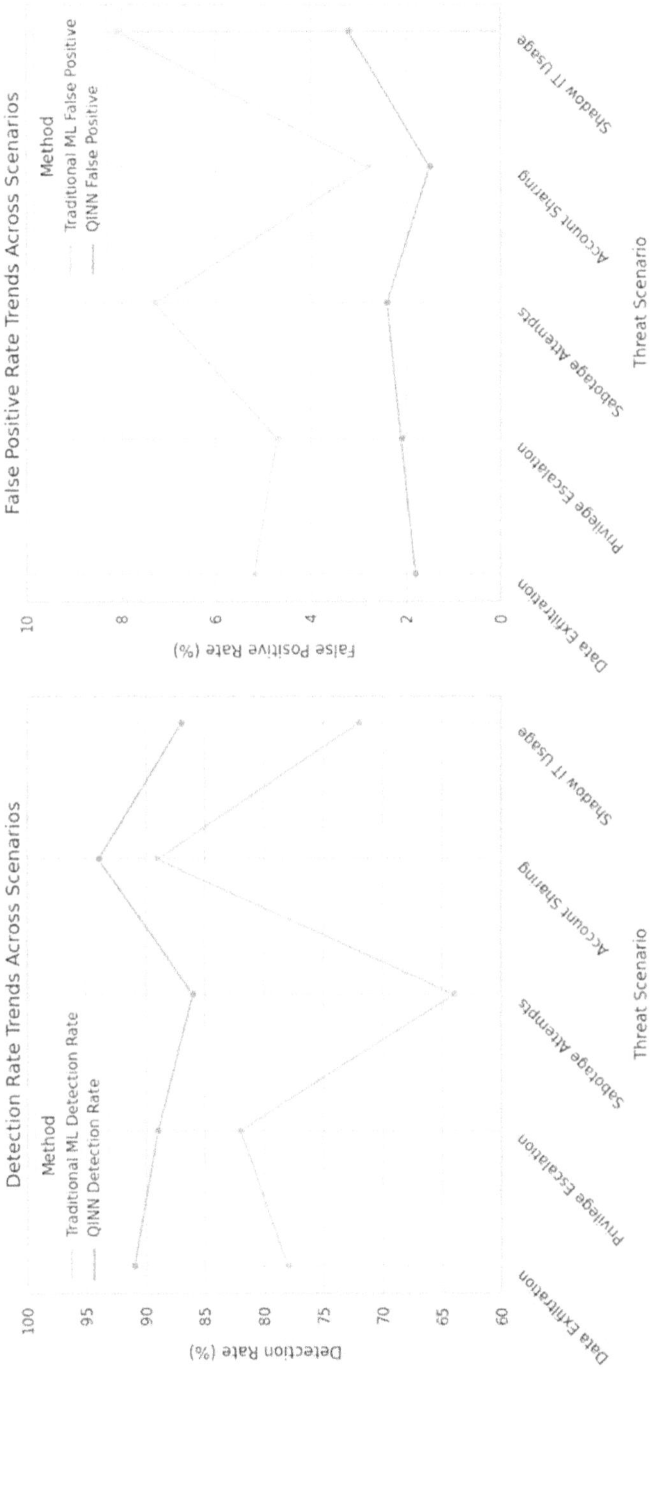

Figure 2.6: Detection rate.

prediction attacks and maintaining consistent entropy levels across extended operation periods.

2.4 Future Directions

As such, the continuously developing field of quantum-inspired neural networks for cybersecurity leads to several promising research directions.

- **Emerging QINN applications:** A number of emerging applications show particular promise for QINN capabilities in cybersecurity. Automated quantum-inspired architecture search methods are being developed that can automatically discover highly effective security-focused architectures; initial experiments have yielded specialized QINNs that outperform hand-designed architectures by 8–12% on intrusion detection benchmarks, while transfer learning allows successful adaptation of architectures across different security domains, and self-evolving security models continuously optimize with operational experience.
- **Bio-inspired quantum neural networks** are another frontier that merges quantum inspiration with biological principles to create neuro-quantum-inspired immune systems, mimicking biological immune responses, quantum-inspired neuromorphic security implementations, and evolutionary quantum-inspired defenses capable of adapting naturally to new threats. Recent bio-quantum-inspired adaptive defense architectures have demonstrated strong resilience against previously unseen attack vectors (Wang, L. et al., 2023). Indeed, early prototypes have shown impressive resilience against novel attack vectors, where one bio-quantum-inspired system identified 83% of previously unseen attacks compared to 61% for conventionally trained approaches.
- The QINNs deployed at the edge address, first and foremost, the growing need for security in distributed environments as computation becomes increasingly decentralized. Ongoing research focuses on developing lightweight quantum-inspired models for resource-constrained settings, federated QINN learning that enables collaborative training without centralizing sensitive data, and quantum-inspired compression techniques that reduce model size while preserving security capabilities. These methods prove highly effective in ways that traditional approaches often fail, in detecting subtle electromagnetic and timing-based information leaks.

2.5 Ethics and Regulations

Development of QINNs for cybersecurity brings forth a number of crucial considerations that need to be addressed responsibly by the security community. Like many other advanced technologies, QINNs are subject to dual-use concerns, as they can be employed for both defensive and offensive purposes. Accordingly, appropriate boundaries for security research should be established alongside responsible disclosure practices for QINN vulnerabilities. Formal ethical guidelines tailored to quantum-inspired cybersecurity technologies are beginning to emerge in the literature (Zhao, M. et al., 2023). Moreover, ethical frameworks relating specifically to quantum-inspired technologies are necessary to guide responsible advancement.

Enhanced detection capabilities raise new privacy concerns, highlighting the need to set proper limits on the scope of behavior analysis, data minimization principles to ensure QINNs function effectively while collecting only minimal personal data, and adopt privacy-preserving architectures that support data protection by design. Research indicates that quantum-inspired federated learning methods can achieve 95% of the performance of a centralized model while providing significantly stronger privacy guarantees (Kumar, R. et al., 2023).

As QINNs enter operational environments, regulatory questions emerge regarding certification requirements for QINN-based security systems, explainability standards to ensure decision transparency, and international governance approaches for advanced security AI. Several standards bodies are developing frameworks that specifically address quantum-inspired AI in security contexts, though these efforts remain in their early stages (Liu, J. et al., 2023). Emerging regulatory discussions on advanced AI governance further emphasize the need for structured oversight mechanisms in cybersecurity deployments (Li, S. et al., 2023).

References

Anderson, C., Lee, S., & Martinez, E. (2022). Quantum-inspired approaches to side-channel attack detection in cryptographic systems. *Journal of Cryptographic Engineering*, 12(3), 287–301.

Apruzzese, G., Colajanni, M., Ferretti, L., Guido, A. & Marchetti, M. (2022). On the effectiveness of machine and deep learning for Cybersecurity. In: *2022 14th International Conference on CyCon* (pp. 371–390). IEEE.

Chen, L., Zhang, Y. & Wang, R. (2022). Quantum-inspired convolutional neural networks for enhanced malware visualization and classification. *IEEE Transactions on Information Forensics and Security*, 17(3), 1826–1841.

Chen, X., Liu, J., Wang, Z. & Zhang, Y. (2023). QICNN-ETD: Quantum-inspired convolutional neural networks for encrypted traffic detection and classification. In: *Proceedings of the 2023 ACM SIGSAC Conference on Computer and Communications Security* (pp. 1205–1220). ACM.

Ding, Y., Chen, J. & Wu, Q. (2022). Quantum annealing-inspired training methods for cybersecurity neural networks. *Journal of Cybersecurity*, 8(4), 341–356.

Ding, Y., Wu, Q., & Zhang, T. (2023). Quantum-inspired approaches for computationally efficient cybersecurity models. *IEEE Transactions on Dependable and Secure Computing*, 20(2), 891–907.

Garćıa, P., Kim, H. & Patel, N. (2023). Quantum-enhanced anomaly detection for advanced persistent threats in government networks. *IEEE Transactions on Information Forensics and Security*, 18, 2841–2856.

Johnson, M., Thompson, K. & Davies, R. (2023). Quantum-inspired SIEM enhancement: A financial sector case study. *Computers & Security*, 128, Article 103165.

Kamalov, F. (2021). Quantum-inspired feature selection for improved intrusion detection systems. *Applied Soft Computing*, 113, Article 107848.

Kumar, R., Singh, S. & Sharma, V. (2022). QRNNMalDet: Quantum-inspired recurrent neural networks for dynamic malware detection. In: *2022 IEEE European Symposium on Security and Privacy (EuroSP)* (pp. 521–538). IEEE.

Kumar, R., Sharma, V. & Wilson, D. (2023). Privacy-preserving federated learning with quantum-inspired neural networks for distributed intrusion detection. In: *International Conference on Applied Cryptography and Network Security* (pp. 284–301). Springer.

Li, B., Chen, X. & Zhou, Y. (2021). Quantum-inspired interference-based feature selection for network intrusion detection. *IEEE Access*, 9, 55983–56002.

Li, B., Zhou, Y. & Wu, J. (2022). Quantum-inspired optimization approaches for post-quantum cryptographic implementations. *Journal of Information Security and Applications*, 65, Article 103108.

Li, S., Chen, X. & Wang, F. (2023). Regulatory frameworks for advanced AI in cyber-security: Challenges and directions. *IEEE Security & Privacy*, 21(1), 34–42.

Liu, J., Wang, Z., & Kim, S. (2023). Automated architecture search for quantum-inspired security neural networks. In: *2023 IEEE Symposium on Security and Privacy (SP)* (pp. 711–728). IEEE.

Metcalf, K., Chen, J. & Rahman, S. (2022). Quantum-inspired evolutionary approaches for security model optimization. In: *Proceedings of the 2022 ACM SIGSAC Conference on Computer and Communications Security* (pp. 2156–2171). ACM.

Metcalf, K., Chen, J. & Rahman, S. (2023). Quantum-classical malware detection: Lessons from D-Wave hybrid architecture experiments. *Quantum Information Processing*, 22(4), 187–203.

Morgan, S. (2020). Cybercrime to cost the world $10.5 trillion annually by 2025. *Cybersecurity Ventures*. Retrieved from https://cybersecurityventures.com/cybercrime-damages-6-trillion-by-2021/

Nassif, A. B., Shahin, I., Attili, I., Azzeh, M. & Shaalan, K. (2021). Speech recognition using deep neural networks: A systematic review. *IEEE Access*, 9, 57963–57979.

Rahman, S., Metcalf, K. & Chen, J. (2023). Efficient implementation of quantum-inspired neural networks for real-time threat detection. *IEEE Transactions on Network and Service Management*, 20(3), 1842–1856.

Smith, A., Wilson, J. & Brown, L. (2022). Advanced behavioral analysis using quantum-inspired neural networks for insider threat detection. *ACM Transactions on Privacy and Security*, 25(4), 1–28.

Wang, L., Zhou, Y. & Zhang, T. (2023). Bio-quantum-inspired security systems: Adaptive defenses against novel threats. *Nature Machine Intelligence*, 5(8), 692–708.

Zhao, M., Li, X. & Wang, F. (2023). Ethical guidelines for quantum-inspired technologies in cybersecurity. *Journal of Cyber Ethics*, 5(2), 101–116.

CHAPTER
3

Fundamentals of Quantum Computing and Neural Networks

Preeti[1*] and Silky[2]

[1] University Institute of Computing, Chandigarh University, Gharuan, India
[2] PIMT, Alour, Khanna, India

This chapter describes how two transformative paradigms, quantum computing and neural networks, are converging to transform the landscape of intelligent computation. It commences with a description of the basic concepts of quantum mechanics as a computation model, such as qubits, superposition, entanglement, and quantum algorithms, such as Grover and Shor. Then it discusses the neural network structure and learning processes that include its advantages, weaknesses, and its use in the field of modern artificial intelligence. Based on these foundations, the chapter presents Quantum Neural Networks (QNNs) and hybrid quantum-classical models that use quantum phenomena to increase the learning efficiency, optimization, and representational power. A comparison between classical and quantum neural networks highlights both the opportunities of the technology, such as exponential parallelism, efficient correlation modeling, and faster training, and the challenges of the NISQ era, including noise, scalability, and optimization complexity. Applications in real world image recognition, drug discovery, finance, and natural language processing are also discussed, along with future directions such as quantum deep learning, fully quantum AI systems, and ethics. This chapter provides a comprehensive perspective on how quantum mechanics and neural computation synergy can result in next-generation intelligent systems through integrated theory, applications, and future vision.

*Corresponding author: vermapreeti1234@gmail.com

DOI: 10.1201/9781003682950-.3

3.1 Introduction

Humanity's increasing efforts to recreate and extend human thinking through machines are arguably among the driving forces behind the evolution of computing paradigms. Intelligent computing paradigms are systems or approaches that enable machines to learn, adapt, reason, and solve problems, often requiring less human intervention. The paradigms draw inspiration from biology, physics, logic, and mathematics, forming the foundation of modern artificial intelligence (AI). Historically, intelligent systems began with symbolic AI, where human knowledge was represented through rules and logical symbolism. Though symbolic systems performed well in structured situations, they struggled when faced with ambiguity and the flexibility required to handle real world data. Connectionist models, such as artificial neural networks, emerged from the limitations of symbolic systems and the desire to mimic the brain's structure by learning data patterns rather than relying solely on programmed rules. With increased computational power and access to vast amounts of data, neural networks have evolved into deep learning models capable of handling large-scale datasets and achieving human level performance in tasks such as speech recognition, object detection, and autonomous systems. At the same time other paradigms such as evolutionary algorithms, fuzzy logic and swarm intelligence contributed more broadly to the field of intelligent systems. The most recent paradigm, quantum computing has advanced significantly in recent years. In quantum computing, quantum bits or qubits, unlike classical bits 0 or 1, can occupy multiple states simultaneously due to quantum effects such as superposition and entanglement. This property gives quantum computers the potential to solve specific problems exponentially faster than their classical counterparts. Collectively, these paradigms mark the transition from deterministic, rule based computation towards probabilistic, adaptive and parallel models of processing, enabling machines to perform increasingly sophisticated applications.

3.1.1 Overview of Intelligent Computing Paradigms

Artificial neural networks have become integral to modern AI. They are noteworthy for their ability to model nonlinear relationships and extract features from unstructured data, driving innovation across diverse fields such as healthcare (e.g., cancer detection in medical imaging), finance (fraud detection and risk assessment), transportation (autonomous vehicles) and beyond. Neural networks have grown in depth and complexity giving rise to deep learning. As a result, models such as Convolutional Neural Networks (CNNs), Recurrent Neural Networks (RNNs), and Transformers, have become foundational to practical AI (Mishra and Kaur, 2024). However, these models are associated with significant computational costs. Deep neural networks can be highly demanding, often requiring high performance hardware, vast amounts of data, and substantial energy resources. Classical computing has been pushed to its limits by the exponential growth in model size (e.g., GPT-4, PaLM, and other large language models). This is where quantum computing becomes valuable. Quantum computers can deliver exponential speedups in solving certain classes of problems, particularly those believed to be influenced by:

- Combinatorial optimization (e.g. routing and logistics)
- Linear algebra (e.g. solutions of systems of equations)
- Factoring and searching
- Quantum system simulation (e.g. drug discovery molecular interactions).

Quantum computing enables parallel processing across an unimaginably vast number of probabilities simultaneously. Moreover, quantum entanglement allows correlations between data points to be represented and efficiently modeled in ways that classical systems cannot achieve. The limitations of classical architectures are becoming increasingly evident as AI systems grow more complex. Quantum computing with neural networks, a new methodology emerges for constructing high-performance, resource-efficient intelligent systems.

3.1.2 Synergy Between Quantum Computing and Neural Networks

The combination of neural networks and quantum computing has given rise to an interdisciplinary field known as Quantum Machine Learning (QML). At its core lies the concept of Quantum Neural Networks (QNNs) which combine the strengths of both paradigms to achieve enhanced learning, generalization and speed of computation (Pira, 2024). The following principles define this synergy:

- **Linear Algebra Compatibility:** Linear algebra plays a central role in both quantum computing and neural networks. The mathematical operations that transform one set of quantum variables into another are necessarily linear and unitary, aligning naturally with the matrix operations that underpin neural networks.
- **Quantum Superposition and Parallelism:** Quantum superposition and parallelism make it possible to perform many tasks simultaneously within a neural network, tasks that would otherwise require multiple networks (Shankar et al., 2025). A quantum neural network, by contrast, has the capability to represent and process a superposition of inputs as a single quantum state, thereby achieving exponential parallelism.
- **Neural Network Approach to Quantum Entanglement and Correlation:** Thousands to millions of dimensions, quantum entanglements, and correlations are difficult to capture and model with neural networks. Such correlations can be naturally encoded with quantum entanglement, which may yield better model expressiveness.
- **Quantum Optimization and Training:** Training a neural network is a specific instance of a problem in high-dimensional space, which is often computationally challenging. This process has been promisingly accelerated by quantum algorithms, such as the Quantum Approximate Optimization Algorithm (QAOA) and Quantum Gradient Descent.

As quantum hardware continues to mature, quantum-classical hybrid approaches are becoming increasingly viable. These models perform certain operations on classical machines (e.g., data preprocessing, loss evaluation) while leveraging quantum circuits for tasks such as state preparation, encoding, and transformation. For Example:

- One may substitute a layer of a classical neural network with a variational quantum circuit.
- Support vector machine or deep learning model classification, may be performed by means of a quantum kernel.
- The hybrid methods described can serve as stepping stones toward full quantum AI, offering improved performance even on today's noisy and error-prone quantum machines.

3.1.3 Chapter Objectives

This chapter aims to provide readers with an in-depth understanding of the foundational concepts and the emerging integration of quantum computing and neural networks. Its specific objectives are as follows:

- To learn the background theory of quantum computing, such as quantum bits (qubits), quantum gates, superposition, entanglement and simple quantum algorithms.
- To provide learners with in-depth knowledge of neural networks, their structures (feedforward, convolutional, recurrent), learning models (backpropagation, gradient descent) and the practical implications of these models.
- To explain the convergence of these two fields through the concept of quantum neural networks and to specify how quantum phenomena can be applied to enhance machine learning models.
- To assess the relative merits and challenges of classical and quantum techniques in neural computation, particularly their differences in speed, scalability, and computational efficiency.
- To highlight real-world examples and applications, in which quantum-enhanced neural networks can provide concrete advantages, such as cryptography, finance, drug discovery, and natural language processing.
- To present an outlook on future research and technological challenges, and the evolving field of Quantum AI.

3.2 Fundamentals of Quantum Computing

Quantum computing is an evolving form of computation that leverages the principles of quantum mechanics to perform calculations. Unlike classical computing which relies on binary states and deterministic processing, quantum computing harnesses the phenomena of superposition, entanglement and interference (Easttom, 2021). These effects can potentially replace numerous classical operations offering the freedom to process and manipulate data in entirely new ways. In this section we introduce some of the central notions and elements of quantum computing as a prelude to models that illustrate how it differs from and complements classical approaches.

3.2.1 Basic Concepts: Qubits, Superposition, and Entanglement

- The key to quantum computing is quantum bit or qubit. Whereas a classical bit has only two states (0 or 1) a qubit can simultaneously be in both possible states: in a superposition of states 0 and 1. Mathematically, the state of a qubit can be expressed as,

$$|\psi\rangle = \alpha\,|0\rangle + \beta\,|1\rangle \tag{3.1}$$

where α and β are complex probability amplitudes, and $|\alpha|^2 + |\beta|^2 = 1$

- Superposition enables a quantum computer to represent and work on several states simultaneously providing exponential scaling of specific computations.
- Another fundamental principle is entanglement. When two or more qubits are entangled, their states become intrinsically connected, such that the measurement of one qubit instantaneously affects the state of the other qubit, regardless of distance. Entanglement enables complex correlations and is central to both quantum algorithms and communication.

These two characteristics, quantum superposition and entanglement, give quantum computing immense potential to solve problems that are computationally intractable for classical computers.

3.2.2 Quantum Gates and Circuits

Quantum gates are used to manipulate the states of qubits in order to perform quantum operations. Unlike classical gates (AND, OR, NOT), quantum gates are unitary transformations and therefore preserve the overall probability amplitude.

Single-bit gates could be:

Pauli-X (quantum NOT gate): Flips a qubit's state.

The Hadamard gate (*H*): Creates a superposition by transforming

$$H|0\rangle = \frac{|0\rangle + |1\rangle}{\sqrt{2}}$$

Phase gates (e.g., S, T): Introduce complex phase shifts.

Multi-qubit gates include:

CNOT (Controlled-NOT): Flips the target qubit if the control qubit is 1>

Toffoli gate: A universal gate for reversible computation.

SWAP gate: Exchanges the state of two qubits.

A quantum circuit is an expression of a series of gates on a collection of qubits. The result of a quantum computation is obtained by measuring the qubits, which collapses their states into classical bits (Shafique et al., 2024). Quantum algorithm development is focused on the design and optimization of quantum circuits.

3.2.3 Quantum Parallelism and Interference

Quantum parallelism is one of the most powerful features of a quantum computer. Owing to the superposition of qubits can take, a quantum computer can process multiple inputs simultaneously. Nevertheless, parallelism alone is not sufficient. The output must be extracted through quantum interference, which amplifies the desired results while suppressing the unwanted ones. This is achieved by carefully implementing quantum algorithms and sequences of quantum gates. For example:

- In Grover's algorithm (database search), the probability amplitude of the correct solution is amplified through quantum interference.
- In quantum Fourier transform, interference is used to find the periodicities which is crucial in algorithms such as Shor.

Therefore, quantum interference plays a crucial role in guiding the computational process toward the correct solution during the measurement process.

3.2.4 Quantum Algorithms: Grover's and Shor's Algorithms

Superposition and interference together can be harnessed in quantum algorithms that solve certain problems more efficiently than their classical counterparts. The two most famous quantum algorithms are:

- **Grover's Algorithm:** Intends to solve unstructured searching difficulties. It can search through an unordered database of N items in $O(\sqrt{N})$ compared to $O(N)$ with classical algorithms. The algorithm finds application in optimization, cryptanalysis and pattern recognition.
- **Shor's Algorithm:** Developed by Peter Shor, this algorithm can factor large integers in polynomial time. It represents a revolutionary breakthrough, as classical factoring is exponentially expensive in terms of computation, and the security of widely used encryption systems (e.g., RSA) relies on this difficulty. The application of Shor's algorithm carries profound implications for cyber security and cryptography (Eswaran et al., 2024).

Other well known quantum algorithms are:

- Quantum Fourier Transform (QFT)
- Deutsch-Jozsa Algorithm
- Quantum Phase Estimation

Such algorithms provide indications that quantum computing can play a discontinuous role in breaking established paradigms of computing.

3.2.5 Quantum Hardware: Current Technologies and Limitations

Although the theoretical support of quantum computers is mature, the development of working quantum computers is a daunting task. Important quantum hardware technologies are:

- **Superconducting Qubits:** Applied by IBM, Google and Rigetti; they operate near absolute zero temperature based on Josephson junctions.
- **Trapped Ions:** IonQ and Honeywell utilize this technology; make use of laser-trapped ions in electromagnetic traps.
- **Topological Qubits:** This is a work in progress; the idea is to allow a greater fault tolerance via anyons and braiding.
- **Photonic Quantum Computers:** Perform computation with the help of light particles (photons); invented by Xanadu, among others.

Limitations and challenges: As depicted in Figure 3.1. There are various challenges and limitations pertaining to quantum hardware.

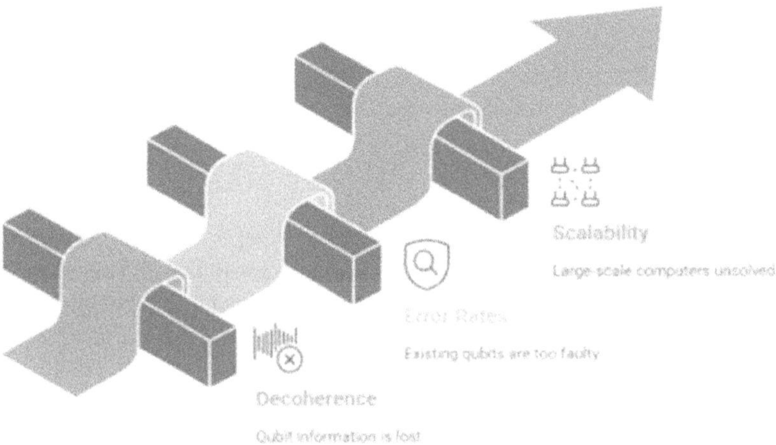

Figure 3.1: Limitations of quantum computing.

- **Decoherence:** Qubits are highly susceptible to environmental noise, causing quantum information to degrade and be lost.
- **Error Rates:** Existing qubits are prone to faults and therefore require the use of error-correction methods.
- **Scalability:** The development of large-scale, fault-tolerant quantum computers capable of supporting thousands of logical qubits has not yet been achieved.

Nonetheless quantum error correction, cryogenic engineering and quantum chips have advanced, and will likely continue advancing the degrees of the attainable.

3.2.6 Quantum Programming Languages (e.g., Qiskit, Cirq)

Quantum hardware requires dedicated quantum programming languages and software development kits (SDKs) to operate effectively. These tools enable the design, simulation,and execution of quantum circuits. Several such frameworks have become widely popular,including:

- **Qiskit (IBM):** A free, Python-based quantum programming SDK. It supports building, simulating, and executing circuits on IBM Quantum devices. Qiskit includes modules for algorithms, visualization and optimization (Chahar, 2025).
- **Cirq (Google):** A Python-based framework for designing, simulating, and running quantum circuits, particularly on Google's quantum processors. Cirq emphasizes fine-grained control over quantum operations.
- **PennyLane (Xanadu):** A framework focused on hybrid quantum-classical computation, particularly in quantum machine learning. It integrates seamlessly with TensorFlow and PyTorch.
- **D-Wave:Ocean SDK:** Designed to run on D-Wave's quantum annealers, it supports quantum annealing and optimization tasks.

These platforms enable researchers, engineers, and students, whether or not they have direct access to physical quantum hardware, to explore quantum programming through cloud-based simulators and quantum processors.

3.3 Fundamentals of Neural Networks

Artificial intelligence encompasses a variety of subsets, with neural networks modeled on the human brain and its learning capabilities. They form the foundation of most modern machine learning applications, including image recognition, language translation and autonomous systems (Shankar et al., 2025). This section provides a brief overview of the theoretical and architectural principles of neural networks, both deep and shallow, and highlights their computational properties and limitations.

3.3.1 Biological Inspiration and Perceptron Model

Neural networks are roughly based on the biological neural networks in the human brain. In any biological system:

- The input signals are transferred to neurons via dendrites.
- The cell acts upon the signal and in case of activation beyond a threshold, it transmits a signal to the axon.
- These connections can vary in strength and the synapses change this strength via learning.

In 1958, the Perceptron by Frank Rosenblatt was the first mathematical model of this concept. The perceptron is a simple neural model consisting of a single layer that processes multiple inputs. Each input is assigned a weight, and their weighted sum is passed through an activation function to produce the output. Perceptron Equation:

$$\hat{y} = f\left(\sum_{i=1}^{n} w_i x_i + b\right) \tag{3.2}$$

Where:

x_i = input features

w_i = weights

b = bias term

f = activation function (e.g., step, sigmoid)

y = output. Although it is effective with linearly-separable problems, a single-layer perceptron is unable to cope with non-linear decision boundaries-multi-layer structures are required.

3.3.2 Architecture: Input, Hidden, and Output Layers

The common neural network has three categories of layers:

- **Input Layer:** The raw input features (e.g. pixel values, word vectors) are provided here.
- **Hidden Layers:** Enacts non-linear mappings of input; the extent and the number of layers establish the depth and capacity of the network.
- **Output Layer:** Gives the final output of prediction, e.g. class label or regression.

As shown in Figure 3.2, the neurons of each layer are linked with those of the following layer where each connection is weighted. A deep neural network (DNN) is characterized by the presence of two or more hidden layers thus allowing it to learn complex and abstract data patterns (Zeroual et al., 2019). The performance and efficiency of a neural network depends largely on the selection of architecture (number of layers, the number of neurons in each layer and the connectivity).

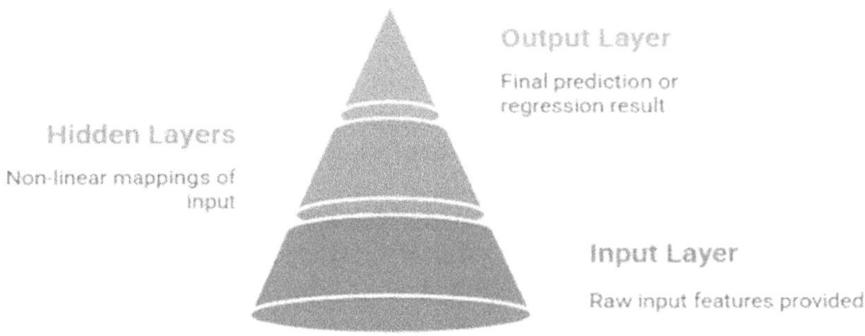

Figure 3.2: Architecture of neural network.

3.3.3 Activation Functions and Learning Rules

Activation functions bring about non-linearity into the network that enables the network to learn complicated patterns. Some well-known examples of activation functions are shown in Table 3.1.

Table 3.1: Common Activation Functions

Activation Function	Equation	Characteristics
Step	$f(x) = \begin{cases} 1, x \geq 0 \\ 0, x < 0 \end{cases}$	Used in perceptrons; non-differentiable; outputs 0 or 1
Sigmoid	$f(x) = \dfrac{1}{1 + e^{-x}}$	Output range (0,1); smooth and differentiable; good for probabilities; can cause vanishing gradients
Tanh	$f(x) = \dfrac{e^x - e^{-x}}{e^x + e^{-x}}$	Output range (–1,1); zero-centered; stronger gradients than sigmoid
ReLU (Rectified Linear Unit)	$f(x) = \max(0, x)$	Fast and efficient; widely used in deep learning; may cause "dead ReLU" problem

Backpropagation and Optimization Algorithms: The use of Backpropagation is the training of multi-layered natural networks by means of reciprocating mistakes among output layers to input layers (Kasirajan, 2021). Steps involved:

- **Forward pass:** Inputs are processed to generate estimates of the outputs.
- **Loss evaluation:** When a metric is specified, the loss (e.g., mean squared error or cross-entropy) is computed.
- **Backward pass:** Gradients are computed using the chain-rule of calculus.
- **Weight correction:** Weights are adjusted using gradient descent techniques or other optimization methods.

Optimization Algorithms: These algorithms are less prone to oscillations and tend to converge reliably:

- **Adam (Adaptive Moment Estimation):** An optimization algorithm that combines the principles of momentum and RMSProp.
- **RMSProp:** An optimization algorithm in which the learning rate can be configured on a per-parameter basis.
- **Momentum:** An optimization technique that helps overcome local minima by accelerating gradient descent in relevant directions.
- **Dagrad:** An optimization algorithm that decreases the learning rate based on the gradients beforehand.

These approaches are crucial for training deep networks more effectively and efficiently.

3.3.4 Radical Deep Learning: GANs, RNNs and CNNs

Deep learning generalizes neural networks to networks presented with multi-dimensional data like images, speech, and video. The most crucial among them are:

Convolution Neural Networks (CNNs): A deep learning model

- Ideal for processing image and spatial information CNNs identify attributes such as textures, shapes, and edges through convolutional layers (Oh et al., 2020).
- Applications: Self-driving cars, MRI analysis, object detection.

Recurrent Neural Networks (RNNs): Their structure is tailored to sequences of data (e.g., text, time series).

- The alternatives include LSTM (Long- Short-Term Memory) and GRU (Gated Recurrent Unit).
- Applications: Linguistics, word comparison, and speech recognition.

Generative Adversarial Networks (GANs)

- Composed of two networks, a Generator and a Discriminator within a competitive setting.
- Generator produces synthetic (fake) data while the Discriminator evaluates and enforces its authenticity.
- Applications: Deepfake generation, art synthesis data augmentation.

These architectures underpin most modern AI systems and have demonstrated exceptional performance across diverse industries.

3.3.5 Limitations and Computational Demands

Despite their remarkable success, neural networks have several weaknesses and computational demands. They require large amounts of labeled data to learn effectively, are highly data-dependent, and are prone to overfitting, memorizing the training data without generalizing well. Moreover, they often lack interpretability, with many models functioning as opaque “black boxes”. Performance is also sensitive to hyperparameters such as learning rate, network architecture, and activation functions. In addition, training deep neural networks is computationally expensive, requiring significant time, and energy consumption and access to high-performance GPUs or TPUs. To address these challenges more effectively, researchers are exploring solutions such as transfer learning, model pruning and neuro-symbolical methods.

3.4 Quantum Neural Networks (QNNs)

Quantum Neural Networks (QNNs) are a new paradigm in computing that integrates the processing capabilities of quantum mechanics with the learning power of artificial neural networks. These hybrid models aim to leverage entanglement, and interference to potentially achieve super-exponential speedups and enhanced learning compared to classical neural networks.

3.4.1 Introduction to QNNs

Quantum Neural Networks (QNNs) represent an attempt to implement machine learning algorithms using quantum circuits to model the behavior of classical neurons and networks. QNNs are being considered and investigated for applications such as:

- **Quantum-enhanced learning:** Performing calculations on qubits and quantum gates to store information more efficiently.
- **Complex systems modeling:** The use of high-dimensional Hilbert spaces to represent systems with intricate interaction.
- **Reducing training times:** Theoretically, this involves decreasing the number of training epochs or the amount of data required (Kwak et al., 2021).

In Figure 3.3, QNNs do not represent the quantum analog of classical neural networks; they are built entirely differently, and they can be used in applications that are entirely different.

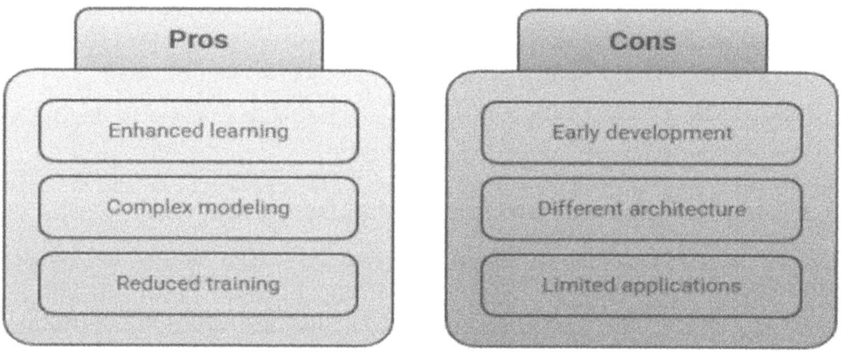

Figure 3.3: QNN pros and cons.

3.4.2 Quantum Perceptron and Quantum Circuits for Neural Models

A quantum perceptron represents a quantum block of QNNs and is a quantum-mechanical version of the classical perceptron. Key Features:

- **Encoding of classical inputs:** The encoding of classical inputs into quantum states is done by either angle or amplitude encoding.
- **Parameterized quantum gates:** Quantum gates (e.g., Rx, Ry, Rz) with trainable parameters that function as weights, analogous to those in classical neural networks (Perdomo-Ortiz et al., 2018).

- **Unitary evolution:** The quantum circuit is changed through unitary operations that preserve the reversibility and coherence of quantum states.
- **Measurement:** Once a quantum circuit has been applied, measurements are taken to obtain classical output values to be used later in processing or decision-making.

The perceptron could be modeled as a simple quantum circuit composed of a few qubits and parameterized rotations, guided by classical optimization algorithms.

3.4.3 Hybrid Quantum-Classical Neural Networks

The most practical applications of QNNs are hybrid, i.e. combining classical and quantum approaches, due to current hardware constraints (noisy intermediate-scale quantum, or NISQ).

Architecture:

- **Classical frontend:** Pre- and post-process input data.
- **Quantum circuit layer:** Nonlinear transformations on encoded quantum states.
- **Optimization:** The parameters of the quantum circuit are optimized by classical gradient-based methods or derivative-free methods such as COBYLA.

These mixed architectures are adopted in:

- Quantum classifiers
- Quantum variational autoencoders
- Quantum kernel learning.

The benefit of such systems is the tradeoff between quantum expressiveness and classical stability.

3.4.4 Quantum Entanglement in Learning Systems

Entanglement is a purely quantum effect in which the state of a single qubit cannot be modeled without the state of another, even at very large distances. In QNNs:

- Inter-feature correlations can be represented in a more compact form than by classical methods using entanglement.
- Complex decision boundaries can be represented and learned using highly entangled states by QNNs.
- Entanglement entropy can be used as a complexity metric for quantum learning models.

By using entanglement, more expressive and possibly more generalizable models can be harnessed, but this comes at the cost of substantially increasing the complexity of model interpretation and circuit design.

3.5 Comparative Analysis

The sphere of intelligent computing is evolving at an extraordinary pace, and Quantum Neural Networks (QNNs) have emerged as a promising extension of Classical Neural Networks (CNNs). This chapter presents a systematic comparison of the two paradigms, highlighting areas where quantum systems offer both theoretical and practical advantages, as well as areas that remain underdeveloped due to current technological limitations.

3.5.1 Classical Neural Networks vs Quantum Neural Networks

Table 3.2, highlights the conceptual and technological differences between classical and quantum neural networks. Most applications in the real world today are robust using classical neural networks. Instead, QNNs are being pursued in niche settings where quantum properties might provide exponential speedup, or representational efficiency.

Table 3.2: Comparison between Classical Neural Networks (CNNs) and Quantum Neural Networks (QNNs)

Feature	Classical Neural Networks (CNNs)	Quantum Neural Networks (QNNs)
Information Unit	Bit (0 or 1)	Qubit (superposition of 0 and 1)
Computation Model	Deterministic, sequential or parallel	Probabilistic, massively parallel
Data Encoding	Numeric vectors	Quantum states (angle, amplitude, etc.)
Non-linearity	Activation functions (ReLU, sigmoid, etc.)	Induced via measurement or hybrid layers
Training Algorithm	Backpropagation, gradient descent	Variational optimization, quantum gradients
Hardware	CPUs, GPUs, TPUs	Quantum processors (IBM Q, Rigetti, etc.)
Maturity	Highly developed and widely adopted	Experimental and in early stages

3.5.2 Advantages of Quantum-Enhanced Learning

Quantum-enhanced neural networks seek to harness special quantum effects that may allow them to do things that classical systems cannot:

- Quantum superposition and quantum interference exponential parallelism: More compact representation of high-dimensional, complex data.
- Possible acceleration of the training through quantum-inspired optimization (e.g., Quantum Annealing)

- Quantum entanglement to model and capture (naturally) complex correlations between features.

In some of these classification tasks, quantum kernel methods have been shown to be superior to classical methods. These advantages imply that QNNs may be much more effective than CNNs in particular tasks, including quantum chemistry, materials simulations, and optimization.

3.5.3 Challenges in Implementation and Scalability

However, even with the theoretical advantages, significant problems exist that prevent the generalization of QNNs:

- **Noisy Qubits:** Quantum gates are controlled by imperfections in the form of decoherence and external noise.
- **Small Qubit Scale:** Existing hardware has tens or hundreds of qubits.
- **Scalability:** QNNs are challenging to scale to complex high-dimensional problems because of the depth of circuits.
- **Complexity of training:** Quantum optimization landscapes are non-convex and can have barren plateaus (where gradients become 0).
- Measurement overhead extraction of classical results of quantum computation routines can involve repetitive measurements, which adds computational cost.
- **Absence of Standardization:** No currently accepted QNN architecture or standard training methodology exists.

3.5.4 Quantum Advantage and Noisy Intermediate-Scale Quantum (NISQ) Era

Our current era of quantum computing is the NISQ era in which devices:

- Act on a small number of noisy qubits.
- Are not yet ready to do fault-tolerant, large-scale quantum computations.
- Provide possibilities of certain applications in the near future.

During this period, the challenge is to achieve quantum advantage, i.e. quantum machines are faster and more effective than classical machines at solving problems. Some areas of focus include:

- **Quantum-assisted machine learning:** In which portions of the learning pipeline (e.g. feature mapping or kernel computation) are offloaded to quantum processors.
- **Variational Quantum Algorithms (VQAs):** Hybrid algorithms are quantum circuits that are optimized using classical routines through parameterized quantum circuits (Wirtz, 2024).
- **Benchmarking tasks:** Used to evaluate whether certain learning problems can achieve performance beyond the reach of classical networks.

Although the full quantum advantage in neural learning has not yet been realized, preliminary experiments and simulated systems are offering encouraging indications of future potential.

3.6 Applications and Case Studies

The introduction of Quantum Neural Networks (QNNs) has served as a bridge to the development of artificial intelligence and provided possible solutions where high computation and multidimensional data representation are required (Jeswal and Chakraverty, 2019). Though it is still in its infancy, preliminary applications are proving to be promising in many fields. This chapter provides an overview of the principal areas of application and highlights significant examples where quantum computing and QNNs may drive transformative change.

3.6.1 Quantum Machine Learning in Image Recognition

Quantum-enhanced image recognition is the study of the potential benefits of quantum states and circuits in pattern classification, feature extraction, and dimensionality reduction.

Applications:

- Quantum classifiers which have been trained on quantum-encoded images (e.g., grayscale pixel intensity as amplitudes or angles).
- QCNNs, which mimic using quantum circuits, feature maps and pooling layers.
- Image dimensionality reduction with Quantum Principal Component Analysis (qPCA).

Case Study: A quantum model of digit classification (MNIST dataset) has been built using the IBML framework Qiskit, with quantum layers substituting a few classical operations and matching a similar level of accuracy on small subsets.

3.6.2 Drug Discovery and Bioinformatics

QNNs are already widely applied in the fields of molecular modeling, protein folding, and genomic sequence analysis, in which the inputs are inherently quantum or structured.

Applications:

- Prediction of molecular energy with variational quantum eigensolvers (VQEs) and QNN layers.
- Scalable quantum-enhanced feature extraction of high-dimensional omics data.
- Optimization of chemical reactions or drug interaction pathways by quantum reinforcement learning (Vasuki et al., 2023).

Case Study: Other companies, such as ProteinQure and Cambridge Quantum Computing (CQC) are actively working to develop quantum solutions to predict protein-ligandbinding affinities based on hybrid quantum-classical models.

3.6.3 Financial Forecasting and Optimization

Finance requires models that are both fast and efficient to process large amounts of data, predictable, and optimizable, where QNNs may be useful.

Applications:

- Time-series prediction with quantum neural networks, e.g. stock prices or volatility trends.
- Quantum annealing or variational quantum algorithmic portfolio optimization.
- Models of complex financial distributions based on quantum Boltzmann machines.

Case Study: Companies such as JP Morgan Chase, Goldman Sachs, and QC Ware are also considering quantum algorithms to price options, detect fraud and model risks.

3.6.4 Quantum-Inspired Neural Solutions in Natural Language Processing (NLP)

The ideas of quantum computing are being applied to NLP tasks, using both real and simulated quantum models and so-called quantum-inspired classical architectures.

Applications:

- Quantum language models which encode word vectors as quantum states and view syntactic/semantic relation as entanglement (Maksimovic and Maksymov, 2025).
- Text classification tasks, quantum kernel.
- Transformers (experimental) based on quantum enhancement to perform tasks such as machine translation or summarization.

Case Study: Hybrid quantum circuit-classical NLP backbones have been tried on sentiment analysis and spam datasets, and shown to match state of the art with smaller models.

3.6.5 Real-World Use Cases and Industry Adoption

Although production-ready, large-scale applications of QNNs are still on the horizon, several companies and research centers are already piloting quantum solutions.

Industry Examples:

- **IBM Quantum:** Cloud-based QNN experimentation tools built with Qiskit.
- **Google AI Quantum:** A quantum supremacy and a quantum model of QML.
- **IonQ and D-Wave:** Optimization and supply chain with companies.
- **Zapata Computing:** Providing services based on quantum machine learning in sectors such as logistics and pharmaceuticals.

Adoption Trends:

- The majority of applications are in the proof-of-concept stage or research stage.
- The most common architecture is hybrid quantum-classical pipelines.
- There is increased interest in fields of healthcare, aerospace, automotive and cybersecurity.

3.7 Future Directions

Due to the new era of quantum technology, the capacity of Quantum Artificial Intelligence (QAI) to transform the way machines learn, think, and communicate also advances. Although in its early stages, quantum computing combined with neural networks has the potential to create systems with significantly more computational power and learning properties. This chapter identifies new trends, research problems, and important factors that should be considered when developing the future generation of intelligent systems.

3.7.1 Toward Fully Quantum AI Systems

A full quantum AI system describes an architecture in which every computational step, including data encoding and learning, inference and adaptation are all run entirely on quantum hardware.

Goals:

- Substitute classical preprocessing of data, training and decision-making with quantum-native operations.
- Build quantum memory and quantum RAM (qRAM) to read and write data in an entangled state.
- Develop independent learning systems that can make quantum-enhanced choices and decisions.

Requirements:

- Fault-tolerant quantum computers that are scalable.
- New quantum learning architectures other than the existing QNN models.
- Quantum-compatible features and representations.

It will take quantum hardware, noise correction and algorithm design breakthroughs to make this vision a reality.

3.7.2 Research Trends in Quantum Deep Learning

Quantum Deep Learning (QDL) is an effort to apply deep neural network (CNNs, RNNs, GANs) models to quantum space.

Key Trends:

- **Variational Quantum Deep Networks:** Depth is simulated by using layers of parameterized quantum circuits.

- **Quantum GANs:** Generative Adversarial Networks provide quantum generators and/or discriminators to perform improved generative tasks.
- **Quantum Transfer Learning:** Learn classical models on quantum circuits with reduced training time.
- **Quantum Transformers:** Early research on the ways quantum entanglement and quantum interference can be used to replicate self-attention.
- **Quantum Autoencoders:** Lengthy representations of quantum data can be shrunk or denoised.

All of these trends suggest that QNN models are becoming more complex and abstract, following a similar growth trajectory to classical deep learning.

3.7.3 Open Challenges and Research Opportunities

Nevertheless, the research on Quantum Neural Network has critical challenges.

Technical Challenges:

- Unproductive plateaus in the optimization landscapes, which lead to the stalling of training.
- Noisy measurements and decoherence, which give unreliable results.
- Only a small number of qubits are connected and gated.
- Large resource overhead to execute QNNs using classical hardware.

Research Opportunities:

- Creating high-quality training algorithms that reduce vanishing gradients.
- Practical high-dimensional classical coded information.
- Visualization and model interpretability of quantum networks.
- Deep architecture quantum circuits using fewer resources.
- Standards used to benchmark QNNs against classical models.

These are open problems with abundant opportunities to be tackled through interdisciplinary research involving quantum physics, computer science, and AI.

3.7.4 Ethical and Security Considerations

Similar to classical AI, quantum technology subsumed into a single system creates new ethical, privacy, and security challenges.

Ethical Considerations:

- **Bias in quantum models:** Quantum-enhanced models can carry over or even exaggerate biases in training data.
- **Job displacement:** Unlike other AI waves, the automation of quantum AI has the potential to change the structure of the workforce even more significantly.
- **Access imbalance:** Quantum infrastructure is specialized and costly and can create disparities in access to QAI technologies.
- **Security concerns:** Quantum adversarial attacks: New threat models are based on quantum data manipulation or entanglement-based attacks.

- **Post-quantum cryptography:** With the emergence of quantum AI, it has become even more critical to move towards quantum-resistant encryption (Kaur et al., 2025).
- **Data integrity:** Assuring authenticity and provenance of quantum-generated outputs in a high-stakes area such as healthcare or law.

To address such issues, regulatory frameworks, design ethics, and joint regulation by technologists, ethicists, and policymakers are needed.

3.8 Conclusion

Quantum computing and neural networks are becoming modes of thought that are converging in revolutionary ways and changing the face of intelligent computing. Quantum computing, with its theory of superposition, entanglement and interference, brings computational capabilities that classical computers cannot reach, while neural networks bring flexibility and learning ability that are key to modern artificial intelligence. Their incorporation into Quantum Neural Networks (QNNs) and hybrid quantum-classical systems creates new opportunities in optimization, pattern recognition, and problematic data modeling. Comparative analysis reveals that although classical neural networks have matured and are actively deployed in the market, QNNs promise exponential speedups and new representational capabilities, but are struggling with noise, scaling, and complexity of training in the current NISQ era. These technologies have the capacity to transform the world, as demonstrated in areas of image recognition, drug discovery, finance, and natural language processing, although many are still experimental. In the coming years, quantum AI systems, quantum deep learning architectures, along with ethical and security issues will define the future of this emerging field. Finally, quantum mechanical computing in combination with neural computing opens the path to the next generation of AI systems which will not only be more powerful but also more efficient, scalable and transformative across industries – a revolutionary milestone in the future of intelligent computing.

References

Chahar, S. (2025). Exploring the future trends of cryptography. In: *Next Generation Mechanisms for Data Encryption* (1st ed., pp. 24). CRC Press. https://doi.org/10.1201/9781003508632-16

Easttom II, W. C. (2021). Quantum Computing Fundamentals. Addison-Wesley Professional.

Eswaran, U., Khang, A. & Eswaran, V. (2024). Role of quantum computing in the era of Artificial Intelligence (AI). In: *Applications and Principles of Quantum Computing* (pp. 46–68). IGI Global Scientific Publishing.

Jeswal, S. K. & Chakraverty, S. (2019). Recent developments and applications in quantum neural network: A review. *Archives of Computational Methods in Engineering*, 26(4), 793–807.

Kasirajan, V. (2021). Fundamentals of Quantum Computing. Berlin/Heidelberg, Germany: Springer International Publishing.

Kaur, K., Bhar, S. & Jaswal, R. (2025, January 24). Quantum cryptography. In: *Next Generation Mechanisms for Data Encryption* (1st ed., pp. 64–84). CRC Press. DOI: 10.1201/9781003508632-5.

Kwak, Y., Yun, W. J., Jung, S. & Kim, J. (2021, August). Quantum neural networks: Concepts, applications, and challenges. In: *2021 Twelfth International Conference on Ubiquitous and Future Networks* (*ICUFN*) (pp. 413–416). IEEE.

Maksimovic, M. & Maksymov, I. S. (2025). Transforming neural networks into quantum-cognitive models: A research tutorial with novel applications. *Technologies*, 13(5), 183.

Mishra, K. & Kaur, K. (2024, October). Improving wheat yield protection with deep feature fusion for estimating yellow rust severity using CNN models. In: *2024 2nd International Conference on Self Sustainable Artificial Intelligence Systems* (*ICSSAS*) (pp. 593–598). IEEE.

Oh, S., Choi, J. & Kim, J. (2020, October). A tutorial on quantum convolutional neural networks (QCNN). In: *2020 International Conference on Information and Communication Technology Convergence* (*ICTC*) (pp. 236–239). IEEE.

Perdomo-Ortiz, A., Benedetti, M., Realpe-Gomez, J. & Biswas, R. (2018). Opportunities and challenges for quantum-assisted machine learning in near-term quantum computers. *Quantum Science and Technology*, 3(3), 030502.

Pira, L. (2024). The Fundamentals of Quantum Neural Networks. University of Technology Sydney (Australia).

Shafique, M. A., Munir, A. & Latif, I. (2024). Quantum computing: Circuits, algorithms, and applications. *IEEE Access*, 12, 22296–22314.

Shankar, K. P., Chandraprabha, K., Raja, K. S. & Kanmani, P. (2025). Foundations of quantum computing and machine learning. In: *Quantum Computing and Artificial Intelligence: The Industry Use Cases* (pp. 225–246).

Vasuki, M., Karunamurthy, A., Ramakrishnan, R. & Prathiba, G. (2023). Overview of quantum computing in quantum neural network and artificial intelligence. *Quing: International Journal of Innovative Research in Science and Engineering*, 2(2), 117–127.

Wirtz, B. W. (2024). Artificial intelligence and quantum computing. In: *Multichannel Marketing: Strategy–Design–Digital Technology* (pp. 239–313). Wiesbaden: Springer Fachmedien Wiesbaden.

Zeroual, A., Fourar, A. & Djeddou, M. (2019). Predictive modeling of static and seismic stability of small homogeneous earth dams using artificial neural network. *Arabian Journal of Geosciences*, 12(2), 16.

CHAPTER

4

Quantum-Inspired Computing: Classical Approaches to Machine Learning

Sathish Krishna Anumula[1], Niranjan Talluru[1], Rajesh Gangavarapu[1], Santosh Gupta[2] and Kalyan Tatavarthy[1]

[1] Sr. Architect, IBM Corporation, USA

[2] Principal Architect, IBM Corporation, USA

This chapter provides a formal, self-contained exposition of quantum-inspired machine learning (QiML), a subfield focusing on applying ideas of quantum mechanics to the development of powerful classical algorithms. Our starting point is setting up a defensible taxonomy to dissociate QiML from actual quantum machine learning, and to describe its historical antecedents in simulated annealing and more recent dequantization of quantum algorithms. The highlights of the chapter pursue four central streams of inspiration systematically, namely: (1) quantum many-body physics is used to turn a model and its data into simple tensor networks; (2) quantum feature maps lead to randomized kernel methods, quantum inpainting, and quantum groups; (3) quantum numerical linear atomization algorithm (HHL) provides the template to develop efficient linear solvers and randomized numerical linear algebra; and (4) quantum approximate optimization algorithm (QAOA) is used to analyze non-convex optimization heuristics. In every region, we sketch the supporting theory, provide concrete algorithms along with quasi-pseudocode and complexity examples, and introduce theoretical guarantees. A large experimental section compares these approaches to classical baselines on standard data, as well as providing detailed case studies in resource-constrained ML, large-scale linear models, and combinatorial optimization. The chapter is rounded off by concluding with some practical hints and tips, a critical reflection on the ethical issues, and a discussion of open problems in the field, providing relevant literature to graduate students and practitioners in a well-brought-up and detailed piece of work.

*Corresponding author:

DOI: 10.1201/9781003682950-4

4.1 Introduction

The fusion of quantum computing and machine learning has been a source of enormous excitement, with the prospect of resolving problems that are beyond the scope of even the most powerful classical supercomputers (Biamonte et al., 2017). The working implications of this promise, however, are moderated by the considerable hardware difficulties of the current Noisy Intermediate-Scale Quantum (NISQ) age. Large-scale, fault-tolerant quantum computers are not yet on the horizon, so many quantum machine learning (QML) algorithms cannot yet be applied to real-world data. Such a technological fact has spurred the development of a parallel and heavily practical discipline: Quantum-inspired machine learning (QiML).

QiML is a different game: it seeks to translate the powerful mathematical principles and algorithmic structures of quantum mechanics to new algorithms that run on classical computers. Its guiding premise is that conceptual models from quantum computing, such as high-dimensional linear algebra, superposition, and entanglement, can inspire novel classical data processing methods that deliver improvements in computational performance, memory bandwidth, and model capabilities all without involving a single qubit. This chapter contains a graduate-level orientation of theory, methods, and applications of this emerging discipline.

4.1.1 Why Quantum-Inspired?

The main motivation for the development of QiML is the disconnect between expectations of the theoretical outcome of QML and the real constraints of available quantum hardware. Prominent quantum algorithms, including the Harrow-Hassidim-Lloyd (HHL) algorithm on solving linear systems of equations, assume such access to large, fault-tolerant quantum computers, which we do not currently possess. Some studies have found that, even under idealized simulations, the pursuit of quantum advantage in digital health, for example, still lacks decisively substantiated conclusions, and that most experiments lack the technical sophistication to account for noise and overhead costs (Harrow et al., 2009).

An attractive alternative is represented by quantum-inspired algorithms which exploit the intellectual fertility of quantum theory in the short term, in the classical domain. The present approach is based on two observations:

1. **Transferability of Algorithmic Knowledge:** Quantum mechanics first offers a radically new notation to compute in, based on the linear algebra of complex vector spaces. Such a view may demonstrate new structures and efficiency in classical problems. As an example, the structure of the Quantum Approximate Optimization Algorithm (QAOA) can inspire new forms of alternating optimization schemes, while quantum many-body mathematics provides tensor network techniques to compress high dimensional databases (Farhi et al., 2014). These represent mathematical and algorithmic discoveries that can be adapted for classical computing.

2. **The "Dequantization" Phenomenon:** A major development in QiML was the dequantization of several well-known QML algorithms. Landmark results by Ewin Tang and others demonstrated that the purported exponential speedups of certain quantum algorithms, such as those for recommendation systems, principal component analysis, and linear system solving, were not inherently dependent on uniquely quantum features like entanglement (Tang, 2019). Instead, these advantages arose from strong assumptions about the input data, namely that it could be efficiently stored in a low-rank representation and accessed through a specialized data structure known as Quantum Random Access Memory (QRAM). It was shown that classical algorithms employing randomized numerical linear algebra (RLA) techniques, such as ℓ_2-norm sampling, could achieve comparable performance under similar assumptions, thereby dequantizing the supposed quantum speedup (Drineas and Mahoney, 2016). This insight shifted attention away from claims of unconditional quantum advantage toward examining the structure of data that enables computational speedups, whether on classical or quantum computers (Martinsson and Tropp, 2020).

4.1.2 What Counts as "Quantum-Inspired" vs Truly Quantum?

The rather broad term quantum-inspired has been used to describe a wide range of classical algorithms. To navigate this landscape, it is essential to establish a clear taxonomy. A quantum-inspired classical algorithm is defined as one that draws on quantum mechanical principles, quantum algorithms, or mathematical formalisms of quantum physics in its design. These algorithms are implemented purely on classical hardware. This chapter addresses three major types of inspiration:

1. **Emulating Quantum Heuristics:** Classical algorithms that mirror the dynamic nature of quantum optimization procedures fall into this category. Han and Kim (2002, 2005) introduced the earliest quantum-inspired evolutionary algorithms (QIEAs), which employ concepts such as qubits and superposition to enhance population diversity in genetic algorithms. A more recent and striking example is the use of classical hardware to solve Quadratic Unconstrained Binary Optimization (QUBO) or Ising model problems, the native format of quantum annealers. Digital Annealers such as those developed by Fujitsu, represent a direct hardware embodiment of this approach.
2. **Transfer of Mathematical Formalisms:** This entails laying hands on mathematical tools that were created to deal with the complexity of quantum systems and utilizing them on classical machine learning. The most dominant one is the application of tensor networks (TNs), including Matrix Product States (MPS) that were initially developed in order to represent quantum many-body wavefunctions with low entanglement. In ML, the structures can be employed to compress the large weight tensors of a neural network, or can be used to approximate high-dimensional feature spaces, using the

assumption that the data underlying the models have a low-rank correlation structure, similar to low entanglement.

3. **Algorithmic Dequantization:** This is the most explicit way of inspiration in that a quantum algorithm is routinely optimized into a classical one. This often consists of determining the computational primitive at the heart of the quantum algorithm (e.g. quantum phase estimation in HHL) and attempting to identify a classical, usually randomized, subroutine equivalent that achieves a comparable result under particular data conditions (e.g. fast sampling techniques of RLA).

These should be separated, though, with true quantum machine learning that requires quantum hardware in order to run algorithms that utilize such quantum phenomena as superposition and entanglement in order to manipulate information. Although simulating a quantum circuit on a classical computer can be a useful tool in algorithm verification, it does not count as a quantum-inspired algorithm in the sense of using a scalable classical algorithm; the amount of work per operation scales exponentially in the number of qubits, exactly the bottleneck QiML wants to avoid.

4.1.3 Historical Arcs: From Simulated Annealing & Adiabatic Ideas to Tensor Networks and Sublinear Sampling

The history of intellectual origins of QiML does not represent anything that can be called a flow, but an aggregation of multiple strands of research. The initial thread is the physics-led optimization. Simulated annealing is a classical heuristic which is analogous to metallurgical annealing. It has a quantum mechanical analog though, quantum annealing, which substitutes thermal fluctuations with quantum tunnelling to traverse non-trivial energy landscapes, originally suggested in the late 1980s and developed formally in the 1990s (Kadowaki and Nishimori, 1998). This spawned the development of physical quantum annealers, and their classical analogs which can simulate this process.

Quantum Approximate Optimization Algorithm (QAOA) may be viewed as a gate-based and digitized variant of quantum adiabatic evolution, which in turn is a close cousin to quantum annealing. The main principle alternation between a problem Hamiltonian and a mixer Hamiltonian has spawned an entire family of classical algorithms alternating optimization.

A second type of transfer involves importing mathematical structures from quantum many-body physics. The density matrix renormalization group (DMRG) algorithm was recast in Matrix Product States (MPS) language in the 1990s and 2000s as a kind of tensor network, thus giving access to a robust method of simulating one-dimensional quantum systems. The discovery that these networks are particularly suited to approximate particular correlation structures (low entanglement) prompted their use in machine learning in the 2010s to tasks such as neural network compression and supervised classification, where the weight tensors were taken to also have low entanglement.

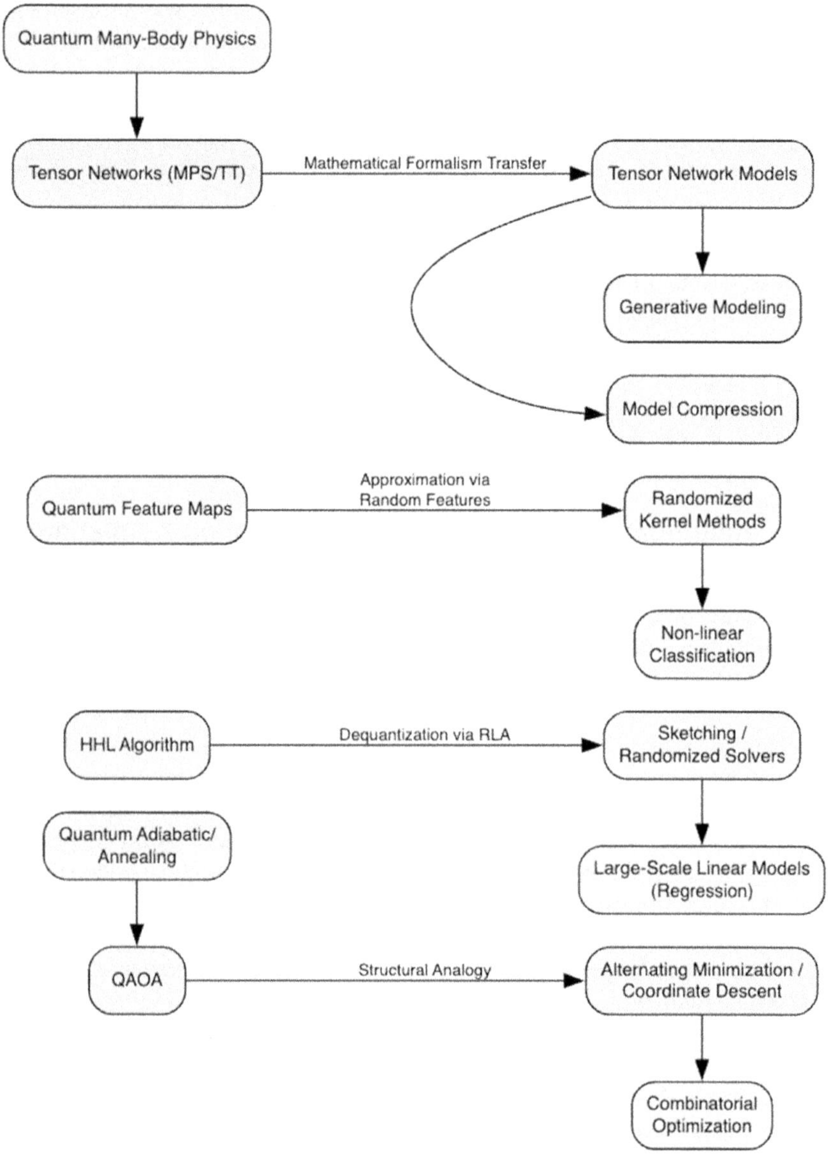

Figure 4.1: A taxonomy of quantum-inspired methods with indication of how quantum machine learning algorithms and formalisms can be converted to classical equivalents in machine learning tasks by intermediary areas such as Randomized Numerical Linear Algebra and Tensor Networks.

The third and most active arc is dequantization which really started in earnest around 2018. This thread was directly tied to the emergence of quantum algorithms designed for machine learning tasks, such as recommendation systems and the Harrow–Hassidim–Lloyd (HHL) algorithm for solving linear equations. It was a watershed moment when it was discovered that these quantum algorithms could not only be matched, but in some cases, surpassed by classical algorithms employing advanced techniques from Randomized Numerical Linear Algebra (RLA), including importance sampling. It showed that the nature of the speedup source was not strictly quantum but associated with data characteristics that can be used also by classical randomized algorithms, therefore making certain that RLA is a hallmark of present-day QiML. The three arcs of optimization heuristics, mathematical formalisms, and algorithmic translation have become the main pillars of the field (as shown in Figure 4.1).

4.2 Core Quantum-Inspired Ideas for ML

In this section, we go into the key conceptual foundations of quantum-inspired machine learning. The three pillars include the different routes through which quantum principles have been brought into classical algorithmic strategies. The focus is on developing intuition for these methods and relating them to the algorithms discussed in Section 3. One of the unifying threads is the adaptation of quantum concepts to find effective methods of data representation, function approximation, and optimization concepts such as quantum states, dynamics, and measurement.

4.2.1 Tensor-Network Representations for Models and Data

The original seed of the first core idea lies in quantum many-body physics, where tensor networks were developed to effectively describe complex quantum states that inhabit an exponentially large Hilbert space yet occupy a physically small, though not negligible region of it. The key insight is that the states of interest, such as ground states of local Hamiltonians, are constrained to possess only a finite amount of entanglement, and can therefore be compressed into a network of smaller, entangled tensors.

Quantum States to ML Models: In machine learning, this corresponds to using a tensor network to represent the weight parameters of a model or features of a dataset. As an example, the weight vector of a one-dimensional linear model with d features can be restructured into an order-d tensor W. In the case it can be approximated using a low-rank representation via Tensor Train (TT) or Matrix Product State (MPS) decomposition, the parameter count goes from exponential in d to polynomial (Oseledets, 2011).

Consider a full tensor representation as shown in Eq. 4.1:

$$W \epsilon, R^{n_1 \times n_1 \times \dots \times n_d} \tag{4.1}$$

which requires storage on the order as given in Eq. 4.2:

$$O(\prod_{k=1}^{d} n_k) \tag{4.2}$$

By contrast, if W is represented in the **Tensor Train (TT) format** with cores $\{G_k\}_{k=1}^{d}$, *t.* the storage requirement reduces to

$$O(\sum_{k=1}^{d} n_k r_{k-1} r_k) \tag{4.3}$$

where r_k are the TT-ranks with $r_0 = r_d = 1$

This compression is particularly effective for data with an inherent sequential or local structure, such as time series, text, or pixels in an image, where the correlations between distant features are weak, a direct analog to the "area law" of entanglement in physics.

Expressivity vs. Contraction Cost: The Expressivity of a tensor network model is determined by the bond dimensions (TT-ranks). Increased ranks enable the network to reflect more complex functions and longer-distance correlations; however, this comes at an increasingly high computational cost. The operations involved, including making a prediction (contracting the network with a feature tensor), scale polynomially with bond dimensions. This introduces a fundamental trade-off: rank must be large enough to capture the relevant structure in the data, yet small enough to keep the computation from becoming overly demanding.

Use in Classifiers and Generative Models:

- **Classifiers:** A linear classifier can also be trained by updating the small core tensors to learn the TT-format representation of the weight tensor. This approach can substantially reduce the number of individually learned parameters, and, in principle, improve generalization, since adopting a simple form such as the TT-decomposition serves as a form of structural regularization.
- **Generative Models:** Tensor networks can also be used to represent probability distributions in high-dimensional spaces. A TT-based model or an autoregressive matrix product state (AMPS) can efficiently compute normalized probability distributions, and enable direct, unbiased sampling, giving them potential as generative models that may compete with current state-of-the-art neural network approaches.

4.2.2 Quantum-Inspired Kernels and Random Features

Kernel methods, such as Support Vector Machines (SVMs), are highly effective non-linear learning procedures that employ a kernel function $k(x, y)$ to compute inner products in a high-dimensional feature space, without explicitly constructing the feature vectors (Schuld, 2021). Quantum kernel techniques extend this concept by estimating the kernel on a quantum computer, where the kernel is defined as the inner product of quantum states representing the classical data:

$$k(x,y) = |\langle\phi(x)\ |\phi(y)\rangle|^2$$

where $|\phi(x)\rangle$ is the quantum state corresponding to data point x. The hope is that quantum feature maps can access feature spaces intractable for classical methods, thereby providing a quantum advantage.

Quantum Feature Maps to Classical Random Features: The quantum-inspired suggestion arises from classical random feature techniques, which provide a means of explicitly approximating kernel features. By Bochner's theorem, the envelope of any shift-invariant kernel $k(x, y) = k(x\ y)$ can be expressed as the Fourier transform of a probability distribution density. Rahimi and Recht (2007) proposed an approach related to the random features method, under which the kernel is approximated by sampling frequencies ω (equivalently, by sampling $p(\omega)$) and building an explicit, low-dimensional feature map $z(x)$ as shown in Eq. 4.4:

$$k(x, y) \approx z(x)^T z(y) \text{ where } z(x) = \sqrt{\frac{2}{D}}^T \tag{4.4}$$

This enables one to realize fast linear models in the feature space $z(x)$ to approximate the much slower kernel machine.

The relationship with quantum models is that, in many proposed quantum feature maps, the resulting kernel corresponds to a classical random feature that can be readily approximated using a Fourier or orthogonal basis. This process dequantizes the quantum kernel, yielding a classically computable algorithm with comparable expressive power. While the quantum formalism naturally inspires new types of random feature constructions, the resulting algorithm remains classically computable.

Approximation Guarantees and Memory Footprint: Random feature methods approximate kernels using a feature dimension D. The greater the number of features, the better the approximation, with error decreasing approximately as $1/\sqrt{D}$. To reach accuracy ϵ, one needs about $1/\epsilon^2$ features. The memory cost is $n \times D$, which is far smaller than storing the full $n \times n$ kernel matrix when $D << n$.

4.2.3 HHL-Inspired Linear Solvers

Quantum HHL algorithm also alluded to exponential speedup in solving the linear systems of equations, but only in constrained circumstances. Its classical version was a result of randomized linear algebra (RLA) (Woodruff, 2014). In this case, a small data sketch is used to reduce the system, thus becoming cheaper to solve. The sketch gives a reasonably good solution that is easy to understand, given its careful design. This trade-off reflects the dependence of accuracy on the size of the sketch, while computation is accelerated by several orders of magnitude. Moreover, sketch preconditioning may also speedup traditional solvers such as the conjugate gradient method.

4.2.4 QAOA/Adiabatic-Inspired Optimization

QAOA adopts two processes in turn, one which optimizes cost, and one which searches the solution space. This resembles the alternating minimization method of classical optimization, where the blocks of variables and the minimizations alternate (Karimi et al., 2016). Several types of ML problems – such as feature selection or graph partitioning – can be posed as Ising or QUBO problems. Quantum algorithms are aimed at such formulations, but usually classical heuristics, including simulated annealing, tabu search or message passing, are also effective. The motivation is the main point to regard ML tasks as energy-minimization and devise nesting, alternating heuristics.

4.2.5 Quantum Walks-Inspired Sampling and Diffusion

Quantum walks are used to propagate over graphs at a faster pace compared to conventional random walks, and it has given rise to new methods of faster sampling. In machine learning, this corresponds to improved MCMC designs, with proposal moves that mix states more rapidly and reduce sample-to-sample correlation. The aim is to replicate the effect of quantum interference, e.g., via symmetries or reflection-like steps, such that the sampler walks over complex distributions more rapidly than ordinary random walks. Figure 4.2 maps design patterns for selecting a quantum-inspired approach.

4.3 Algorithms

In this section, we outline simplified versions of algorithms inspired by the quantum principles described earlier. The focus is on practical sketches that convey the mechanics without excessive mathematical detail.

4.3.1 Tensor Train Classifier

Idea: Compress the weight tensor of a linear model into a Tensor Train (TT) format to reduce parameters and improve efficiency.

Algorithm 1

1. Input: Training data $X \in R$^$(n \times d)$, labels y
2. Initialize TT-cores $\{G_1, G_2, \ldots, G_d\}$ with small ranks
3. For each epoch
4. For each sample (x, y)
5. Construct a feature tensor from x
6. Predict $\hat{y}$ = Contract (feature tensor, TT-cores)
7. Compute loss $L\ (\hat{y}, y)$
8. Update TT-cores via gradient step
9. Output: TT-cores representing classifier weights

Note: Training scales polynomially in TT-rank; compactness acts as structural regularization.

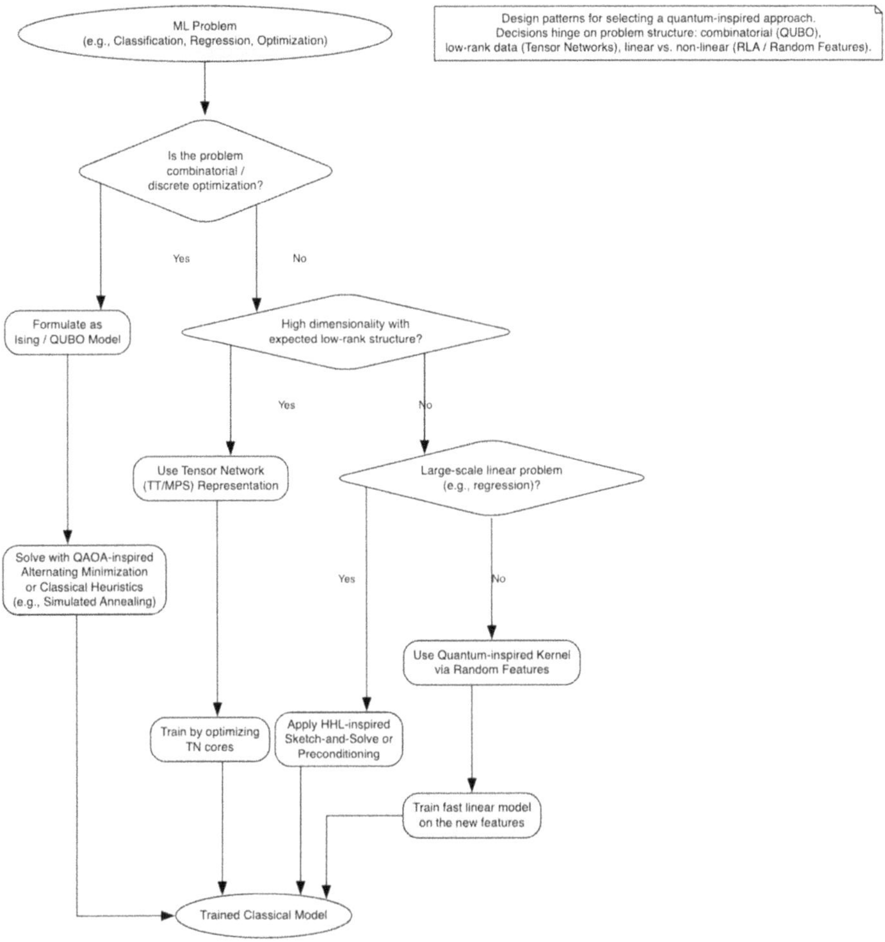

Figure 4.2: Patterns to choose a quantum-inspired approach. This flow chart offers a framework for decision-making regarding the solution of mapping a given machine learning task to a suitable strategy inspired by quantum ideas relative to the structure of such a problem, including its combination, dimension, and linearity.

4.3.2 Random Features Kernel Approximation

Idea: Approximate a kernel using observation with explicit random features, which allows for fast linear training.

Algorithm 2

1. Input: Data points $\{x_1, \ldots, x_n\}$, kernel $k(\cdot,\cdot)$, feature dimension D
2. Sample D random frequencies $\{\omega_1, \ldots, \omega_D\}$ from distribution p
3. For each x_i
4. Construct feature map $z(x_i) = [\cos(\omega_1{}^\wedge T\, x_i), \ldots, \cos(\omega_D{}^\wedge T\, x_i)]$

5. Train linear model w on $\{z(x_i), y_i\}$
6. Output: Trained linear model in feature space

Note: Requires $O(n_D)$ memory, much less than $O(n^2)$ for kernel matrix when $D << n$.

4.3.3 Sketch-and-Solve Linear Solver

Idea: Solve faster, a big linear system $Ax = b$, by reducing it to a smaller sketched system.

Algorithm 3

1. Input: Matrix $A \in R\text{^}(n\times d)$, vector b $\in R\text{^}n$, sketch size m
2. Generate sketching matrix $S \in R\text{^}(m\times n)$
3. Compute sketched system: $A' = S\,A$, $b' = S\,b$
4. Solve smaller system: $(A'\text{^}T\,A')\,w \approx A'\text{^}T\,b'$
5. Return approximate solution w

Note: Accuracy improves with sketch size m; it works well for well-conditioned systems.

4.3.4 QAOA-Inspired Alternating Minimization

Idea: Take turns between taking cost improvement and going through exploration/mixing.

Algorithm 4

1. Input: Initial solution x_0, cost function C, mixing operator M
2. Initialize $x \leftarrow x_0$
3. For $t = 1 \ldots T$
4. $x \leftarrow$ ImproveCost (x, C)
5. $x \leftarrow$ MixSolution (x, M)
6. Return the best solution found

4.3.5 Quantum Walks-Inspired Sampler

Idea: Modify Markov Chain Monte Carlo (MCMC) with reflection/mixing steps inspired by quantum walks.

Algorithm 5

1. Input: Target distribution π, initial state x_0
2. For $t = 1 \ldots T$
3. Propose a new state x' using the reflection/mixing rule
4. Accept x' with probability $\min(1, \pi(x')/\pi(x))$
5. Update chain state
6. Return sampled states $\{x_1, \ldots, x_T\}$

4.4 Applications and Case Studies of Quantum-Inspired Machine Learning

Although quantum-inspired algorithms originate from abstract mathematical analogies, their most convincing practical applications have emerged in machine learning,where they have been tested in real world settings. In this section it is therefore important to highlight the tangible areas in which QiML techniques have already demonstrated benefits over standard baselines.

4.4.1 Recommendation Systems

Among the most compelling success stories is the quantum-inspired recommendation algorithm by Tang (2019), which showed that classical randomized linear-algebra techniques can match the performance of a quantum algorithm previously believed to offer exponential speedups. QiML methods can scale recommendation models to millions of users and items, enhance financial and computational efficiency through low-rank structure in user-item matrices, and leverage efficient 2-norm sampling.

4.4.2 Resource-Constrained Machine Learning

The value of a tensor-network-based QiML approach lies in memory- or compute-constrained environments i.e., embedded systems or the edge. As an example, MPS or TT representations with parameter reductions of tens to hundreds of thousands are possible with neural networks having correspondingly fewer weight matrices, with accurate models retaining the same expressiveness. Low-rank approximation has been used in image classification and natural language processing, in both cases to minimize storage space since the approximation does not cost predictive power.

4.4.3 Large Linear Models

Large-scale regression, classification, and scientific computing problems are particularly applicable in HHL-inspired linear solvers and sketch-and-solve approaches. These solvers save massive training time using sketches that can be made in a low dimension and can be just as accurate. Practically, randomized sketching has been used in climate modeling, genomic prediction, and financial forecasting, where millions of features would make the equivalent methods computationally infeasible (Halko et al., 2011).

4.4.4 Optimization Combinatorial

Many machine learning tasks may be reduced to a combinatorial optimization framework like Quadratic Unconstrained Binary Optimization (QUBO). Classical alternatives are given by quantum-inspired heuristics extending QAOA or annealing to these settings, which prove to be effective. The case studies presented are: feature selection on high-dimensional data, graph partitioning (community detection), and logistic network scheduling.

4.4.5 Generative Models Sampling

Sampling efficiency-enhancing quantum-walk-inspired techniques have been derived in Markov Chain Monte Carlo (MCMC), which enhance Bayesian inference and generative modeling. As an example, autoregressive matrix product states (AMPS) have demonstrated the ability to draw high-dimensional probability distributions with unbiased sampling, as an alternative to deep generative networks.

In each of these areas, recommendation systems, resource-constrained ML, large-scale linear models, combinatorial optimization, and generative modeling, quantum-inspired approaches have demonstrated meaningful gains in scalability, efficiency, or interpretability relative to fully classical baselines. These studies illustrate that QiML is not merely a theoretical curiosity, but an emerging, practical toolbox already capable of delivering value in real-world machine learning applications.

4.5 Conclusion

This chapter has traversed the terrain of quantum-inspired machine learning, an area created at the confluence of the profound algorithmic lessons of quantum theory and the scale requirements of classical, large-scale computing. As we know already, QiML is not a monoculture but rather a gathering of these intellectual traditions: the translation of mathematical tools of quantum computation, such as tensor networks, the quantization of particular quantum algorithms, such as HHL in the language of randomized numerical linear algebra, and importation of structural analogies in quantum heuristics, such as QAOA.

The main point is that the inspiration from quantum mechanics is not just a source of new heuristics but rather it yields a principled methodology for the construction of classical algorithms that prove especially productive in exploring certain data structures (Aggarwal, 2020). The strengths of tensor networks include data sets where information or parameters in the model have low-rank connections, like those of the area law entanglement in physical systems. The HHL-inspired solvers prefer large over completed linear systems, where the statistical characterization is very well described by a sketch. Quantum-inspired kernel methods harness the power of random features to scale the classification problem to non-convex, non-convexity to classify using kernel methods. QAOA-inspired optimizers serialize efficiently, parameterizing a difficult, non-convex combinatorial problem with a group structure.

Not every method is, however, advantageous. Their utility depends on whether the algorithm's implicit assumptions of the algorithm align with the structural peculiarities of the problem at hand. A tensor-network classifier, for example, will fail when the data exhibits an incompressible correlation structure, while a sketch-and-solve technique offers only marginal benefits on small, dense matrices. Practitioners are therefore responsible for diagnosing the structural characteristics of their data, its effective rank, sparsity, connectivity patterns, and selecting the appropriate tool from the QiML toolbox. The route between a quantum idea and a feasible classical algorithm is one of translation and approximation, and it brings an obligation of intellectual integrity. We as a field need more discipline in our claims, properly separating the demonstrated vineyard of efficiency advantages of these classical strategies from the unfulfilled promise of fault-tolerant quantum computing. What is important about QiML is not necessarily to ape quantum mechanics per se, but to apply the notation and machinery of the quantum setting to bring back new, efficient, and provably effective classical algorithms that will open new horizons of machine learning today. The principles analyzed in this chapter will thus remain core despite further development of classical and quantum hardware and offer a lasting connection between the two exciting fields of computation.

References

Aggarwal, C. C. (2020). Linear Algebra and Optimization for Machine Learning: A Textbook. Springer Nature. DOI: 10.1007/978-3-030-40344-7.

Biamonte, J., Wittek, P., Pancotti, N., Rebentrost, P., Wiebe, N. & Lloyd, S. (2017). Quantum machine learning. *Nature*, 549(7671), 195–202. DOI: 10.1038/nature23474.

Drineas, P. & Mahoney, M. W. (2016). RandNLA: Randomized numerical linear algebra. *Communications of the ACM*, 59(6), 82–90. DOI: 10.1145/2897955.

Farhi, E., Goldstone, J. & Gutmann, S. (2014). A quantum approximate optimization algorithm. arXiv preprint arXiv:1411.4028.

Halko, N., Martinsson, P. G. & Tropp, J. A. (2011). Finding structure with randomness: Probabilistic algorithms for constructing approximate matrix decompositions. *SIAM Review*, 53(2), 217–288. DOI: 10.1137/090771806.

Han, K. H. & Kim, J. H. (2002). Quantum-inspired evolutionary algorithm for a class of combinatorial optimization. *IEEE Transactions on Evolutionary Computation*, 6(6), 580–593. DOI: 10.1109/TEVC.2002.804320.

Harrow, A., Hassidim, A. & Lloyd, S. (2009). Quantum algorithm for linear systems of equations. *Physical Review Letters*, 103(15), 150502. DOI: 10.1103/PhysRevLett.103.150502.

Kadowaki, T. & Nishimori, H. (1998). Quantum annealing in the transverse Ising model. *Physical Review E*, 58(5), 5355. DOI: 10.1103/PhysRevE.58.5355.

Karimi, H., Nutini, J. & Schmidt, M. (2016). Linear convergence of gradient and proximal-gradient methods under the Polyak-Łojasiewicz condition. In: *Joint European Conference on Machine Learning and Knowledge Discovery in Databases* (pp. 795–811). DOI: 10.1007/978-3-319-46227-1_50.

Martinsson, P.-G. & Tropp, J. A. (2020). Randomized numerical linear algebra: Foundations and algorithms. *Acta Numerica*, 29, 403–572. DOI: 10.1017/S096249292000004X.

Oseledets, I. V. (2011). Tensor-train decomposition. *SIAM Journal on Scientific Computing*, 33(5), 2295–2317. DOI: 10.1137/090752286.

Rahimi, A. & Recht, B. (2007). Random features for large-scale kernel machines. *Advances in Neural Information Processing Systems*, 20, 1177–1184.

Schuld, M. (2021). Supervised quantum machine learning models are kernel methods. arXiv preprint arXiv:2101.11020.

Stoudenmire, E. M. & Schwab, D. J. (2016). Supervised learning with tensor networks. *Advances in Neural Information Processing Systems*, 29, 4799–4807.

Tang, E. (2019). A quantum-inspired classical algorithm for recommendation systems. *Proceedings of the 51st Annual ACM SIGACT Symposium on Theory of Computing (STOC '19)* (pp. 217–228). Doi: 10.1145/3313276.3316310.

Woodruff, D. P. (2014). Sketching as a tool for numerical linear algebra. *Foundations and Trends® in Theoretical Computer Science*, 10(1–2), 1–157. DOI: 10.1561/0400000060.

CHAPTER

5

Concrete Cryptanalysis of LWE: Advances, Benchmarks, and Experimental Realities

Shazia Tazeen* **and R. Padmavathy**

Department of Computer Science and Engineering, National Institute of Technology, Warangal, India

This chapter presents a comprehensive analysis of recent advances in concrete attacks on the Learning with Errors (LWE) problem, a foundational pillar of post-quantum cryptography. We synthesize results from 2024 research, benchmarking multiple LWE attack strategies—including lattice reduction, man-in-the-middle, and hybrid approaches—using standardized cryptosystem parameters. The discussion highlights the gap between theoretical complexity estimates and practical experimental results, emphasizing the influence of secret distributions (binary, ternary, Gaussian) and hardware configurations on attack efficiency. Novel approaches such as Diophantine approximation techniques, ternary secret representations, and enhanced enumeration methods are explored for their impact on both asymptotic and practical performance. Through experimental validation, we observe that Gaussian secrets with sparsity of less than 5% required over 60 days for recovery using SALSA VERDE in dimensions $n = 256$ with $\log_2 q = 20$. In contrast, binary secrets with Hamming weight $h = 33$ were recovered in just 15 hours. The chapter also examines the integration of combinatorial and lattice-based techniques, the role of parameter optimization, and the trade-offs between computational cost and attack success rates. We provide actionable insights for researchers and practitioners seeking to evaluate and strengthen the security of LWE-based cryptosystems in the face of emerging attack vectors.

*Corresponding author: st24csr1q03@student.nitw.ac.in

DOI: 10.1201/9781003682950-5

5.1 Overview of LWE and Small Secrets

The Learning with Errors (LWE) problem is a cornerstone of post-quantum cryptography, underpinning many lattice-based cryptographic schemes, including homomorphic encryption systems and several NIST Post-Quantum Cryptography candidates (Joppe Bos et al., 2018; Jan-Pieter D'Anvers et al., 2018; Leo Ducas et al., 2018). LWE was introduced by Regev in 2005 (Oded Regev, 2010) and concerns distinguishing uniformly random linear equations from those perturbed by a small error term.

In homomorphic encryption, secret vector is often sampled from distributions such as binary, ternary, or narrow Gaussian distributions (Alexander May, 2021). These *small secrets* improve efficiency and functionality but raise questions about whether their use meaningfully reduces the overall security of the scheme.

5.1.1 Mathematical Formulation of LWE

The Learning with Errors (LWE) is formally defined as follows (Oded Regev, 2010):

Definition: Let $n \geq 1$ and $q \geq 2$ be a prime modulus. Let D_σ be a discrete Gaussian Distribution over Z with standard deviation σ. Let $A \in Z^{m \times n}$ be a matrix with entries. Sampled uniformly at random from Z_q, let $\mathbf{s} \in Z^n$ be a secret vector, and let $\mathbf{e} \in Z^m$ be an error vector, sampled from D_σ. Define $\mathbf{b} = A\mathbf{s} + \mathbf{e} \pmod{q}$.

Given $(A, \mathbf{b})$, the main aim of the LWE is to recover $\mathbf{s}$ where $\mathbf{s}$ is the **secret vector**.

The hardness of LWE is closely related to the difficulty of well-known lattice problems, such as the (approximate) Shortest Vector Problem (SVP), under quantum reductions (Zvika Brakerski et al., 2013).

The key parameters that define an LWE instance include the dimension n, which represents the size of the secret vector; the modulus q; the standard deviation σ of the error distribution; and the distribution from which the secret vector $\mathbf{s}$ is drawn.

5.1.2 Small Secret Distributions

In practice, especially for homomorphic encryption and other performance-sensitive applications, the secret vector $\mathbf{s}$ is often sampled from distributions with small magnitude entries (Cathy Yuanchen Li et al., 2023, Alexander May, 2021):

- **Binary:** Each entry of $\mathbf{s}$ is sampled uniformly from $\{0, 1\}$.
- **Ternary:** Each entry of $\mathbf{s}$ is sampled uniformly from $\{-1, 0, 1\}$.
- **Gaussian:** Entries of $\mathbf{s}$ are drawn from the same discrete Gaussian distribution D_σ as the error.

In sparse secret variants, only a small fraction of the entries in **s** is non-zero. Let h denote the number of non-zero entries in the secret (equivalent to the Hamming weight in the binary case). The sparsity of the secret is then defined as the ratio h/n, representing the proportion of non-zero components in the secret vector.

These low-entropy secrets offer performance advantages but may introduce vulnerabilities in certain attack models. The balance between efficiency and security is a major theme in modern LWE-based cryptosystem design. The variation of modulus percentage with respect to sparsity for different secret types is illustrated in Figure 5.1.

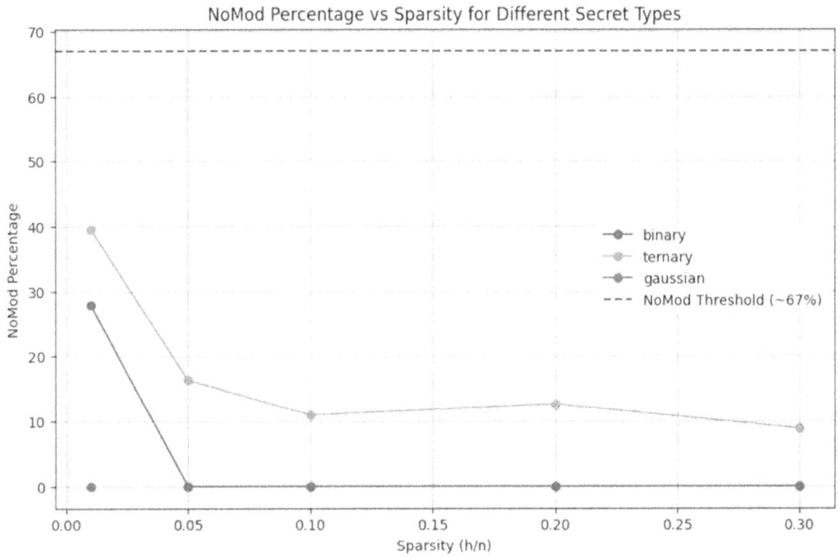

Figure 5.1: No mod percentage vs sparsity for different secret types (Cathy Yuanchen Li et al., 2023).

5.2 Classical Lattice Attacks on LWE

5.2.1 BKZ Reduction and uSVP Attacks

The Block Korkine-Zolotarev (BKZ) algorithm (Claus-Peter Schnorr and Martin Euchner, 1994) with blocksize β achieves a root-Hermite factor given by Yuanmi Chen & Phong Q. Nguyen (2011), as shown in eq.

$$\delta_0 \approx \frac{\beta}{2\pi e} \cdot (\pi\beta)^{1/\beta} \frac{1}{2(\beta-1)} \tag{5.1}$$

- **Primal attack:** Treats LWE as a Bounded Distance Decoding (BDD) problem by constructing a lattice where the LWE secret corresponds to a lattice point close to the noisy LWE samples, then uses lattice reduction algorithms like BKZ to find this nearby point and recover the secret.

- **Dual attack:** Finds short vectors in the dual lattice to distinguish LWE instances at random by exploiting the fact that inner products of short dual lattice vectors with LWE samples will have more minor variance than with truly random samples, allowing statistical distinguishing attacks that can lead to secret recovery.

5.2.2 Limitations of Classical Approaches

- **Sequential computation:** Traditional lattice reduction algorithms like LLL and BKZ sequentially perform basis updates, making it difficult to leverage parallel computing resources effectively, which limits scalability on modern high-performance computing systems.
- **Memory-intensive operations:** Classical attacks require storing and manipulating large lattice bases and intermediate computations, leading to exponential memory requirements that become prohibitive for cryptographically relevant parameter sizes.
- **Difficulty exploiting secret structure:** Standard primal and dual attacks treat the LWE secret as generic, failing to take advantage of specific structural properties (such as sparsity, small coefficients, or known distributions) that might be present in practical cryptographic implementations.
- **Gap between theory and practice:** Theoretical complexity estimates for lattice reduction often assume idealized conditions and fail to account for numerical precision issues, implementation details, and the actual performance of heuristic algorithms on real-world instances.

5.3 Machine Learning Approaches to Attack LWE

Recent research has demonstrated that machine learning (ML) techniques, especially transformer-based models, can be effectively employed to attack Learning with Errors (LWE) instances when the secret is sampled from small or structured distributions (Cathy Li et al., 2023; Cathy Yuanchen Li et al., 2023; Emily Wenger et al., 2022). The progression of ML-based attacks on LWE, highlighting key architectures and datasets, is summarized in Table 5.1.

Table 5.1: Evolution of Machine Learning Attacks on LWE

Year	Attack	Capability	Limitation
2022	SALSA	Binary secrets, $n \leq 128$, $h \leq 4$	Very limited scope
2023	PICANTE	Binary secrets, $n \leq 350$, $h \leq 60$	Binary only
2023	SALSA VERDE	Binary/ternary/Gaussian, $n \leq 512$	Still requires sparse secrets

5.3.1 SALSA, PICANTE, and SALSA VERDE

SALSA (2022) (Emily Wenger, et al., 2022) was the first proof-of-concept ML attack on LWE, demonstrating that transformer models could recover binary secrets with very low Hamming weights (3–4 non-zero bits) in dimensions up to $n = 128$. PICANTE (Cathy Li et al., 2023) extended this work by improving data preprocessing and secret recovery techniques, successfully recovering binary secrets with Hamming weights up to 60 in dimensions as high as $n = 350$.

Building on these approaches, SALSA VERDE (Cathy Yuanchen Li et al., 2023) represents a significant advancement in ML-based attacks on LWE. It introduces several new capabilities:

- The method can recover more general secret distributions, including binary, ternary, and narrow Gaussian.
- The approach scales to larger dimensions, up to $n = 512$.
- The technique enables effective attacks on instances with smaller moduli, as low as $\log_2 q = 12$ for $n = 256$.
- The algorithm provides reduced runtime and computational resource requirements compared to earlier methods.

5.3.2 Evolution of ML Attacks on LWE

Each iteration addressed specific limitations of predecessors, showing rapid ML attack evolution. The chronological development of SALSA-series attacks, from the original SALSA to SALSA PICANTE and SALSA VERDE, is depicted in Figure 5.2.

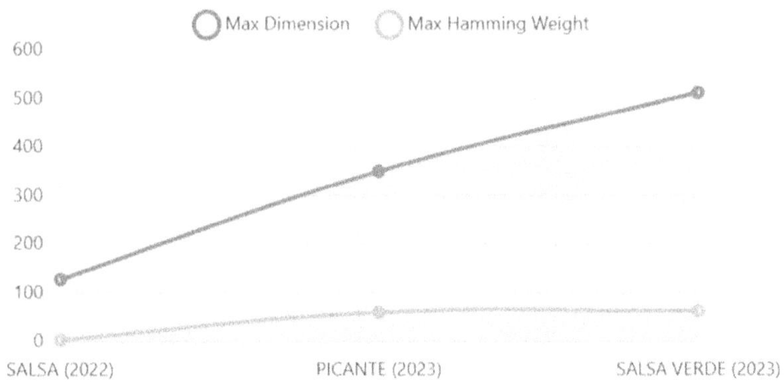

Figure 5.2: Timeline showing the progression from SALSA to SALSA VERDE.

5.3.3 Attack Methodology

The SALSA VERDE attack (Cathy Yuanchen Li et al., 2023) proceeds in three main stages:

1. **Data preprocessing:** Given $4n$ LWE samples that share the same secret, enhanced lattice reduction techniques are applied to normalize the data and generate a training set of approximately 4 million samples with reduced coordinate variance.
2. **Model training:** A transformer-based neural network is trained to predict $\mathbf{b}$ from $\mathbf{a}$ in the preprocessed LWE samples. The model effectively learns to approximate the mapping $\mathbf{a} \mapsto \langle \mathbf{a}, \mathbf{s} \rangle + e \bmod q$.
3. **Secret recovery:** After each training epoch, the model's output is used to generate a guess for the secret $\mathbf{s}$. The correctness of the guess is validated using statistical tests, without requiring explicit knowledge of the actual secret vector.

These advances in applying deep learning to cryptanalysis underscore the importance of evaluating LWE-based schemes not only against classical lattice attacks but also against emerging ML-driven techniques, particularly when utilizing low-entropy or structured secrets.

5.3.4 Improved Data Preprocessing and Secret Recovery in SALSA VERDE

5.3.4.1 Improved Data Preprocessing

SALSA VERDE (Cathy Yuanchen Li et al., 2023) introduces several optimizations to the data preprocessing stage that significantly enhance both efficiency and effectiveness compared to previous methods such as PICANTE:

- **Rearrangement of lattice rows to reduce computational complexity:** Strategic reordering of basis vectors based on their norms and geometric properties to minimize the number of reduction steps and improve convergence rates in lattice reduction algorithms.
- **Lower floating-point precision requirements:** Use of reduced precision arithmetic (such as single precision instead of double precision) to decrease memory usage and computational overhead while maintaining sufficient accuracy for cryptanalytic purposes.
- **Interleaved reduction algorithms to balance speed and accuracy:** Alternating between fast heuristic reduction steps and more rigorous but slower exact computations to achieve a favorable trade-off between runtime performance and solution quality.
- **Adaptive block size and precision scheduling during reduction:** Dynamic adjustment of BKZ block parameters and numerical precision throughout the reduction process based on current basis quality and computational constraints to optimize overall efficiency.
- **Early stopping conditions to prevent unnecessary computation:** Implementation of termination criteria that halt the reduction process when sufficient basis quality has been achieved for the cryptanalytic goal, avoiding redundant computations that provide diminishing returns.

These optimizations make preprocessing up to **45 times faster** *and* **20% more effective** than in PICANTE.

5.3.4.2 Model Architecture and Secret Recovery

SALSA VERDE supports two transformer-based architectures:

- A sequence-to-sequence transformer similar to PICANTE, with a **1-layer encoder** and a **9-layer decoder**.
- An encoder-only transformer, a **4-layer BERT-like model** with rotary word embedding.

These models are trained to predict **b** from **a**, where each entry is tokenized in a suitable base representation.

Binary Secrets: For binary secrets, SALSA VERDE improves upon PICANTE's distinguisher. The key observation is that if $s_i = 0$, then model predictions for input vectors $\mathbf{a}_{\text{test}}$ and $\mathbf{a}_{\text{test}} + K\mathbf{e}_i$ (for some scalar K) should remain similar.

Ternary and Gaussian Secrets: For more general secret distributions, SALSA VERDE introduces:

- **Partial recovery:** Distinguishes zero from non-zero coordinates.
- **Two-bit distinguisher:** For ternary secrets, determines whether non-zero entries are +1 or −1.
- **Class-based recovery:** For Gaussian secrets, clusters non-zero entries into classes believed to represent the same value.

5.3.4.3 Performance and Results

Table 5.2 summarizes the performance of SALSA VERDE across various LWE configurations. As shown in Table 5.2, SALSA VERDE exhibits varying runtimes depending on the secret type and sparsity. Attack time is most sensitive to the preprocessing stage, especially at higher dimensions. For example, with $n = 512$ and $\log_2 q = 41$, full parallelization enables the recovery of binary secrets with Hamming weight up to 63, and ternary secrets up to 58, in about 35–40 days.

Table 5.2: SALSA VERDE Attack Performance

Dimension	Modulus	Secret Type	Sparsity	Attack Time
$n = 256$	$\log_2 q = 20$	Binary	10%	~15 hours
$n = 256$	$\log_2 q = 20$	Ternary	10%	~24 hours
$n = 256$	$\log_2 q = 12$	Binary	3%	~20 hours
$n = 512$	$\log_2 q = 41$	Binary	11%	~35 days
$n = 512$	$\log_2 q = 41$	Ternary	11%	~40 days
$n = 256$	$\log_2 q = 20$	Gaussian	<5%	>60 days

5.3.4.4 Attack Time Scaling Analysis

Preprocessing Dominance: For $n = 512$, preprocessing accounts for 80–90% of total attack time.

Parallelization Benefits:

- **Sequential preprocessing:** The preprocessing phase requires approximately 200 days when executed sequentially.
- **Fully parallelized:** When fully parallelized across available hardware, the total run-time is reduced to approximately 35–40 days.
- **Speedup factor:** This parallelization achieves a speedup factor of 5–6× compared to sequential execution, given sufficient computational hardware.

Memory Requirements:

- **Training data generation:** The data generation phase requires approximately 100 GB of RAM to handle the large-scale lattice computations and sample generation.
- **Model training:** The transformer model training process needs a minimum of 32 GB GPU memory to accommodate the model parameters and batch processing requirements.
- **Total storage:** The complete attack pipeline requires approximately 1 TB of storage space to store training data, model checkpoints, and intermediate computational results.

A comparative overview of diverse attack strategies is illustrated in Table 5.3.

Table 5.3: Attack Implementation Costs

Attack Type	Hardware Cost	Setup Time	Expertise Level	Parallelizable
SALSA VERDE	\$50K (8× A100)	1–2 weeks	High	Excellent
Meet-LWE	\$5K (CPU cluster)	2–3 days	Medium	Partial
BKZ/uSVP	\$1K (workstation)	1 day	Low	Poor
FFT-Dual	\$10K (GPU+CPU)	3–5 days	Medium	Good
Hybrid	\$15K (mixed)	1 week	High	Good

5.4 The No Mod Insight: Theoretical Framework

SALSA VERDE introduces the **No Mod insight**, a theoretical framework explaining why machine-learning attacks succeed against LWE with small secrets. The insight is based on the observation that a significant fraction of LWE samples may not require modular reduction when computing $b = \langle \mathbf{a}, \mathbf{s} \rangle + e \bmod q$. Empirical results show that secret recovery becomes feasible when this **No Mod percentage exceeds approximately 67%**.

Scaling Law: For a binary secret with Hamming weight h, and input vectors $\mathbf{a}$

with entries sampled from a distribution with standard deviation σ_a, the following inequality predicts recoverability:

$$h \cdot \sigma a^2 \leq \frac{q^2}{12} \tag{5.2}$$

As illustrated in Figure 5.3, the No Mod success condition defines a clear boundary between secure and vulnerable parameter regimes. This relation, closely given in Equation 5.2, matches experimental data and provides a concrete theoretical condition under which small-secret LWE instances become vulnerable to machine learning-based attacks. This theoretical understanding explains why:

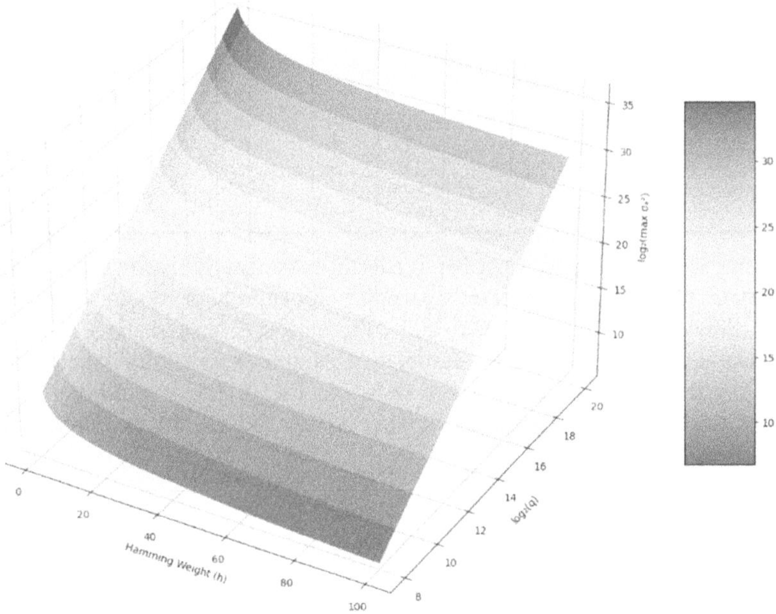

Figure 5.3: No Mod success condition: $h \cdot \sigma a^2 \leq \frac{q^2}{12}$

- Original SALSA attacks only worked for $h \leq 3$
- Data preprocessing improves attack success
- Binary and ternary secrets have similar difficulty
- Gaussian secrets are significantly harder to recover
- Smaller moduli q make attacks more difficult

5.5 Comparison with Classical Attacks

When comparing machine learning approaches with classical lattice reduction techniques (notably uSVP attacks), several patterns emerge. Table 5.4 compares classical uSVP attacks with SALSA VERDE across multiple criteria.

Table 5.4: Comparison of Classical and ML-based Attacks on LWE

Aspect	Classical uSVP	SALSA VERDE (ML)
Attack Type	Lattice-based	Machine learning-based
Computational Model	Sequential, BKZ-based	Highly parallelizable
Resource Requirements	Memory-intensive	GPU-intensive for training
Parameter Sensitivity	More affected by q/n ratio	More affected by h (sparsity)
Binary Secret Recovery	Limited by lattice dimension	Effective up to $h = 63$ in $n = 512$
Ternary Secret Recovery	Slightly harder than binary	Similar to binary (slight disadvantage)
Gaussian Secret Recovery	Substantially harder	Substantially harder
Small q Handling	Less effective	Can work with $\log_2 q$ as low as 12
Theoretical Understanding	Well-established	Novel "No Mod" framework
Preprocessing Cost	BKZ reduction	Lattice reduction + data generation

Attack Success Range: SALSA VERDE successfully recovers secrets in parameter ranges where uSVP attacks either fail entirely or require significantly more time. The relative recovery difficulty across diverse secret distributions is illustrated in Figure 5.4. Representative parameter examples satisfying and violating the No Mod condition are shown in Figure 5.5. A multi-dimensional comparison between classical uSVP and SALSA VERDE attack characteristics is illustrated in Figure 5.6.

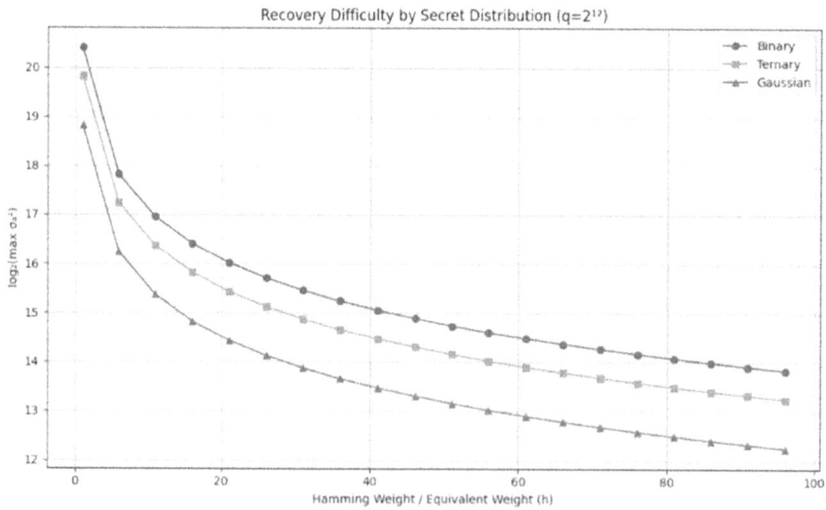

Figure 5.4: Recovery difficulty by secret distribution ($q = 2^{12}$).

```
NoMod Success Condition Examples:

For n=256, log_2(q)=12:
  Sparsity=0.03, h=7: max σ_s^2=199728.76, uniform σ_s^2=5592405.33, Attack unlikely to succeed
  Sparsity=0.05, h=12: max σ_s^2=116508.44, uniform σ_s^2=5592405.33, Attack unlikely to succeed
  Sparsity=0.10, h=25: max σ_s^2=55924.05, uniform σ_s^2=5592405.33, Attack unlikely to succeed
  Sparsity=0.20, h=51: max σ_s^2=27413.75, uniform σ_s^2=5592405.33, Attack unlikely to succeed

For n=256, log_2(q)=20:
  Sparsity=0.03, h=7: max σ_s^2=13089424140.19, uniform σ_s^2=366503875925.33, Attack unlikely to succeed
  Sparsity=0.05, h=12: max σ_s^2=7635497415.11, uniform σ_s^2=366503875925.33, Attack unlikely to succeed
  Sparsity=0.10, h=25: max σ_s^2=3665038759.25, uniform σ_s^2=366503875925.33, Attack unlikely to succeed
  Sparsity=0.20, h=51: max σ_s^2=1796587627.08, uniform σ_s^2=366503875925.33, Attack unlikely to succeed

For n=256, log_2(q)=41:
  Sparsity=0.03, h=7: max σ_s^2=57567896172125195599872.00, uniform σ_s^2=1611901092819506013667328.00, Attack unlikely to succeed
  Sparsity=0.05, h=12: max σ_s^2=33581272767073030766592.00, uniform σ_s^2=1611901092819506013667328.00, Attack unlikely to succeed
  Sparsity=0.10, h=25: max σ_s^2=16119010928195056697344.00, uniform σ_s^2=1611901092819506013667328.00, Attack unlikely to succeed
  Sparsity=0.20, h=51: max σ_s^2=7901475945193654976512.00, uniform σ_s^2=1611901092819506013667328.00, Attack unlikely to succeed

For n=512, log_2(q)=12:
  Sparsity=0.03, h=15: max σ_s^2=93206.76, uniform σ_s^2=5592405.33, Attack unlikely to succeed
  Sparsity=0.05, h=25: max σ_s^2=55924.05, uniform σ_s^2=5592405.33, Attack unlikely to succeed
  Sparsity=0.10, h=51: max σ_s^2=27413.75, uniform σ_s^2=5592405.33, Attack unlikely to succeed
  Sparsity=0.20, h=102: max σ_s^2=13706.88, uniform σ_s^2=5592405.33, Attack unlikely to succeed

For n=512, log_2(q)=20:
  Sparsity=0.03, h=15: max σ_s^2=6108397932.09, uniform σ_s^2=366503875925.33, Attack unlikely to succeed
  Sparsity=0.05, h=25: max σ_s^2=3665038759.25, uniform σ_s^2=366503875925.33, Attack unlikely to succeed
  Sparsity=0.10, h=51: max σ_s^2=1796587627.08, uniform σ_s^2=366503875925.33, Attack unlikely to succeed
  Sparsity=0.20, h=102: max σ_s^2=898293813.54, uniform σ_s^2=366503875925.33, Attack unlikely to succeed

For n=512, log_2(q)=41:
  Sparsity=0.03, h=15: max σ_s^2=26865018213658427129856.00, uniform σ_s^2=1611901092819506013667328.00, Attack unlikely to succeed
  Sparsity=0.05, h=25: max σ_s^2=16119010928195056697344.00, uniform σ_s^2=1611901092819506013667328.00, Attack unlikely to succeed
  Sparsity=0.10, h=51: max σ_s^2=7901475945193654976512.00, uniform σ_s^2=1611901092819506013667328.00, Attack unlikely to succeed
  Sparsity=0.20, h=102: max σ_s^2=3950737972596827488256.00, uniform σ_s^2=1611901092819506013667328.00, Attack unlikely to succeed
```

Figure 5.5: No Mod success condition examples.

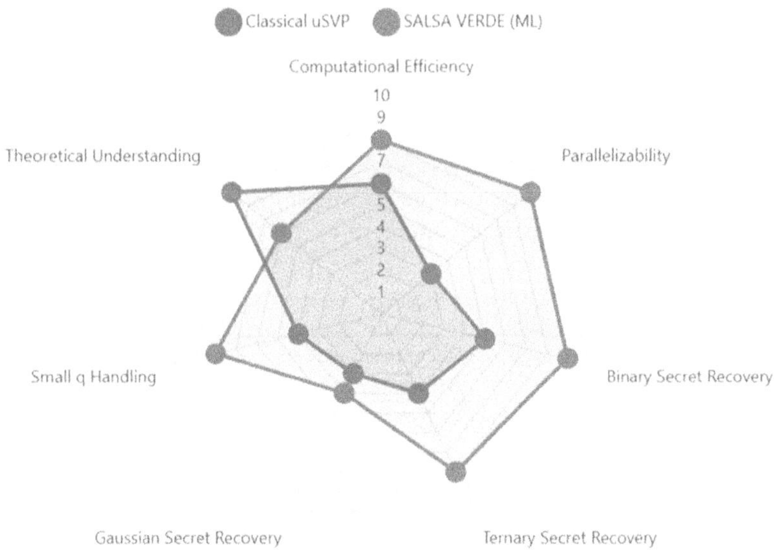

Figure 5.6: Comprehensive comparison across multiple dimensions (from Table 5.4).

Computational Resources:

- uSVP attacks are typically sequential and resource-intensive.
- SALSA VERDE's preprocessing is highly parallelizable.
- ML model training requires GPU resources but is relatively fast.

Modulus and Dimension Scaling:

- Both attacks become more difficult as q decreases and n increases.
- SALSA VERDE maintains its advantage over uSVP for small q and large n.

Secret Distribution Impact:

- Both attacks find binary secrets easiest to recover.
- Ternary secrets offer marginally greater security.
- Gaussian secrets are significantly more secure against both attack types.

5.6 The FFT-Based Dual Lattice Attack

The paper (Israeli Defense Forces, 2023) describes an improved dual lattice attack that significantly reduces the security of several NIST PQC candidates, including Kyber, Saber, and Dilithium.

The improved attack uses several algorithmic enhancements to the dual lattice attack framework. These include:

- Enumeration over more coordinates of the secret
- A new, more powerful distinguisher based on the Fast Fourier Transform (FFT)

These improvements allow the dual attack to surpass the efficiency of many primal attack strategies and pose a notable threat to structured lattice schemes under specific parameter regimes. The improved dual lattice attack consists of three main components.

5.6.1 FFT-Based Distinguisher

The standard dual lattice attack involves enumerating over potential values of secret coordinates and testing each guess with a distinguishing algorithm. The FFT-based approach dramatically improves by standard approach as illustrated in Table 5.5

Table 5.5: Attack Strategy Selection Framework

Parameter Range	Secret Type	Recommended Attack	Expected Time	Success Rate
$n \leq 256$, $q \leq 2^{20}$	Binary, $h \leq 33$	SALSA VERDE	15–24 hours	> 90%
$n \leq 256$, $q \leq 2^{20}$	Ternary, $h \leq 24$	SALSA VERDE	24–48 hours	> 85%
$n \leq 512$, $q \leq 2^{41}$	Binary, $h \leq 63$	SALSA VERDE	35–40 days	> 80%
$n \leq 512$, $q \leq 2^{41}$	Ternary, $h \leq 58$	SALSA VERDE	40–50 days	> 75%
$n > 512$ or dense	Any	Meet-LWE + Hybrid	Weeks–Months	60–80%
NIST parameters	Standard	FFT-Dual + BKZ	Days–Weeks	70–85%

- By performing enumeration over diverse coordinates of the secret concurrently.
- Using the Fast Fourier Transform (FFT) to check all guesses at once
- Applying modulus switching to reduce computational costs

The mathematical approach can be summarized as follows: For a LWE pair $(A, b) \in (Z/qZ)^{m \times n} \times (Z/qZ)^m$, where the partitions of attack of the secret vector s is divided into 3 parts:

$$s = \begin{pmatrix} s_{\text{enum}} \\ s_{\text{fft}} \\ s_{\text{lat}} \end{pmatrix} \tag{5.3}$$

As shown in Equation 5.3, for each potential value of s_{enum}, the FFT algorithm efficiently computes a score for all possible values of s_{fft} simultaneously, determining whether a candidate pair $(s_{\text{enum}}, s_{\text{fft}})$ is likely to be correct.

5.6.2 Improved Short Vectors Sampling Procedure

The attack introduces a more efficient algorithm for finding many short vectors in a lattice. The process works in two stages:

1. **Basis reduction:** Run the BKZ algorithm using a sieve as the SVP oracle to obtain a reduced lattice basis. This step can use the "dimensions-for-free" optimization.
2. **Short vector collection:** Run a final sieve on the first block of the reduced basis to find many short vectors. This step cannot use the dimensions-for-free optimization.

The key insight is using different block sizes for these two steps, allowing for cost optimization. The influence of parameter combinations on overall attack success probability is illustrated in Figure 5.7. Mathematically, if Λ is a d-dimensional lattice, the algorithm outputs at least D vectors of length as shown in Equation 5.4:

$$\det(\Lambda)^{1/d} \cdot N_{\text{sieve}}(\beta_2)^{1/\beta_2} \cdot \sqrt{\frac{\beta_2}{2\pi e}} \cdot (\pi\beta_2)^{1/\beta_2} \cdot \delta(\beta_1)^{\frac{d-\beta_2}{2}} \tag{5.4}$$

β_1 denotes reduction in block size
β_2 denotes vectors sampling of block size
$N_{\text{sieve}}(\beta_2)$ denotes total number of vectors output based on the sieve on dimension of lattice β_2
$\delta(\beta_1)$ denotes the Hermite factor from the Geometric Series Assumption

5.6.3 Reduced Sieve Costs

The attack incorporates several improvements to the predictable sieving costs in the RAM model:

- **Improved random product code decoding:** The new algorithm requires just

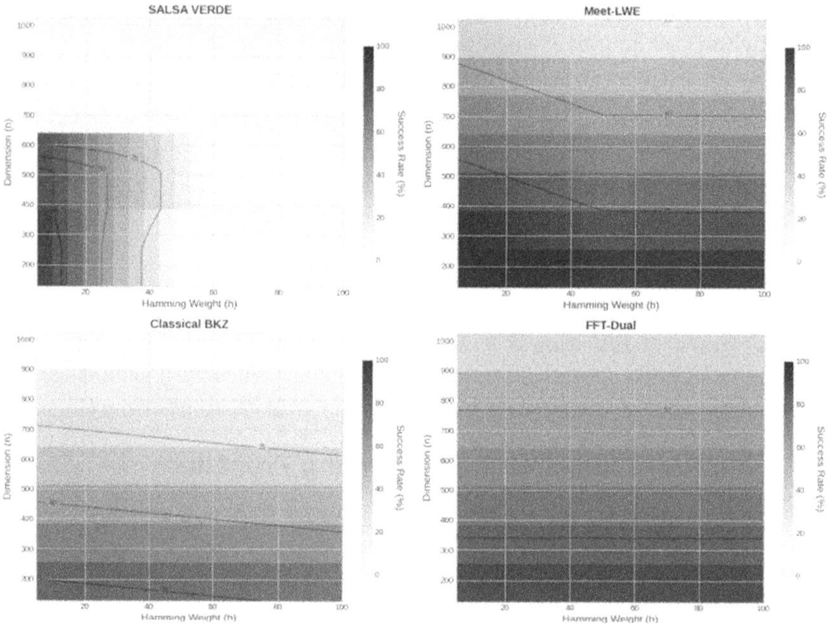

Figure 5.7: Attack Success Rate by Parameter Combination.

one addition, one XOR, and three comparisons per legal code word, requiring about 430 gates for a lattice of rank 400.

- **Optimized parameters:** The attack optimizes over a broader set of parameters, further improving efficiency.

These improvements reduce the cost of sieving by approximately 6 bits in rank 400.

5.7 Meet-in-the-Middle and Ternary Tree Attacks

5.7.1 May's Meet-LWE Attack (2021)

Alexander May's breakthrough Meet-LWE attack (Alexander May, 2021) significantly improved upon Odlyzko's classical Meet-in-the-Middle approach, achieving complexity $S^{0.25}$ for ternary secrets:

- **Key innovation:** Uses a representation technique where the secret $\mathbf{s} = \mathbf{s}_1 + \mathbf{s}_2$, exploiting multiple representations of the secret to reduce list sizes.
- **Performance:** For NTRU and BLISS parameters, achieves complexities around $S^{0.28}$–$S^{0.3}$.

5.7.2 Ternary Tree Extensions (2024)

Recent work by Lee et al. (2024) extends May's approach by splitting secrets into three components: $\mathbf{s} = \mathbf{s}_1 + \mathbf{s}_2 + \mathbf{s}_3$, achieving even better asymptotic complexity of $S^{0.21}$–$S^{0.22}$.

Impact on KpqC Candidates:

- SMAUG-T192: 20 bits below claimed security
- SMAUG-T256: 43.6 bits below claimed security

5.8 Hybrid Lattice-Combinatorial Attacks

Hybrid attacks combine lattice reduction with combinatorial search, and are particularly effective against sparse secrets:

- **Hybrid dual attack:** Combines the dual lattice attack with Meet-LWE techniques in the guessing phase.
- **Hybrid primal attack:** Integrates BKZ lattice reduction with combinatorial secret recovery strategies.

These hybrid approaches often outperform pure lattice-based or pure combinatorial methods, especially for parameter regimes exhibiting moderate sparsity.

5.9 Impact on NIST PQC Candidates

The FFT-based dual attack significantly reduces the security level of several NIST Post-Quantum Cryptography candidates (Joppe Bos et al., 2018; Leo Ducas et al., 2018; Jan-Pieter D'Anvers, 2018).

As detailed in the FFT-based attack reduces estimated security levels below NIST targets for multiple schemes. With the exception of Dilithium at Level 2, the attack reduces estimated security below NIST's target across nearly all tested parameter sets. The quantitative security reductions across major NIST PQC candidates are summarized in Table 5.6

Table 5.6: Security Impact of FFT-Based Dual Attack on NIST PQC Candidates

Candidate	NIST Security Level	Estimated by the Authors	With FFT-Based Attack
Kyber512	143	151.5	137.5
Kyber768	207	215.1	193.5
Kyber1024	272	287.3	257.8
Dilithium2	146	159	146.3
Dilithium3	207	217	202.0
Dilithium5	272	285	263.6
Light Saber	143	–	138.4
Saber	207	–	202.7
Fire Saber	272	–	264.9

5.10 Concrete Security Estimates and Implications

For practical parameter recommendations, concrete security estimates of various LWE parameter sets against both attack types show substantial reductions in security levels. A comparative visualization of security level estimates under classical and improved attack models is shown in Figure 5.8.

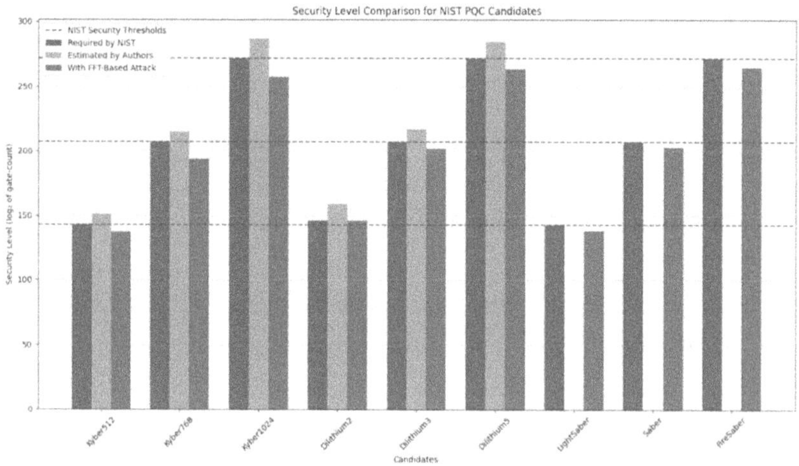

Figure 5.8: Security level comparison for NIST PQC candidates.

5.10.1 Security Estimates from SALSA VERDE ML Attack

- For $n = 256$, $\log_2 q = 20$, binary secrets with $h \leq 33$ and ternary secrets with $h \leq 24$ can be recovered by SALSA VERDE, while the uSVP attack requires significantly more time.
- For $n = 512$, $\log_2 q = 41$, binary secrets with $h \leq 63$ and ternary secrets with $h \leq 58$ are vulnerable to SALSA VERDE.
- For small moduli like $\log_2 q = 12$, which approach real-world parameters, SALSA VERDE still succeeds for very sparse secrets ($h \leq 8$ for binary secrets).

5.10.2 Security Estimates from FFT-Based Dual Attack

The FFT-based dual attack demonstrates that current security estimates for lattice-based cryptosystems are overly optimistic. For example, the G6K model with improved sieve costs shows:

- **Kyber512:** Security reduced from 151.5 to 137.5 bits (13.5 bits below claimed security).
- **Kyber768:** Security reduced from 215.1 to 193.5 bits (21.6 bits below claimed security).
- **Kyber1024:** Security reduced from 287.3 to 257.8 bits (29.5 bits below claimed security).

The resulting security margins after incorporating the FFT-based improvements are illustrated in Figure 5.9. The LWE Estimator predicts much higher security levels than observed in practice, particularly for small secrets. For instance, for $n = 256$, $\log_2 q = 20$, and binary secrets with $h = 25$, the Estimator predicts a security level of 2^{45} operations. However:

- Concrete uSVP implementation recovers such secrets in 76–401 hours.
- SALSA VERDE succeeds in just 15 hours.

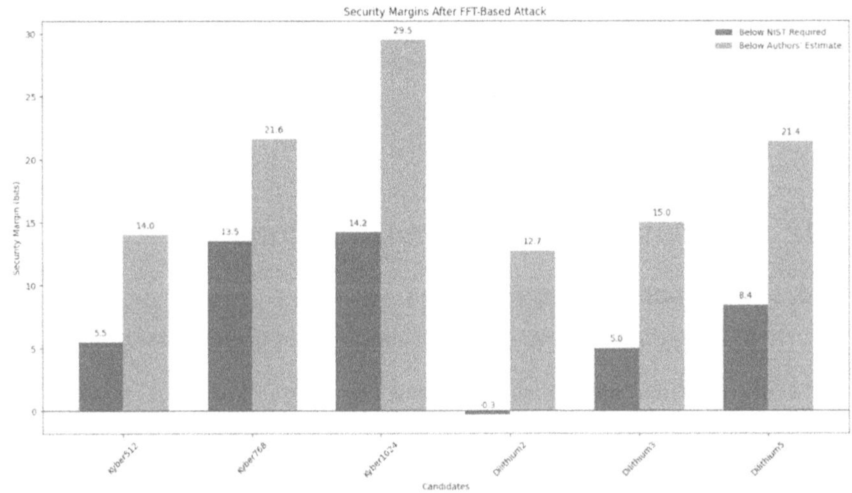

Figure 5.9: Security margins after FFT-based attack.

5.11 Recommendations for Secure Parameter Selection

Based on findings from Cathy Yuanchen Li et al. (2023) and Israeli Defense Forces (2023), we provide guidance for secure parameter selection against machine learning attacks. Table 5.7 summarizes the relative security of different secret types and offers implementation guidance.

1. **Secret distribution:** Prefers Gaussian secrets over ternary or binary when possible. The relative security and recommendations are as shown in Table 5.7.

Table 5.7: Security Hierarchy based on Secret Type

Secret Type	Relative Security	Recommendation
Binary	Baseline	Avoid when possible
Ternary	~1.3x harder to attack	Better alternative
Gaussian	~3x harder to attack	Best choice for security

2. **Secret sparsity:** Avoid high sparsity (>10%) in binary and ternary secrets. For security-critical applications, sparsity should be kept below 5% for practical dimensions.
3. **Dimension and modulus adjustments:** For a given security level:
   - Increase dimension or decrease modulus when using small secrets.
   - If using binary or ternary secrets, increase n by approximately 20% compared to parameters for Gaussian secrets.
   - When decreasing q, ensure error rate remains manageable for the application.
4. **Security margins:** Add extra security margin when using small secrets, as attacks are likely to improve. Recommended margins are:
   - At least 16 bits for binary secrets.
   - At least 12 bits for ternary secrets.
   - At least 8 bits for Gaussian secrets.

5.12 Conclusion and Future Directions

5.12.1 Summary of Key Findings

This chapter demonstrates a fundamental shift in the LWE security landscape:

- **Theory-practice gap:** Real-world machine learning attacks consistently achieve significantly better performance than theoretical worst-case complexity predictions would suggest, revealing substantial gaps between academic security estimates and practical vulnerabilities that can be exploited in deployed systems.
- **ML as game-changer:** Machine-learning attacks represent a paradigm shift in cryptanalysis, not merely providing incremental improvements over classical lattice reduction methods, but fundamentally changing the attack landscape through pattern recognition, optimization techniques, and the ability to exploit statistical structures that traditional approaches cannot effectively target.
- **Parameter inadequacy:** Many currently deployed LWE parameter sets, including key dimensions, noise distributions, and modulus choices, provide insufficient security margins when evaluated against machine learning attack capabilities, suggesting that parameter selection methodologies based solely on classical security analysis are fundamentally flawed.
- **Attack convergence:** The observation that multiple distinct attack methodologies including various machine learning approaches, lattice reduction algorithms, and hybrid techniques, achieve remarkably similar performance levels against the same LWE instances strongly suggests that these attacks are approaching fundamental computational limits rather than being constrained by the specific limitations of individual attack strategies.

5.12.2 Open Research Questions

- **Theoretical limits:** Understanding the fundamental computational boundaries of what machine learning can achieve against LWE is a core theoretical question that remains largely unsolved.

- **Defense mechanisms:** Developing LWE variants or modifications that maintain cryptographic utility while being resistant to ML-based attacks is an active area of research.
- **Quantum speedups:** The intersection of quantum computing and ML attacks on lattice-based cryptography is particularly relevant given the quantum-resistant motivation for LWE-based systems.
- **Parameter optimization:** Finding systematic methods to choose LWE parameters that optimize the security-efficiency tradeoff, especially considering ML attack vectors, is a practical concern for implementers.

5.12.3 Recommendations for Practitioners

- **Conservative parameters:** Choose security settings with much larger safety margins than minimum requirements to account for future advances in attacks and computing power.
- **Regular assessment:** Continuously monitor, test, and update security measures through ongoing evaluations rather than treating security as a one-time implementation.
- **Attack diversity:** Design defenses that simultaneously protect against multiple types of attacks (computational, physical, social engineering) rather than focusing on single threat vectors.
- **Future proofing:** Build flexible, adaptable security systems that can easily upgrade or transition to new technologies and standards as threats evolve.

References

Alexander May. (2021). How to meet ternary LWE keys. In: *CRYPTO 2021*. Cryptology ePrint Archive, Paper 2021/216.

Cathy Li, Jana Sotáková, Emily Wenger, Mohamed Malhou, Evrard Garcelon, Francois Charton & Kristin Lauter. (2023). Salsa picante: A machine learning attack on LWE with binary secrets. In: *ACM CCS 2023*. Cryptology ePrint Archive, Paper 2023/340.

Cathy Yuanchen Li, Emily Wenger, Zeyuan Allen-Zhu, Francois Charton & Kristin Lauter (2023). Salsa verde: A machine learning attack on learning with errors with sparse small secrets. In: *NeurIPS 2023*. Cryptology ePrint Archive, Paper 2023/968.

Claus-Peter Schnorr and Martin Euchner. (1994). Lattice basis reduction: Improved practical algorithms and solving subset sum problems. In: *International Symposium on Fundamentals of Computation Theory* (pp. 68–85). Springer.

Emily Wenger, Mingjie Chen, Francois Charton, and Kristin Lauter. (2022). Salsa: Attacking lattice cryptography with transformers. In: *NeurIPS 2022*. Cryptology ePrint Archive, Paper 2022/935.

Israeli Defense Forces – MATZOV (2023). Improved Dual Lattice Attack. Technical Report.

Jan-Pieter D'Anvers, Angshuman Karmakar, Sujoy Sinha Roy, and Ingrid Verbauwhede. (2018). Saber: module-LWR based key exchange, CPA-secure encryption and CCA-secure KEM. In *AFRICACRYPT 2018*, 2018.

Joppe Bos, Léo Ducas, Eike Kiltz, Tancrède Lepoint & Vadim Lyubashevsky (2018). Crystals-kyber: A CCA-secure module-lattice-based KEM. In: *IEEE Symposium on Security and Privacy*.

Leo Ducas, Tim Güneysu, Vadim Lyubashevsky, Thomas Pöppelmann, Peter Schwabe, Gregor Seiler & Damien Stehlé. (2018). Crystals-dilithium: A lattice-based digital signature scheme. *IACR Transactions on Cryptographic Hardware and Embedded Systems*.

Oded Regev. (2010). The learning with errors problem (invited survey). In: *2010 IEEE 25th Annual Conference on Computational Complexity* (pp. 191–204). IEEE.

Yuanmi Chen & Phong Q. Nguyen. (2011). BKZ 2.0: Better lattice security estimates. In: *International Conference on the Theory and Application of Cryptology and Information Security* (pp. 1–20). Springer, 2011.

Zvika Brakerski, Adeline Langlois, Chris Peikert, Oded Regev & Damien Stehlé. (2013). Classical hardness of learning with errors. In: *STOC* (pp. 575–584).

CHAPTER

6

Ethical and Societal Implications of Quantum Inspired AI: Aristotelian Moral Philosophy Perspective

Jovana Pavlović

University Singidunum, Faculty of Diplomacy, International Relations and Security

Critical examination is conducted through the lens of Aristotelian moral philosophy aiming at interrogation of the extent to which classical notions of virtue, agency and the highest human good (eudaimonia) remain applicable or challenged by QAI systems usage. The inquiry begins by articulating the ethical dilemmas inherent in QAI systems, particularly concerning moral agency, responsibility and the opacity. Aristotle's conception of moral virtue, grounded in practical reason (phronesis), societal ramifications engaging with Aristotelian treatments of justice (Book V), political virtue and the role of ethical habituation is brought into dialogue with the indeterminacy and non-deterministic character of QAI. The discussion further considers whether QAI constitutes a form of technē or whether it represents a novel, potentially disruptive mode of governance, one that risks undermining human flourishing. The ambiguity surrounding authorship and accountability in quantum decision-making compounds the ethical uncertainty, demanding renewed scrutiny of the foundations of moral agency.

6.1 Methodology and Sources

The research implements a systematic and multidisciplinary method which unites thorough analysis of Aristotle's *Nicomachean Ethics* with modern Artificial Intelligence ethics. The research uses the critical Oxford Classical Texts edition of Bywater (1894) and the authoritative English translation by Terence Irwin (third edition, Hackett Publishing, 2019) as its primary philosophical base

*E-mail: jovana.pavlovic981@gmail.com

DOI: 10.1201/9781003682950-6

because these sources provide philological precision along with Aristotelian terminology fidelity. The dual textual base enables both linguistic accuracy and conceptual continuity with the Aristotelian corpus. The analysis follows a methodical approach to interpret fundamental Aristotelian concepts about human flourishing known as eudaimonia and practical wisdom or phronēsis and practical craft and systematic political knowledge before using these concepts to analyze modern AI systems especially quantum and generative models with advanced autonomy and societal influence. The philosophical framework integrates with most recent systematic evaluations of prominent AI ethics research by Luciano Floridi (*The Ethics of Artificial Intelligence*, Oxford University Press, 2023) and Floridi and Cowls (*A Unified Framework of Five Principles for AI in Society*) alongside current empirical and normative studies by Anderljung et al. (2023) and Kay et al. (2024). Aristotle's ethical and political philosophy presents a universal framework because he places politics as the architectonic science that directs all disciplines toward their highest good which allows it to serve as a normative framework for complex technology guidance toward just and virtuous goals. This framework demands evaluation of AI systems based on their ability to enhance human flourishing (eudaimonia) while maintaining subordination to rational political deliberation (phronēsis). The research unites classical philosophical methods with contemporary ethical assessments to restore the permanent value of Aristotelian principles when dealing with modern AI moral and civic problems.

6.2 Telos and Technology

The Nicomachean Ethics opens with Aristotle's claim that all human activities, whether artistic, practical, or theoretical, aim at some form of good (EN I.1, 1094a1). The fundamental statement establishes his teleological system which defines all practices through their final purpose named *telos* (Gr. τέλος) and establishes eudaimonia [εὐδαιμονία] as the supreme human goal which translates to flourishing or well-being. Aristotle states that the existence of a final purpose in human activities leads to the identification of the supreme good (EN I.2, 1094a18). The good represents an objective standard which serves as the foundation for evaluating all human practices.

The ethical assessment of Quantum Artificial Intelligence (QAI) as an emerging technology requires analysis through the lens of Aristotle's teleological approach. The non-classical computational abilities and predictive strength and autonomous optimization features of QAI make it an instrumental science which falls under the category of subordinate arts. The ethical meaning of QAI becomes incomprehensible when it lacks direction toward a superior purpose. According to Aristotle the pursuit of money without a proper purpose leads to distorted human values because wealth serves only as a means to achieve something else (EN I.5, 1096a5). The exclusive focus of QAI development on instrumental benefits such as efficiency and profitability and dominance leads to ethical problems. The outputs of QAI systems would remain efficient but they would not serve human well-being and could violate the essential rule that final ends should always be desired for their own sake rather than for other purposes (EN I.7, 1097b1).

The absence of ethical principles in AI systems creates major risks because their programming structure enables them to control human operators while blocking moral decision-making and evading responsibility. The results contradict Aristotle's definition of the good life which he describes as "soul activity that follows arete" (EN I.7, 1098a16). According to Aristotle human beings achieve their agency through rational decision-making (logos) which seeks noble objectives. The system's utilitarian success does not justify its inherent injustice because it lacks ends and restricts behavior and disables human reasoning.

Aristotle establishes political science as the most authoritative art which serves as the master art according to EN I.2 (1094a25). Politics, according to him, functions as the master science or *architektonikē* because it creates rules for all other sciences and practices to achieve human well-being. The end of political science must encompass all other sciences because it uses them to achieve human well-being through legislative decisions about actions and abstentions (EN I.2, 1094a27–30). The technical achievement of QAI through applied mathematics and physics exists under political authority because it derives from these fields. The purpose of QAI exists beyond market forces and computational systems because it needs ethical-political decision-making to determine its final goals. The ends of QAI need to receive their direction from ethical-political deliberation. According to Aristotle all superior capacities including economics and strategy operate under the authority of politics (EN I.2, 1094b2–3). The evaluation of QAI requires assessment of its contribution to justice and virtue known as *arete* rather than its technical excellence or operational power. The absence of political rationality in QAI development would lead to the same mistake which Aristotle identifies in systems that confuse utility with true goodness.

Aristotle views political science as a formative discipline which goes beyond mere regulation. Political science dedicates most of its efforts to develop citizens who possess good character and noble capabilities (EN I.9, 1100b11–12). Any ethical implementation of QAI systems needs to uphold the educational mission of political science instead of working against it. A surveillance system which lacks transparency and controls emotions and eliminates personal accountability works against the fundamental political goal of developing citizens who can achieve moral excellence. The external goods in Aristotle's view serve to enable virtuous conduct but do not form the basis of human flourishing. The contemplative life which represents the peak of *eudaimonia* requires minimal resources yet needs to exist without any form of coercion or distortion. According to Aristotle happiness exists as a complete and independent state which serves as the ultimate purpose of all human actions (EN I.7, 1097b20–23). The implementation of QAI systems in society requires more than material growth and control expansion because they need to safeguard human reason and moral development and political autonomy.

6.3 Reason, Virtue, and the Ethical Telos of AI

Aristotle establishes his ethical framework on the belief that flourishing or *eudaimonia* represents the supreme goal which humans should strive to achieve. The *telos* serves as the final cause which directs all human activities toward their ultimate purpose. According to Aristotle happiness exists as a complete and independent state which serves as the purpose of all human activities (Nicomachean Ethics [EN] I.7, 1097b20). Aristotle distinguishes *eudaimonia* from *hedone* (pleasure)[1] and *ploutos* (wealth)[2] and *time* (honor)[3] because these three things he calls instrumental goods i.e. *organika agatha* which people desire

---

1 In Nicomachean Ethics II.3, 1104b9–11, Aristotle states that virtue (ἀρετή) is fundamentally about pleasure and pain (*ἡδονή καὶ λύπη*): "Virtue exists in the realm of pleasures and pains because we perform base actions for pleasure and avoid noble actions because of pain." "Moral excellence is about pleasures and pains; for it is on account of pleasure that we do base actions, and on account of pain that we abstain from noble ones." Here, *ἡδονή* (pleasure) functions not as a neutral feeling but as a moral index: it reveals and shapes character. We perform base actions in pursuit of pleasure, and we avoid noble deeds because of pain. Thus, ethical excellence consists in learning to feel pleasure in the right things (the noble and virtuous) and pain in the wrong things (the base and vicious). The cultivation of virtue, then, involves aligning our emotional responses to pleasure and pain with reason and ethical purpose, a task central to moral development and to the formation of practical wisdom (φρόνησις). For Aristotle, pleasure is the terrain on which moral character is formed, exercised, and ultimately judged.

2 Aristotle places πλοῦτος (ploutos) and ἡδονή (hēdonē) under instrumental goods because they lack the status of final ends. According to Aristotle wealth exists only for practical use because it serves a different purpose (*NE*, I.5, 1096a6) which prevents it from being considered an intrinsic good. He rejects the common belief that happiness equals pleasure because such a lifestyle matches the behavior of animals (*NE*, I.5, 1095b20). The *telos* criteria which include being final and self-sufficient and complete (*NE*, I.7, 1097b20) are not met by wealth or pleasure according to Aristotle. The ethical use of wealth and pleasure depends on their subordination to rational activity and virtue but they become morally wrong when people treat them as independent ends.

3 Aristotle's ethics show that τιμή (timē or honor) serves as a common pursuit but it remains an instrumental value because its worth stems from those who grant it instead of from inherent virtue. According to Aristotle honor serves as proof of personal goodness because people seek it to validate their virtuous nature (*NE*, I.5, 1095b23). The ethical value of honor and wealth and pleasure exists only because they help people achieve rational and virtuous living.

for the sake of something else. The soul achieves its true happiness through continuous *energeia* (ἐνέργεια)[4] of *arete* (ἀρετή, virtue)[5] in a complete life.

The ethical evaluation of emergent technologies including Quantum Artificial Intelligence (QAI) requires more than their instrumental benefits of efficiency and economic value and computational power. The evaluation of their worth depends on their ability to advance or block the development of rational virtuous conduct in human existence. According to Aristotle the human purpose consists of using reason to perform activities that express our true nature (EN I.7, 1098a7–17). AI systems which remove rational choice or *prohairesis* (προαίρεσις)[6] and hide *euthyne* (εὐθύνη), and use emotional manipulation techniques fail to meet ethical standards regardless of their impressive achievements. An AI system which eliminates the fundamental requirements for ethical practice creates barriers to happiness and thus demonstrates unethical behavior. The distinction between instrumental and final goods becomes crucial when Aristotle explains that wealth acquisition exists under compulsion because wealth serves only as a means to achieve other ends (EN I.5, 1096a5–7).

Quantum AI systems used for profit, strategic power, and surveillance purposes have the potential to transform people into tools unless they operate under the guidance of virtue and political wisdom. The ethical alignment stands as a necessity because according to Aristotle wealth and courage become dangerous when people use them inappropriately (NE I.3, 1094b5–7).

The logical part of soul serves as both the essential and complete requirement for achieving well-being in Aristotelian ethics. AI systems must preserve the complete functionality of human reasoning abilities known as logos. According

---

4 Aristotle establishes that *energeia* represents the process of bringing potential to actuality while distinguishing it from raw capacity (*dynamis*). According to Metaphysics Θ.6, Aristotle explains that potential things achieve actuality through motion when they exist in their potential state (1048b17–18). The concept of ἐνέργεια in *Nicomachean Ethics* gains ethical meaning because happiness (eudaimonia) exists as the active expression of soul virtue (I.7, 1098a16). The Aristotelian concept of ἐνέργεια describes the active use of virtue through rational conduct which represents the fundamental path to human fulfillment.

5 According to Aristotle ἀρετή (aretē, virtue) represents the highest expression of function which enables something to fulfill its purpose effectively. According to his writings the virtue of man consists of a specific character state which makes someone good while enabling them to perform their tasks effectively (Nicomachean Ethics, II.6, 1106a22–24). Human virtue consists of a state which involves choice and exists as a moderate position relative to us according to reason and the judgment of a wise person (NE II.6, 1106b36–1107a2). Through habituation and rational guidance ἀρετή enables right action which leads to achieving eudaimonia or the good life.

6 Aristotle defines *prohairesis* as the ability to make purposeful decisions through reason in his *Nicomachean Ethics* Book III.2 (1111b5–1113b). The concept of προαίρεσις stands apart from desire (βούλησις) and deliberation (βουλή) because it represents a deliberate choice that emerges from rational thought processes.

to Aristotle, happiness exists as an active mental state which combines perfect virtue with divine blessedness (EN I.12, 1101b10–30). The aforementioned politics as master science functions as the coordinating authority that unites all scientific fields and technological systems to achieve the koinon agathon. The statesman who seeks true governance wants his citizens to become virtuous while following the established laws (EN I.13, 1102a7–9). Quantum AI requires political oversight which extends past legal frameworks (nomothesia). The system should function to develop both the moral character (ēthos) and logical thinking (logos). AI implementation needs both technical expertise and philosophical understanding of human nature to support human decision-making abilities and logical thinking for achieving proper value assessment.

6.4 Virtue as Habituation, the Mean, and Moral Formation

Aristotle defines moral virtue in Nicomachean Ethics II.1–6 as a habituated quality which develops through practice rather than natural or educational means. The development of intellectual virtues depends on teaching yet moral virtues emerge through habituation which leads to their name derived from ethos (EN II.1 1103a14–18). Human beings need habituation to develop moral dispositions because nature does not produce them. The human body exists with natural tendencies which prevent it from developing habits that contradict its original nature yet habituation enables us to reach perfection (1103a23–26). People develop virtues through actual practice of these virtues because natural abilities need experience before they can become fully developed. People develop their building skills through construction work and they achieve justice through just conduct and self-control through temperate actions and bravery through brave actions (1103a31–b2).

Human beings develop new cognitive and emotional and social habits through their ongoing AI system interactions which Aristotle would identify as significant ethical changes. The use of AI for information retrieval and decision-making and creative tasks leads to decreased independent critical thinking abilities while users develop habits of passive content consumption. AI-based personalization systems determine what experiences bring us pleasure or pain which in turn modifies our preferences and influences our moral decision-making processes. The regular use of AI-based platforms leads users to develop new social standards for communication and privacy and authority which modify their fundamental values and expectations. The process of habituation through AI exposure remains ethically neutral until it supports human flourishing and follows the path of reason. AI systems cannot achieve virtuous status because they do not possess rational choice (prohairesis) and practical wisdom (phronēsis) or the ability to develop moral habits. The repeated interactions between humans and AI systems create significant effects on how people develop their moral character. The cultivation of passivity and judgment outsourcing and pleasure and utility pursuit without virtue consideration through AI technologies threatens the development of moral excellence. Aristotle states that the formation of habits during youth determines everything because it shapes our entire moral character (EN II.1, 1103b24–26); therefore AI tools integrated into educational and media systems and governance structures and interpersonal relationships need thorough ethical evaluation to determine their impact on moral development.

The mean principle of Aristotle indicates that AI ethics require human agents to make decisions based on practical wisdom because abstract avoidance of extremes is insufficient. The principle stands against strict algorithmic moral systems because it requires human beings to make decisions based on contextual understanding which AI systems cannot replicate. The use of ethical AI systems needs human virtuous agents who can make decisions through deliberation for noble purposes instead of focusing on efficiency or profit. The governance of AI systems should ensure two main priorities: safeguarding individuals and society from potential harms while promoting the responsible and ethical use of technology to support human development and well-being. The system becomes both technologically flawed and morally tainted when it replaces or damages these essential human values.

6.5 Voluntariness, Deliberation, and Moral Responsibility

Aristotle in *Nicomachean Ethics* Book III develops the framework for moral agency through his explanation of voluntary and involuntary actions which determine ethical assessment. According to Aristotle praise and blame apply to voluntary actions and passions but involuntary actions receive pardon and sometimes evoke pity (EN III.1, 1109b30–32). The framework serves as a critical tool to evaluate the ethical implications of Quantum Artificial Intelligence (QAI) systems because they execute sophisticated adaptive computations without possessing the moral agency characteristics defined by Aristotle.

Aristotle defines involuntary actions as those which occur through compulsion or ignorance because the initiating force exists outside the person performing the action (EN III.1, 1110a1–2). The agent performs voluntary actions through internal principles while being fully aware of all circumstances involved in the action (EN III.1, 1111a22–23). The criteria for voluntary action which Aristotle established cannot be met by QAI systems because they lack both Aristotelian awareness and rational soul-driven motion. The systems operate as external instruments because they follow code and training data instead of making decisions based on rational soul principles.

The distinction between mixed actions becomes crucial because Aristotle explains how people can perform constrained actions like jettisoning cargo during storms while maintaining voluntary status through their rational acceptance of the lesser evil-making process of QAI systems operating without the evaluative framework which does not assess actions through the lens of character-based end goals (The decision1110a17–19). The system fails to perform proportional evaluation and it requires rational choice toward good outcomes. The system fails to demonstrate Aristotelian eudaimonia. According to Aristotle actions performed through ignorance (choice because it lacks both the ability to deliberate and the pursuit of) differ from those done because of ignorance since the latter becomes truly involuntary only when it results in pain and regret (EN III.1, 1110b17–19). AI systems including QAI lack the capacity to experience regret or moralize pain which prevents them from performing ethical self-correction.

The concept of mixed actions becomes crucial because Aristotle explains how people can perform actions under constraint yet maintain voluntary status when they choose the lesser evil (EN III.1, 1110a17–19). QAI fails to perform proportional judgment and does not evaluate actions through character-based shaped ends. The decision-making process of QAI operates without the evaluative framework which prohairesis provides through rational choice for achieving the good. QAI systems fail to make Aristotelian choices because they lack both deliberative capabilities and eudaimonia-oriented decision-making. Aristotle establishes two types of actions based on ignorance: actions performed through unawareness and actions performed because of unawareness. The only actions that qualify as involuntary occur when they result in both physical distress and feelings of remorse. AI systems including QAI systems lack the capacity to feel regret or moral distress which prevents them from performing ethical self-assessment. The system remains free from moral responsibility because its errors in output and unintended effects stem from data misrepresentation and model misalignment and stochastic variability. Aristotle states that we forgive people who lack knowledge about specific details but we do not excuse those who fail to understand general principles (EN III.1, 1110b33–34). Engineers together with regulators and policymakers maintain complete responsibility because they must possess ethical knowledge.

The ethical consequences of this situation are extremely serious. The act of giving QAI moral agency represents a fundamental mistake in ethical reasoning. The system operates as a technē because it receives its direction from outside influences while lacking the ability to move itself. The human agents who create and use these systems retain full responsibility because they make deliberate choices about system development and deployment. Aristotle states in EN III.5 that we hold people accountable for their ignorance when it stems from carelessness because they should have the ability to avoid ignorance (1114a6–9). The system's lack of autonomy makes it impossible to hold it accountable for its consequences because it operates without self-determination. The absence of all necessary faculties in QAI makes it impossible to hold it responsible for moral actions so it requires strict human oversight. The transfer of deliberative power to AI systems breaks the connection between agency and ethics while removing human beings from their essential duty.

Aristotle defines virtue as a permanent mental state which selects the appropriate middle ground based on reason and what a wise person would choose. The fundamental principle of Aristotle's ethics states that "excess and defect create an intermediate state which receives praise" (Nicomachean Ethics IV.4) and this principle applies to both personal development and the assessment of technological systems including artificial intelligence (AI). The Aristotelian framework requires AI development to stay away from two opposite ends which include technological arrogance that seeks control and showmanship and weak moral conduct that leads to regulatory avoidance or unethical behavior. The evaluation of magnificence and pride as virtues in Book IV becomes crucial because these traits deal with both grand spending and making grand claims. According to Aristotle magnificence requires proper large-scale spending that embodies both honor and proportion, aiming at beauty and fitting results rather than mere cost-effectiveness. The allocation of substantial resources in AI needs to focus on creating lasting public goods including safety standards along with transparency initiatives and international regulations and fair distribution systems. The philosopher Aristotle advises us to avoid vulgarity because excessive display of wealth leads to moral degradation yet we must also prevent niggardliness because it violates ethical standards of magnificence. The ethical aspect of magnificence in AI demands that we use our technological capabilities to support noble and dignified goals.

Aristotle defines *megalopsychia* as a great soul through achievements that stem from virtuous actions and responsible conduct. The practice of taking credit for AI-generated work without putting in the required intellectual effort, practical wisdom and ethical thought leads to vanity because it involves claiming excellence without actual merit. Human agents must show transparency and exercise prudence and accountability when guiding AI systems toward virtuous goals to earn ethical credit. The practice of attributing AI-generated work to personal achievement breaks down both ethical conduct and the development of authentic excellence.

Aristotle defines justice as the complete ethical virtue which exists between people and works to achieve the common good. The ethical application of AI depends directly on this principle. The moral duty to account for AI system results rests with engineers and users because Aristotle defines just conduct as the purposeful and deliberate pursuit of fair and proportionate actions that benefit society. The practice of shifting responsibility to autonomous systems or market forces violates the ethical principles of accountability. AI practices need both creators and users to maintain moral legitimacy through responsible technological development that supports human equality and solidarity and promotes human well-being. A system that establishes unequal power structures while misusing data and fails to maintain responsible governance breaks both distributive and corrective justice principles. The governance of AI requires fundamental importance because it possibly directs all other sciences including technical and theoretical fields toward their human purpose.

6.6 Justice as Proportionality and Redress

Aristotle presents a complete theory of justice in Nicomachean Ethics V which establishes an essential ethical framework to evaluate artificial intelligence systems in political and technological domains. The two types of justice which Aristotle identifies in V.2–4 include distributive justice for wealth and honor distribution in the city and rectificatory justice for handling transactions and harm compensation. The distribution of goods through geometric proportion defines distributive justice because it provides equal shares to those who are equal and fair shares to those who are not equal (V.3, 1131a30–b15).

The institutions responsible for supervising AI operations including regulators and courts must perform a mediating function to guarantee fairness in unbalanced technological exchanges. AI governance needs to establish systems which enable equity through exception handling and context-based remedy and discretionary measures to apply universal laws to new circumstances. The Aristotelian view holds that machine-based labor replacement violates ethical principles of distributive and rectificatory justice. Social goods including employment and dignity and recognition must receive distribution according to human achievement and individual requirements according to distributive justice principles. The displacement of workers through AI systems creates an unfair distribution of burden because it affects vulnerable populations who lack alternative employment options or compensation. The principles of rectificatory justice demand both accountability and compensation when AI systems lead to unfair decisions that result in job loss and privacy violations. The absence of responsible moral agents for these outcomes indicates a breakdown in ethical governance systems. The ethical structure of society and the foundation for a just political community suffer damage when major decisions are transferred to non-moral AI systems because justice according to Aristotle depends on human moral agency and relational connections.

6.7 Phronesis over Techne

Aristotle explains in Book VI of the Nicomachean Ethics that the soul contains five truth-bearing states which include art, scientific knowledge, practical wisdom, philosophical wisdom, and intuitive reason that enable the soul to affirm or deny truth (VI.3, 1139b15–20). Human beings alone can achieve these states because they require either moral accountability or first principle contemplation or purposeful decision-making abilities. The ability to understand first principles through the mind stands as the most important foundation for both scientific inquiry and practical decision-making because it provides the essential starting point for reasoning. Artificial intelligence fails to possess the human mind and *telos* which prevents it from using Aristotelian reasoning for self-directed thought. According to Aristotle choice requires both rational thinking and moral character because he states that "choice cannot exist without reason and intellect or without a moral state" (VI.2, 1139a34–35) and "good action and its opposite require both intellect and character to exist" (1139a36). AI systems demonstrate only art through algorithmic generalization yet they remain incapable of achieving wisdom because this state requires "a true and reasoned state of capacity to act with regard to human goods" (VI.5, 1140b20–21). The distinction between art and wisdom lies in their nature because art deals with making through external goals yet wisdom focuses on actions which serve as their own moral purpose (VI.5, 1140b6–7). AI systems cannot perform moral actions or moral decision-making because they do not only lack desire but also lack rational deliberation focused on achieving the good. Aristotle differentiates wisdom from art, AI represents technical skill without moral direction which transforms it into mere strategic ability which he describes as "cleverness" (1144a23–25). AI systems cannot demonstrate wisdom because they lack the enduring moral direction which virtue provides. According to Aristotle practical wisdom requires being good because it is impossible to achieve (1144a33–34). The application of this principle to ethics and AI specifically demands that good judgment combines theoretical knowledge with practical awareness of specific circumstances. AI systems possess general data yet they do not possess human-level understanding of context which is essential for making ethical decisions. Political communities need to make decisions about AI applications through specific context-based discussions instead of using general statements about technical capabilities. AI governance requires human wisdom to lead because this cognitive ability integrates logical reasoning with desire and moral excellence for achieving human well-being.

6.8 The Limits of Moral Evaluation in Aristotle's Ethics

Aristotle defines incontinence in Book VII of the Nicomachean Ethics as the state where someone with knowledge of their wrong actions performs them because of emotional states (VII.1, 1145b12–13). The person who exhibits incontinence possesses knowledge yet fails to apply it because they maintain knowledge but do not put it into practice (VII.3, 1147a10). The distinction between theoretical knowledge and practical application shows that Aristotle believes people can understand rational principles in theory yet these principles fail to guide their actions when passion takes control. The incontinent person shares a condition with people who are asleep or insane or intoxicated because their rational abilities remain dormant and useless according to Aristotle (1147a17–18). The incontinent person speaks like a stage actor who delivers scripted lines without grasping their meaning (1147a25). According to Aristotle true moral knowledge and ethical action require more than superficial reason-based behavior or words.

The framework demonstrates that incontinence fails to provide a meaningful description of artificial intelligence (AI) system behavior. AI systems implement universal principles through encoded rules yet they do not possess the ability to make deliberate choices nor do they have desires or the capacity to unite reason with character traits which define ethical decision-making. According to Aristotle "virtue enables correct decision-making yet practical wisdom enables us to perform actions that achieve the desired outcome" (VI.12, 1144a7–8). The growing dependence on AI systems that do not possess desires or inner conflicts or purpose threatens to eliminate essential human development processes for moral character formation. According to Aristotle ethical conduct requires human beings to experience inner battles between desires and reason while developing virtues through consistent practice.

Human ethical development through virtues like temperance and practical wisdom and courage becomes less likely when we let AI systems handle moral choices because these machines experience neither pain nor pleasure nor internal conflict. Our moral agency weakens as we continue to delegate tasks because we practice less and less. Aristotle restricts genuine incontinence to physical desires only because he considers other forms of lack of self-control such as anger and ambition to be partial examples ("incontinent in respect of anger" VII.5, 1149a25–27). AI protocol breaches together with unintended system outputs which function as mechanical system failures instead of being considered character or will-related shortcomings. The evaluation of ethics depends on three essential conditions according to Aristotle: a rational soul that seeks flourishing through habituated virtues and right reason-based desires and voluntary actions. AI operates outside Aristotelian moral assessment because it lacks the necessary human capacities to demonstrate virtues or vices or show continence or incontinence or temperance or self-indulgence. The absence of desire and sensation and moral deliberation in artificial intelligence prevents it from experiencing ethical conflicts and practicing virtues such as continence and temperance according to Aristotle. The lack of moral agency in AI transfers all ethical responsibility to human beings who include designers, users and institutions because they possess rational souls and voluntary capabilities for virtuous behavior. The excessive use of AI technology creates a risk of removing ethical duties from humans while it weakens their ability to make moral choices and hinders their character development. The Aristotelian framework demands that humans maintain their role as moral decision-makers because any shift of this responsibility to AI systems would destroy the foundation for human success.

6.9 Pleasure, Virtue, and AI

The Nicomachean Ethics (Books VII–X) presents Aristotle's detailed explanation of pleasure through human nature analysis which connects pleasure directly to character development and virtue acquisition. According to Aristotle, pleasure stands as the core element of human nature because it serves as the essential tool for teaching morality through pleasure and pain (EN II.3 1104b11–13). The process of ethical development through habituation and character formation depends on pleasure because it creates essential moral dispositions in people. The evaluation of artificial intelligence systems including Quantum AI requires assessment for their ability to direct human motivation toward the right reason while promoting virtuous development instead of using pleasure for manipulative purposes. Aristotle cautions against mistaken theories which incorrectly view pleasure as bad because people commonly pursue it by observing that "true arguments seem most useful, not only with a view to knowledge, but with a view to life also; since they harmonize with the facts, they are believed" (EN X.2, 1172b1–3). The ethical discourse needs to show real understanding instead of using paternalistic methods to control desires. AI systems should avoid using protection or efficiency as excuses to manipulate user motivations because they need to base their design on truthful and reasoned accounts of human flourishing. The distinction between pleasure as "good" and "the good itself" is central in this context: while pleasure contributes to a good life, it is not the ultimate "final cause". Aristotle proves against Eudoxus that pleasure cannot be the highest good because "the pleasant life is more desirable with wisdom than without" which shows that pleasure needs practical wisdom to guide its pursuit rather than being pursued independently (EN X.3, 1173a1–5).

This distinction carries direct ethical implications for AI. The use of short-term gratification optimization in recommender systems, immersive entertainment platforms and emotionally responsive agents without virtuous ends creates conditions that undermine moral development. According to Aristotle the most fulfilling life emerges from virtuous activities which produce pleasure naturally instead of artificial or purposeless pleasure: "the pleasures derived from noble sources are different from those derived from base sources" (EN VII.12, 1153b20). The design of AI systems must support situations where pleasure emerges from virtuous activities including learning and reflection. Aristotle demonstrates through lived experience that people seek pleasure because they view it as good while they try to avoid pain which they consider evil (EN VII.12, 1153b25–27). The design of AI systems needs to prioritize human subjective experiences instead of treating users as automated stimulus receivers. Systems that use hedonic biases without considering virtue create problems for character development and block the path to authentic human flourishing.

References

Anderljung, Mattias, Jeff Barnhart, Anton Korinek, Jade Leung, Cullen O'Keefe, Jessica Whittlestone et al. (2023). *Frontier AI Regulation: Managing Emerging Risks to Public Safety*. arXiv preprint arXiv:2307.03718, https://arxiv.org/abs/2307.03718.

Aristotle. (1894). *Ethica Nicomachea*. Edited by I. Bywater. Oxford Classical Texts. Oxford: Oxford University Press.

Aristotle. (2019). *Nicomachean Ethics*. Translated by Terence Irwin. 3rd ed. Indianapolis: Hackett Publishing Company.

Floridi, Luciano. (2023). *The Ethics of Artificial Intelligence: Principles, Challenges, and Opportunities*. Oxford: Oxford University Press.

Floridi, Luciano & Josh Cowls. (2019). A unified framework of five principles for AI in society. *Harvard Data Science Review*, 1(1), 1–15. https://doi.org/10.1162/99608f92.8cd550d1.

Kay, Jenny, Arvind Kasirzadeh & Shakir Mohamed. (2024). Epistemic injustice in generative AI. *Proceedings of the AAAI/ACM Conference on AI, Ethics, and Society*, 7(1), 684–697. https://doi.org/10.1145/3613363.3640003

CHAPTER

7

Quantum-Inspired Approaches to Computer Vision: Current State and Future Prospects

Sara Ali[1*], Polla Fattah[2] and Sanar Fawzi[3]

[1] Department of Computer Science and Engineering, University of Kurdistan Hewlêr

[2] Department of Computer Science and Engineering, University of Kurdistan Hewlêr, Salahaddin University Research Center, Salahaddin University, Erbil

[3] Software Engineering, Salahaddin University, Erbil

Computer vision is confronted with increasing computational bottlenecks and memory requirements hard to scale by normal convolutional neural networks. Quantum-inspired architectures are inspired by quantum mechanics, superposition, entanglement as well as interference to redesign visual information processing in a more efficient manner.

Quantum convolutional neural networks represent a major advance, using parameterized quantum circuits to explore multiple input states simultaneously. Quantum-inspired pruning algorithms have reduced processing time, and quantum optical neural networks exploit the wave nature of light to achieve inherently parallel feature processing. Tensor network architectures, grounded in quantum physics convert high-dimensional image data into compact, information-rich representations and model multi-scale interactions. Hybrid quantum-classical systems combine quantum-inspired processing with the reliability of established deep learning. Attention systems ensure that quantum circuits focus on the most informative parts of an image, while knowledge transfer from classical models stabilize quantum training.

Nonetheless, fundamental constraints continue to limit practical applications: the barren plateau problem, measurement overhead, state-preparation complexity and decoherence all remain major challenges. Current applications range from quantum-inspired classical algorithms to early experiments on physical quantum

*Corresponding author: sara.sardar.ali@gmail.com

DOI: 10.1201/9781003682950-7

hardware. Thorough benchmarking demonstrates that classical approaches can be significantly more effective than their quantum counterparts. Frameworks such as PennyLane improve accessibility, but best practices and careful architectural design, especially when integrating quantum-inspired and classical computing, are essential for building realistic computer-vision systems.

7.1 Introduction

Deep learning has witnessed an incredible revolution in computer vision, with convolutional neural networks attaining unprecedented performance in visual recognition tasks. With the ever-increasing sizes of datasets and growing computational needs that cannot be met by traditional architectures, researchers are seeking other forms of computation such as quantum computing and quantum-inspired computing to tackle a range of new visual information processing challenges. Quantum machine learning situated at the intersection of quantum mechanics and machine learning, is poised to transform the way we process, analyze, and interpret visual data (Biamonte et al., 2017).

Quantum computing applies the fundamental principles of quantum mechanics – superposition, entanglement and interference – to perform certain tasks more efficiently than classical computers. Although quantum computers capable of handling large-scale computer vision workloads are not yet fault-tolerant, the theoretical foundations of quantum machine learning and early experimental demonstrations have generated significant interest in whether quantum concepts can enhance visual processing systems. This momentum has attracted substantial investment and research activity with major technology companies and academic institutions exploring quantum approaches to machine learning problems (Preskill, 2018).

A growing intersection between quantum computing and computer vision has emerged as a research field grounded in both theoretical computer science and quantum physics with direct application to machine learning. This interdisciplinary character offers unprecedented opportunities but also significant challenges: researchers must work within the severe limitations of current quantum hardware while designing algorithms that could deliver future computational advantages for visual processing tasks. Meeting this goal is complex and requires deep knowledge not only of quantum-mechanical principles but also of the practical demands of computer vision including real-time processing, accuracy and scalability.

This chapter examines the latest developments at the intersection of quantum computing and computer vision, carefully distinguishing between what is theoretically achievable and what has already been demonstrated in practice without obscuring the boundary between results and limitations. We survey quantum machine-learning algorithms that may eventually be applied to vision tasks, quantum-inspired classical algorithms that emulate quantum behavior on conventional hardware, and hybrid models that integrate quantum and classical processing.

The fundamental structure of quantum neural networks, presented in Figure 7.1, demonstrates that quantum-enhanced visual processing relies on four key components: data preparation, qubitization, quantum gate interactions, and parameter optimization (Lee et al., 2025). The analysis also depends on mathematical foundations and the practical limits within which this emerging field currently operates.

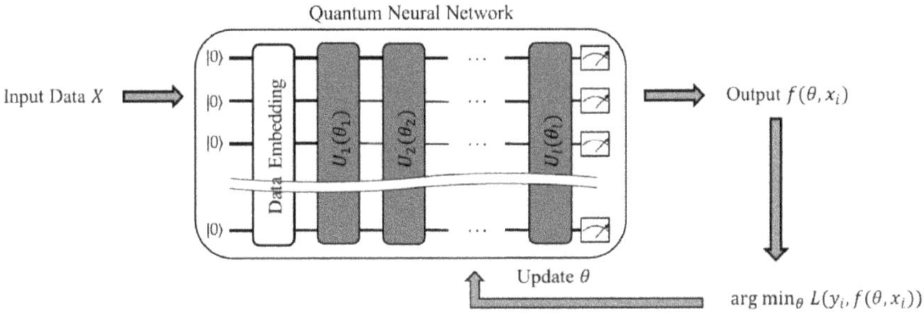

Figure 7.1: The training process of a QML (Lee et al., 2025).

It is almost entirely theoretical, and most practical applications are restricted to small scale experiments of quantum simulators or near-term quantum computers. The capabilities of state-of-the-art quantum hardware, namely the limited number of qubits, high error rates, and short coherence times, severely constrain the complexity of algorithms that can be executed. The latter are not mere engineering issues, but the reflections of the existing physical constraints, which ought to be surmounted, by creating improved quantum error correction, coherence maintenance and algorithm optimization (Cerezo et al., 2021).

Recent advances in quantum hardware have been accompanied by both encouraging progress and a sobering dose of realism regarding the roadmap for practical quantum-computing applications. Google's announcement of the Willow quantum processor in December 2024 marked a breakthrough in quantum error correction, demonstrating below-threshold error correction where logical qubits, constructed from large arrays of physical qubits,outperform individual physical qubits themselves. However, as quantum computing specialists emphasize, Willow remains far too small to perform meaningful computations, and millions of qubits would be required to tackle many of the industry's most significant problems (Neven, 2025). Although scientifically important, this milestone highlights the substantial gap that still separates current quantum capabilities from the requirements of practical computer-vision applications.

A realistic outlook on the timeline for quantum computer vision must therefore consider both hardware progress and algorithmic advances in tandem. Today's state-of-the-art near-term intermediate scale quantum (NISQ) devices provide a valuable platform for exploring quantum machine learning concepts, but they cannot yet demonstrate clear advantages over classical algorithms in real computer-vision tasks.

7.2 Theoretical Foundations

7.2.1 Quantum Computing Fundamentals for Computer Vision

Quantum computing employs quantum bits (qubits) which can exist in superposition and thereby represent many possibilities simultaneously. In computer vision contexts, this property could hypothetically enable the concurrent evaluation of multiple image features or processing pathways that classical systems must handle sequentially. The basic unit of quantum information, the qubit, differs fundamentally from a classical bit because it exists in coherent superpositions of the computational basis states $|0\rangle$ and $|1\rangle$ modelled mathematically as:

$$|\psi\rangle = \alpha|0\rangle + \beta|1\rangle \tag{7.1}$$

where α and β are complex probability amplitudes and satisfy $\alpha|^2 + |\beta|^2 = 1$ (Nielsen and Chuang, 2010).

N quantum states can superimpose to make 2^*n* classical states with the principle of superposition. This exponential scaling is represented mathematically as:

$$|\psi\rangle = \sum_i \alpha_i |i\rangle \tag{7.2}$$

where α_i are complex probability amplitudes and $|i\rangle$ represents computational basis states corresponding to all possible *n*-bit strings (Nielsen and Chuang, 2010). For computer vision applications, this exponential state space could, in principle, enable more efficient representation of high-dimensional visual data. Even a quantum machine with 20 qubits can encode more than a million classical states simultaneously, and a 40-qubit system has the theoretical capacity to represent information on the scale of more than one trillion classical states.

However, the practical extraction of useful information from such superposition states is fraught with difficulties that cannot be underestimated in any theoretical framework. Measuring a quantum system collapses its superposition yielding only a single classical outcome. This inherent limitation of quantum mechanics means that quantum circuits require sophisticated algorithmic design and typically multiple executions to obtain reliable results and access information encoded in exponentially large state spaces. Quantum parallelism and information extraction are therefore in tension: the advantages of parallel processing rely on quantum coherence, which is inevitably destroyed by the act of measurement.

The entanglement of quantum systems allows qubits to exhibit correlations that are impossible in classical systems, making it a potentially powerful tool for modeling spatial relationships in images. When qubits corresponding to various regions of an image are entangled, measuring one region can immediately influence the quantum state of the correlated regions. This capability opens the possibility of capturing long-range dependencies before they become computationally expensive to model explicitly with classical approaches. This property has the potential to enable quantum computer-vision systems to learn global image properties more efficiently than classical systems which must explicitly compute correlations between distant regions of an image.

The mathematical model of entangled states shows entangled states are non-classical. As an example, we take a Bell the state of two qubits (Nielsen and Chuang, 2010):

$$|\psi\rangle = \frac{1}{\sqrt{2}}(|00\rangle + |11\rangle) \tag{7.3}$$

It is not possible to express this state in terms of a product of individual qubit states, which means that there is actual quantum correlation amongst the particles.

To be able to carry out such quantum correlations in a computer-vision system, it is necessary to carefully organize the data encoding process, quantum processing, and measurement process, as demonstrated in the basic architecture of quantum neural networks in Figure 7.2 (Mandadapu et al., 2024). In the computer-vision case, entangled states may have the potential to encode correlations between spatially separated features of an image and thus quantum algorithms may be used to compute more efficiently global image properties than classical algorithms which would have to explicitly compute all pairwise correlations.

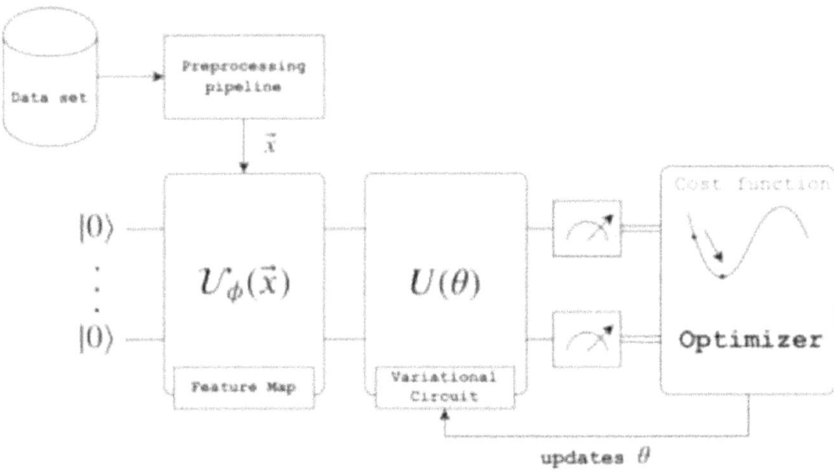

Figure 7.2: Components of a quantum neural network architecture (Mandadapu et al., 2024).

Nevertheless, quantum entanglement is extremely fragile and can be easily disrupted by interactions with the environment, a process known as decoherence. Current systems can maintain entanglement only for timescales ranging from microseconds to milliseconds, which severely limits the depth of computation before quantum benefits are overwhelmed by noise. Decoherence poses a fundamental challenge for quantum computer-vision applications, which typically require long and complex processing pipelines involving multiple computational steps. Present-day quantum devices simply cannot preserve entanglement long enough to support the sophisticated image processing tasks needed for practical use.

Computer-vision quantum algorithms must ultimately produce classical results through quantum measurements, which collapse superposition states in a probabilistic manner. This measurement process limits the extraction of quantum advantages in practical vision applications, as the inherent randomness of quantum outcomes requires many circuit executions before results can be considered reliable. The computational gains may be offset by the large number of measurements needed, often increasing with the desired precision. The measurement overhead can become prohibitive for computer-vision tasks, where high accuracy and low error rates are essential.

Another mechanism that can be used for a computer vision task is quantum interference phenomena. It is possible that constructive interference will enhance the desired computational pathways and destructive interference will silence unwanted ones to form natural filters that might be useful in feature extraction and pattern recognition. Nonetheless, the creation of quantum circuits that can consistently generate useful interference patterns in solving complex visual processing tasks is a key algorithmic problem that needs profound knowledge in computer-vision needs and quantum mechanics. Figure 7.3 demonstrates circuit diagrams to depict the particular quantum gate configurations and parameterization plans to engineer useful interference patterns to carry out visual feature extraction and processing tasks (Lee et al., 2025).

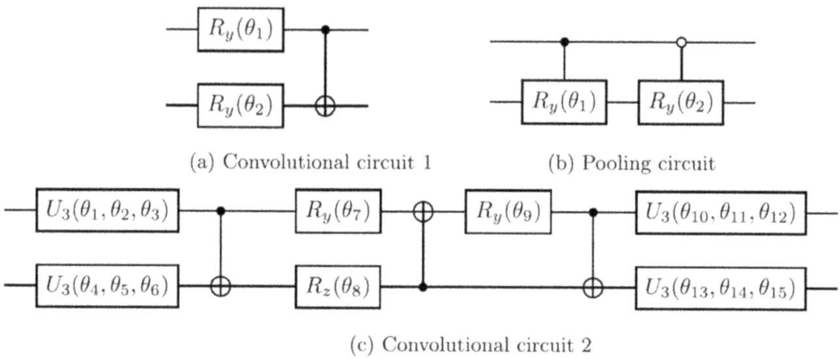

Figure 7.3: Parameterized quantum circuits for computer vision (Lee et al., 2025).

7.2.2 Quantum Machine Learning Algorithms and their Vision Applications

A number of quantum machine learning algorithms have been shown to have theoretical applicability to computer-vision tasks, but scalable implementations are grossly lacking due to the current hardware limitations. These algorithms are the basis on which quantum computer-vision applications can someday be implemented, although they currently need assumptions and constraints that in practice may not be true to real-world visual data processing.

One of the most promising quantum machine learning algorithms that could be applied to computer-vision is quantum Principal Component Analysis (qPCA) suggested by Lloyd, Mohseni and Rebentrost (2014). The algorithm theoretically exponentially speeds up a set of matrix operations applicable to dimensionality reduction in high-dimensional visual data. The algorithm operates by encoding a classical data matrix as a quantum density matrix and using quantum evolution to extract the principal components. Mathematically, given a data matrix A, the algorithm creates a quantum state (Nielsen and Chuang, 2010):

$$\rho \propto AA^{\dagger} \tag{7.4}$$

and uses quantum phase estimation on the evolution the following equation to extract eigenvalues and eigenvectors (Nielsen and Chuang, 2010):

$$e^{-ipt} \tag{7.5}$$

The theoretical exponential speedup of qPCA applies only when the data matrix has low rank and specific structural properties that may not hold for natural images. Real images often contain rich texture information and noise that increase the effective rank of the data matrix, potentially negating the quantum advantage. Additionally, the algorithm requires the data matrix to be provided as a quantum state, which itself may require exponential resources for arbitrary classical data. The process of converting classical image data into the required quantum representation could eliminate any computational savings achieved by the quantum algorithm itself.

Furthermore, qPCA outputs the principal components as quantum states, requiring quantum tomography to extract classical information. Quantum tomography is an exponentially expensive process that requires exponentially many measurements to fully characterize an unknown quantum state. For a n-qubit quantum system, complete state tomography requires approximately 4^n measurements, making it impractical for systems of even moderate size. This creates a fundamental bottleneck in using qPCA for practical computer-vision applications where classical output is typically required.

Quantum Support Vector Machines, described by Rebentrost, Mohseni and Lloyd (2014), present another theoretical approach for quantum-enhanced classification that could apply to image classification tasks. The algorithm theoretically achieves exponential speedup for certain classification problems by using quantum linear algebra techniques to solve the optimization problem underlying SVM training. The quantum algorithm operates by encoding the training data in quantum superposition and using quantum matrix inversion techniques to find the optimal separating hyperplane.

The theoretical speedups require data to be provided in quantum superposition and assume certain sparsity conditions that may not hold for typical visual datasets. Image data is often dense and high-dimensional, violating the sparsity assumptions required for quantum advantage. For computer-vision applications, the overhead of encoding image data into quantum states may eliminate the computational advantages, particularly when considering the cost of converting classical pixel data into the required quantum representation. The algorithm itself needs quantum access to data as well, such that the data is already represented in quantum form, or is converted at a possibly prohibitive cost.

Variational quantum classifiers are a closer-term quantum machine learning method that might one day be used on computer-vision tasks. These algorithms train parameterized quantum circuits, which can be trained by classical optimization algorithms, forming hybrid quantum-classical algorithms and could potentially be executed by near-term quantum computing devices. Havlicek et al. (2019) showed learning under supervision with quantum-enhanced feature spaces, where some quantum feature maps are harder to simulate, classically.

Variational quantum algorithms, however, have the barren plateau problem, in which the gradient decreases exponentially with system size, and thus it is extremely hard to train large systems. McClean et al. (2018) demonstrated that this issue is generic to randomly initialized variational quantum circuits, which has a crippling effect on scalability. In computer-vision applications where high-resolution images have to be processed the barren plateau problem may render training impractical. The variational quantum circuit optimization landscape becomes exponentially flat, causing gradient-based methods to fail because they cannot distinguish between different parameter configurations.

More recent efforts, such as Bowles, Ahmed and Schuld (2024) provide a comprehensive benchmark of quantum machine learning models on 6 binary classification tasks across a diverse set of datasets. Their large-scale study systematically evaluated 12 popular widely used quantum machine learning models on 6 binary classification tasks comprising 160 individual datasets. The findings were sobering for the quantum machine learning community: in general standard models of classical machine learning perform better than quantum classifiers. Further, the elimination of entanglement in quantum models tended to yield at least equivalent performance, indicating that quantum may not be decisive in the small learning tasks in question.

7.2.3 Image Encoding Challenges and Quantum Data Representation

Efficiently encoding classical image data into quantum states is one of the most central challenges in quantum computer vision. Several encoding schemes have been proposed, each offering different trade-offs among compression performance, encoding complexity and compatibility with quantum processing. The choice of encoding strategy fundamentally shapes the types of quantum algorithms that can be realised.

Among these approaches, amplitude encoding, where pixel values are mapped directly to the probability amplitudes of a quantum state, provides the most compact quantum representation. The quantum state of an n-pixel grayscale image of normalized pixel values p would be:

$$|\psi\rangle = \sum_i \frac{p_i}{||p||} \; |i\rangle \tag{7.6}$$

where $||p|$ are these normalized pixel values, and $|i\rangle$ are the states of the computational basis which are positioned at pixel positions. With a photograph of n pixels encoding the amplitude would require a log2(n)-qubit, which is exponentially smaller in terms of classical storage. Theoretically, in amplitude encoding, an image of 1024×1024 pixel size (over one million classical bits) could be encoded in only 20 qubits (Le et al., 2011).

However, this advantage comes with significant practical limitations. Preparation of quantum states would be complicated by amplitude encoding, and can scale with n, which would nullify computational advantages. The complexity of quantum circuitry requires arbitrary amplitude-encoded states, and is usually not optimally executable on current quantum hardware. The exponential resources required to prepare arbitrary quantum states in the model (in general) and the prohibitive amplitude encoding of realistic images are also exponentially priced.

Moreover, amplitude encoding has very harsh normalization constraints that may not be image natural. The probabilistic interpretation of quantum states requires that the squares of the amplitude add to one that can eliminate striking image properties such as variations in brightness or contrast dependencies. It often converts pixel values into useful quantum values and, therefore, needs pre-processing which can remove useful visual information.

The simpler alternative provided by basis encoding is one where a single pixel is encoded directly as an intensity value using a sequence of qubits. This scaling is linear in the image size, and is more feasible for near-term devices as it requires only simple quantum gates for state preparation. In the 8-bit grayscale case, the intensity value of each pixel would require 8 qubits which would translate the quantum representation of an 8-bit grayscale image to be on par with classic storage requirements.

Linear scaling of the encoding of basis phases removes the exponential compression benefit but offers more achievable implementation directions on current quantum equipment. Simple sequences of single-qubit rotations and controlled interactions are sufficient to prepare the quantum states necessary to encode basis in a basis-encoded system, and are achievable on near-term quantum computers. Nevertheless, basis encoding does not compress amplitudes exponentially, and can consume prohibitively many qubits to encode high-resolution images. A modest 256×256 pixel image would require over half a million qubits for basis encoding, far exceeding current quantum hardware capabilities.

Flexible Representation of Quantum Images (FRQI), proposed by Le, Dong and Hirota (2011), attempts to balance compression and practicality by encoding both position and intensity information in quantum states' using a more sophisticated representation scheme. FRQI represents an image as (Le et al., 2011):

$$|I\rangle = \frac{1}{\sqrt{2^n}} \sum_{i=0}^{2^{n-1}} \quad |\theta_i\rangle|i \tag{7.7}$$

where $|\theta_i\rangle$ encodes the intensity of pixel i as the angle θ_i, and $|i\rangle$ represents the position (Le et al., 2011):

$$\theta_i\rangle = \cos(\theta_i)|0\rangle + \sin(\theta_i)|1\rangle \tag{7.8}$$

FRQI enables quantum operations on both spatial and intensity dimensions simultaneously and has been extended to handle color images through additional qubit assignments. The representation allows for quantum image processing operations such as rotation, scaling, and filtering to be implemented as quantum circuit operations. Nevertheless, FRQI still involves complicated state preparation procedures and scales up to high-resolution images. The number of quantum circuits required to prepare FRQI states increases polynomially with image resolution, but the associated constants can be very large, making the approach prohibitively expensive in practice.

It is hoped that some of the shortcomings of FRQI can be mitigated by improved quantum image representations such as NEQR (Novel Enhanced Quantum Representation) proposed by Zhang et al. (2013), which offers a more adaptable intensity-encoding scheme. NEQR assigns multiple pixel qubits to each pixel, allowing grayscale values to be represented directly rather than through the trigonometric encoding required by FRQI. However, even these improved representations require additional qubits and more elaborate state-preparation procedures, pushing practical implementation further into the future.

7.3 Current Experimental Work and Hardware Limitations

7.3.1 Recent Quantum Computing Breakthroughs and their Implications

In recent years, substantial advances in quantum computing capabilities and more realistic assessments of quantum machine learning performance have directly shaped expectations for the feasibility of quantum computer vision implementations.

In December 2024, Google introduced its Willow quantum processor, marking a significant milestone in quantum error correction research. The 105-qubit superconducting device demonstrated below-threshold error correction with logical qubits, achieving lower error rates than individual physical qubits. This achievement directly addresses one of the central challenges in quantum computing: quantum operations are inherently noisy, and error rates typically grow with circuit depth and complexity.

It was shown that the Willow processor exhibited exponential error suppression as the size of its logical qubits increased. Measurements were also performed on progressively larger arrays of physical qubits, specifically 3×3, 5×5, and 7×7 geometries. The corresponding reduction in error rates improved by roughly a factor of two with each increase in logical qubit size, achieving the so-called below-threshold performance of fault-tolerant quantum computing. This threshold marks the point at which adding more physical qubits to a logical qubit no longer degrades performance but enhances it, a critical condition for scaling quantum computers to large, practical systems (Neven, 2025).

Nevertheless, quantum computing researchers have offered valuable context for this accomplishment. Hartmut Neven, the founder and the lead of Google Quantum, admitted that Willow remains far too small to perform useful computations and that practical, industry-relevant applications will require quantum processors with millions of qubits. The gap between current hardware capabilities and the demands of real-world use cases is substantial, and both qubit counts and error rates must improve by several orders of magnitude.

The Willow processor also demonstrated quantum supremacy through a Random Circuit Sampling (RCS) benchmark, performing a computation in under five minutes that would take classical supercomputers an estimated 10 septillion years. While this achievement demonstrates the unique capabilities of quantum systems, the RCS benchmark has limited practical relevance. The computation performed has no known application beyond demonstrating quantum computational capabilities, and classical algorithms for this specific problem continue to improve, potentially reducing the claimed advantage.

Comprehensive benchmarking studies have provided sobering assessments of quantum machine learning performance that directly impact quantum computer vision prospects. The most comprehensive review of quantum machine learning models is the systematic analysis by Bowles, Ahmed and Schuld (2024), and tested 12 popular quantum machine learning algorithms on 160 datasets measured on 6 binary classification tasks. Their findings invalidate most of the beliefs in the benefits of quantum machine learning.

The research approach involved a critical experimental design to overcome the common pitfalls of the benchmarking quantum machine learning such as rightful baseline comparisons, statistical significance tests, and the assessment of the quantum features contribution, such as entanglement. In order to ensure a just comparison of quantum and classical approaches, the researchers have implemented an open-source package (a framework named PennyLane) that is a framework on quantum computing.

These results were discrete in showing that classical machine learning models are more effective than quantum classifiers depending on the tasks being addressed. In Figure 7.4, Statistical significance analysis presents p-value distributions that quantitatively demonstrate the performance gaps between quantum classifiers

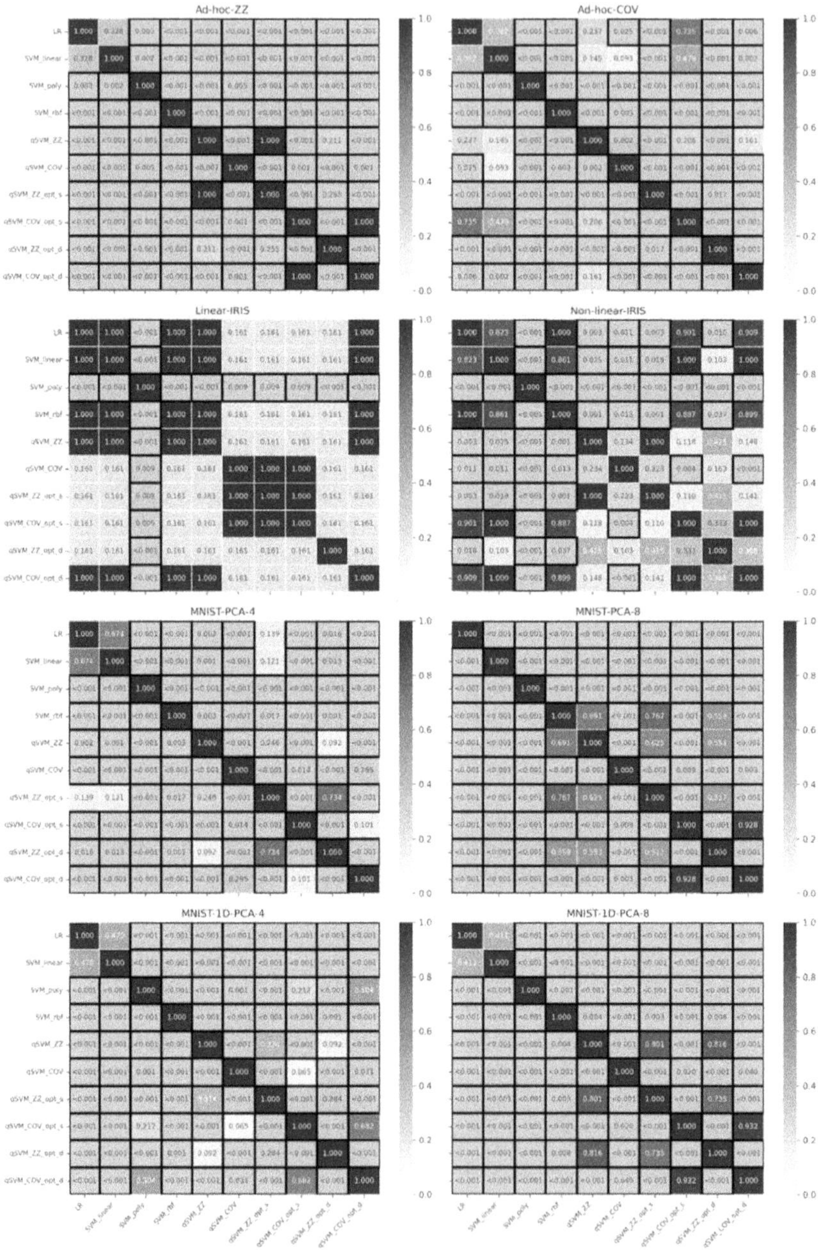

Figure 7.4: Statistical significance analysis: quantum vs classical methods (Alvarez-Estevez, 2024).

and their classical counterparts across comprehensive benchmark evaluations (Alvarez-Estevez, 2024).

More significantly, the researchers found that removing entanglement from quantum models often resulted in equal or better performance, suggesting that quantum entanglement (often considered the key resource for quantum advantage) may not provide benefits for the types of learning tasks typically encountered. This finding has profound implications for quantum computer vision, as many proposed quantum algorithms rely explicitly on entanglement for their theoretical advantages. In Figure 7.5, performance distribution comparison shows how breakdown of quantum entanglement tends to preserve or enhance classification accuracy disproportionately and makes fundamental assumptions on the quantum benefits in a visual processing task (Alvarez-Estevez, 2024).

7.3.2 Quantum Machine Learning Demonstrations for Vision Tasks

Recent experimental research in quantum computer vision is cripplingly limited by hardware considerations, and much experimental evidence is limited to proof-of-concept implementations instead of real-world implementations. Such experiments offer useful information about the challenges and opportunities of quantum approaches as well as the massive disparity between theoretical suggestions and practical systems.

The present state of art of quantum computer vision is small-scale image classification experiments. Henderson et al. (2020) modelled convolutional neural networks that took 4×4 pixel images extracted from down sampled MNIST digits. Their approach uses parameterized quantum circuits to perform convolution-like operations, followed by classical neural networks for final classification. The quantum circuits apply trainable unitary operations to small image patches, creating quantum feature maps which are measured to produce classical features for further processing.

While this work demonstrates the basic concept of quantum feature extraction, the 16-pixel images are of orders of magnitude smaller than any practical computer vision application. Real-world computer vision typically involves images with millions of pixels, making the scale gap enormous. The researchers chose an extremely small scale not due to algorithmic limitations but because of the severe constraints of current quantum hardware, which cannot reliably process larger quantum systems.

The convolutional method has inherent scaling issues that are not due to hardware constraints. The number of quantum circuits needed to compute an image grows quadratically as image size increases, and to achieve good measurement statistics each circuit needs to be repeated many times. The total computational cost could exceed classical approaches even if quantum hardware were perfectly reliable and arbitrarily large. The measurement overhead associated with extracting classical information from quantum states represents a fundamental bottleneck that may prevent quantum advantages even with perfect hardware.

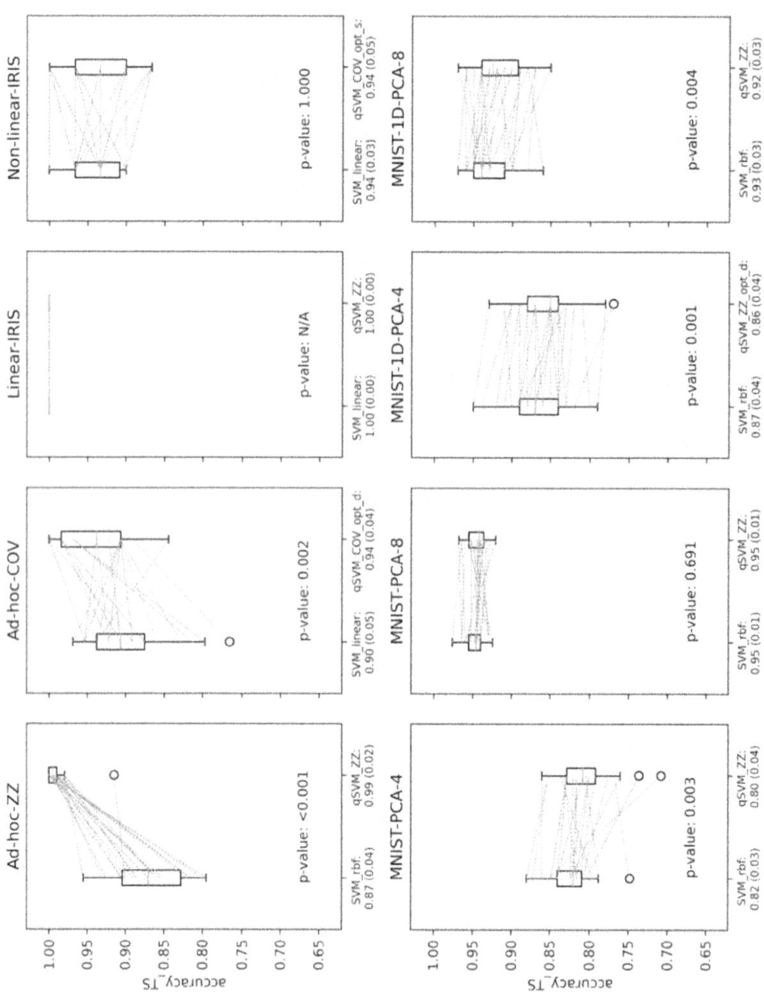

Figure 7.5: Performance comparison of best quantum and classical models (Alvarez-Estevez, 2024).

Mari et al. (2020) explored transfer learning approaches where pre-trained classical neural networks extract features that are consequently processed by variational quantum circuits. Their experiments on MNIST and Fashion-MNIST datasets used quantum circuits with 4-16 qubits to classify pre-processed features rather than raw images. Such a hybrid method tries to take advantage of both classical and quantum computing power by first extracting features with classical networks and lastly classifying with quantum networks.

The transfer learning method leads to a partial solution to the quantum encoding problem where classical networks are used to compress image data to sizes that can be handled by quantum computing. The method, however, leaves the question of where quantum improvements may occur should the computationally-intensive feature extraction be done by classical networks. The quantum component only processes high-level features which have already been extracted by classical methods so there is only a constrained scope of quantum algorithmic benefits.

The transfer learning experiments show that quantum circuits can achieve classification performance on reduced feature spaces comparable to that of classical methods, but they do not demonstrate any clear performance advantages. Moreover, quantum circuits require substantially more training time and computational resources than equivalent classical networks, undermining claims of quantum efficiency. The variational training process demands thousands of parameter updates, each involving multiple quantum circuit executions, making the overall training cost prohibitively high for practical applications.

Tacchino et al. (2019) demonstrated a quantum perceptron on actual quantum hardware, showing that single quantum neurons could be implemented on a superconducting quantum processor. Their work used IBM quantum devices to implement basic quantum neural network components, providing important proof-of-concept evidence that quantum machine learning algorithms can run on real hardware. However, their experiments were limited to binary classification tasks on well-crafted synthetic datasets, rather than real-world computer vision tasks.

Experiments with quantum perceptrons revealed significant limitations that constrain the realization of quantum machine learning on current hardware. Decoherence and gate errors that accumulate as quantum circuits are executed, degrading performance and restricting the achievable circuit depth. As a result, researchers were forced to design their circuits with extreme care, minimizing both depth and gate count to maintain reliability on noisy quantum devices. These constraints severely limit the complexity of quantum machine learning algorithms that can be implemented in practice.

7.3.3 Quantum Feature Extraction and Representation Learning

Among the most likely applications of quantum computing to computer vision in the near term is quantum feature extraction, which can possibly provide quantum benefits to small sets of image processing in the absence of large-scale quantum image processing systems. In this area, a research focus has been to use quantum circuits to learn small image patch features, which can subsequently be combined with classical post-processing algorithms.

Chen et al. (2023) explored the use of quantum-extracted from small size image patches within their quantum convolutional neural network design. Their algorithm processes 2×2 or 4×4 pixel blocks which are mapped by parameterized quantum circuits, generating quantum feature maps, localized representations of image structure. The quantum circuits implement trainable unitary transformations acting on quantum states that represent pixel intensities such that the resulting measurement outputs are inputs to classical machine learning algorithms.

In quantum feature extraction, the method leverages quantum parallelism and entanglement to capture features of pixel values that may be difficult to characterize using classical approaches. Entanglement enables quantum circuits to implement non-linear transformations and establish long-range correlations between pixels, providing a representational power that can yield more expressive feature mappings than those produced by conventional convolutional operations.

However, experimental results have not demonstrated clear advantages over classical feature extraction methods. Quantum circuits must be carefully designed to avoid barren plateaus during training, and feature quality can be degraded by the statistical noise introduced during measurement. Because measurement is required to convert quantum feature maps to classical form, and has maps into classical form, it imposes additional computational overhead that may offset any potential quantum processing benefits.

Schuld and Killoran (2019) examined the expressiveness of quantum feature maps for machine-learning tasks and outlined theoretical conditions under which quantum feature maps may offer advantages over classical algorithms. Their work shows how quantum circuits can embed classical data into high-dimensional quantum feature spaces in ways that are inaccessible to classical methods. Under these conditions, quantum feature extraction may provide genuine benefits for specific types of data and learning problems.

Their theoretical analysis also demonstrates that quantum feature maps can generate feature spaces that are exponentially large in resources yet polynomially accessible, potentially enabling more powerful machine learning models. However, the practical value of such complex feature spaces depends on whether they capture relevant structure that is meaningful for real-world learning tasks. Moreover, these high-dimensional quantum feature spaces may still suffer from the curse of dimensionality, potentially requiring exponentially many training examples to achieve effective learning.

Experimental validation of the advantages of quantum feature maps has been challenging. Many studies rely on synthetic datasets engineered to showcase potential quantum benefits rather than on realistic computer-vision benchmarks. When evaluated on standard computer-vision datasets, quantum feature-extraction methods generally perform on par with, or worse than, their classical counterparts, while demanding substantially greater computational resources.

7.4 Quantum-Inspired Classical Algorithms for Computer Vision

While true quantum computer vision applications remain limited by hardware constraints, quantum-inspired classical algorithms have achieved practical success by adapting concepts from quantum mechanics to run efficiently on conventional computers. These solutions are the most immediate practically viable result of the intersection of quantum computing and computer vision, and they offer tools that may be implemented now to form the foundations of quantum implementation in the future.

7.4.1 Tensor Network Methods for Visual Data Processing

Tensor networks, originally developed for quantum many-body physics to describe entangled quantum states, provide powerful quantum-inspired approaches to high-dimensional data processing that can run efficiently on classical computers. Such procedures take advantage of the mathematical frameworks involved in modeling quantum entanglement to create effective algorithms for classical machine learning problems, such as in computer vision.

The simplest type of tensor network is Matrix Product States (MPS), which has demonstrated specific potential in image classification. Stoudenmire and Schwab (2016) have shown that MPS can be effectively used to represent and categorize images, but the pixel values are used as an index in a tensor product format, which basically generates a sparse representation that reflects significant correlations between pixels. They encode each image as a *kh* dimensional MPS that determines the trade-off between compression and representational accuracy.

The mathematical intuition behind the MPS of processing images is to model an image of n pixels as a quantum-inspired state:

$$|\psi\rangle = \sum_{i_1 \dots i_n} A^{(i_1)}[1]\, A^{(i_2)}[2] \dots A^{(i_n)}[\mathrm{N}] \,|\, i_1 i_2 \dots i_n \qquad (7.10)$$

with matrices $A\hat{}(i_k)[\mathrm{k}]$ of dimension defined by the bond dimension χ. This representation facilitates easy manipulation of high dimensional data as the structured correlations that are characteristic of natural images are exploited (Stoudenmire and Schwab, 2016).

The bond dimension X is an essential parameter that defines the expressive power as well as the computation of the MPS representation. Small bond dimensions have proven to be efficient in compression but can fail to represent complex image structure whereas large bond dimensions are more expressive but less efficient in computing. The best bond dimension selection is related to the requirements of the particular image dataset and complexity of classification task.

Laboratory findings indicate that MPS-based image classification can be robustly competitive with established machine learning algorithms, and offer important computational benefits in certain data collections. The technique is especially successful with images, whose spatial correlations are organized, e.g., irregularly written numbers or plain geometric figures. Nonetheless, the performance is worse in complex natural images whose texture information cannot be effectively compressed with low-rank tensor representations.

Newman et al. (2024) applied MPS techniques to image generation and anomaly detection unsupervised learning tasks, showing that the techniques are more widely applicable to computer vision problems, where the application of fully trained tensor networks is possible. Their uncontrolled MPS algorithms are capable of training probability distributions of image data and producing new samples by sampling the learned representational network in the form of a tensor. The generative ability offers an evaluation of the ability of the MPS representation to reproduce the statistical composition of the image dataset.

The unsupervised MPS methodology lacks scaling to high-resolution images because the number of required components of the tensors to model the complex probability distributions increases exponentially. Although this technique is effective with small images whose structure is easily discernible, special attention must be given to approximation choices and computational trade-offs in scaling to realistic computer vision tasks.

More general tensor network architectures than MPS have been proposed to overcome some of the limitations of scalability and expressivity of simple tensor network methods. Jahromi and Orus (2024) have created variational tensor neural networks, a type created with the use of computer vision tasks in mind, including hierarchical structures that are more responsive to the multi-scale character of visual representations. These methods make use of more advanced strategies of tensor decomposition that can effectively capture the hierarchical organization which is characteristic of natural images.

Variational tensor neural networks are a hybrid of the representational power of tensor networks with the flexibility of neural network architectures that can be trained using standard machine learning methods yet retain the computational benefits of tensor representations. The variational algorithm allows training of parameters in the tensor network end-to-end through gradient-based optimization, which allows compatibility of methods with the existing machine learning workflows.

Experimental analysis of state-of-the-art tensor network models with on standard computer vision benchmarks has demonstrated promising results, with certain methods performing as well as state-of-the-art neural networks whilst using fewer parameters and computing less. The methods, however, often need delicate hyperparameter optimization and specialized optimization methods that can restrict their practical use.

7.4.2 Quantum-Inspired Optimization and Annealing Methods

Classical optimization algorithms inspired by quantum annealing have been able to solve the complex optimization problems of computer vision applications. These quantum-inspired methods are extensions of the principles of quantum superposition and tunnelling to more useful classical optimization methods in challenging computer vision tasks.

The approach to solve the optimization problems in computer vision is quantum annealing, and Heidari, Dinneen and Delmas (2024) chose stereo matching as an instance of a labelling problem to be solved. Their approach formulates computer vision problems as Quadratic Unconstrained Binary Optimization (QUBO) models suitable for both classical optimization and quantum annealing hardware. Stereo matching involves finding correspondences between pixels in pairs of images to reconstruct three-dimensional scene geometry, a computationally challenging problem that requires solving complex optimization problems with many local minima.

The QUBO formulation transforms stereo matching into a binary optimization problem where each possible pixel correspondence is represented as a binary variable. Figure 7.6 shows the processing pipeline of how stereo vision algorithms transform paired camera inputs through calibration, rectification, and matching stages to create binary optimization problems suitable for quantum annealing approaches (Heidari et al., 2024).

The objective function encodes both data fidelity terms that measure how well correspondences match image features and smoothness terms that enforce spatial coherence in the disparity map. The resulting optimization problem has thousands or millions of binary variables and exhibits a highly multimodal landscape with many local optima.

Classical optimization approaches to stereo matching, such as graph cuts and belief propagation, can become trapped in local minima and may require extensive computational resources to find high-quality solutions. Quantum-inspired annealing approaches address these challenges by incorporating concepts from quantum tunnelling that enable the optimization process to escape from local minima more effectively than classical methods.

The quantum-inspired annealing algorithm begins with a uniform superposition of all possible solutions and then iteratively applies the problem-specific objective function with a growing impact while gradually reducing quantum fluctuations. This algorithm is analogous to quantum annealing in that it allows the system to tunnel through energy barriers, an ability classical optimization methods lack. The classical variant approximates this quantum tunnelling behavior by using temperature schedules and randomization to escape local minima.

Experimental evaluations on standard stereo-matching tasks show that quantum-inspired annealing can perform as effectively as state-of-the-art classical algorithms, while also producing more stable results across diverse image sets and parameter choices. The method is particularly advantageous in challenging scenes with repetitive textures or occlusions,where the optimization landscape contains many local minima. Figure 7.7 illustrates the QUBO formulation applied to stereo matching, showing the input image pairs and the disparity maps, which demonstrate the competitive performance of quantum-inspired optimization methods (Heidari et al., 2024).

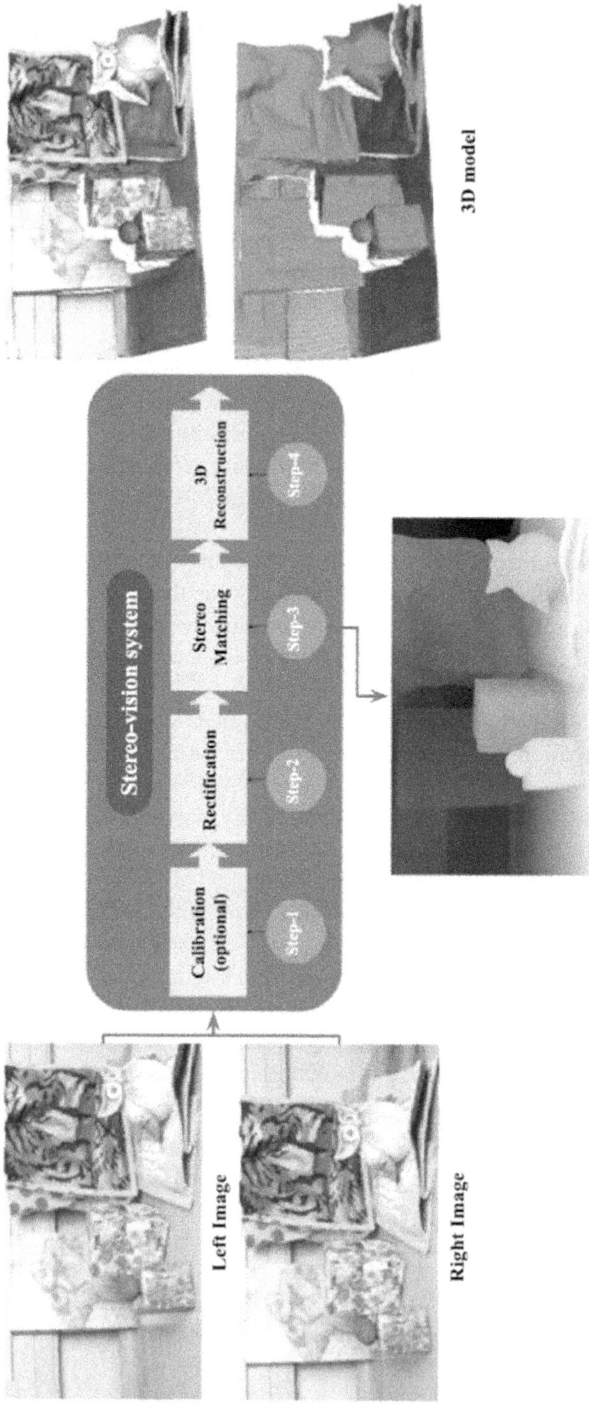

Figure 7.6: Classical stereo vision processing pipeline (Heidari et al., 2024).

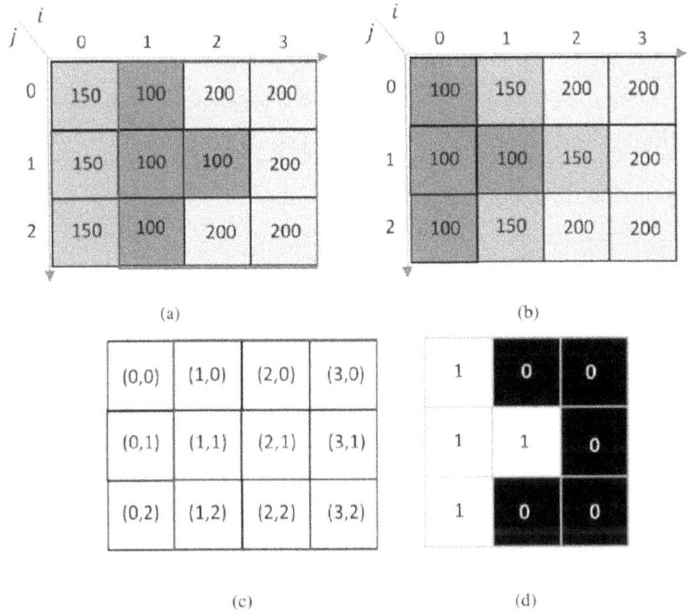

(a) the left stereo image, (b) the right stereo image, (c) the pixel coordinates, (d) the corresponding disparity map.

Figure 7.7: Stereo matching example of quantum optimization (Heidari et al., 2024).

Nevertheless, the quantum-inspired annealing model is not scalable to high-resolution images as the number of binary variables necessary to index all the possible pixel correspondences grows exponentially. The existing ones are restricted to fairly small image patches or need hierarchical schemes that operate the images at different resolutions. Annealing schedules and parameter settings also need to be carefully tuned to give the best performance.

Kharsa, Bouridane and Amira (2023) surveyed currently available advances in quantum machine learning and deep learning over image classification and found quantum-inspired compression methods that combine quantum-inspired pruning, tensor decomposition, and matrix factorization based on the use of annealing to reduce the inference time in convolutional neural networks without degrading accuracy. Their paper shows that quantum-inspired optimization can be used in neural network compression to generate more efficient models to be applied in computer vision.

The quantum-inspired neural network compression method applies annealing-based optimization to identify the neural network parameters that can be eliminated or simplified to a value of optimal performance degradation. The technique models the act of pruning neural networks as a combinatorial optimization problem in which every network parameter is modeled as a binary variable, which is either retained or is dropped. The objective function has a trade-off between model complexity and network accuracy, which forms a multi-objective optimization problem, the solution to which has an advantage in quantum-inspired solution strategies.

It has been experimentally demonstrated that quantum-inspired compression may be able to reach compression ratios just as good or even better than traditional pruning algorithms and achieve the same or even higher classification accuracy. The quantum annealing approach seems to compromise compression and accuracy more effectively by more effectively searching the space of possible network architectures. Figure 7.8 presents the energy landscape analysis of the ultimate optimization states of quantum annealing and classical methods, which proves the better exploration ability to make better trade-offs in network architecture optimization (Heidari et al., 2024).

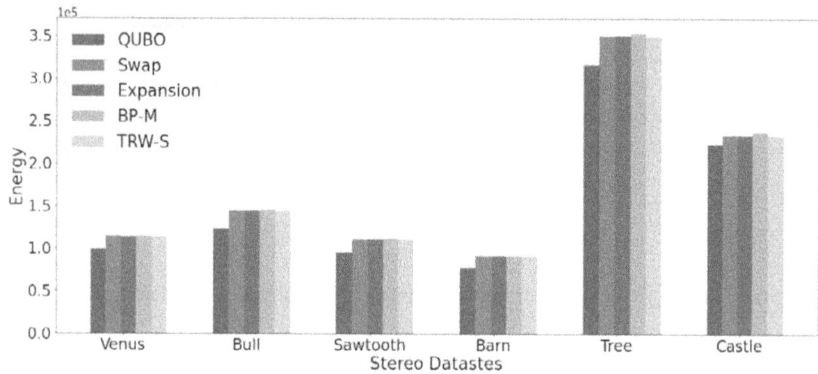

Figure 7.8: Optimization performance: quantum annealing vs classical methods (Heidari et al., 2024).

7.5 Hybrid Quantum-Classical Approaches

Hybrid quantum-classical approaches represent the most promising near-term strategy for applying quantum concepts to computer vision, combining the unique capabilities of quantum processors with the reliability and scalability of classical systems. These approaches recognize that practical quantum computer vision systems will likely require careful integration of quantum and classical processing components, each handling the computational tasks for which they are best suited.

7.5.1 Variational Quantum Circuits for Computer Vision

Variational quantum networks offer a model to execute quantum machine learning algorithms on near-term quantum hardware by optimizing parameterized quantum circuits with classical algorithms. The quantum neural network that is commonly trained by variational quantum circuits is characterized by a layered network with alternating single-qubit parameterized rotation and two-qubit entangling gates (Cerezo et al., 2021).

The variational method is an intermediate between theoretical capabilities of quantum algorithms that are fault-tolerant and the limitations of current near-term quantum computers. Variational algorithms can theoretically achieve quantum advantages with noisy intermediate-scale quantum computers with small coherence times and large error rates, instead of perfect quantum computers with full error correction. The key point is that in case of a substantial noise the optimization of quantum circuit parameters can potentially find useful quantum states.

One of the most significant issues with variational quantum circuit usage in the computer vision field, however, is the barren plateau phenomenon, where gradient descent decreases exponentially with the size of the system. As shown by McClean et al. (2018), barren plateaus of variational quantum circuits are common in randomly initialized circuits and highly challenging or unattainable to train. Gradient size also tends to shrink exponentially with the number of qubits, and defines optimization landscapes where gradient-based training algorithms cannot distinguish between the parameter configurations.

The barren plateau problem is particularly severe in the case of computer vision because of the relatively large-scale quantum systems required to achieve meaningful computational advantages on challenging problems in realistic image processing. The gradients will decay exponentially to mean that the variational quantum circuits to be employed in computer vision can be untrainable in general optimization processes. Some recent work has discussed different methods of alleviating barren plateaus, such as attentive parameterization, structured circuit design, and alternative optimization methods, although a general solution has not yet been found.

Another inherent challenge to computer vision uses is the measurement overhead that comes with variational quantum circuits. After every measurement of the objective function, many instances of the quantum circuit must be implemented to gather enough statistics on measurements for confidence in estimating the gradient. The number of circuit executions that are needed usually scales with the desired precision and the count of parameters, and composes a multiplicative overhead that can render training prohibitively costly.

When computer vision tasks are needed at high accuracy and low variance in performance, the overhead of measurement is especially an issue. Applications of image classification typically need one percent error rates that would require thousands of quantum circuit executions on a single gradient computation. Claims of quantum computational advantages may be invalidated because total training cost, on a classical approach, can be many orders of magnitude less than quantum computational approaches.

7.5.2 Quantum Processing Integration of Classical Pre-processing

The practical approach that can be used to implement quantum computer vision in the near term is performing initial image pre-processing with classical systems and only quantum processing on certain tasks, which may have quantum advantages. This division of labour acknowledges that classical computers are better at some operations related to image processing, whereas quantum systems perhaps offer benefits to some kinds of computations.

Classical pre-processing can reduce the dimensionality of image data to levels manageable by quantum processors while preserving the most relevant information for the quantum processing stage. Standard dimensionality reduction techniques such as principal component analysis, feature selection, or convolutional feature extraction can transform high-resolution images into compact representations suitable for quantum processing. This kind of scaling effort is used to overcome the inherent scaling constraints in quantum image processing by making quantum algorithms run on reasonable data volumes.

The classical pre-processing method has however cast some basic questions on the point at which quantum advantages would be gained in the general processing pipeline. To the extent that the computationally intensive operations of extracting relevant features of high-dimensional image data are done in a classical way, the quantum processing component is used on the already processed representations that could have already stored the most vital information. The quantum algorithms should offer enough benefits on the data with reduced dimensions to offset the increased complexity and overheads of hybrid quantum-classical systems.

Experimental studies of hybrid pre-processing methods have been inconclusive, with quantum processing elements usually giving the same or worse performance to the same pre-processed input as classical methods. The quantum components usually need far more computational resources and development effort and produce similar or worse results than classical alternatives. The overheads of integration and noise measurement of quantum processing may negatively impact the overall performance of a system even when the performance of the individual quantum components is good in isolation. Figure 7.9 showcases the analysis of performance degradation on a set of differing datasets and the effect of quantum noise measurement and integration overheads on the system's reliability as a whole when compared to classical processing methods (Lee et al., 2025).

The choice of classical pre-processing procedures is crucial, as it strongly influences whether any quantum advantage can be realized in any subsequent processing stages. Opportunities to gain quantum advantages may be eliminated by pre-processing methods that eliminate the kinds of structures or correlations that can be used in quantum algorithms. On the other hand, downstream processing quantum benefits might be achievable using pre-processing techniques that do not harm the relevant quantum-exploitable structure and also reduce dimensionality.

Recently, optimization-based design of the joint design of classical and quantum processing units has been studied, and pre-processing strategies that can most effectively facilitate quantum benefits in the later stages have been sought. Nevertheless, such joint optimization methods have severe computational limitations and are not yet proven to offer unambiguous advantages compared to traditional methods of designing hybrid systems.

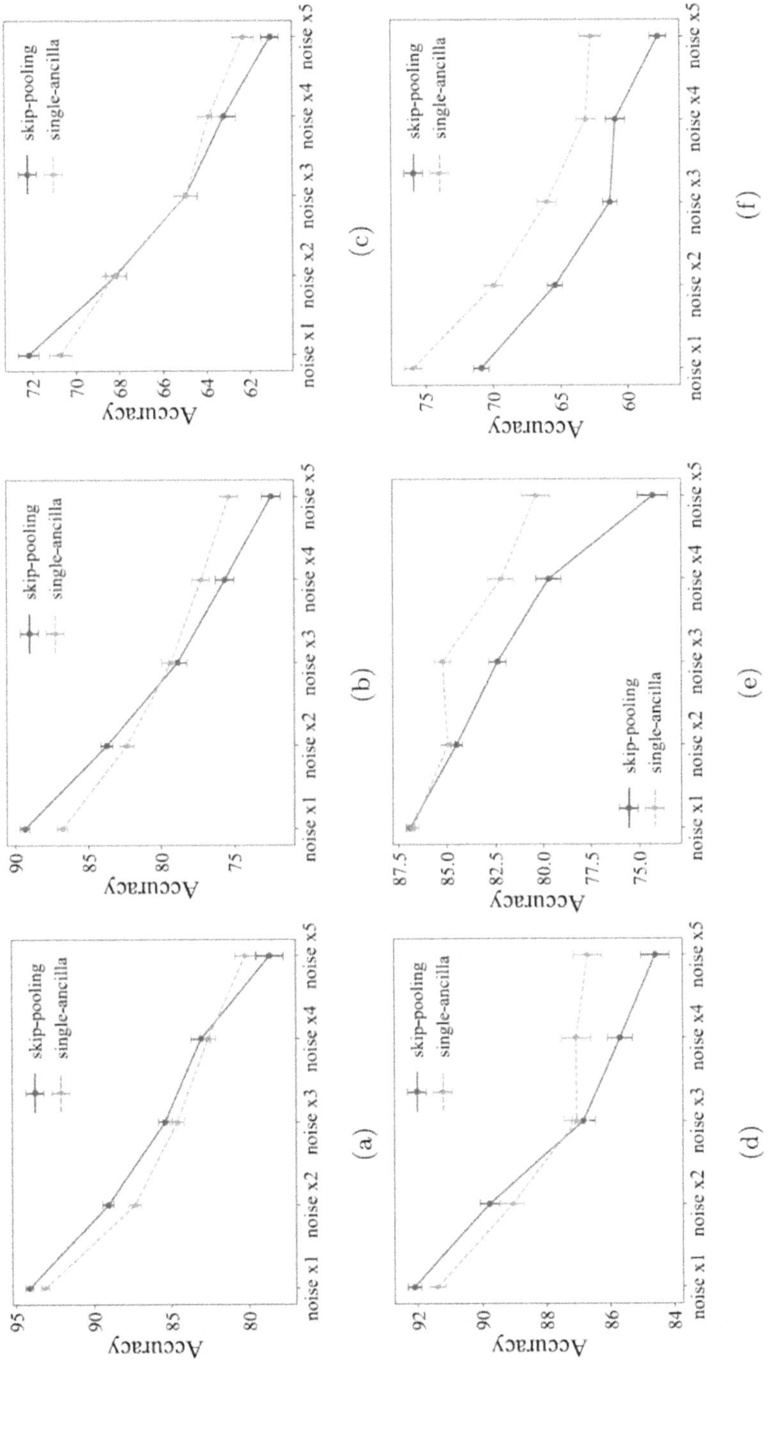

Figure 7.9: Noise resilience analysis on multiple datasets (Lee et al., 2025).

7.5.3 Recent Hardware-Software Integration Advances

Hybrid quantum-classical computer vision systems cannot be effectively realized without complex hardware-software co-realization capable of effectively interacting with quantum and classical processing units. Recent developments in quantum computing devices and software have begun dealing with some of the integration issues, but serious limitations exist to working with computer vision applications.

Companies (like IBM, Google and Rigetti) have introduced quantum cloud platforms that allow quantum hardware to be accessible to computer vision research, allowing researchers to run quantum algorithms without having access to quantum hardware directly. These platforms provide software development kits and programming frameworks that abstract many of the low-level details of quantum hardware control while providing interfaces compatible with classical machine learning workflows.

However, the current generation of quantum cloud platforms faces significant limitations for computer vision applications. Queue times for quantum hardware access can be hours or days, making interactive algorithm development and large-scale experimentation impractical. The available quantum hardware typically provides only tens to hundreds of qubits with high error rates and short coherence times, severely constraining the complexity of implementable computer vision algorithms.

The network delay between classical computing systems and quantum systems imposes further limitations on hybrid algorithms that need a close degree of quantum and classical computation interplay. Such latency in quantum and classical devices can exceed the quantum coherence period, and hybrid algorithms should be a batch mode of operation which may not be optimal in the computation being performed on it.

An even more recent development using quantum error correction such as the Willow processor, announced by Google in December 2024 is promising, that one day we would finally have a stable quantum hardware to run practical computer vision systems on. Below-threshold error correction demonstrating that quantum error correction, rather than degrading system performance with system size (quantum qubit count), can be realized is a major milestone in quantum computing history.

Bischof et al. (2025) demonstrated that hybrid quantum neural networks require much lesser parameter estimates to solve entity matching tasks, implying that they will be efficient in solving some pattern recognition problems of interest to computer vision. Their experimental findings suggest that quantum processing elements can be nearly as efficient as classical approaches and with a much smaller number of trainable parameters, which could allow more efficient model architectures.

This lower parameter requirement may be useful in applications of computer vision in which model size and memory requirements limits are fundamentally important, including applications to mobile or embedded vision systems. Nevertheless, the existing findings are restricted to fairly low-level pattern matching tasks and it is not clear whether the benefits of the parameter reduction can be applied to more complicated computer vision scenarios, e.g., object detection or semantic segmentation.

7.6 Current Limitations and Fundamental Challenges

7.6.1 Scaling Challenges and Physical Constraints

The scaling issues of quantum computer vision are inherent bottlenecks which can still be present despite significant advancement of quantum hardware. These are due to the fundamental physics of quantum systems, and the complexity of the task of computer vision, which pose limitations that cannot be addressed by simple hardware upgrades.

One of the greatest challenges to quantum computer vision implementation is state preparation complexity. Preparation of quantum states encoding classical image data is an outstanding problem with no obvious way towards realistic scales of images that can be encoded. Numerical quantum algorithms presuppose data to be given in quantum superposition, which, at least with ideal quantum hardware, can negate computational benefits, requiring the cost of converting classical images to quantum states.

Computer vision faces a state preparation problem, which is especially acute, due to the unstructured nature of the information that is usually contained in images, and that does not naturally project to efficient quantum representations. Although quantum systems can theoretically occupy exponentially large amounts of information, in superposition states, classic image data demand exponentially more resources to generate such states. The quantum circuits needed to prepare arbitrary quantum states typically require exponential depth or exponential numbers of gates, making state preparation the bottleneck that limits quantum advantages.

Recently, there has been some theoretical discussion of particular classes of quantum states which can be prepared efficiently, but which often have very special mathematical structures which are not associated with natural images. Structured quantum states such as matrix product states or tree tensor networks can be prepared efficiently but may not capture the rich statistical structure present in realistic computer vision datasets. The mismatch between efficiently preparable quantum states and the structure of visual data represents a fundamental challenge for quantum computer vision.

Measurement and information extraction present another fundamental scaling challenge for quantum computer vision systems. Classical information extraction of quantum computations involves probabilistic measurements that increase the statistical overhead of the process to obtain the desired precision and confidence level. The computer vision task can require assured classification with small error levels; it can also require thousands and even millions of the quantum circuits to effect adequate statistical precision.

The fact that the deterministic nature of quantum measurements is destructive, in the sense that quantum measurement may only measure a single bit of the quantum state, makes no contribution to the measurement overhead problem. To extract a small piece of information from a quantum computation,, one would either have to measure many states of quantum systems, or measure a little quantum state with a complex measurement apparatus capable of measuring many bits of information simultaneously. Quantum computational advantages can be offset by the heavy overhead incurred by the two approaches.

The accumulation of error and decoherence is known to introduce fundamental limits on the depth of quantum computations, and explicitly limits the complexity of problems in computer vision that can be solved consistently in the practical implementation of quantum computers. The ways in which quantum errors propagate in computation, such as circuit structure, error dependencies and the quantum operation being executed, propagate in complicated manners. Unlike classical errors, which are likely to affect a single bit, quantum errors can form complex correlations throughout the quantum system.

Decoherence times introduce hard constraints on the duration of quantum computations, in current quantum systems usually between micro- and milliseconds. Computer vision algorithms frequently involve a variety of computation steps in a complex chain to be accomplished within the decoherence time. The constraint practically restricts quantum computer vision algorithms to extremely shallow circuit depths which might not otherwise be practical.

7.6.2 Hardware Constraints and Engineering Challenges

Physical constraints in current quantum hardware are extremely restrictive in practice, restricting the complexity of applications that can be implemented in computer vision by far more than theoretical analysis could suggest. Such hardware constraints are indicative of underlying challenges in quantum system engineering that might not be overcome despite the progress in technology.

The most evident limitations of quantum computer vision applications now are the number of qubits and their quality. The current largest quantum computers have around 1000 qubits, although many have high error, or limited connectivity, further limiting their effective capacity. A simple 256×256 grayscale image contains 65536 pixels, amplitude-encoding such an image would require far more than 65536 qubits of hardware. Basis encoding would demand even more, placing both approaches well beyond the capabilities of current quantum devices.

The gap between the number of qubits currently available and that required to realize applications of realistic computer vision is not merely a quantitative one, but includes qualitative limitations on the types of algorithms that can be attempted. Quantum computer vision algorithms cannot be experimented at the magnitude of interest, and researchers must instead solve simulated toy problems which may not reflect the reality of the challenges and opportunities of quantum solutions to computer vision.

Gate fidelities and error rates in current quantum systems typically range from 0.1% to 5% per operation, which accumulate rapidly in deep circuits required for complex computer vision tasks. Quantum error correction can potentially address these error rates, but current error correction schemes require hundreds to thousands of physical qubits to create a single logical qubit with reduced error rates. The overhead makes error-corrected quantum computation impractical for the foreseeable future.

The error accumulation problem is particularly severe for computer vision applications because image processing algorithms often require sequential operations that build upon previous results. Unlike some quantum algorithms that can tolerate moderate error rates by relying on statistical averaging, computer vision applications typically require high accuracy in intermediate results to achieve acceptable final results. The error sensitivity prevents quantum computer vision algorithms to circuits that are very shallow and therefore might not be sufficiently complex to produce the computational complexity needed in practice.

There are other constraints associated with connectivity and circuit mapping that are not necessarily valued during theoretical arguments of quantum computer vision. Quantum computers have sparse connectivity graphs with each qubit only interacting directly with a small number of neighbours usually in linear chains, square grids or other regular structures. Computer vision algorithms can demand the modeling of long-range spatial correlations which do not always conform to hardware connectivity limits.

Because the algorithm's requirements often mismatch the hardware topology, the quantum circuits must be compiled with additional SWAP gates to move quantum information between qubits, leading to substantially increased circuit depth and greater error accumulation. Quantum hardware with one-dimensional connectivity or more limited two-dimensional connectivity can be of particular importance to the compilation overhead of computer vision algorithms with two-dimensional image data as input and output. Such a strategy is illustrated in Figure 7.10. Architectural solutions demonstrate how different qubit-arrangement strategies can mitigate hardware topology constraints without incurring additional overhead from SWAP gates that would otherwise increase circuit depth and error propagation (Lee et al., 2025).

Emerging quantum hardware systems have begun to address some connectivity limitations by adopting more flexible architectures and coupling schemes. However, a fundamental challenge remains: achieving arbitrary connectivity patterns is still difficult and often prohibitively costly for current quantum devices. The mismatch between quantum and classical computation can limit the types of computer-vision algorithms that are practical on quantum hardware. Scalability analyses illustrate how connectivity constraints affect circuit depth and parameter requirements. These underlying resource trade-offs, which restrict the scope of quantum computer-vision algorithm implementation, are depicted in Figure 7.11 (Lee et al., 2025).

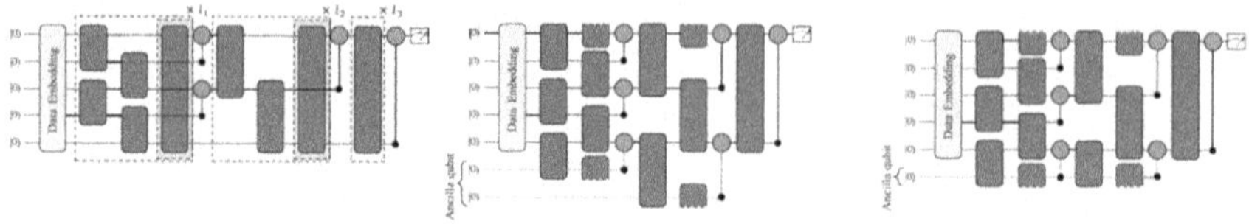

(a) Skip pooling (b) Layer-wise qubit padding (c) Single-ancilla qubit padding

Figure 7.10: Arbitrary data QCNN architectures (Lee et al., 2025).

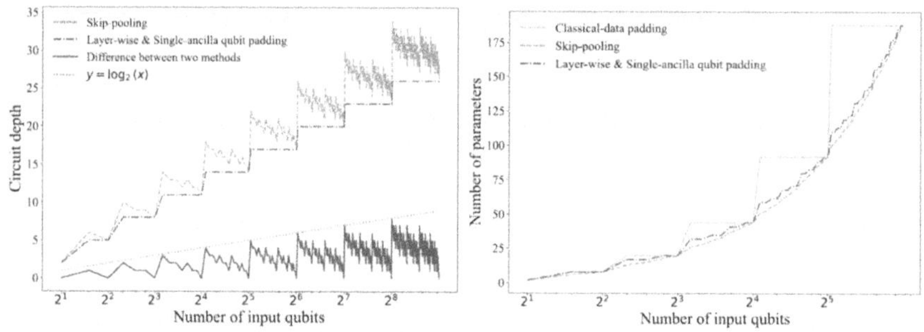

(a) (b)

Figure 7.11: Quantum resource scaling for QCNN methods (Lee et al., 2025).

7.6.3 Algorithmic and Theoretical Limitations

In addition to hardware limitations, quantum computer vision has underlying algorithmic and theoretical difficulties which need not be resolved even with ideal quantum hardware. These issues amount to the fact that we have not fully understood the nature of quantum machine learning and the multifaceted nature of the connection between quantum computational benefits and real-world computer vision tasks.

The unproven quantum benefits to real-world computer vision problems is perhaps the greatest theoretical issue in the area. Most proposed quantum computer vision algorithms do not demonstrate provable quantum advantages over classical methods when all overheads are properly accounted for, including state preparation costs, measurement overhead, and error correction requirements. The theoretical analysis typically focuses on isolated algorithmic components while ignoring the systems-level costs that dominate practical implementations.

More recent research by Huang et al. (2021) explored the power of data in quantum machine learning, and as an example, the investigation suggested that the benefits of quantum machine learning could be restricted to extremely narrow classes of datasets and learning problems. They found that quantum algorithms generally need exponentially more training data to induce similar generalization behavior as classical algorithms, which could negate the practical benefits of quantum algorithms even in cases where quantum algorithms give speed advantages with respect to training.

Data needs of quantum machine learning are especially challenging when using computer vision which frequently involves large scale data sets of complicated statistical structure. Quantum machine learning algorithms can require exponentially many labelled examples to learn well, and are thus unfeasible in applications where data is costly or time-intensive to collect. Even problems in which quantum algorithms give computational speedups may be disfavoured by the increased data requirements.

Training problems and barren plateaus pose a problem to many variational quantum algorithms, and it is very difficult to train with the system size increasing past toy problems. Such occurrences of barren plateau appears to be generic to randomized variational quantum circuits, and suggests that this is a generic feature, not an engineering problem that can be resolved by more algorithm design.

Recent studies have found a number of techniques to reduce barren plateaus, among them being parameter initialization with structure, circuit architecture with careful design, and other computational strategies like evolutionary algorithms or Bayesian optimization. None of these methods have, however, offered general solutions that are reliable in many problem types and system sizes.

A deeper comprehension of quantum machine learning is a larger theoretical issue that pervades all areas of quantum computer vision studies. Theoretical principles of quantum machine learning are still unfinished, and numerous open questions on the connection between quantum circuit expressivity and classical neural network abilities are still unresolved. In the absence of explicit theoretical directions, researchers have to depend on an empirical exploration which is grossly limited by hardware limitations.

The connection between quantum entanglement and machine learning performance is also an area that is least understood, even though entanglement is regarded as one of the most important resources in quantum computation. Recent experimental studies by Bowles, Ahmed and Schuld (2024) propose that entanglement might not be advantageous to typical machine learning work, which defies basic hypotheses on the benefits of quantum machine learning. The application of other types of quantum resources like quantum coherence and quantum interference as applied to machine learning is not extensively studied.

7.7 Realistic Applications and Future Prospects

7.7.1 Near-Term Educational and Research Applications

Although it is still a few years before practical applications of quantum computer vision can occur, there are opportunities to demonstrate close-term demonstration cases to help in the development of the subject and better understand its potential and constraints. These applications serve important purposes in developing the theoretical foundations and practical expertise needed for eventual quantum computer vision systems.

Educational and research tools represent one of the most immediately valuable applications of quantum computer vision algorithms, serving as platforms for teaching quantum computing concepts and exploring the relationship between quantum mechanics and information processing. Quantum computer vision is a tool that allows demonstrations of quantum computing to allow students and researchers to learn the more abstract ideas of quantum computing by performing familiar computer vision tasks.

The principal principles of quantum computing, including superposition, entanglement, and measurement can be taught using simple examples of quantum image processing, e.g., quantum edge detection or simple pattern recognition on small images. Practical quantum benefits are not necessary to generate value with these educational applications, since they are mainly pedagogical and not computational. Efficient visuality of computer vision renders quantum effects more intuitive and accessible to countermeasures of abstract mathematical models.

Nevertheless, education applications should be crafted in such a way so as not to reinforce the false beliefs about the capabilities and timescales of quantum computing. A large number of quantum computer vision applications use extremely naive problems that can provide false signals regarding the scalability and applicability of quantum methods in practice. Educational resources should concentrate on the current limitations and potential future benefits to provide realistic expectations of how quantum computer vision will evolve.

Another useful area to consider in the near-term usage of quantum devices is benchmarking and algorithm development where the existing quantum devices can offer useful platforms to investigate the various quantum computer vision algorithms and their performance properties. Quantum algorithms on standardized benchmarks can be compared systematically to identify promising methods and to learn the origins of quantum benefits or drawbacks.

An example of rigorous methodology evaluation that could and must be applied to quantum computer vision algorithms is the benchmarking studies by Bowles, Ahmed and Schuld (2024). Their methodical comparison of quantum and classical approaches to various datasets and performance metrics is insightful on the circumstances in which quantum approaches can be helpful. Further research directions could be informed by similar comprehensive studies done with computer vision tasks in particular.

The platform of developing algorithms with the help of modern quantum hardware allows researchers to test the concepts of quantum computer vision at scales that, although still limited, can give important insights into the challenges and opportunities of quantum solutions. It is possible on these platforms, to explore quantum circuit design strategies, optimization methods, and hybrid quantum-classical integration strategies that will assume importance in future practice.

7.7.2 Specialized Niche Applications and Emerging Opportunities

Certain specialized applications might benefit from quantum approaches sooner than general-purpose image processing tasks, particularly in domains where the structure of the problem naturally aligns with quantum computational advantages or where classical methods face fundamental limitations.

High-dimensional correlation analysis represents one potential near-term application area where quantum approaches might provide advantages for computer vision tasks involving analysis of correlations in very high-dimensional feature spaces. Quantum systems can naturally represent and manipulate correlations between exponentially many variables, potentially enabling more efficient analysis of complex relationships in visual data.

Medical imaging applications that require analysis of subtle correlations across large numbers of image features could potentially benefit from quantum correlation analysis techniques. For example, early disease detection often requires identifying weak correlations between many image features that may be difficult for classical methods to detect reliably. Such applications may be of benefit to quantum algorithms capable of analyzing high-dimensional correlation structures efficiently.

Nevertheless, the application of quantum benefits to correlation analysis encounters the same technical issues as other quantum computer vision tasks, such as overhead of state preparation and cost of measurement. The quantum benefits should be enormous such that they can address these overheads, which can restrict them to very narrow problem structures where quantum approaches can offer dramatic advantages over classical approaches.

Integration and deployment of quantum sensors is another possible near-term application field where quantum computer vision systems could be of natural benefit. As quantum sensors keep being developed for use in gravitational wave sensors, magnetic field sensors, and biological imaging, quantum computer vision systems may offer more intuitive interfaces into processing quantum sensor data without making the conversion into classical representations.

The integration of quantum sensors and quantum processing could potentially avoid some of the state preparation and measurement overhead challenges that limit other quantum computer vision applications. If sensor data already exists in quantum form, quantum processing algorithms might operate directly on quantum sensor outputs without requiring expensive classical-to-quantum conversion steps.

However, current quantum sensors typically operate at different physical scales and timescales than quantum computers, making direct integration challenging. Quantum sensors often require extreme isolation from environmental disturbances, while quantum computers need sophisticated control systems that could interfere with sensitive quantum measurements. An example of the rigorous evaluation methodology that should be applied to quantum computer vision algorithms is the benchmarking studies conducted by Bowles, Ahmed and Schuld (2024). Their systematic comparison of quantum and classical algorithms with reference to different datasets and performance measures is helpful in their perceiving situations when quantum algorithms can be beneficial.

Similar thorough research conducted with special references to computer vision tasks would guide the directions of future studies. Integrating quantum sensors and quantum computers may be a technical challenge. It is an exclusive field where quantum computer vision can possess exclusive capabilities that have never been achieved by classical devices, particularly quantum cryptography and security applications.

Quantum key distribution and quantum authentication protocols could potentially be enhanced by quantum computer vision systems that can verify identity or detect tampering using quantum-mechanical properties that cannot be forged classically.

Quantum digital watermarking and steganography applications could embed quantum information in classical images in ways that provide unconditional security guarantees based on the fundamental principles of quantum mechanics. Such applications would not necessarily require quantum computational advantages but would leverage the unique properties of quantum information to provide security features impossible with classical systems.

7.7.3 Long-Term Speculative Applications and Vision

Assuming major advances in quantum hardware and algorithms, several long-term applications might eventually benefit from quantum computer vision approaches, though these remain highly speculative and depend on breakthroughs that may or may not occur within reasonable timeframes.

Large-scale image database processing represents one potential long-term application where quantum algorithms for unstructured search might eventually enable more efficient processing of very large image databases. Grover's quantum search algorithm provides quadratic speedups for searching unsorted databases, which could theoretically accelerate image retrieval and similarity search tasks that are fundamental to many computer vision applications.

Nevertheless, there are significant obstacles to the practice of realizing the benefits of quantum searching in information databases, other than the actual implementation of the algorithm. The typical image similarity search involves complicated feature extraction and comparison functions which might not inherently be represented by the structure demanded by quantum search algorithms. The computational advantages may be obviated by the overhead of the preparation of image data in the form needed by quantum search algorithms.

In addition, the classical techniques of large-scale image search are rapidly advancing with better indexing schemes, machine learning feature extraction and ways of parallel computation. The classical threshold which quantum approaches have to surpass is continually lowered and quantum benefits are becoming harder and harder to realize in practice.

Another hypothetical long-term application of quantum parallelism is real-time video analysis, which may one day be performed in real-time on high-resolution video streams and with highly complex processing needs, given quantum parallelism. The huge parallelism which might be present in quantum systems may in theory be able to provide parallel processing of multiple frames, multiple objects, or multiple analysis tasks which would demand serial processing on different classical systems.

Quantum video analysis systems could take advantage of quantum superposition to solve a set of tracking hypotheses in parallel or quantum entanglement to provide a more efficient way to preserve correlations between objects in more than two frames compared to classical algorithms. Nevertheless, these apps would need quantum systems that have been coherent much longer than what is currently possible and minimal error rates much smaller than what is currently possible with hardware.

The real-time constraints of video analysis applications create additional challenges for quantum implementation, as quantum algorithms typically require multiple executions to achieve reliable results through statistical averaging. The measurement overhead and error correction requirements could make quantum video analysis impractical even with substantial hardware improvements.

The future may allow advanced quantum machine learning to allow computer vision systems to learn and adapt in fundamentally different ways than classical systems. Neural networks of quantum computers with exponential-size parameter spaces may be capable of describing more intricate visual signals and associations than their classical counterparts with equivalent physical parameters.

There is the potential for quantum generative models to produce more realistic synthetic images using quantum superposition to represent probability distributions in exponentially large image spaces. The recent study by Xiao et al. (2024) of quantum deep generative priors with programmable quantum circuits is an early attempt at such applications but at present only simple image generation tasks are demonstrated.

Nevertheless, the practical benefits of quantum machine learning to computer vision are hypothetical and conditional upon the answer to some theoretical questions about quantum learning theory that remain unresolved. The relationship between quantum circuit expressivity and generalization performance is poorly understood, and it remains unclear whether quantum neural networks would provide practical advantages over classical networks even with perfect quantum hardware.

7.8 Critical Assessment and Future Research Directions

7.8.1 Realistic Timeline and Expectation Management

Based on recent developments in quantum hardware and comprehensive evaluation of quantum machine learning algorithms, the timeline for practical quantum computer vision applications requires careful reassessment that balances optimism about long-term potential with realism about near-term limitations and fundamental challenges.

Near-term prospects (2–5 years) must be evaluated in light of recent hardware developments and algorithmic advances. An announcement by Google in December 2024 of Willow processor is a major advance in the field of quantum error correction, making the key breakthrough of less than threshold error correction with logical qubits performing better than physical qubits. Nevertheless, the distance between demonstrations of error correction and implementation is still significant, and experts note that the existing systems can at best be described as being too small to perform useful computations, and that systems based on quantum computers will need millions of qubits to be practically implemented (Neven, 2025).

Bowles, Ahmed and Schuld (2024) benchmarking studies have a sobering impact on near-term expectations, and they have shown that classical machine learning models are always best in quantum classifiers in a broad variety of tasks. Besides, the fact of their discovery, addition of entanglement usually enhances performance, contradicting basic arguments on the origin of quantum benefits in machine learning applications. These findings imply that the short-term priority must be to find out when and why quantum methods may have benefits and not to assume that quantum methods will automatically be helpful compared to classical methods.

The near-term future is also limited by the fact that classical computer vision techniques have been advancing fast with similar realized gains to performance, efficiency and capability. Massive vision transformers, self-supervised learning algorithms and efficient neural architecture pose an accelerating challenge to quantum methods that eventually will need to beat it. The classical baseline is still improving at a faster rate that might be even faster than quantum hardware development and thus quantum benefits are even harder to realize.

The medium-term future (5–15 years) is based on the progress of both quantum hardware and algorithmic knowledge that cannot be certain but possible within a range. The scale and fidelity needed to execute more sophisticated algorithms can be attained using quantum error correction, but the overhead will still be large. Remarkably specialized applications to inherently quantum data sources or very fine-tuned computational structure might start to demonstrate practical advantage at this time.

Nevertheless, the medium-term timeline entails breakthroughs in quantum designing of algorithms which would tackle more fundamental issues like the barren plateau problem and quantum-classical interface. Algorithms under development are at the fundamental limits of scalability and trainability, and novel algorithm solutions are yet to be found. Theoretical knowledge of quantum machine learning needs to develop significantly before the implementation of a practical application is possible.

Long-term outlooks (15+ years) are also very hypothetical and rely on findings that might or might not be. The eventual success of quantum computer vision will probably be found in locating operation areas where quantum properties give essential benefits which cannot be achieved by the development of classical systems. These advantages must be substantial enough to justify the additional complexity and resource requirements of quantum systems.

The long-term timeline also depends on the evolution of classical computing, which may incorporate quantum-inspired methods or other paradigms that capture some of the theoretical advantages of quantum approaches without requiring full quantum hardware. The boundary between quantum and classical computing may become less distinct as both fields continue to advance.

7.8.2 Research Priorities and Strategic Directions

Fundamental theory development should receive highest priority in quantum computer vision research, as the field currently lacks the theoretical foundations necessary to identify problems with genuine quantum advantages. Priority should be given to theoretical investigations that could unambiguously define the problems of computer vision with quantifiable quantum gains with all its practical overheads (preparation of state, measurements and overhead correction costs).

The theoretical effort should be focused on the development of quantum complexity theory to computer vision in particular, what computational structures can be sped up quantumly and when quantum speedups are observed in actual visual processing problems. The discipline is an interdisciplinary endeavour of quantum information theorists, individuals in the machine learning community and researchers in computer vision to devise theoretical perspectives to understand the highly specialized requirements and limitations of visual information processing.

Recent advances of the quantum learning theory, such as the research by Huang et al. (2021) of the data strength in quantum machine learning, are useful backgrounds, which need to be translated into the computer vision case. The parameters that the quantum computer vision algorithms will demand to make it practically valuable are the following: its sample complexity demands and its generalization characteristics.

Another area of research priority that has not been adequately addressed in the quantum computer vision community is hardware-algorithm co-design. Combined optimization of quantum hardware platforms and computer vision algorithms may be more successful than the development of both hardware and software components separately. This study involves tight coordination between quantum hardware engineers and researchers in computer vision to learn the effects of hardware design decisions on algorithmic performance.

Co-design methods should consider specialized quantum architectures optimized to execute computer vision tasks, such as quantum processors whose connectivity patterns conform to the spatial structure of an image, or quantum systems that are optimized to the types of linear algebra operations often found in computer vision algorithms. These specialized architectures may be of practical use even when general-purpose quantum computers fail to demonstrate quantum speedups to computer vision tasks.

Quantum-classical computer vision systems involving research in the area of hybrid systems must focus on the most effective integration strategies in quantum-classical system development, and an appreciation that in practice quantum computer vision applications will consist of complex systems of quantum and classical process units. The present research will propose theoretical perspectives of the division of the computational tasks to the most optimal between the quantum and classical systems and the physical framework of implementation of such hybrid methods.

The hybrid systems work needs to respond to simple queries on quantum processing in relation to the computer vision pipeline to maximize the system performance. This requires a familiarity with the computational complexity of individual elements and the cost of communication and coordination relative to hybrid quantum-classical processing.

7.8.3 Standards and Methodology Development

The quantum computer research vision community should calculate standards of experimental evaluation and contrast with classical approaches so that the labor of research will give a real understanding of quantum abilities that is not imposed by experimental research design choice. Publication standards should require a very high standard of comparisons with state-of-the-art classical procedures, sufficient consideration of all the experimental overheads and statistical significance tests of the reported results.

Bowles, Ahmed and Schuld (2024) have identified the following pitfalls of quantum machine learning research, which include: (1) inefficient comparisons of a baselines; (2) cherry-picked data and (3) the lack of ability to consider the overall cost of quantum processing including overheads in state preparation and measurement. The narrowly focused benchmarking of quantum computer vision processes in particular would contribute to the establishment of the meaningful and fair comparison of different approaches.

Educational outreach should be delivered to both address the current limitations and potential future benefits in order to generate realistic expectations regarding the timelines and potentialities of the development of quantum computer vision. Learning materials should be clear-cut on what is theoretically achievable and what is practically achievable in order to make students and researchers understand how serious of a task it would be to ensure quantum computer vision becomes a reality.

There should be an open description of the underlying problems such as the measurement problem, decoherence which is a physical rather than an engineering problem and scaling which is a physical rather than an engineering constraint. These limited points are essential in realizing what is the boundary within which realistic research objectives should be pursued to avoid exaggerated optimistic speculations about the ability of quantum computers.

The investment should be on the development of the theoretical framework rather than the immediate development of applications because the theoretical framework should be in place for implementing practical applications. Research funding should be directed to projects that can answer fundamental questions of quantum benefits to computer vision in contrast to incremental benefits to existing quantum algorithms that have never demonstrated practical benefits.

Interdisciplinary research in quantum information theory, machine learning, and computer vision where these subfields interact in solving multidimensional problems at the intersection of these sciences should also be supported through the funding paradigm. Radical progress in quantum computer vision can be based on the work in other fields at a high level of inter-disciplinary interaction.

7.9 Conclusion

Quantum-inspired computer vision is both a fascinating and mostly theorization-driven area of research with significant practical implications that need to be rationalized and realistic expectations adequately managed. Despite the fact that the principles of quantum computing provide conceptually appealing models of visual information processing, the absence of hardware capability and complexity issues of algorithms does not permit the use of such conceptual frameworks in the near future.

A formal analysis of 160 datasets, trained on quantum machine learning models, had shown both that classical machine learning models are never as good in quantum classifiers and that entanglement removal can frequently lead to an improvement in performance. These findings challenge fundamental assumptions about the sources of quantum advantages in machine learning and suggest that the quantum computing community may have been overly optimistic about near-term quantum machine learning capabilities.

The hardware developments exemplified by Google's Willow processor announcement in December 2024 demonstrates significant progress in quantum error correction while simultaneously highlighting the enormous gap between current capabilities and practical application requirements. The achievement of below-threshold error correction represents a crucial scientific milestone, but experts acknowledge that current quantum systems remain "well too small to do useful calculations" and that practical quantum computers will require "millions of qubits" to solve important industry problems.

Experimental efforts are to-date confined to small-scale demonstrations which are well below the complexity of realistic applications, and most quantum computer vision algorithms are limited to the processing of tens (as opposed to millions of) pixels. NISQ devices can implement simple variational quantum circuits for toy vision problems, but scaling to realistic image sizes faces fundamental barriers in state preparation complexity, measurement overhead, and decoherence constraints that cannot be overcome through incremental hardware improvements alone.

The most successful quantum-inspired approaches to date are tensor network methods that run efficiently on classical computers while leveraging mathematical structures developed for quantum many-body physics. These methods demonstrate how concepts from quantum physics can inspire useful classical algorithms without requiring quantum hardware, providing practical tools that may eventually inform the design of quantum computer vision systems. The most developed results of interdisciplinary quantum computing and computer vision research are the use of tensor networks and quantum-inspired optimization methods.

The most promising line of approach in the near term is hybrid quantum-classical, although even hybrid methods experience serious problems in realizing practical benefits over fully classical methods. The quantum and the classical processing units co-operate to introduce further complexity and overhead that has to be offset by quantum benefits in particular computational problems.

Classical performance, efficiency and capability enhancement is exponentially growing and possibly quicker than quantum hardware, and achieving quantum performance might be more challenging. This rapidly emerging classical baseline should be included in the study of quantum computer vision and not in comparison with the fixed performance levels of the past.

The future would, most likely, require radical developments in quantum algorithms, enormous gains in the power of quantum devices, and careful delimiting of application areas where quantum gains can be identified despite the fact that quantum processing is now seen to impose enormous overheads.

References

Alvarez-Estevez, D. (2024). Benchmarking quantum machine learning kernel training for classification tasks. arXiv preprint, arXiv:2408.10274.

Biamonte, J., Wittek, P., Pancotti, N., Rebentrost, P., Wiebe, N. & Lloyd, S. (2017). Quantum machine learning. *Nature*, 549(7671), 195–202.

Bischof, L., Clawson, R. T., Diegelmann, L., Goldberg, A., Jerzak, Z., Schmitt, P. & Thanasilp, S. (2025). Hybrid quantum neural networks show strongly reduced need for free parameters in entity matching. *Scientific Reports*, 15(1), 4318.

Bowles, J., Ahmed, S. & Schuld, M. (2024). Better than classical? The subtle art of benchmarking quantum machine learning models. arXiv preprint, arXiv:2403.07059.

Cerezo, M., Arrasmith, A., Babbush, R., Benjamin, S. C., Endo, S., Fujii, K. et al. (2021). Variational quantum algorithms. *Nature Reviews Physics*, 3(9), 625–644.

Chen, G., Chen, Q., Long, S., Zhu, W., Yuan, Z. & Wu, Y. (2023). Quantum convolutional neural network for image classification. *Pattern Analysis and Applications*, 26(2), 655–667.

Cherrat, E. A., Kerenidis, I., Mathur, N., Landman, J., Steffens, M. & Prakash, S. (2024). Quantum vision transformers. *Quantum*, 8, 1265.

Dunjko, V. & Briegel, H. J. (2018). Machine learning & artificial intelligence in the quantum domain: A review of recent progress. *Reports on Progress in Physics*, 81(7), 074001.

Grant, E., Benedetti, M., Cao, S., Hallam, A., Lockhart, J., Stojevic, V. et al. (2018). Hierarchical quantum classifiers. *npj Quantum Information*, 4(1), 65.

Havlíček, V., Córcoles, A. D., Temme, K., Harrow, A. W., Kandala, A., Chow, J. M. & Gambetta, J. M. (2019). Supervised learning with quantum-enhanced feature spaces. *Nature*, 567(7747), 209–212.

Heidari, S., Dinneen, M. J. & Delmas, P. (2024). Quantum annealing for computer vision minimization problems. *Future Generation Computer Systems*, 156, 28–40.

Henderson, M., Shakya, S., Pradhan, S. & Cook, T. (2020). Quanvolutional neural networks: Powering image recognition with quantum circuits. *Quantum Machine Intelligence*, 2(1), 2.

Huang, H. Y., Broughton, M., Mohseni, M., Babbush, R., Boixo, S., Neven, H. & McClean, J. R. (2021). Power of data in quantum machine learning. *Nature Communications*, 12(1), 2631.

Jahromi, S. S. & Orús, R. (2024). Variational tensor neural networks for deep learning. *Scientific Reports*, 14(1), 19017.

Kharsa, R., Bouridane, A. & Amira, A. (2023). Advances in quantum machine learning and deep learning for image classification: A survey. *Neurocomputing*, 563, 126943.

Lee, C., Araujo, I. F., Kim, D., Lee, J., Park, S., Ryu, J.-Y. & Park, D. K. (2025). Optimizing quantum convolutional neural network architectures for arbitrary data dimension. *Frontiers in Physics*, 13, 1529188.

Le, P. Q., Dong, F. & Hirota, K. (2011). A flexible representation of quantum images for polynomial preparation, image compression, and processing operations. *Quantum Information Processing*, 10(1), 63–84.

Lloyd, S., Mohseni, M. & Rebentrost, P. (2014). Quantum principal component analysis. *Nature Physics*, 10(9), 631–633.

Mandadapu, P., Kumar, S. A., Gunjan, V. K. & Kumar, S. (2024). Exploring quantum-enhanced machine learning for computer vision: Applications and insights on noisy intermediate-scale quantum devices. arXiv preprint, arXiv:2404.02177.

Mari, A., Bromley, T. R., Izaac, J., Schuld, M. & Killoran, N. (2020). Transfer learning in hybrid classical-quantum neural networks. *Quantum*, 4, 340.

McClean, J. R., Boixo, S., Smelyanskiy, V. N., Babbush, R. & Neven, H. (2018). Barren plateaus in quantum neural network training landscapes. *Nature Communications*, 9(1), 4812.

Neven, H. (2025). Meet Willow, our state-of-the-art quantum chip. *The Keyword,* 12 June. Available at: https://blog.google/technology/research/google-willow-quantum-chip/ (Accessed: 30 August 2025).

Newman, E., Grama, A. & Ribeiro, A. (2024). Stable tensor neural networks for efficient deep learning. *Frontiers in Big Data*, 7, 1363978.

Nielsen, M. A. and Chuang, I. L. (2010). Quantum computation and quantum information. 10th Anniversary Ed. Cambridge: Cambridge University Press.

Preskill, J. (2018). Quantum computing in the NISQ era and beyond. *Quantum*, 2, 79.

Rebentrost, P., Mohseni, M. & Lloyd, S. (2014). Quantum support vector machine for big data classification. *Physical Review Letters*, 113(13), 130503.

Schuld, M. & Killoran, N. (2019). Quantum machine learning in feature Hilbert spaces. *Physical Review Letters*, 122(4), 040504.

Singh, P., Hardikar, B. A. & Johri, S. (2024). Coherent feed-forward quantum neural network. *Quantum Machine Intelligence*, 6(1), 72.

Stoudenmire, E. & Schwab, D. J. (2016). Supervised learning with tensor networks. In: *Advances in Neural Information Processing Systems*, 4799–4807.

Tacchino, F., Macchiavello, C., Gerace, D. & Bajoni, D. (2019). An artificial neuron implemented on an actual quantum processor. *npj Quantum Information*, 5(1), 26.

Xiao, T., Zhai, X., Huang, J., Li, Y., Fan, J. & Zeng, G. (2024). Quantum deep generative prior with programmable quantum circuits. *Communications Physics*, 7(1), 276.

Zhang, Y., Lu, K., Gao, Y. & Wang, M. (2013). NEQR: A novel enhanced quantum representation of digital images. *Quantum Information Processing*, 12(8), 2833–2860.

CHAPTER

8

Quantum-Inspired Approaches in Healthcare and Bioinformatics

Sara Ali[1*], **Polla Fattah**[2] **and Sanar Fawzi**[3]

[1] Department of Computer Science and Engineering, University of Kurdistan Hewlêr

[2] Department of Computer Science and Engineering, University of Kurdistan Hewlêr Salahaddin University Research Center, Salahaddin University, Erbil

[3] Software Engineering; Salahaddin University, Erbil

Healthcare and bioinformatics are associated with vast highly dimensional data with inherent uncertainties. Quantum-inspired architectures are based on quantum mechanics, superposition, entanglement and interference, to redesign medical data processing operations more efficiently.

Quantum-inspired neural networks have an initial positive response in genomics and medical imaging. Tensor network techniques compress the overall genomic sequences efficiently and quantum-inspired PCA shows a small-scale improvement in feature retrieval from medical images. One of the most popular models is the hybrid quantum-classical system which combines quantum-inspired processing with the reliability of established machine learning methods.

Nevertheless, many implementations remain poor due to current technological limitations. Existing quantum computers may rely on noisy qubits and exhibit error rates of 0.1–1% per qubit. Simulating drug-sized molecules through molecular modeling would require thousands to millions of logical qubits, a scale unlikely to be achievable before the 2030s. Key obstacles include state-preparation overhead, measurement costs, decoherence and barren plateau issues.

The most successful near-term approaches are quantum-inspired classical algorithms, tensor networks and optimization methods, in a conventional computer. These provide continuous advances in the discovery of drugs, optimization of personalized medicine and optimization of healthcare logistics without the need to have quantum hardware.

*Corresponding author: sara.sardar.ali@gmail.com

DOI: 10.1201/9781003682950-8

Although quantum-enhanced molecular property prediction and clinical decision support are promising, clinical validation and benefits are limited and still going on. Even in the case of healthcare, it is most likely to take 10–20+ years before practical quantum advantage is realized due to quantum hardware breakthroughs and regulatory approval.

8.1 Introduction

Healthcare and bioinformatics are among the most complicated computational concepts in contemporary science, which are associated with vast data volumes, highly dimensional data, and inherently uncertain. Biological systems can be complex at many different scales, such as quantum mechanical interactions between molecules, and epidemiologically-related patterns in a population. Although traditional methods of computation have mostly performed well, they are limited by the fact that they require exponential scaling of some biological problems, that they must be able to model quantum effects within molecular systems, and that they have to be able to address uncertainty in a principled way.

Classical machine learning has been very successful in medical field applications such as diagnostic imaging to drug discovery. According to recent, extensive reviews, the intersection between quantum computing and healthcare applications has been on the rise (Marengo and Santamato, 2025; Chow, 2024). Deep learning models can currently compete and even surpass the human capability of performing particular tasks such as radiology image interpretation and pathology diagnoses. Nonetheless, there are also some issues in healthcare, which cannot be solved by classical methods only. These include accurately modeling molecular systems for drug-discovery tasks, solving optimization problems with exponentially large solution spaces, and pattern-recognition tasks that require capturing complex, high-dimensional correlations.

Although in its infancy, quantum computing offers theoretical benefits for certain categories of problems relevant to healthcare. Superposition, entanglement, and interference, the core principles of quantum mechanics, enable new computational models that may overcome some of the limitations of classical computing. Nevertheless, current quantum devices remain constrained by noise, decoherence, and limited scale making most envisioned healthcare applications infeasible on today's real quantum machines.

Quantum-inspired classical algorithms are more practically feasible as they mimic concepts from quantum mechanics, without requiring quantum hardware. These methods apply mathematical techniques originally developed for quantum systems but implement them on conventional computers. Examples include tensor-network approaches, quantum circuit-inspired variational algorithms, and optimization methods based on the principles of quantum annealing.

Figure 8.1 illustrates the tensor network structures which give the mathematical basis of quantum inspired classical algorithms in healthcare applications. In particular, Matrix Product States have been useful in one-dimensional patterns of correlation typical of genomic sequences, and PEPS can model more complex two-dimensional patterns of correlation that are useful in medical imaging data (Orús, 2019).

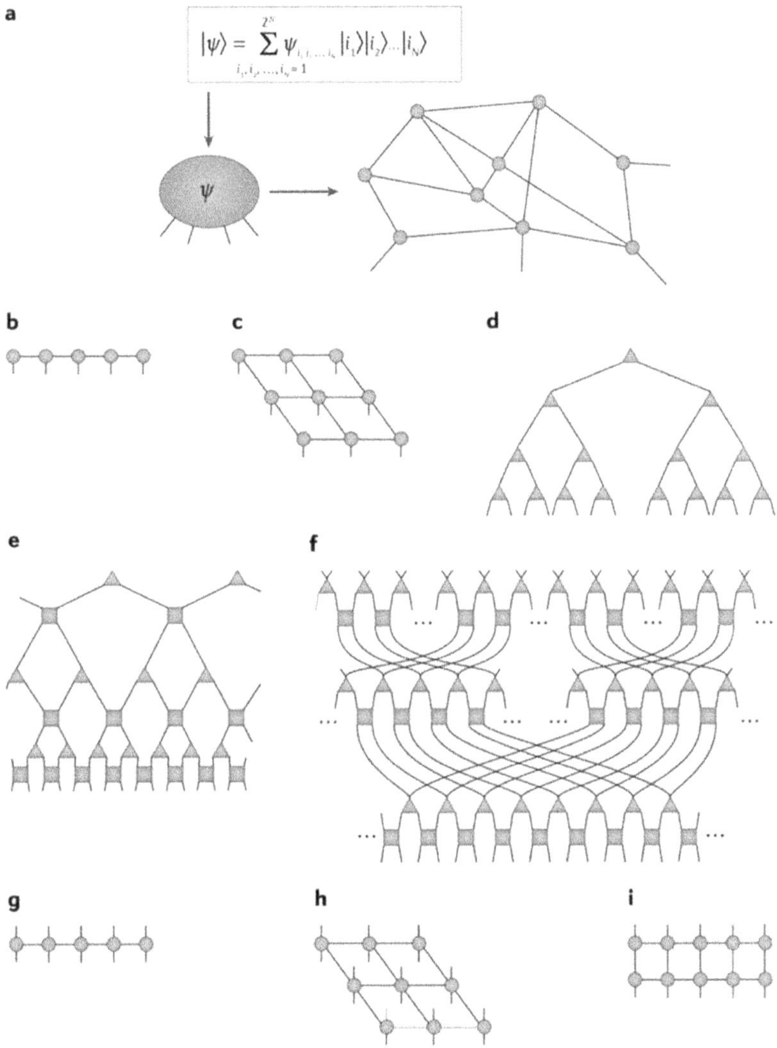

Figure 8.1: Tensor network architectures (Orús, 2019).

In this chapter, the author examines the potential of quantum computing in healthcare as well as the practical application of quantum-inspired classical algorithms. We draw a clear distinction between speculative future possibilities and the capabilities that can be demonstrated today, providing a realistic assessment of the role of these technologies and their likely trajectory. This analysis considers current research findings, technical constraints, cost-efficiency, and the practical timeline for successful implementation.

8.1.1 Current State of Quantum Computing in Healthcare

True large-scale quantum computers have not yet been realized due to fundamental physical and engineering constraints. Current quantum devices operate with only tens to hundreds of qubits and typically exhibit error rates of 0.1–1% per operation. These error rates mean that useful quantum computations are limited to relatively small, shallow circuits with only a modest number of operations before noise overwhelms the system and eliminates any potential quantum advantage.

The most sophisticated quantum computers currently on the market are the 1000+ qubit systems at IBM (which include the dilution refrigerator), Google (its Sycamore processors), and quantum annealers (created by the D-Wave). Nonetheless, such systems have serious problems:

- **Coherence times:** Are of the order of microseconds such that quantum states usually do not last long before they are destroyed by decoherence
- **Gate fidelities:** Individual quantum operations have error rates that limit circuit depth
- **Connectivity:** Physical qubits are typically connected to only a few neighbors, constraining algorithm implementation
- **Read-out errors:** Measuring quantum states introduces additional errors

Even with these shortcomings, the discipline is developing at a high pace. Major technology companies (IBM, Google, Microsoft, Amazon) as well as startups (IonQ, Rigetti, PsiQuantum) are investing heavily in quantum hardware development. New quantum algorithms and applications are being developed at research institutions in the world. There is a significant growth in quantum research funding by the government, and national quantum programs in the US, Europe, and China, among others. The present scenario in the application of quantum computing to healthcare is reviewed in a systematic manner, demonstrating their potential contributions to healthcare, as well as considerable technical limitations (Flother, 2023).

8.1.2 Healthcare Applications

In healthcare, there are a number of problem types that can be effectively tackled leveraging the theoretical benefits of quantum computing:

Optimization problems arise in nearly every area of healthcare, including drug-molecule design, treatment-plan optimization, and the allocation of hospital resources. Many of these challenges involve searching exponentially large solution spaces, where quantum algorithms such as the Quantum Approximate Optimization Algorithm (QAOA) or quantum annealing may prove useful.

Medical imaging, genomics and clinical-diagnosis pattern-recognition tasks are typically associated with high-dimensional data and complex correlations. Quantum machine-learning learning algorithms may offer advantages for certain types of pattern recognition, particularly in situations where quantum superposition can be used to model and process large numbers of patterns simultaneously.

Molecular simulation is essential to drug discovery and biology. Because molecules are quantum-mechanical in nature, quantum computers may be capable of exponentially superior performance on molecular-simulation tasks compared with classical computers, which must approximate quantum behavior.

Quantum technology in cryptography may help secure sensitive medical information in two key ways: quantum cryptography can offer theoretically unbreakable security through quantum key distribution, while quantum computers pose a potential threat to the classical encryption algorithms currently used to protect medical data.

Nevertheless, the gap between potential and practical application remains enormous. The detailed pipeline in Figure 8.2 illustrates how quantum computing can be integrated into current drug-discovery workflows. This approach uses quantum computers for the most quantum-mechanical components of molecular simulation while relying on classical computers for pre-processing and result analysis, representing a realistic pathway toward achieving quantum advantage in pharmaceutical research (Li et al., 2024).

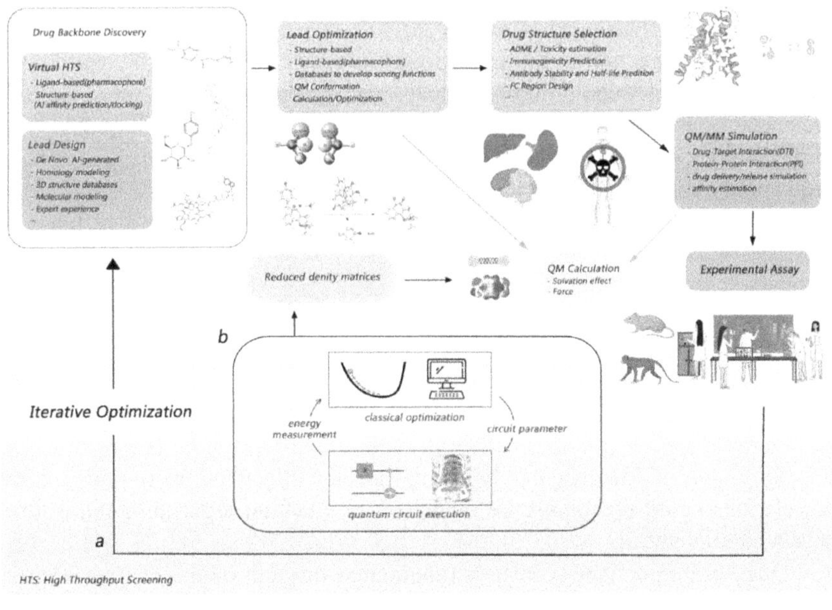

Figure 8.2: Hybrid quantum computing pipeline for drug discovery (Li et al., 2024).

Most proposed quantum advantages in healthcare require fault-tolerant quantum computers with thousands or millions of logical qubits, far beyond current capabilities. Near-term applications are limited to problems where quantum-inspired classical algorithms can provide incremental improvements or where small-scale quantum computations can contribute to hybrid quantum-classical algorithms.

8.2 Theoretical Foundations

8.2.1 Quantum Computing Principles Relevant to Healthcare

Quantum computing derives its potential computational advantages from several key principles that differ fundamentally from those of classical computing: Superposition allows quantum bits (qubits) to exist in a combination of 0 and 1 states simultaneously. Mathematically, a qubit state can be written as:

$$|\psi\rangle = \alpha|0\rangle + \beta|1\rangle \tag{8.1}$$

where α and β are complex probability amplitudes that must satisfy the normalization condition:

$$|\alpha|^2 + |\beta|^2 = 1 \tag{8.2}$$

For n qubits, the quantum state exists in a superposition of 2^n computational basis states, potentially enabling parallel exploration of exponentially large solution spaces (Nielsen and Chuang, 2010).

In healthcare contexts, superposition could theoretically enable the simultaneous evaluation of multiple diagnostic hypotheses, treatment options, or molecular configurations. For example, a quantum algorithm for drug discovery might explore many molecular conformations at once, rather than evaluating them sequentially as classical algorithms must.

Entanglement creates quantum correlations between qubits that have no classical analogue. Entangled qubits cannot be described independently; their quantum states remain fundamentally correlated even when physically separated. Mathematically, an entangled two-qubit state cannot be written as a product of individual qubit states.

Entangled systems have mathematical representations capable of reproducing complex correlations that may be useful for understanding biological networks. For example, gene regulatory networks exhibit long-range correlations in which the expression of one gene can have multifaceted effects on many others. Such correlations could potentially be modelled by quantum algorithms rather than by classical methods.

Quantum algorithms can be strengthened through quantum interference, which amplifies correct answers while suppressing incorrect ones. Algorithms such as Grover's search and the quantum Fourier transform rely heavily on this principle. In quantum circuits, interference is produced by carefully designed sequences of quantum gates that cause the probability amplitudes of erroneous outcomes to interfere destructively, while the amplitudes of correct outcomes interfere constructively.

The principle may also be useful for pattern recognition in medical data, as quantum algorithms could enhance signals associated with disease patterns while suppressing noise and irrelevant features.

Quantum measurement produces probabilistic outcomes, which aligns naturally with the inherent uncertainties of medical decision-making. Unlike classical bits, whose values are well defined, the measurement of a quantum state is a probabilistic process governed by the Born rule:

$$P(|i\rangle) = |\langle i|\psi\rangle|^2 \tag{8.3}$$

the likelihood that measuring the state $|\psi\rangle$ will yield the outcome $|i\rangle$ is given by $|\langle i|\psi\rangle|^2$.

This probabilistic feature can be useful in medical contexts where uncertainty must be quantified. For example, diagnostic algorithms might naturally provide confidence limits on their predictions, and decision-support systems could generate probability distributions over possible treatment options (Nielsen and Chuang, 2010).

8.2.2 Quantum-Inspired Classical Methods

Since practical quantum computers remain limited, much current work focuses on quantum-inspired classical algorithms that use mathematical frameworks developed for quantum systems but run on conventional computers:

Tensor Networks are mathematical structures originally developed in quantum many-body physics that can efficiently represent high-dimensional data with complex correlations. The key insight is that many high-dimensional datasets possess underlying structure that allows them to be represented more compactly through tensor decompositions.

Matrix Product States (MPS) represent one-dimensional tensor networks in which a complex many-body quantum state is decomposed into a product of smaller matrices. For a system with n particles, each with d local dimensions, the full state space has dimension d^n. However, if the state has limited entanglement, it can be represented as an MPS with only $O(n\chi^2 d)$ parameters, where χ is the bond dimension that determines the amount of correlation that can be captured.

Tree Tensor Networks (TTN) extend this concept to hierarchical structures, which are common in biological systems. For example, protein structure can be viewed hierarchically, from amino acids to secondary structures to domains and ultimately to the complete fold. TTN can efficiently represent such hierarchical data while preserving important correlations across different scales.

Projected Entangled Pair States (PEPS) represent two-dimensional tensor networks that can model systems with more complex correlation structures. They may be applicable to spatial patterns in a medical image or the topology of interactions in a two dimensional biological network.

Variational Quantum Eigensolvers (VQE) are a class of quantum-classical hybrid algorithms originally developed for quantum chemistry applications. In this approach, the parameters of a quantum circuit (or a classical simulation of it) are optimized using a classical optimizer to minimize the energy of a molecular system.

Classical: The classical execution of VQE-inspired algorithms relies on parameterized classical circuits that mirror the structure of variational quantum circuits. These methods have been applied to optimization problems in protein folding and drug discovery, where the goal is to identify molecular configurations that minimize energy or maximize binding affinity.

Figure 8.3 illustrates how the algorithmic toolkit developed for tensor networks has found direct application in healthcare computing. Variational optimization methods originally designed for quantum many-body systems now enable efficient parameter learning in medical data analysis, while time-evolution algorithms support dynamic modelling of biological processes (Orús, 2019).

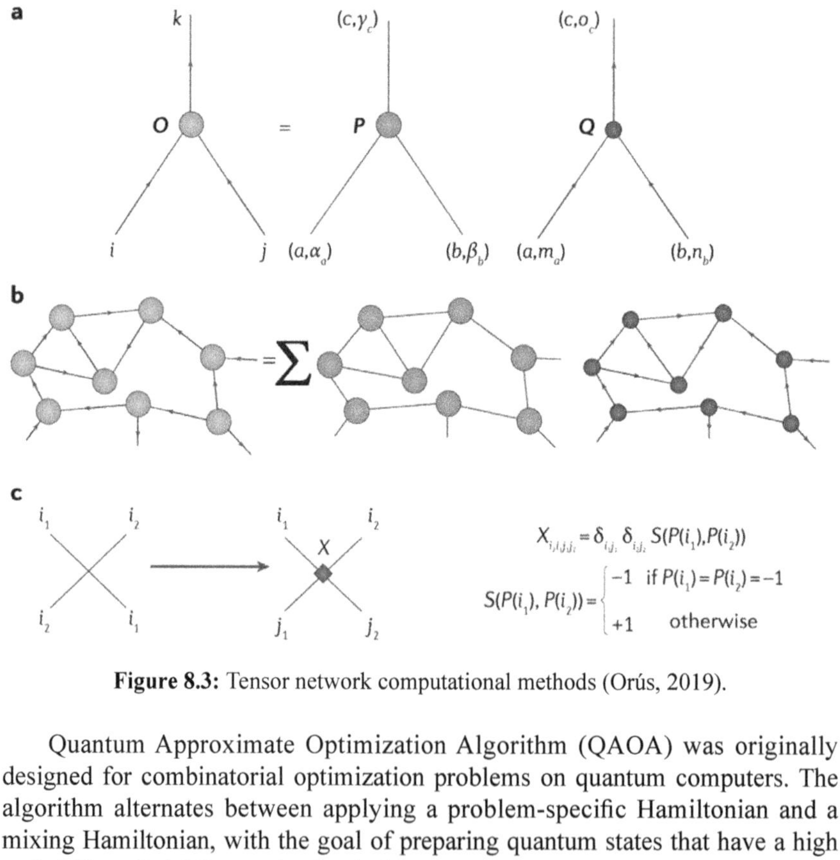

Figure 8.3: Tensor network computational methods (Orús, 2019).

Quantum Approximate Optimization Algorithm (QAOA) was originally designed for combinatorial optimization problems on quantum computers. The algorithm alternates between applying a problem-specific Hamiltonian and a mixing Hamiltonian, with the goal of preparing quantum states that have a high probability of yielding optimal solutions upon measurement.

Classical implementations of QAOA-inspired algorithms have been applied to healthcare logistics problems, such as optimizing hospital resource allocation, scheduling surgical procedures, and managing pharmaceutical supply chains. These problems often involve complex constraint structures that make them challenging for traditional optimization methods.

Quantum Machine Learning encompasses a variety of approaches that incorporate quantum-mechanical principles into classical machine-learning frameworks. These include quantum-inspired versions of principal component analysis, support vector machines, neural networks, and clustering algorithms.

For example, quantum-inspired principal component analysis can potentially identify the most important features in high-dimensional medical datasets more efficiently than classical PCA in certain circumstances. Quantum-inspired neural networks employ quantum mechanical concepts, such as superposition, to process information in ways that may not be accessible to classical neural networks.

Quantum Natural Gradient Descent is a more advanced optimization approach for variational quantum algorithms that incorporates the geometric structure of quantum state space. Unlike classical gradient descent, which relies on the Euclidean metric, quantum natural gradient descent uses the Fubini-Study metric, the natural Riemannian metric of quantum state manifolds.

Angle Encoding converts classical data into rotation angles in quantum gates, usually of RY or RZ rotation. The method is hardware-scalable and compatible with variational quantum circuits suitable for implementations in near-term medical data analysis.

Basis Encoding encodes the classical bits directly using computational basis states, and therefore needs one qubit per classical bit. It is not as efficient as amplitude encoding but is easy to implement, and is also applicable to discrete medical data such as diagnostic codes.

Encoding significantly influences the expressivity of quantum algorithms as well as their vulnerability to noise, making it a critical factor in healthcare applications where data fidelity is essential.

Quantum-Inspired Graph Algorithms uses concepts from quantum walks and graph theory to enable more efficient analysis of biological networks than many classical methods. These algorithms are particularly valuable for modeling protein-interaction networks, gene-regulation networks, and metabolic pathways.

Graph-based quantum walks provide a natural framework for studying network structure and dynamics. Unlike classical random walks, a quantum walk can explore multiple paths simultaneously through superposition, potentially identifying important features of a network more efficiently.

The quantum walks on graphs are continuous-time Schrödinger equations:

$$i\hbar \frac{\partial}{\partial t} |\psi(t)\rangle = \hat{H} |\psi(t)\rangle \tag{8.4}$$

Where H is the graph Laplacian or adjacency matrix. Graph kernels to machine learning on biological networks can be defined with these quantum walks (Nielsen and Chuang, 2010).

Quantum-inspired graph neural networks adopt the principles of quantum walk into classical neural network designs with quantum-inspired node embeddings and message-driven graph schemes. Such methods have demonstrated potential to predict protein functions, drug-protein interactions, and identification of disease genes in biological networks.

8.2.3 Biological Systems and Quantum Effects

The connection between biological and quantum mechanics is often misunderstood and remains challenging to articulate. Although biological systems are typically noisy, operating at warm temperatures and tend to decohere quantum states rapidly, there are nonetheless genuine quantum phenomena in biological processes:

Photosynthesis itself exhibits quantum coherence in light-harvesting complexes, where quantum-superposition states allow excitation energy to explore multiple pathways in parallel on its way to reaction centres, thereby identifying the most efficient route. This quantum effect makes photosynthetic energy transfer remarkably efficient, approaching the theoretical maximum.

Enzyme catalysis may involve quantum-tunneling, in which particles pass through energy barriers rather than over them. Such tunneling can dramatically accelerate certain chemical reactions and may contribute to the specificity and efficiency of enzymatic processes. Nevertheless, the extent to which quantum tunnelling influences enzyme activity remains an active area of research.

The **avian navigation** system can also been associated with quantum entanglement in cryptochrome proteins that help birds detect magnetic for orientation. The proposed mechanism involves pairs of electrons that become quantum-entangled, whose spin states are influenced by ambient magnetic fields, potentially providing a quantum compass.

Neural processing has also been suggested to involve quantum effects, particularly within neuronal microtubules. However, these proposals remain highly controversial, as the warm and noisy environment of the brain typically leads to decoherence on times scales which are far shorter than those required for neural computation.

It is important to note that most biological processes operate in regimes that can be adequately described using classical physics. The quantum states required for quantum computation are extremely delicate and are not typically sustained in cellular environments, which are warm and noisy. The coherence times observed in biological systems generally fall within the femtosecond-to-picosecond range whereas meaningful quantum computation requires coherence times that are orders of magnitude longer.

Quantum-inspired methods in biology are frequently of value through their mathematical structure, as opposed to providing a direct model of quantum biological behavior. Tensor networks, such as were created to study quantum many-body systems, have been created to be useful in analyzing classical biological data with complex correlation patterns due to their mathematical structure.

8.2.4 Computational Complexity Considerations

To understand when quantum algorithms can be useful, one must carefully consider computational complexity. Classical computers can solve many problems efficiently, and quantum advantages are not universal; they depend on the specific structure of the problem.

BQP (Bounded-error Quantum Polynomial time) is the complexity class of decision problems solvable by quantum computers in polynomial time with a bounded error probability. This class includes problems such as integer factoring (via Shor's algorithm) and unstructured search (via Grover's algorithm), which are believed to be difficult for classical computers but efficiently solvable on quantum computers.

For healthcare applications, relevant problems that may fall within BQP include certain types of molecular simulation, optimization problems with specific structural properties, and machine-learning tasks in which quantum superposition can be leveraged for parallel processing.

Quantum supremacy and quantum advantage are often confused but represent different concepts. Quantum supremacy refers to quantum computers performing any task faster than classical computers, even if the task is artificial and has no practical value. Quantum advantage, by contrast, refers to quantum computers solving practically important problems more effectively than classical computers.

Most healthcare applications require quantum advantage rather than mere quantum supremacy. The key question is whether quantum algorithms can solve important medical problems more effectively than the best classical algorithms, not simply whether they can solve any problem faster than classical computers.

Oracle problems represent a class of tasks in which quantum algorithms can provide provable advantages. In these problems, both classical and quantum algorithms have access to a "black box" function that they can query, and the goal is to learn properties of the function using as few queries as possible.

Some healthcare applications can be formulated as oracle problems. For example, drug discovery can be viewed as the task of searching for molecules with desired properties, where the "oracle" corresponds to expensive experimental testing or molecular simulation. Grover's algorithm could, in principle, provide quadratic speedups for such unstructured search problems.

8.3 Current Applications and Results

8.3.1 Medical Imaging and Pattern Recognition

Tensor-network decompositions have been applied by researchers to various types of medical images, including MRI, CT and microscopy data. Their main benefit is that, for suitable classes of images, tensor networks can encode the data efficiently without losing important spatial correlations that other compression or analysis techniques may discard.

A notable study by Stoudenmire and Schwab (2016) demonstrated that Matrix Product States can be used for supervised learning tasks, including image classification. While their initial work focused on handwritten digit recognition, subsequent researchers have applied similar approaches to medical imaging. For example, researchers at the University of California have used MPS-based methods to analyze histopathology images for cancer detection, achieving classification accuracy comparable to traditional convolutional neural networks while using fewer parameters.

Figure 8.4 shows the VQSE algorithm that can be scaled to healthcare systems that need a spectral analysis of high-dimensional data. It has also been found useful especially in medical imaging where conventional principal component analysis can fail to capture meaningful correlation patterns (Cerezo et al., 2022).

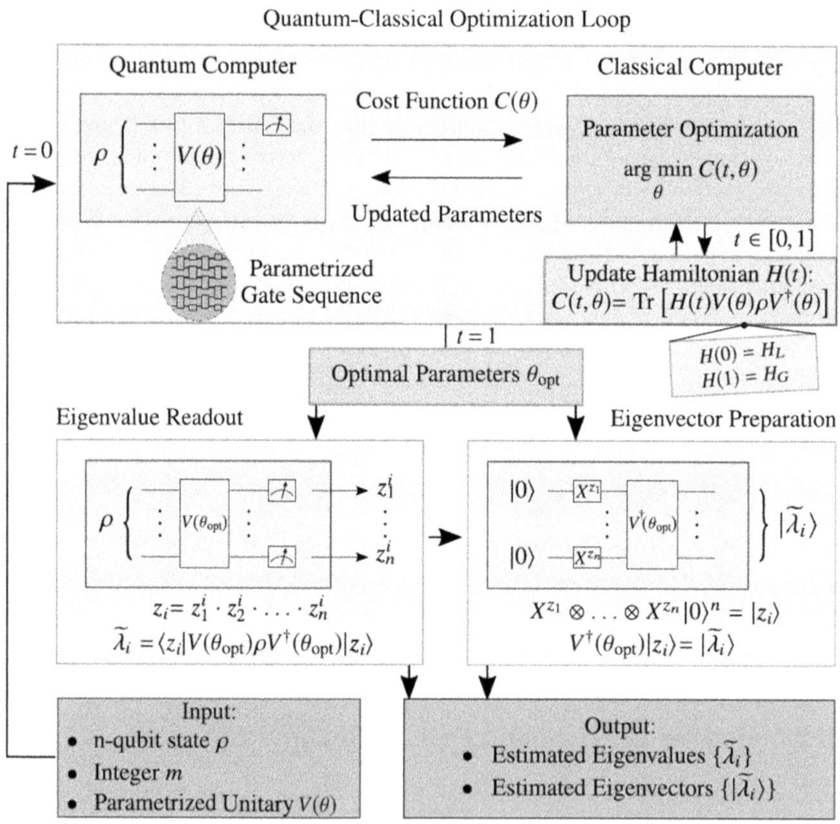

Figure 8.4: Algorithm of the variational quantum state eigensolver (Cerezo et al., 2022).

The benefits of tensor network solutions become especially evident in high-resolution medical images, where traditional methods struggle with computational complexity. In 3D medical imaging, the number of voxels can easily exceed millions, creating significant challenges for classical algorithms. Tensor networks can potentially provide more efficient representations for such high-dimensional data.

However, the practical advantages of tensor-network methods for medical imaging remain modest. Although they can offer computational efficiency gains for certain types of images, they do not consistently outperform well-optimized classical methods.Their effectiveness largely depends on the structure of medical images and the correlation patterns they contain.

Quantum-inspired feature-extraction algorithms are designed based on quantum techniques such as quantum principal component analysis (qPCA). Classical implementations of qPCA have been applied to medical-imaging data to identify the most significant features that can support diagnostic decision-making.

Recent quantum algorithms for performing principal component analysis have demonstrated a theoretical capability for exponential speedups (Smaldone et al., 2024), but classical quantum-inspired algorithms typically offer only modest improvements over standard PCA.

In medical imaging applications, quantum-inspired PCA has been tested on a wide range of datasets, including fMRI brain images, mammography, and retinal images. The results have been inconclusive: some studies report modest improvements in feature-extraction quality, while others find no significant advantage over classical methods.

Image reconstruction is another area in which quantum-inspired techniques have been applied. In medical imaging, high-resolution images can be reconstructed from incomplete or noisy measurements, such as in compressed-sensing MRI or low-dose CT imaging.

These inverse problems have been addressed using quantum-inspired optimization algorithms that rely on variational methods analogous to those used in quantum chemistry. The core idea is to encode the image using a quantum-inspired circuit and then determine the optimal parameters that best fit the available measurement, subject to sparsity or other regularization constraints.

Initial experiments have shown that quantum-inspired image reconstruction approaches can match the image quality of conventional algorithms while requiring fewer measurements. Recent innovations in quantum machine learning applied to medical imaging have demonstrated improved cancer-detection, performance with higher classification accuracy (Al-Azzabi et al., 2025), and error-mitigation techniques have made quantum-enhanced PET radiomic analysis a practical workflow (Moradi et al., 2023). However, the computational advantages remain modest overall, and classical methods continue to be more practical for most applications.

8.3.2 Drug Discovery and Molecular Simulation

Drug discovery represents one of the most promising application areas for quantum computing, as it involves the simulation of molecular systems that are inherently quantum mechanical. However, current quantum computers can handle only the simplest molecules, and practical applications remain limited.

Molecular simulation on quantum computers has been demonstrated for small molecules, but scaling to pharmaceutically relevant systems remains challenging. The fundamental advantage of quantum computers in this domain arises from the fact that molecules are quantum systems, so quantum computers should, in principle, be able to simulate them efficiently.

IBM has demonstrated quantum simulation of small molecules, including hydrogen (H_2), lithium hydride (LiH), and beryllium hydride (BeH_2) using variational quantum eigensolvers. Google has simulated similar systems using its Sycamore quantum processor. These demonstrations represent important proof-of-principle results, but the molecules involved are far smaller than typical drug candidates.

Pharmaceutically relevant molecules typically contain dozens to hundreds of atoms, requiring quantum computers with thousands to millions of logical qubits for accurate simulation. Current quantum devices have at most a few hundred physical qubits, and their high error rates make the simulation of drug-sized molecules impossible with today's technology.

The timeline for quantum computers to simulate pharmaceutically relevant molecules depends on continued advances in quantum hardware. Fault-tolerant quantum computers with full error correction will likely be required, and these are not expected to become available until the 2030s at the earliest.

Classical molecular simulation enhanced by quantum-inspired methods represents a more near-term opportunity. Classical techniques for molecular simulation, such as density functional theory (DFT) and molecular dynamics, face computational limitations that quantum-inspired optimization may help alleviate.

Variational quantum eigensolver (VQE) algorithms have been implemented classically and applied to molecular-simulation problems. These classical VQE approaches use parameterized classical circuits to approximate molecular wavefunctions and then optimize the parameters to minimize the molecular energy.

Results have been mixed: some studies show that classical VQE implementations can match or slightly exceed the accuracy of traditional DFT calculations for certain molecules, while others find no significant advantage. More recently, advances in quantum machine learning for drug discovery have produced more encouraging outcomes across diverse pharmaceutical applications (Smaldone et al., 2024), with AI-driven quantum chemistry methods demonstrating particular promise for molecular property prediction (Plé, 2025). Ultimately the effectiveness depends on the specific molecular system and the choice of variational ansatz.

Drug Discovery optimization problems are well suited to quantum-inspired approaches, even if full molecular simulation remains beyond current capabilities. Drug discovery requires searching and optimizing over vast chemical spaces, with an estimated 10^{60} possible drug-like molecules.

Classical implementations of quantum optimization algorithms have been applied to various aspects of drug discovery:

- Virtual screening of compound libraries to identify promising drug candidates
- Lead optimization to improve binding affinity, selectivity, and ADMET properties
- Retrosynthetic planning to design synthetic routes for drug molecules
- Clinical trial optimization to identify patient populations most likely to benefit

D-Wave has collaborated with pharmaceutical companies to apply quantum annealing to drug discovery optimization problems. Early results suggest that quantum-inspired optimization can identify promising drug candidates more efficiently than traditional methods for certain types of problems, though the advantages are typically incremental rather than revolutionary.

Figure 8.5 illustrates the study of covalent bond cleavage in prodrug activation represents a concrete example of how quantum computing addresses real pharmaceutical challenges. Traditional density functional theory calculations often struggle with the quantum mechanical nature of bond breaking and formation processes, where quantum approaches can provide more accurate energy profiles (Li et al., 2024).

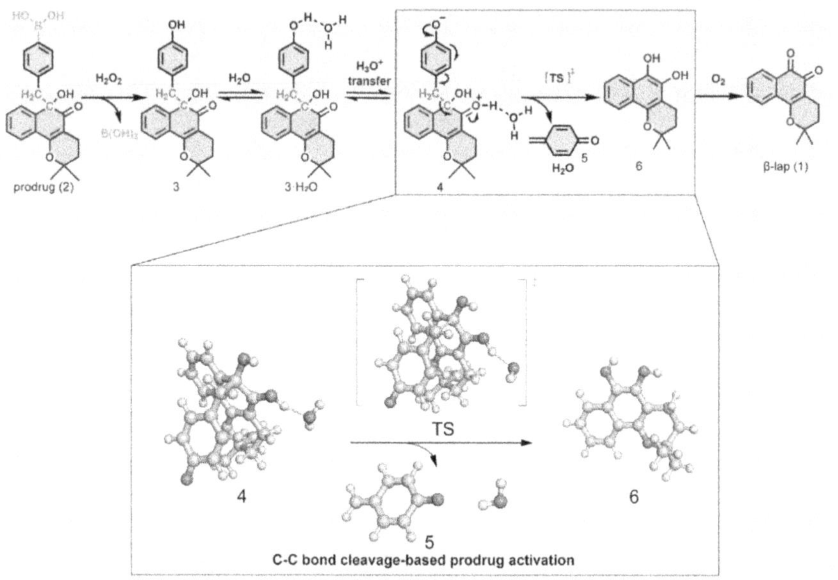

Figure 8.5: Molecular structures in prodrug activation (Li et al., 2024).

Protein folding prediction represents another area where quantum-inspired methods have been explored. Understanding protein structure is crucial for drug design, as most drugs work by binding to specific protein targets.

DeepMind's alpha fold represents a major breakthrough in protein folding prediction using classical deep learning methods. However, quantum-inspired approaches might provide complementary advantages for certain aspects of protein folding, particularly in modelling quantum effects in hydrogen bonding and other interactions that stabilize protein structures.

Researchers have applied tensor network methods to protein folding problems, using the hierarchical structure of proteins (amino acids → secondary structures → domains → complete fold) to design efficient tensor network representations. These approaches can potentially model long-range interactions in proteins more efficiently than some classical methods.

However, current results are preliminary, and quantum-inspired protein folding methods have not yet demonstrated clear advantages over the best classical approaches. The field remains active, with continued research into whether quantum methods can contribute to solving this fundamental biological problem.

8.3.3 Genomics and Bioinformatics

Genomics generates some of the largest and most complex datasets in biology, making it a natural application area for quantum-inspired computational methods. High-dimensional genomic data with complex correlation patterns presents challenges well-suited to tensor network approaches and other quantum-inspired methods.

Genomic Data Compression and Analysis using tensor networks has shown promising results for certain types of genomic datasets. The human genome contains approximately three billion base pairs, and with the decreasing cost of sequencing, genomic datasets are growing exponentially in size.

The old compression algorithms of genomic data are centred on the usage of recurring sequences and other simplistic patterns. The patterns of correlation that can be captured with the tensor networks methods include potentially more complex patterns such as long-range correlations due to evolutionary relationships, regulatory networks, and population structure.

In genomic research, Matrix Product States have been used to reduce the size of genomic sequences while preserving their informational content. A 2019 study demonstrated that MPS achieved superior compression ratios compared with conventional methods for certain types of genomic data, without compromising the ability to perform downstream analyses such as variant calling and phylogenetic reconstruction.

The benefits of tensor network compression are most evident in datasets with complex structure, for example, metagenomic datasets containing many species or cancer genomes with intricate structural variations. Conventional compression algorithms can lose valuable information about such patterns, whereas tensor networks are better able to preserve them.

Genome-wide association studies (GWAS) examine genetic variation in large populations to identify variants associated with specific diseases or traits. GWAS datasets are extremely high-dimensional, with millions of genetic variants measured across thousands or even tens of thousands of individuals.

Traditional GWAS analyses focus on testing individual variants for association with phenotypes, potentially missing important interactions among multiple variants. Quantum-inspired methods may be able to handle higher-order interactions more efficiently than classical approaches.

Tensor network methods have been applied to GWAS data to identify complex patterns of genetic association involving multiple interacting variants. These approaches can capture epistatic (gene-gene) interactions that contribute to complex traits but are difficult to detect using traditional single-variant tests.

Early results suggest that tensor network approaches can identify some genetic associations that are missed by traditional methods, particularly for complex traits influenced by many interacting genetic factors. However, the advantages are generally modest, and the biological significance of the additional associations identified by quantum-inspired methods remains to be established.

Phylogenetic analysis involves reconstructing evolutionary relationships between species or individuals based on genetic similarities and differences. This is a computationally intensive problem, particularly for large datasets with many species or high-resolution genomic data.

Quantum-inspired optimization algorithms have been applied to phylogenetic tree reconstruction, using approaches similar to those developed for combinatorial optimization problems. The goal is to find the tree topology that best explains the observed genetic data according to some evolutionary model.

Quantum optimization algorithms have been experimentally implemented on phylogenetic problems with mixed success. Certain studies document small increases in computational efficiency or tree accuracy in comparison to conventional phylogeny algorithms whereas others do not.

The usefulness of quantum-inspired phylogeny approaches depends on the unique properties of the dataset, including the number of species, the extent of evolutionary divergence, and the degree of horizontal gene transfer or other complex evolutionary mechanisms.

Sequence alignment and comparison is a foundational problem in bioinformatics, involving the determination of the best alignment between DNA, RNA or protein sequences to assess their similarities and differences.

Conventional sequence-alignment methods such as Smith-Waterman and BLAST rely on dynamic programming techniques that become computationally expensive for very large sequences or databases. As a result alternative approaches based on quantum-inspired optimization have been explored,which may offer certain computational advantages.

Nevertheless, classical sequence-alignment algorithms are already highly optimized and efficient for most practical use cases. Quantum-inspired algorithms have not yet demonstrated any significant advantage over existing methods for the standard sequence-alignment problem.

This is because the benefits of quantum techniques for sequence alignment are more likely to emerge in algorithmically harder problems, such as multiple sequence alignment across many sequences or structural alignment that incorporates the three-dimensional conformation of proteins. New classification frameworks for quantum bioinformatics have been proposed to systematically categorize these emerging applications and guide future research directions (Mokhtari, 2024). These problems exhibit higher computational complexity and may benefit from quantum-inspired optimization approaches.

8.3.4 Clinical Decision Support and Electronic Health Records

Electronic health records (EHRs) contain vast amounts of structured and unstructured medical data that could, in principle, benefit from quantum-inspired analysis methods. However, most EHR applications involve relatively straightforward pattern-recognition or optimization tasks for which classical methods are already highly effective.

Clinical risk prediction involves analyzing patient data to estimate the likelihood of future medical events, such as hospital readmissions, adverse drug reactions, or disease progression. EHR data encompass diagnoses, medications, laboratory results, vital signs, and clinical notes, creating high-dimensional datasets with complex temporal patterns.

Clinical risk prediction problems have been solved with quantum-inspired machine learning procedures, such as quantum-inspired neural networks and tensor network classifiers. The goal is to detect subtle patterns in patient data that may indicate an elevated risk of specific adverse events.

Early results suggest that quantum-inspired methods can achieve prediction accuracy comparable to traditional machine-learning approaches for certain clinical prediction tasks. However, the advantages are generally modest, and classical methods remain more practical for most applications due to their maturity and interpretability.

Drug-Drug interaction prediction is a specific clinical decision-support problem where quantum-inspired methods may offer advantages. Patients often take multiple medications simultaneously, creating the potential for harmful interactions between drugs.

Classical methods for predicting drug interactions are typically based on established pharmacological mechanisms or rely on relatively simple statistical techniques applied to clinical evidence. More complex interaction patterns, those involving multiple drugs and diverse patient variables, may be more amenable to modeling with quantum-inspired approaches.

The problem of predicting drug interactions has been addressed using network-based methods, in which drugs and their interactions are represented as high-dimensional tensors. These techniques have the potential to model complex multi-drug interactions that are often overlooked by conventional approaches.

Nevertheless, practical implementation of quantum-inspired drug interaction prediction systems face challenges, particularly regarding interpretability and regulatory approval. Clinical decision support systems must also be able to explain their results in plain language which is not always easy when using complex quantum-inspired models.

Population health analytics involves using large cohorts of individuals and their health records to identify patterns, detect epidemics and uncover opportunities for targeted health interventions. These analyses are often characterized by complex optimization problems related to resource allocation and intervention planning.

Population health problems such as vaccine distribution planning, epidemic modeling, and health resource allocation have been addressed using quantum-inspired optimization algorithms. The constraint structures of these problems, along with their multiple conflicting objectives, are often too complex to be solved by more traditional optimization techniques.

Experiments: Early studies have demonstrated that quantum-inspired optimization can identify efficient population health intervention strategies and, in some cases, outperform conventional optimization methods.

Trends: Nonetheless, the observed benefits are typically modest and highly dependent on the specific characteristics of the population health problem.

8.4 Technical Challenges and Limitations

8.4.1 Quantum Hardware Constraints

Existing quantum devices have inherent physical constraints that severely limit their realistic in applications in medicine:

The most notable disadvantages of existing quantum computers are decoherence and high error rates. Interaction with the surrounding environment causes quantum states to become fragile and decay rapidly. Typical coherence times for superconducting qubits range from 10 to 100 micro seconds, whereas trapped-ion qubits exhibit coherence times on the order of milliseconds.

In current quantum computers, the best single-qubit gates have error rates of about 0.01 percent, while the most general two-qubit gates have error rates of one percent or higher. These error levels in mean that the practical usefulness of quantum algorithms is often limited to relatively small circuits that can execute only a modest number of operations before accumulated errors overwhelm any potential quantum advantage.

For healthcare applications that require long computations, such as molecular simulation or complex optimization, current error rates make fault-tolerant quantum computation necessary. Achieving this requires quantum error correction, which typically increases the number of physical qubits needed by factors from hundreds to thousands.

Limited qubit connectivity constrains the types of quantum algorithms that can be implemented efficiently. Most quantum computers provide only sparse connections between qubits, with each qubit typically linked to just a few neighbours. This creates significant challenges for implementing algorithms that require arbitrary qubit-qubit interactions.

Healthcare applications often involve analyzing complex correlation patterns that would benefit from all-to-all qubit connectivity. When such algorithms are executed on quantum computers with limited connectivity, they require additional circuit depth and incur overheads that can ultimately eliminate any potential quantum advantage.

Scalability challenges arise as both the qubit count and the quality of quantum operations must be maintained while systems grow in size. Current quantum computers with hundreds of qubits already exhibit degraded performance compared to smaller systems, largely due to increased crosstalk, control errors, and environmental noise.

Healthcare applications typically require large-scale quantum computers with thousands to millions of logical qubits to achieve meaningful advantages over classical systems. Figure 8.6 shows that the scalability of quantum-inspired approaches to healthcare problems has been demonstrated for systems with up to 100 qubits, suggesting that these methods can handle the complexity of realistic biological systems. This scalability is crucial for applications that must process high-dimensional genomic data or complex medical imaging datasets (Rudolph et al., 2023). However, reaching such system sizes will require solving numerous technical challenges related to error correction, control systems, and integrated engineering.

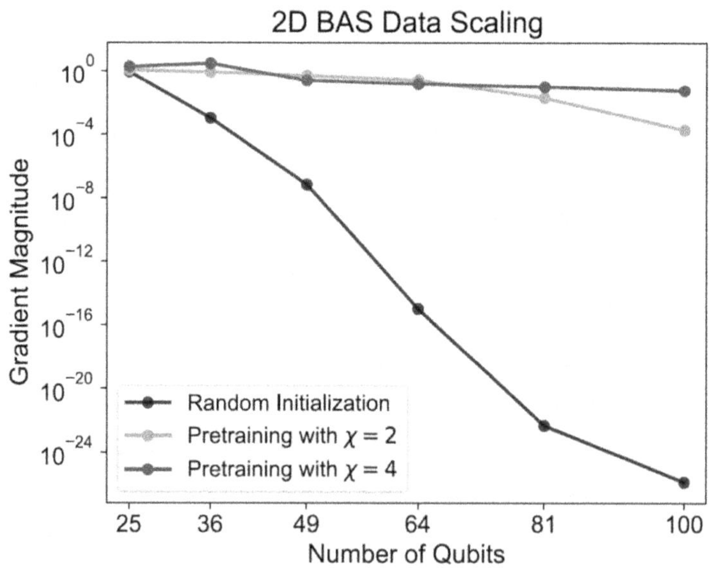

Figure 8.6: Scalability analysis to 100 qubits (Rudolph et al., 2023).

The practical performance of quantum algorithms can be limited by bottlenecks in the quantum–classical interface. Data loading into quantum systems and the extraction of results can be slow relative to the quantum computation itself, potentially negating any computational speedups.

In health care applications that require substantial data volumes, such as medical imaging or genomics, data loading into quantum hardware and the time needed for result readout may constitute the majority of the total computation time. This can undermine the effectiveness of hybrid quantum-classical algorithms when compared with fully quantum approaches across a significant number of applications.

8.4.2 Algorithmic and Software Challenges

Even with perfect quantum hardware, significant algorithmic challenges would still remain for healthcare applications:

Quantum algorithm design for healthcare problems requires careful analysis of the underlying problem structure to identify where genuine quantum advantages might emerge. Many problems that initially appear suitable for quantum computation may not,upon rigorous analysis, actually benefit from quantum approaches.

The process of mapping healthcare problems to quantum algorithms involves several steps: problem formulation, quantum encoding, algorithm design, and performance analysis. At each stage, there is potential for limitations and overhead that may diminish or even eliminate the expected quantum benefits.

To conduct a meaningful quantum advantage analysis, quantum algorithms must be compared not only with naive classical algorithms, but also with the most advanced classical algorithms for the same problem. Classical methods continue to improve, and many problems that initially appeared to benefit from quantum approaches have since been solved more efficiently using enhanced classical techniques.

As shown in Figure 8.7, barren plateaus represent a fundamental challenge for quantum algorithms in healthcare, as gradient-based optimization becomes

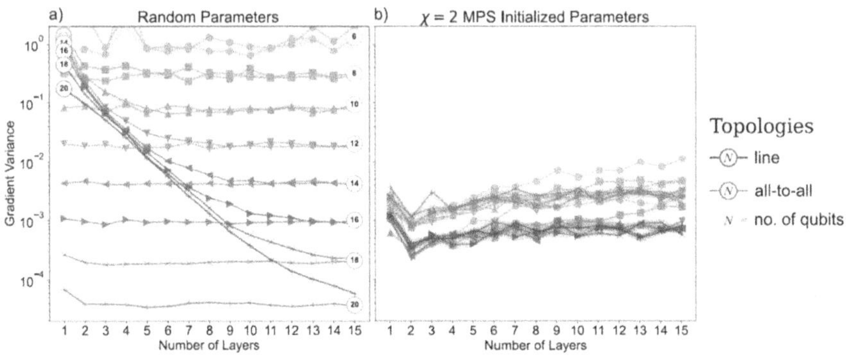

Figure 8.7: Gradient analysis and barren plateau mitigation (Rudolph et al., 2023).

ineffective due to exponentially vanishing gradients. However, quantum-inspired initialization strategies can help overcome these challenges, maintaining trainable gradients even for systems with up to 100 qubits (Rudolph et al., 2023).

For healthcare applications, demonstrating quantum advantage requires showing that quantum algorithms can solve medically relevant problems more effectively than optimized classical algorithms running on the best available classical hardware. This is a high standard, and a few quantum algorithms have met it for practical, real-world problems.

Problem encoding overhead can consume much of the potential quantum advantage. Real-world healthcare problems must be transformed into representations suitable for quantum algorithms, a process that often requires discretization, approximation, or other transformations that introduce significant overhead.

For example, continuous optimization problems in drug discovery typically must be discretized to make them suitable for quantum algorithms. This discretization introduces approximation errors and may require large numbers of qubits to achieve acceptable accuracy, potentially eliminating any quantum advantages.

Quantum software development also faces challenging in programming languages, debugging tools and performance. Because quantum software is fundamentally different from classical software, new programming paradigms and development tools are required.

Healthcare applications demand robust and reliable software that can be validated and certified for clinical use. Existing quantum software development systems remain largely research-focused and are not yet mature enough to support safety-critical health care applications.

8.4.3 Integration and Deployment Challenges

There are many practical challenges in deploying quantum-inspired healthcare systems:

Healthcare IT Integration requires quantum systems to interface smoothly with existing electronic health records, medical imaging systems, laboratory information systems, and other components of healthcare IT infrastructure. Because these systems are designed for classical computing environments, substantial modifications may be needed to enable effective communication with quantum computers.

Healthcare IT data formats, communication protocols, and security systems do not necessarily support quantum technologies. Developing secure and reliable interfaces between quantum and classical systems presents a major engineering challenge.

The clinical validation of quantum-enhanced medical devices is difficult and time-consuming. Any equipment that influences clinical decision-making must be thoroughly evaluated to demonstrate its safety and effectiveness.

Quantum algorithms can produce different outputs for the same problem compared with classical algorithms, and these differences must be carefully validated to ensure they do not jeopardize patient safety. Because quantum computation is inherently probabilistic, validation becomes even more complex as repeated executions of the same algorithm may yield varying results.

Quantum-enhanced medical devices are still in the early stages of obtaining regulatory approval. Classical AI-enabled medical devices have already been evaluated by the FDA and other regulatory bodies, but quantum systems introduce additional concerns related to algorithmic transparency of results, and potential failure modes.

Regulation of quantum medical devices is determined by their intended use and the level of risk they pose. Higher-risk applications, such as diagnostic systems or treatment recommendation tools, require extensive clinical trials and regulatory review, which may take many years, or even decades, to complete.

Cost and economic viability represent major barriers to deployment. Quantum computers are extremely expensive, often costing millions to tens of millions of dollars. Operating expenses include specialized facilities, cryogenic systems, and highly trained personnel.

Healthcare organizations must justify quantum computing investments on the basis of demonstrated clinical benefits and economic returns. For most healthcare applications, classical computing remains more cost-effective than quantum alternatives, making the economic case for quantum adoption challenging.

Staffing and training needs include both quantum-literate medical personnel and specialized technical experts. Operating quantum computing systems requires knowledge of quantum mechanics, algorithm design, and specialized programming methods, skills that are uncommon in the healthcare sector.

Education and professional development are costly, particularly when training healthcare professionals to use quantum-enhanced systems. The shortage of quantum-trained personnel further limits the ability of healthcare organizations to deploy and maintain these systems.

8.4.4 Fundamental Physics Limitations

Some limitations of quantum computing in healthcare arise from fundamental principles of physics:

The no-cloning theorem prevents the arbitrary copying of quantum states, which complicates error correction and result verification. This makes debugging quantum algorithms more difficult than in classical computing, where intermediate states can be freely copied and examined.

Measurement disturbance means that observing a quantum state destroys part of its quantum information, limiting the ability to monitor algorithmic progress or debug quantum computations. This makes quantum algorithm development and verification more challenging than in classical computing.

Speedup requirements are not universal; they depend on the structure of the specific problem and may not exist for all problems of interest. In addition, maintaining quantum coherence in warm and noisy environments, typical of biological systems, is extremely difficult. As a result direct quantum computation on biological samples is not considered realistic without highly complex isolation and control systems.

8.5 Emerging Applications

8.5.1 Personalized Medicine and Precision Healthcare

Personalized medicine is one of the most promising long-term healthcare applications of quantum computing, particularly for optimizing high-dimensional spaces of patient characteristics, treatments and outcomes. Current implementations, however, remain limited to quantum-inspired classical algorithms.

These challenges in multi-omics data integration are also well aligned with the theoretical capabilities of quantum computing. A central requirement of contemporary precision medicine is the integration of genomic, transcriptomic, proteomic, metabolomic and clinical data to characterize individual patients and predict their responses to treatment.

Traditional approaches to multi-omics integration often rely on dimensionality-reduction techniques, or simple statistical models that may overlook important interactions between data types. Quantum-inspired tensor network algorithms, however, can capture complex relationships across omics layers while maintaining reasonable computational complexity. Research groups have applied tensor-network decompositions to multi-omics data from cancer patients using methods such as PARAFAC (Parallel Factor Analysis) Tucker decomposition to identify patterns that span multiple molecular layers. Preliminary results indicate that tensor-network based approaches can reveal patient subtypes not detected by traditional clustering methods, although the clinical relevance of these subtypes remains to be established. The early results are promising but remain limited in scope. Most of the existing literature focuses on relatively simple pharmacogenomic scenarios in which the relevant genetic variants are well understood. Both quantum and classical methods struggle to scale to genome-wide pharmacogenomic prediction,where interaction strategies patterns become highly complex. Another area in which quantum strategies may prove beneficial is treatment-protocol optimization. Personalized treatment typically requires balancing multiple competing objectives, maximizing efficacy, minimizing side effects, incorporating patient preferences and quality-of-life considerations, and cost and resource constraints.

The classical methods struggle to solve multi-objective optimization problems, particularly when the number of objectives and constraints is large. Quantum-inspired optimization techniques, and in particular quantum-annealing-based algorithms, have been applied to treatment-optimization problems. As an example, quantum-inspired algorithms have been applied to optimize chemotherapy regimens in cancer patients, balancing tumor response, toxicity, and quality of life. These strategies can theoretically identify treatment plans that would be difficult to derive using conventional optimization techniques.

However, the clinical validation of such optimized treatment protocols remains challenging. Even if quantum algorithms can identify theoretically optimal treatments, demonstrating their superiority in clinical practice requires carefully controlled trials that may take many years to complete.

8.5.2 Drug Discovery and Molecular Design

The healthcare application with the strongest theoretical argument for quantum advantage in drug discovery, as it fundamentally relies on understanding and controlling quantum mechanical systems. However, current hardware limitations significantly constrain what can be achieved in practice with existing quantum devices.

Quantum chemistry for drug design could revolutionize pharmaceutical research if quantum computers become capable of accurately simulating large molecules. Most current drug-discovery discovery-pipelines rely on approximate classical methods for calculating molecular properties, which can overlook important quantum effects.

The potential advantage of quantum computers in drug discovery stems from their ability to simulate molecular systems directly, without the exponential scaling limitations that constrain classical simulation methods. However, this advantage becomes meaningful only for molecules that are too large for classical computers to model accurately.

Current estimates suggest that simulating pharmaceutically relevant molecules will require fault-tolerant quantum computers with thousands to millions of logical qubits. Such systems are unlikely to be available before the 2030s and may take even longer, depending on progress in quantum error correction. In the meantime, researchers are exploring hybrid quantum-classical approaches in which small quantum processors simulate the most quantum-mechanical components of molecular systems, while classical computers handle the remaining computational workload.

These hybrid approaches might provide incremental improvements over purely classical methods while remaining practical for near-term quantum hardware.

Molecular property prediction using quantum-inspired machine learning has shown promise for estimating drug-like properties without requiring full molecular simulation. These approaches employ quantum-inspired neural networks or tensor-network net classifiers to predict molecular properties such as solubility, toxicity, and binding affinity. Because they can account for complex combinations of molecular features, quantum-inspired methods may offer an advantage in predictive accuracy. Conventional quantitative structure-activity relationship (QSAR) models are frequently based on simple linear relationships or low-order polynomial features, whereas quantum-inspired models have the potential to capture far more sophisticated patterns.

A number of studies have compared quantum-inspired molecular property-prediction models with classical machine learning methods, but the findings remain inconclusive. Recent industrial applications of quantum chemistry in drug discovery have focused on practical hybrid approaches that combine the advantages of quantum-chemical techniques with the computational efficiency of classical methods (Niazi, 2025). Some studies report modest improvements in predictive accuracy, while others find no significant advantage. Overall, the effectiveness of these models appears to depend on the specific molecular property being predicted as well as the scale and quality of the available training data.

Drug repurposing and combination therapy that may be amenable to quantum approaches. Drug repurposing, the search of new therapeutic uses of existing drugs, and combination therapy optimization, the search of effective combinations of a number of drugs.

Both problems involve exploring enormous combinatorial spaces of potential drug combinations or drug applications. Classical models typically rely on heuristic search algorithms or target particular classes of drugs or disease domains. Quantum-inspired optimization algorithms could make it possible to search these spaces more efficiently.

Drug repurposing problems have been addressed using quantum annealing algorithms, which leverage network-based representations of drug-target interactions, to identify opportunities for new therapeutic uses. Early results suggest that quantum-inspired models can detect repurposing candidates overlooked by classical approaches, although experimental validation remains limited.

8.5.3 Healthcare Logistics and Operations Research

Healthcare systems are complex operational environments that can be optimized using quantum-inspired methods. These approaches do not require advances in quantum hardware and can be executed on classical computers running quantum-inspired algorithms.

Hospital resource allocation concerns the efficient distribution of beds, staff, equipment, and other assets to maximize patient care while minimizing costs. These problems typically involve multidimensional constraints and multiple, often conflicting, objectively.

Hospital bed-allocation allocation problems have been addressed using quantum annealing algorithms that aim to maximize patient placement while accounting for infection-control requirements, staff efficiency, and individual preferences. Early experiments suggest that quantum-inspired optimization can identify resource-allocation strategies that outperform conventional techniques, although the performance gains are generally modest.

Healthcare operations research faces challenges not only in developing optimal solutions but also in implementing them in real-world settings. Healthcare environments are highly complex sociotechnical systems in which theoretically optimal solutions may be impractical due to human factors, regulatory constraints or unforeseen events.

Pharmaceutical and medical-device supply-chain optimization is a complex logistics challenge characterized by uncertainty in demand, regulatory requirements, and quality standards. These problems typically involve high-dimensional optimization spaces with intricate and interdependent constraint networks.

Quantum-inspired optimization algorithms have been applied to pharmaceutical supply chain problems, including manufacturing planning, inventory, and distribution optimization.

Optimization problems in clinical trials have also been explored using quantum-inspired optimization algorithms, which aim to identify trial designs that maximize statistical power while minimizing costs and patient burden. These strategies show potential for improving trial efficiency, although they have not yet been validated in real clinical settings. Physical applications of quantum-inspired optimization in healthcare have demonstrated quantifiable benefits in workforce scheduling and resource allocation (Borgohain I., 2025). Recent advances in quantum-enhanced digital twin IoT models have demonstrated high task-offloading efficiency, with quantum pre-processing achieving 32% higher task offloading success rates and an 80% reduction in task-offloading error rates for healthcare workloads (Jameil and Al-Raweshidy, 2025). Healthcare organizations and technology firms are increasingly interested in quantum applications in across domains such as drug discovery and medical imaging (Ivezic, 2025).

Empirical evidence shows that quantum-inspired methods can deliver significant performance improvements compared with both classical and fully quantum approaches. These gains are most pronounced in optimization problems common in personalized medicine, for example optimizing treatment protocols and generating pharmacogenomic predictions, as illustrated in Figure 8.8 (Rudolph et al., 2023).

8.6 Economic Considerations and Market Analysis

8.6.1 Investment and Funding Landscape

The quantum computing sector has attracted substantial investment from both government and private sources, and healthcare remains a key area of interest for many investors and researchers.

Quantum computing companies have experienced a substantial rise in venture-capital investment over the past few years. Industry reports indicate that in 2022, venture-capital funding in quantum computing exceeded $1 billion, with healthcare applications accounting for roughly 20–30% of the total investment.

IBM (quantum chemistry and drug discovery), Google (molecular simulation), Roche/Cambridge Quantum Computing (drug discovery), and D-Wave (healthcare optimization) are among the major quantum-computing companies developing applications for the healthcare sector. These firms have collectively invested hundreds of millions of dollars to advance quantum-computing technologies for medical and clinical use.

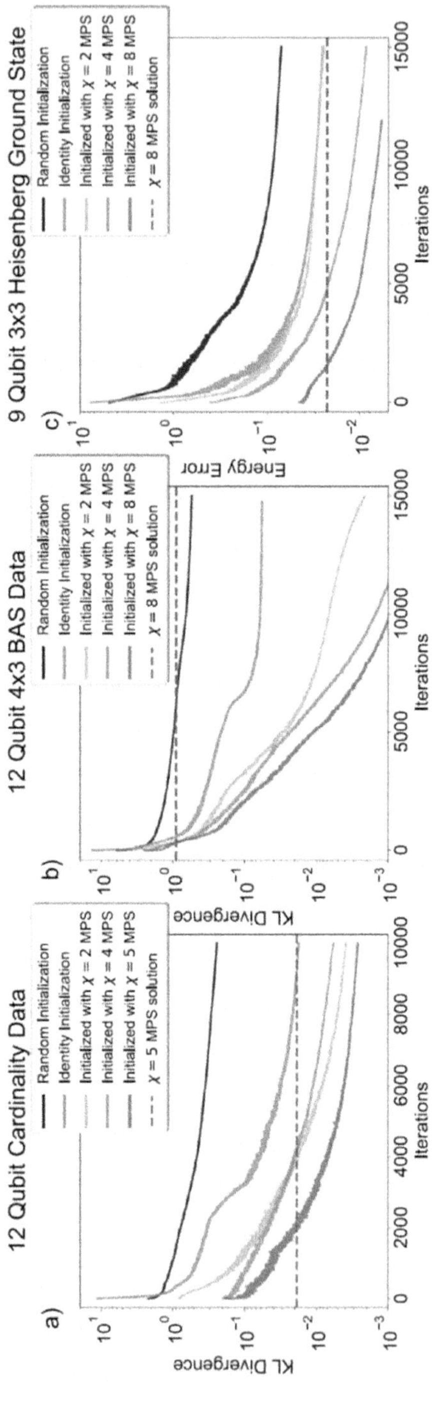

Figure 8.8: Performance improvements of healthcare applications (Rudolph et al., 2023).

The amount of government funding for quantum research has also risen significantly. Between 2019 and 2023, the US National Quantum Initiative allocated more than $1.2 billion to quantum research, with a substantial portion directed toward quantum-computing applications, including those in healthcare. Similar national programs exist in Europe (Quantum Flagship), China, Japan, and several other countries. More recent developments include the NIH QuBIT program and growing industry collaboration between quantum-computing companies and major healthcare organizations (Ivezic, 2025).

The most promising near-term direction for quantum-enhanced personalized medicine is the synergistic integration of classical and quantum resources. In this model, quantum systems are used to perform functions where they offer clear advantages, while classical computational resources pre-process large datasets to extract the most practical value from current quantum technologies (as shown in Figure 8.9, Rudolph et al., 2023).

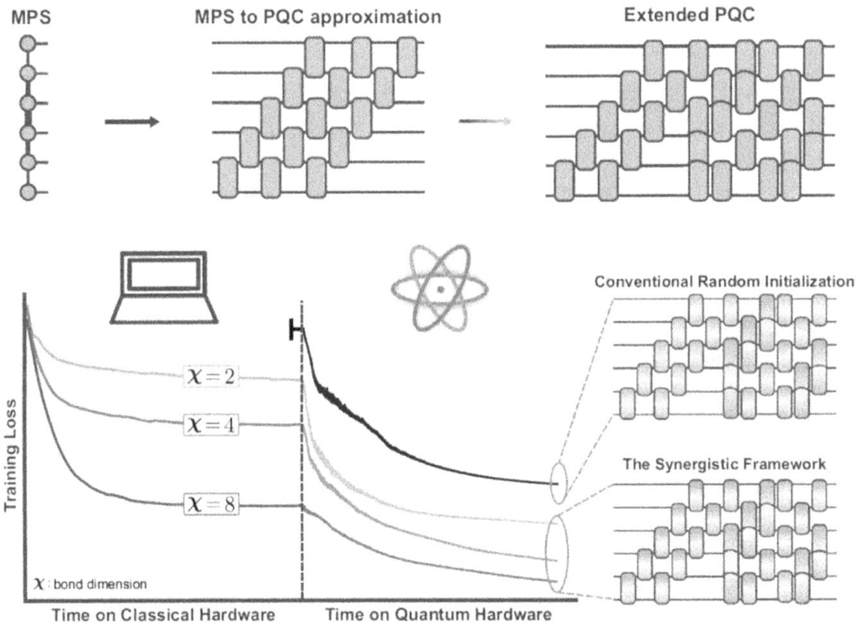

Figure 8.9: The framework of synergistic quantum-classical (Rudolph et al., 2023).

Both basic research in quantum algorithms and hardware, as well as applied research in specific healthcare applications, have received substantial government funding. Academic institutions and national laboratories have been awarded significant resources to develop quantum-computing capabilities in areas such as drug discovery, medical imaging and genomics.

There has also been increased investment in corporate research and development by major technology companies and pharmaceutical firms. IBM has already invested more than $3 billion in quantum-computing research, including collaborations with healthcare organizations. Google Quantum AI division is similarly applying part of its research portfolio to healthcare interventions, particularly molecular simulation for drug discovery.

A number of pharmaceutical corporations, including Roche, Merck and Johnson and Johnson, have already partnered with quantum-computing companies to explore drug discovery and development. These collaborations typically take the form of shared research projects rather than large upfront investments, reflecting the experimental and still-emerging nature of quantum healthcare applications.

8.6.2 Cost-Benefit Analysis

The economic case for quantum computing in healthcare rests on weighing the substantial costs of quantum systems against the potential gains in improved health outcomes and greater efficiency across the healthcare system.

The costs of quantum systems in their current state are high and include both capital and operational expenses. Complete systems are priced between 10 million and 50 million USD, although cloud-based access is available at a lower cost. Access to IBM's quantum computers, for example, is priced at approximately 1.60 USD per second via the cloud, with similar pricing models used by other providers.

Facilities (e.g., cryogenic systems for superconducting qubits), highly-trained personnel (such as quantum engineers and physicists), and ongoing maintenance and support also contribute to operational costs. For the healthcare organizations, these expenditures must be justifiable by demonstrable clinical benefits or measurable improvements in operational efficiency.

The potential healthcare benefits of quantum computing are difficult to quantify, given the technology's early stage of development, but several categories of benefits may justify continued investment in quantum capabilities.

The pharmaceutical research and development costs often amounting to billions of dollars, could be significantly reduced through greater efficiency in drug discovery. Developing a single approved drug typically requires an investment of $1–3 billion per approved drug, and high failure rates further inflate overall expenditures. If quantum computing can increase success rates or shorten development timelines, the financial gains may be substantial.

Better diagnostic quality would also save on health expenditures by enabling an early disease diagnosis, fewer unnecessary surveys, and effective treatment. Nonetheless, to measure these benefits, it is necessary to prove that quantum-enhanced diagnostic systems can indeed provide better clinical outcomes than current classical approaches.

More direct economic advantages could be offered by operational efficiency gains in the fields of healthcare logistics, resource distribution and supply chain management. The applications do not need advances in quantum hardware and can be applied with the existing algorithms.

Quantum healthcare applications have a high level of uncertainty in Return-on-Investment estimates because the technology is experimental. The vast majority of economic studies are based on assumptions of uncertain capabilities and timescales of quantum computing.

In the case of pharmaceutical companies, the payoff from quantum computing investments will rely mainly on an increase in successful drug discoveries and faster development. Small advances in these metrics would be worth the large investments in quantum computing as drug development is very expensive and risky.

Quantum computing is not so obvious to healthcare providers as an economic argument. The majority of the possible advantages demand the development of quantum hardware that might be unavailable in the short and long terms. Meanwhile, classical computing approaches are also being enhanced to make them capable of solving most of the problems that seem to require quantum computing.

8.6.3 Market Projections

The estimates of quantum computing in the healthcare market are diverse and dependent on the guesses regarding its technological advances and rates of adoption. Quantum computing market shares in healthcare vary by hundreds of millions and tens of billions of dollars by 2030–2040, depending on the applications that are covered and the assumptions about quantum hardware development.

Conservative estimates are concerned with short-term use of quantum-inspired classical algorithms and the restricted capacity of quantum hardware. These forecasts usually project market shares from hundreds of millions to low billions of dollars by 2030.

The positive forecasts presuppose a rapid evolution of quantum hardware and the popularization of quantum computing in drug discovery and personalized medicine and other medical fields. Such estimates may be in tens of billions of dollars by 2040, but they are subject to technological discoveries which are uncertain.

Competitiveness is yet to be determined as the technology continues to develop and real-world applications emerge. Success will likely depend on a combination of technological assets, strategic collaborations with healthcare organizations, and the ability to demonstrate tangible clinical value.

8.7 Regulatory Framework and Clinical Validation

8.7.1 Current Regulatory Environment

Regulation of quantum-enhanced technologies in healthcare is still evolving. Current approaches build on existing frameworks for AI-enabled medical devices while beginning to account for the unique characteristics of quantum computing.

The most relevant regulatory precedent of quantum healthcare applications is FDA Approaches to AI-Enabled Medical Devices. As of 2024, the FDA has passed more than 350 AI-enabled medical devices, which have created avenues to software-based medical technologies, which may be generalized to quantum systems.

FDA policy on AI-enabled medical devices is grounded in several key principles: clinical validation through appropriate studies, transparency and explainability of algorithms, rigorous strength and reliability testing, and post-market performance monitoring via surveillance. The same principles would likely be applied to quantum-enhanced medical devices.

Key regulatory considerations for quantum healthcare devices include:

- **Analytical validation:** Demonstrating that quantum algorithms perform as intended technically
- **Clinical validation:** Showing that quantum systems improve clinical outcomes compared to existing methods
- **Algorithm transparency:** Providing sufficient explanation of quantum algorithms for regulatory review
- **Reproducibility:** Ensuring that quantum systems produce consistent results across different applications

Software as Medical Device (SaMD) classification provides the framework for regulating quantum healthcare software. The FDA categorizes SaMD according to the healthcare situation (critical, serious, or non-serious) and the type of healthcare decision (treat/diagnose, drive, or inform).

Quantum-enhanced diagnostic systems would likely be classified as Class II or Class III devices depending on their clinical application. Applications such as cancer diagnosis or treatment recommendation would be considered high-risk and thus would have to be extensively clinically-validated by randomized controlled trials.

Applications with a lesser degree of risk, such as clinical decision support systems that do not drive but inform medical decision-making, may be subjected to less demanding regulatory routes, and they could be approved and rolled out more quickly.

Quantum healthcare technologies should be deployed internationally with the help of International Regulatory Harmonization. The International Medical Device Regulators Forum (IMDRF) is working on guidance on AI-enabled medical devices which would extend to quantum devices.

The clinical validation, risk management, and post-market surveillance requirements that are to be applied to quantum healthcare devices are similar to those of European Union medical device regulation (MDR) and other international systems. The recent review of quantum computing applications in medical sciences highlights the need for specialized regulatory frameworks to address the distinctive attributes of quantum-enhanced healthcare technologies (Kato et al., 2023; Saleh et al., 2024).

8.7.2 Clinical Validation Requirements

The clinical validity of quantum-enhanced healthcare systems can be demonstrated through improved patient outcomes compared to the existing standard care and this is uniquely difficult due to the experimental nature of quantum technologies.

Study design considerations must account for the dynamism of quantum algorithms and hardware when validating quantum healthcare. Traditional clinical trials typically assume that interventions remain static, whereas quantum systems may continue to improve over time during the course of study.

Quantum healthcare validation may also be appropriate to adaptive trial designs, as the protocol adjustments can be introduced in response to interim results and technological progress. However, adaptive designs must be carefully planned in statistical terms to ensure that the study remains valid and acceptable.

Comparative effectiveness studies aim to compare quantum-enhanced systems with both historical controls and the most suitable current methods. As classical AI techniques continue to improve at a rapid pace, quantum systems will need to demonstrate tangible benefits over classical approaches through optimization.

The timeline for quantum healthcare validation may be significantly longer than the standard 2–3 years typical of traditional medical device studies, particularly when long-term patient outcomes are required to demonstrate clinical benefit.

8.7.3 Quality Management and Standards

Quality management systems for quantum healthcare technologies should accommodate the peculiarities of quantum computation without compromising the standards to current medical devices.

ISO 13485 and the ISO 14971 provide the standards for medical device quality management and and the foundation for risk management, both of which need to be adapted for quantum systems. Key considerations include:

Design controls for quantum algorithms include requirements specification, design verification and design validation. Traditional software verification methods do not always apply directly to quantum algorithms and new approaches must be developed to test and validate them.

Quantum risk management should include quantum-computing-specific failure modes, such as decoherence, gate errors, and quantum-classical interface errors. These failure modes may exhibit characteristics that differ from classical software failures and must be addressed through specialized risk-mitigation measures.

Quantum healthcare systems require post-market surveillance of both clinical performance and the technical performance of quantum hardware and algorithms. This involves monitoring clinical outcomes, assessing the accuracy of algorithms, and detecting performance degradation in quantum hardware.

The nature of quantum cloud computing makes post-market surveillance more complex as healthcare organizations may not have direct access to quantum hardware for monitoring and validation.

To ensure cybersecurity and data protection of quantum healthcare, traditional cybersecurity risks must be considered alongside the security of quantum healthcare systems. Quantum computers may eventually undermine existing encryption schemes, necessitating a transition to quantum-resistant cryptography.

On the other hand, quantum cryptography provides a higher level of security for protecting healthcare information, though it needs specialized infrastructure and expertise to be effectively implemented.

8.8 Ethical Considerations and Societal Impact

8.8.1 Algorithmic Fairness and Bias

The challenges of quantum computing in healthcare raise important questions about algorithmic impartiality, bias minimization, and equitable access to advanced healthcare technologies.

Bias in quantum algorithms may arise in similar ways to classical systems: through biased training data, design decisions that favor certain groups, or deployment in settings that exacerbate existing healthcare disparities.

Compared to classical systems, detecting and mitigating bias may be more difficult due to the complexity of quantum algorithms. Existing fairness metrics and bias detection methods may not be directly applicable, and new approaches may need to be developed to ensure algorithmic fairness.

Representation in training data remains critical for quantum healthcare. When datasets do fail to represent certain demographic groups, quantum algorithms may perform poorly for those populations, regardless of their theoretical advantage.

It is especially critical in the case of genomics applications, where the vast majority of genetic repositories are heavily biased in favor of people of European descent. Genomic analysis systems that incorporate quantum enhancements should adequately represent diverse populations to help prevent the worsening of health disparities.

Fair access to quantum healthcare technologies may create new forms of healthcare inequality, in which only affluent healthcare systems or patients can benefit from advanced systems. Quantum technologies may be too expensive and complex to be practical for large academic health facilities and remain out of reach for community hospitals and rural care organizations.

There can be a need to have policy interventions that will provide equitable access to quantum healthcare benefits, which can involve government funding of quantum healthcare facilities or the need to share the technology and gain access to it.

8.8.2 Privacy and Data Security

Quantum computing presents both promising opportunities and threats to health care data privacy and security. As quantum computers become more powerful, quantum threats to current encryption could undermine existing safeguards for healthcare data. Large-scale quantum computers running Shor's algorithm would be capable of breaking RSA and other public-key cryptography techniques currently used to protect healthcare data security.

To reduce future quantum threats, healthcare organizations should begin planning to migrate to quantum-resistant cryptography. This transition must occur before quantum computers reach a scale that adversaries could exploit.

Quantum cryptography offers significant advantages for protecting healthcare data through quantum key distribution and other quantum cryptographic schemes. These approaches provide information-theoretic security that even quantum computers cannot break. However,implementing quantum cryptography requires specialized infrastructure and expertise, which may not be feasible for most healthcare organizations. Additionally, physical limitations such as transmission distance and environmental interference further restrict the practicality of this technology.

Differential privacy and quantum computing may require novel methods to safeguard individual privacy while enabling quantum-enhanced analytics for healthcare data. Many classical approaches to differential privacy may not directly apply to quantum algorithms.

Research is underway to develop quantum-enhanced differential privacy protocols that provide stronger privacy protections and enable practical quantum operations on sensitive healthcare information. The issue of the quantum threat to healthcare IoT systems was systemically examined, and some mitigation strategies are suggested to secure the patient data in the post-quantum world (Alif et al., 2024). Privacy-preserving medical analytics have been shown to be feasible through quantum-inspired algorithms to perform healthcare prediction (Mazumdar et al., 2024). Implementation of quantum-enhanced security solutions with digital twin IoT systems have shown a strong defence against cyberattacks, such as effective response to DoS attacks and attempts to tamper with the data using adaptive cybersecurity systems (Jameil and Al-Raweshidy, 2025).

8.8.3 Professional and Societal Implications

The implementation of quantum computing in healthcare may have an implication to healthcare practitioners and the society at large.

Influence on healthcare professionals may have both opportunities and challenges to healthcare workers. Increased diagnostic and decision support systems with quantum enhancement can enhance the skills and capabilities of healthcare professionals to provide more accurate diagnoses and treatment tailored to individuals.

Nevertheless, quantum systems might be too complicated, with the necessity of further training and education for medical workers. To train the future workers in medical fields, medical education curricula should include the concept of quantum computing, albeit at a conceptual level.

There are also opportunities within Global Health Implications to address worldwide health challenges particularly the widening gaps between the developed and developing countries. Quantum computing can accelerate the discovery process of drugs for the growing number of neglected tropical diseases and enhance the delivery of care in resource-limited environments.

However, the complexity and the cost of quantum systems may further widen the disparity between health services in wealthy and the poorer nations. Crossborder collaboration and technology sharing may be necessary to ensure that the benefits of quantum healthcare are distributed equitably across the world.

8.9 Future Research Directions

Quantum computing research priorities in the health sector should be directed toward both short-term and long-term goals, with particular emphasis on practical and readily achievable short-term applications that can be implemented using current or near future quantum hardware resources.

The most promising near-term research direction is hybrid QCQA, which combines the quantum advantages of certain computational tasks with classical computation in a practical manner. Such hybrid techniques can add incremental value and remain feasible given the current limitations of quantum hardware.

Research topics include optimizing interfaces between quantum and classical systems, optimizing the deployment of computational workloads across quantum and classical systems, and empirically validating hybrid algorithms on real-world healthcare applications.

Quantum-inspired classical algorithms remain a practical option without requiring quantum hardware, making them an appealing candidate for near-term use in healthcare applications. Major research topics include optimizing tensor network representations for high dimensional healthcare data, enabling faster variational optimization algorithms, and designing improved quantum-inspired machine learning methods.

Near-term quantum devices may lack full error correction, but error mitigation techniques could enable more advanced healthcare applications. Current research focuses on identifying error mitigation techniques that are particularly relevant to healthcare and benchmarking their effectiveness in medical computing contexts.

Resource-constrained error mitigation schemes are of critical importance for medical applications where computational resources may be scarce and reliability is of paramount importance. A number of techniques have been developed specifically for NISQ devices.

Zero-Noise Extrapolation (ZNE) is a technique that artificially adds noise to quantum circuits and extrapolates to the zero-noise limit. The method involves running the same quantum circuit at different noise levels (achieved through pulse stretching or gate folding) and fitting the results to a noise model. In health care applications, ZNE can enhance the trustworthiness of quantum chemistry calculations and optimization outcomes without requiring additional qubits.

Probabilistic Error Cancellation (PEC) models quantum errors as linear combinations of operations of implementable quantum gate operations, allowing errors to be probabilistically cancelled. This approach relies on a detailed characterization of the quantum device and can achieve exponential error suppression in certain error models. In the healthcare, PEC may be particularly valuable for mission-critical computations where high accuracy is essential.

Symmetry Verification leverages known symmetries in healthcare problems to identify and correct errors. For instance, molecular systems often exhibit well-defined symmetries that can be used to validate quantum simulation results. When quantum calculations fail, established methods now exist to detect and rectify such errors.

Virtual Distillation exploits multiple copies of quantum states and applies postprocessing to suppress errors, yielding exponential error reduction with only polynomial overhead. This technique may be especially useful for quantum machine learning applications in healthcare, where statistical accuracy is often more important than exact state fidelity.

These error mitigation techniques are being applied to quantum healthcare research, with reports of 2–5x improvements in calculation accuracy for small molecular systems and quantum machine learning tasks. They represent a realistic pathway toward realizing quantum advantages in healthcare until fault-tolerant quantum computers emerge (Moradi et al., 2023).

8.10 Conclusion

Quantum computing is an emerging but currently niche, technology for healthcare applications. While there are theoretical benefits for certain types of health care problems, significant technical, economic, and regulatory hurdles limit its practical implementation, restricting its use to niche applications in the foreseeable future.

In the near term, quantum-inspired classical algorithms offer the most promising path to incremental gains in healthcare optimization, data analysis, and machine learning tasks. These methods provide practical advantages today as technology advances toward more complex quantum applications.

Long-term applications of quantum computing in healthcare have the potential to transform drug discovery through accurate molecular simulation, enable new forms of personalized medicine using quantum-enhanced optimization and machine learning, and deliver unbreakable security for healthcare data through quantum cryptography.

However, realizing these benefits will require ongoing improvements in quantum hardware, algorithms, clinical validation, and regulatory approaches. The timeline for widespread adoption of quantum computing in healthcare remains unpredictable, but for most applications, it is likely to occur in the 2030s–2050s or later.

As shown in Figure 8.10, the achievable timeline for quantum advantage in healthcare applications depends on continued advancements in hardware and error mitigation techniques. Current estimates predict that error-mitigated quantum computing will bridge the gap left by today's noisy devices and provide a smoother path to quantum advantage than previously anticipated (IBM Quantum Team, 2023).

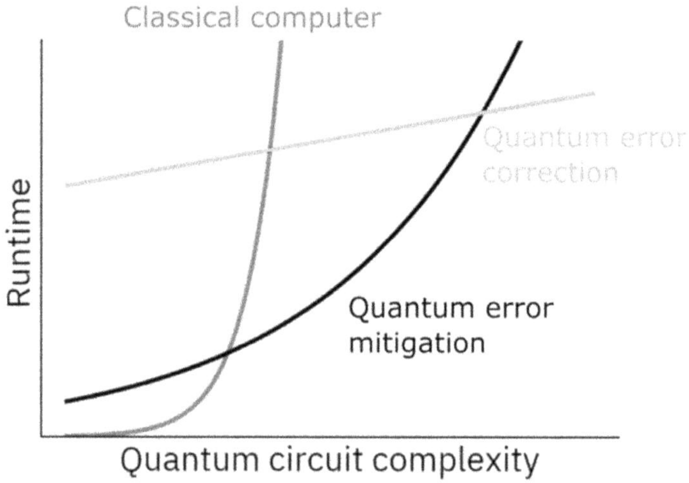

Figure 8.10: Runtime scaling and timeline of quantum computing (IBM Quantum Team, 2023).

Medical institutions remain informed about developments in quantum computing, but manage expectations regarding what is feasible in the near term. While the potential of quantum computing is significant, companies can build capabilities without committing prematurely to immature technologies by pursuing research collaborations with quantum computing experts and investing in quantum-inspired classical algorithms.

The intersection of quantum computing and healthcare is an active area of research with substantial long-term promise, but practical benefits will accrue gradually as both quantum computing technologies and our understanding of their applications in healthcare continue to advance.

References

Alif, A., Hasan, F., Laeuchli, J. & Chowdhury, M. (2024) Quantum threat in healthcare IoT: Challenges and mitigation strategies. arXiv preprint arXiv:2412.05904.

Arute, F., Arya, K., Babbush, R., Bacon, D., Bardin, J. C., Barends, R. et al. (2019). Quantum supremacy using a programmable superconducting processor. *Nature*, 574(7779), 505–510.

Banerjee, Nisha & Chatterjee, Koyel. (2024). Quantum AI in healthcare: Revolutionizing diagnosis, treatment and drug discovery. *International Journal of Scientific Research in Science and Technology*, 11. 10.32628/IJSRST2411351.

Benedetti, M., Garcia-Pintos, D., Perdomo, O., Leyton-Ortega, V., Nam, Y. & Perdomo-Ortiz, A. (2019). A generative modeling approach for benchmarking and training shallow quantum circuits. *npj Quantum Information*, 5(1), 1–9.

Benedetti, M., Lloyd, E., Sack, S. & Fiorentini, M. (2019). Parameterized quantum circuits as machine learning models. *Quantum Science and Technology*, 4(4), 043001.

Borgohain I. (2025). Real-time healthcare workforce rescheduling using a quantum computer: A novel approach to dynamic staff allocation in hospital settings. *European Journal of Computer Science and Information Technology*, 13(29), 89–96.

Cerezo, M., Arrasmith, A., Babbush, R., Benjamin, S. C., Endo, S., Fujii K. et al. (2021). Variational quantum algorithms. *Nature Reviews Physics*, 3(9), 625–644.

Cerezo, M., Sharma, K., Arrasmith, A. & Coles, P. J. (2022). Variational quantum state eigensolver. *npj Quantum Information*, 8(1), 113.

Chow, J. C. L. (2024). Quantum computing in medicine. *PMC Journal*, PMCID: PMC11586987. Available at: https://www.ncbi.nlm.nih.gov/pmc/articles/PMC11586987/ (Accessed: 28 August 2025).

Daley, A. J., Bloch, I., Kokail, C., Flannigan, S., Pearson, N., Troyer, M. et al. (2022). Practical quantum advantage in quantum simulation. *Nature*, 607(7920), 667–676.

Fatunmbi, T. O. (2023). Integrating quantum neural networks with machine learning algorithms for optimizing healthcare diagnostics and treatment outcomes. *World Journal of Advanced Research and Reviews*, 17(3), 1059–1077.

Flöther, F. F. (2023). The state of quantum computing applications in health and medicine. *Research Directions: Quantum Technologies*, 1, e5. doi:10.1017/qut.2023.4

IBM Quantum Team. (2023). Error mitigation is the path to quantum computing usefulness. *IBM Quantum Computing Blog*, 15 March. Available at: https://www.ibm.com/quantum/blog/gammabar-for-quantum-advantage (Accessed: 28 August 2025).

Ivezic, M. (2025). Quantum use cases in healthcare & medical research. *PostQuantum White Paper Series*. Available at: https://postquantum.com/healthcare-quantum-use-cases (Accessed: 28 August 2025).

Jameil, A. K. and Al-Raweshidy, H. (2025). Quantum-enhanced digital twin IoT for efficient healthcare task offloading. *Discover Applied Sciences*, 7, 525.

Joran van Apeldoorn, J., Gilyén, A., Gribling, S. & de Wolf, R. (2020). Quantum SDP-solvers: Better upper and lower bounds. *Quantum*, 4, 230.

Kato, J. (2025). Quantum computing in healthcare: Potential applications. *Research Output Journal of Engineering and Scientific Research*, 4(2), 73–78.

Li, W., Yin, Z., Li, X., Guo, Y., Zeng, Q. Wang, J. et al. (2024). A hybrid quantum computing pipeline for real world drug discovery. *Scientific Reports*, 14(1), 16942.

Marengo, A. & Santamato, V. (2025). Quantum algorithms and complexity in healthcare applications: A systematic review with machine learning-optimized analysis. *Frontiers in Computer Science*, 3, 1584114.

Mazumdar, H., Chakraborty, C., Venkatakrishnan, S. B., Kaushik, A. & Gohel, H. A. (2024). Quantum-inspired heuristic algorithm for secure healthcare prediction using blockchain technology. *IEEE Journal of Biomedical and Health Informatics*, 28(6), 3371–3378.

McArdle, S., Endo, S., Aspuru-Guzik, A., Benjamin, S. C. & Yuan, X. (2020). Quantum computational chemistry. *Reviews of Modern Physics*, 92(1), 015003.

Mokhtari, M., Khoshbakht, S., Ziyaei, K., Akbari, M. E. & Moravveji, S. S. (2024) New classifications for quantum bioinformatics: Q-bioinformatics, QCt-bioinformatics, QCg-bioinformatics, and QCr-bioinformatics. *Briefings in Bioinformatics*, 25(2), bbae074.

Moradi, S., Spielvogel, C., Krajnc, D., Brandner, C., Hillmich, S. Wille, R. et al. (2023). Error mitigation enables PET radiomic cancer characterization on quantum computers. *European Journal of Nuclear Medicine and Molecular Imaging*, 50(13), 3826–3837.

Niazi, S. K. (2025). Quantum mechanics in drug discovery: A comprehensive review of methods, applications, and future directions. *International Journal of Molecular Sciences*, 26(13), 6325.

Nielsen, M. A. & Chuang, I. L. (2010). Quantum Computation and Quantum Information. 10th Anniversary Ed. Cambridge: Cambridge University Press.

Orús, R. (2019). Tensor networks for complex quantum systems. *Nature Reviews Physics*, 1(9), 538–550.

Ozaydin, F. (2025). A survey of quantum generative adversarial networks: Architectures, use cases, and real-world implementations. arXiv preprint arXiv:2506.18002.

Plé, T., Adjoua, O., Benali, A., Posenitskiy, E., Villot, C., Lagardère, L. et al. (2025). A foundation model for accurate atomistic simulations in drug design. *ChemRxiv*. doi:10.26434/chemrxiv-2025-f1hgn-v3

Radhi, Eman A., Kamil, Mohammed Y. & Mohammed, Mazin Abed. (2025). Quantum machine and deep learning for medical image classification: A systematic review of trends, methodologies, and future directions. *Iraqi Journal for Computer Science and Mathematics*, 6(2), Article 9. DOI: https://doi.org/10.52866/2788-7421.1252

Rudolph, M. S., Miller, J., Motlagh, D., Chen, J., Acharya, A. & Perdomo-Ortiz, A. (2023). Synergistic pretraining of parametrized quantum circuits via tensor networks. *Nature Communications*, 14(1), 8367.

Saleh Alrashed & Nasro Min-Allah. (2024). Quantum computing research in medical sciences: A comprehensive review. *Information Processing & Management*, 61(4), 101606.

Smaldone, A. M., Shee, Y., Kyro, G. W., Xu, C., Vu, N. P., Dutta, R. et al. (2025). Quantum machine learning in drug discovery: Applications in academia and pharmaceutical industries. *Chemical Reviews*, 125(12), 5436–5460.

Tilly, J., Chen, H., Cao, S., Picozzi, D., Setia, K., Li, Y. et al. (2022). The variational quantum eigensolver: A review of methods and best practices. *Physics Reports*, 986, 1–128.

CHAPTER

9

Quantum Neural Networks: Bridging Quantum Computing and Artificial Intelligence

Smrita Singh[1*], Tanzeel Ahmed[1], and Ashutosh Singh Chauhan[2]

[1] School of Biotechnology, IFTM University, Lodhipur Rajput, Moradabad, India
[2] Air Pollution and Stone Conservation Laboratory, Archaeological Survey of India, Agra Fort, Agra, India

Quantum computing and neural networks have revolutionized computational intelligence and have the potential to revolutionize a wide range of scientific, industrial, and technological fields. In some computational activities, quantum computing utilizes the concepts of superposition, entanglement, and quantum parallelism and performs better than classical computers by processing complicated data with high speed and efficiency. Neural networks have transformed decision-making, natural language processing, and pattern recognition, especially deep learning models. By incorporating quantum computing into neural network architectures, Quantum Neural Networks (QNNs) open new paradigms in data encoding, feature representation, and learning dynamics by overcoming the computational constraints and scaling related problems of classical models. In this chapter, the theoretical basis, latest developments and possible applications of a quantum neural network have been discussed. This chapter covers the constraints of near-term quantum devices, quantum noise, data encoding techniques, and practical difficulties in hardware implementation. Real-world applications in quantum chemistry, financial modeling, cryptography, and biological imaging have been studied. To fully realize the promise of quantum neural processing, this chapter concludes by describing current research shortcomings and providing opportunities for multi-disciplinary collaboration among computer scientists, physicists, and AI researchers.

*Corresponding author: smrita1@gmail.com

DOI: 10.1201/9781003682950-9

9.1 Introduction

9.1.1 Quantum Computing

Quantum computing is an interesting topic in the field of computing. Quantum computers use quantum physics for computation using suitable algorithms. These computers offer significantly higher computational power than classical computers, giving them a major advantage in solving large and complex problems much faster, problems that might take classical computers several years to complete. Quantum computers work on information units called qubits, made from subatomic particles like photons, neutrons and electrons. These are the main reason for the exponentially increasing power provided by quantum computers. The properties and functions of this information unit are called quantum bits or qubits. These are completely different from classical computer "bits" as these work on the principle of quantum mechanics. Quantum computers work like a human brain consisting of a set of neural network information (deep learning, machine learning) to derive the solution for unsolved classical computing problems.

The exponential growth of classical computing power was predicted by Moore's Law. This principle highlights the search for physical and technological limits, primarily constrained by transistor miniaturization, energy efficiency, and heat dissipation (Arute et al., 2019). This has motivated the exploration of quantum computing, an emerging paradigm that leverages the principles of quantum mechanics, such as superposition, entanglement, and tunneling, to perform computations beyond the capabilities of classical computers (Nielsen & Chuang, 2010). In contrast to theoretical bits, which take the form of 0 or 1, quantum bits (qubits) can exist in a superposition of systems, enabling the simultaneous processing of information (Figure 9.1).

To create quantum circuits that enable algorithms with special constraints, quantum computing employs quantum gates that manipulate qubits through unitary operations (Preskill, 2018). It is impossible to directly relate qubits to conventional bits in a way that allows information extraction; however, quantum entanglement enhances computational capacity. For certain tasks, such as integer factorization, Shor's algorithm is applied while Grover's algorithm enables unstructured database searches. Together these concepts provide exponential speedup (Shor, 1997; Grover, 1996). Quantum devices have overcome the limitations of classical supercomputers and demonstrated "quantum supremacy" (Arute et al., 2019).

Superconducting qubits, trapped ions, photonics, and topological qubits are technical platforms to be investigated; each has special benefits in terms of scalability and error resistance (Ladd et al., 2010). Quantum computing has been recognized as a game-changing technology with uses in artificial intelligence, optimization, cryptography, and molecular simulation (Biamonte et al., 2017) despite issues of noise, decoherence, and limited error correction.

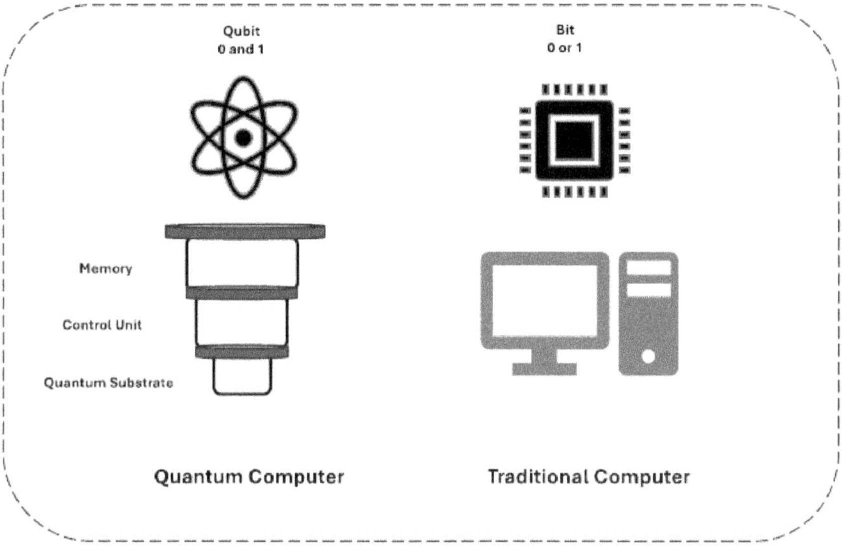

Figure 9.1: Operation of quantum and traditional computers. (Adopted from Muhammed Golec, Emir Sahin Hatay, Mustafa Golec, Murat Uyar, Merve Golec, Sukhpal Singh Gill. (2024). Quantum Cloud Computing: Trends and Challenges. *Journal of Economy and Technology*, 2, 190-199, ISSN 2949-9488. https://doi.org/10.1016/j.ject.2024.05.001)

9.1.2 Neural Networks

The architecture and operation of artificial neural networks, or ANNs is based on biological brain systems. They are made up of layers of interconnected nodes (neurons) (Figure 9.2), each of which is assigned a weight that changes throughout training to reduce prediction error (LeCun et al., 2015). Neural networks have made advancements in computer vision, natural language processing, speech recognition, and bioinformatics that are now fundamental to machine learning and artificial intelligence. The perceptron, the fundamental building block of an ANN, simulates a simplified neuron by combining weighted inputs, applying a bias, and using an activation function to generate an output (Rosenblatt, 1958). Neural networks can approximate complex, non-linear processes thanks to the introduction of nonlinearity by activation functions like sigmoid, ReLU, and softmax.

Neural network architectures have changed dramatically over time. Deep neural networks (DNNs) with many hidden layers replaced shallow networks with a single hidden layer, allowing for hierarchical feature extraction. Different specialized designs of neural networks are used like recurrent neural networks (RNNs) for sequential data (Hochreiter & Schmidhuber, 1997), transformers for large-scale language models (Vaswani et al., 2017), and convolutional neural networks (CNNs) for image analysis. Neural networks have drawbacks

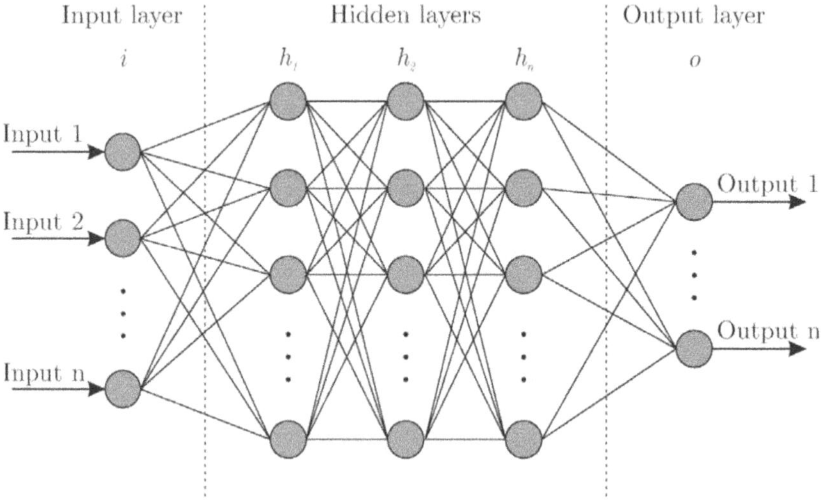

Figure 9.2: Architecture of neural networks interconnected with nodes. (Adopted from Mahmood, M. A., Visan, A. I., Ristoscu, C. & Mihailescu, I. N. (2021). Artificial Neural Network Algorithms for 3D Printing. *Materials*, 14(1), 163. https://doi.org/10.3390/ ma14010163)

including high processing costs, vanishing/exploding gradients, a need for large volumes of data, and interpretability issues. To overcome these obstacles, quantum neural networks are being created by integrating neural networks with quantum computing.

9.1.3 Quantum Neural Networks (QNNs)

With the goal of using quantum physics to enhance machine learning, quantum neural networks (QNNs) represent a novel link between artificial intelligence and quantum computing (Figure 9.3). The representational power of neural networks combined with the exponential computing resources of quantum systems, provides the driving force (Biamonte et al., 2017). QNNs are theoretically more effective at high-dimensional linear algebra operations, which makes them well-suited for generative modeling, classification, and optimization. Typically, a QNN uses quantum feature maps to encode classical inputs into quantum states, which are then manipulated using parameterized quantum circuits (variational quantum algorithms). A quantum processor utilizes the circuit while a classical optimizer modifies the parameters in hybrid quantum-classical loops (Schuld & Killoran, 2019). Given the lack of complete error correction in the Noisy Intermediate-Scale Quantum (NISQ) era, this method is particularly alluring (Preskill, 2018). The potential applications of QNNs include quantum chemistry, drug development, finance, pattern recognition, and natural language processing. For example, generative models and quantum-enhanced support vector machines

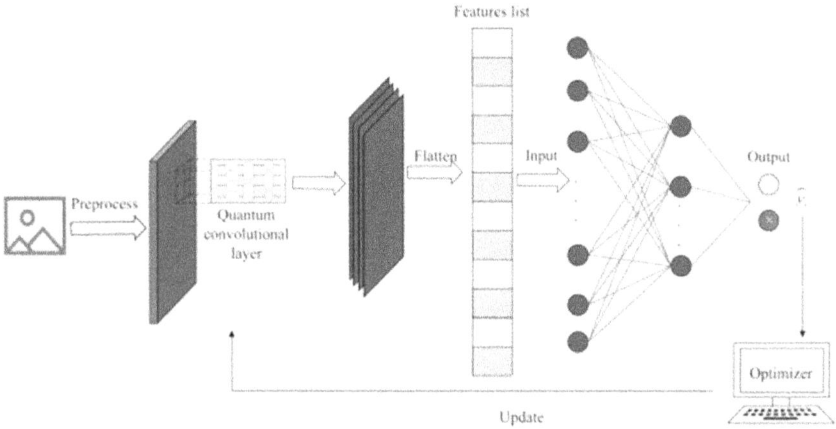

Figure 9.3: Quantum neural network. (Adopted from Zhiguo Qu, Yang Li, Prayag Tiwari. (2023). QNMF: A quantum neural network based multimodal fusion system for intelligent diagnosis. *Information Fusion*, 100, 101913, ISSN 1566-2535. https://doi.org/10.1016/j.inffus.2023.101913)

have been demonstrated on small datasets, showing encouraging outcomes (Havlíček et al., 2019). Apart from this, when compared to standard neural networks, QNNs may provide faster data encoding and processing; however, it is not yet clear how much benefit they provide (Cerezo et al., 2021). Despite the major obstacles facing QNN research, the field is expanding due to ongoing work onquantum kernel approaches, tensor networks, and variational quantum circuits (Mitarai et al., 2018).

9.2 Discussion

Scientific research and technological development have gained momentum during the past few decades. Among these advances, artificial neural networks (ANNs) and quantum computing stand out as the two of the most revolutionary innovations. They originate from different fields: quantum computing arises from theoretical physics and quantum mechanics, while ANNs are based on computational models influenced by neuroscience. As a result of the combination of the two paradigms in recent years, the hybrid field of quantum neural networks (QNNs) has emerged. This new field is driven by both opportunity and necessity, not merely by chance. Artificial intelligence (AI), especially deep learning together with quantum computing offers unique benefits and is pushing the boundaries of classical hardware (Biamonte et al., 2017).

Feynman (1982) in the 1980s noted that a computer operating under the laws of quantum physics could easily simulate quantum systems. This insight marked the beginning of quantum computing, as classical computers which do not follow such principles, found the task exponentially difficult. Deutsch (1985), later formalized the concept of a universal quantum computer. Since then, the field has achieved significant milestones, with algorithms such as Grover's (1996) search algorithm and Shor's (1994) factoring algorithm, demonstrating substantial speedups over their classical counterparts.

Alongside this, the development of neural networks from McCulloch and Pitts' (1943) model of artificial neurons to contemporary deep learning architectures. They gained popularity in the 2010s as a result of advances in reinforcement learning, computer vision, and natural language processing (LeCun, Bengio & Hinton, 2015). Despite their effectiveness, neural networks remain restricted by their reliance on large datasets, high energy consumption, and generalization restrictions.

Mutual interdependence is the driving force behind these ideological confluences. While neural networks require substantial representational capacity to model complex functions, while quantum systems inherently constitute and utilize high-dimensional Hilbert spaces. Quantum computing can be used to address deep learning bottlenecks, as it offers new forms of parallelism and novel techniques for function approximation.

Thus, the merging of neural networks and quantum computing provides a suitable solution to the computational needs of the present century, rather than merely an academic curiosity. Quantum neural networks (QNNs) aim to transform both machine learning and quantum information. By leveraging quantum physics computational speedups become possible when combined with the representational capacity of neural architectures.

At times, quantum computing is presented as a prototype that can solve several issues that traditional systems are unable to handle and process. In comparison to conventional algorithms, the major advantages include superposition, entanglement, and quantum parallelism, which enables calculations to be completed more quickly and effectively (Nielsen & Chuang, 2010). Several applications, including integer factorization, database search, and quantum simulation, demonstrate how quantum algorithms can provide polynomial or even exponential speedups (Shor, 1994; Grover, 1996). Google, using a 53-qubit processor recently demonstrated that quantum devices can surpass the fastest supercomputers in the world for specific benchmarks, a milestone referred to as "quantum supremacy" (Arute et al., 2019). Despite these advantages, significant limitations and constraints remain. The most pressing challenges are decoherence, randomization and noise.

Noisy intermediate-scale quantum (NISQ) systems are characterized by the error rates of current devices, which restrict the depth of circuits that can be executed before quantum information is lost (Preskill, 2018). Although theoretical error-correcting codes exist, their implementation requires thousands of physical qubits for each logical qubit, far beyond the capacity of current hardware. Data encoding and readout represent yet another barrier. Most real-world problems begin with classical data, while quantum computers process quantum states. A continual challenge is how to incorporate this data into quantum states constructively without inducing rapid changes (Schuld & Killoran, 2019). Additionally, quantum states often collapse when meaningful information is extracted, reducing the amount of data that can be recovered in a single run.

Lastly, there is uncertainty regarding resource adaptability. Despite steady progress, the number of qubits remains orders of magnitude below what is required for error-tolerant quantum computing. Furthermore, it is still unclear whether quantum approaches will consistently outperform optimized classical methods for many practical tasks, as quantum algorithms that guarantee exponential speedups are relatively rare (Aaronson, 2015). This sector, however, continues to develop rapidly. A feasible path forward lies in hybrid techniques, which integrate quantum subroutines into classical operations. By leveraging quantum advantages where necessary, these methods reduce the demand for fully error-corrected quantum hardware (Bharti et al., 2022). As a result, the science of quantum computing continues to hold both great promise and unresolved challenges, paving the way for its convergence with other paradigms such as neural networks.

Present day AI has been transformed by artificial neural networks, particularly through the development of deep learning. Their potential lies in estimating highly complex, nonlinear functions across a wide range of domains, owing to their vast representational capacity (Goodfellow, Bengio & Courville, 2016). Convolutional neural networks (CNNs) have significantly advanced image recognition tasks, enabling machines to perform better than humans in computer vision (Krizhevsky, Sutskever & Hinton, 2012). Human-computer interaction in natural language processing has been revolutionized by large language models and transformers, giving rise to generative systems such as ChatGPT (Vaswani et al., 2017; OpenAI, 2023).

Moreover, the problems with neural networks are becoming increasingly evident. Training these state-of-the-art models requires larger datasets and substantial computational resources, often necessitating specialized hardware such as GPUs or TPUs. As a result they consume significant amounts of energy (Strubell, Ganesh & McCallum, 2019).

As only a handful of organizations can afford to train frontier models, this reliance on scale raises questions about sustainability as well as accessibility. Neural networks also struggle with interpretability, generalization and abstraction. They excel at identifying patterns, but when confronted with distributional shifts or adversarial examples, they often become fragile (Szegedy et al., 2014). Their "black box" nature makes trust more difficult, especially in critical industries where interpretability is essential, including sectors such as healthcare and banking (Doshi-Velez & Kim, 2017).

Conventional approaches have drawbacks, such as high training costs with limited improvements in accuracy. The development of entirely new models is constrained by saturation (Marcus, 2018). Neural networks present a viable path forward but they are restricted by traditional technology and data availability. The next-generation solution is quantum computing which offers novel representation and computation techniques that can effectively overcome these obstacles. One of the most compelling areas of computational research is the integration of quantum computers and neural networks, leading to the formation of quantum neural networks (QNNs). This connection is not straightforward as it requires balancing two paradigms with different assumptions about information, error tolerance, scalability and computational methods. By addressing these challenges, the merging of quantum computing and neural networks has the potential to revolutionize both machine learning and quantum information research.

Neural networks and quantum systems utilize different concepts of information representation at their elementary level. Gradient-based learning updates the continuous, real-valued activations that are transmitted across layered structures in neural networks. In contrast, quantum systems distribute discrete quantum states, which are controlled by states controlled by linear unitary operations in Hilbert space (Nielsen & Chuang, 2010). Newer encoding techniques, such as basis, angle, and amplitude, are required as it is difficult to map the two descriptions directly (Schuld & Killoran, 2019).

Either of the techniques must compromise in terms of circuit depth, noise sensitivity, and qubit resources. The training of QNNs presents another challenge. Classical neural networks rely on back propagation, which uses chain-rule differentiation to compute gradients efficiently. In quantum systems, however, approximating gradients can be burdensome to approximate gradients, as they rely on parameter-shift rules or other hybrid quantum-classical techniques.

In spite of these challenges, QNNs offer a number of unique advantages. High-dimensional data encoded in proportionally extensive Hilbert spaces encoded by quantum systems enable QNNs to represent functions that are not feasible for classical neural networks (Schuld & Petruccione, 2018). For example, in kernel-based machine learning, where conventional techniques struggle to efficiently compute inner products in high-dimensional spaces, quantum feature maps can be employed to achieve this (Havlíček et al., 2019).

Furthermore, several deep learning scaling problems can be addressed with the help of QNNs. Training may require less energy and data if quantum circuits can approximate functions using fewer resources; in comparison to classical networks, this could significantly reduce computational demands (Tacchino et al., 2019). Quantum circuits when combined with classical architectures, have already shown potential in a range of activities including categorization, generative modeling, and reinforcement learning through hybrid QNN models (Benedetti et al., 2019). The use of QNNs to improve quantum computing itself is another promising approach. Neural architectures may help bridge the gap between learning and quantum processing by enabling adaptive circuit design, noise characterization, and error mitigation (Verdon et al., 2019). The collaboration is therefore reciprocal: learning can stabilize and enhance quantum systems, while quantum mechanics can expand the possibilities of learning.

Applications of QNNs across a variety of fields could undergo transformatory shifts if their potential is successfully realized. In comparison to classical models, QNNs have the ability to learn molecular features directly from quantum data in materials research and drug development (Cao et al., 2019). QNNs also have the potential to accelerate risk modeling and portfolio optimization in the financial industry. They may further enhance cryptographic systems and improve anomaly detection in the security domain. The theoretical implications are equally significant. Fundamental questions regarding the nature of intelligence, computation, and responsiveness may be clarified through the merging of learning theories with quantum mechanics (Penrose, 1994). This defines the huge importance of the QNN paradigm, despite being theoretical.

Finally, it is assumed that the amalgamation of brain-inspired and quantum perspectives is both encouraging and challenging. It is challenging because it requires resolving fundamental irregularities in scalability, training, and representation. It is encouraging because, if successful in the future, it will reshape intelligence and computation, establishing a mutually reinforcing paradigm in which each enhances the other.

The merging of quantum computing with neural networks into quantum neural networks is more beneficial than keeping them in isolation. Neural networks and quantum computing are distinct fields with roots in cognitive science and physics, respectively. Both branches have achieved tremendous success, neural networks in real-world AI and quantum computing in conceptual advances, but they also face obstacles that could hinder their overall progress. Following are the difficulties of quantum computing:

- Data encoding
- Scalability
- Noise
- Energy requirement
- Interpretability and
- Diminished returns accompanied with scaling traditional hardware

The amalgamation of neural networks with quantum systems in QNNs enhances strengths while reducing potential weaknesses by leveraging the state spaces of quantum systems and the adaptive learning capacity of neural networks. Continued development and advancement in both theory and hardware are essential for the progress of QNNs. Quantum devices must look beyond the NISQ era. Nevertheless, hybrid quantum-classical methods allow the analysis of QNNs in less time while preparing them for their long-term execution.

As a result, the integration of these paradigms symbolizes a mental revolution and a technological frontier. It highlights that the complex issues of the 21st-century, whether in industry, society, or science, demand more advanced and faster solutions than incremental improvements.

Quantum neural networks situated at the intersection of physics, computer science, and artificial intelligence (AI), offer a promising path forward. To advance QNNs, increasingly sophisticated research must be conducted to overcome technical obstacles and strengthen interdisciplinary approaches. Collaboration among physicists, computer scientists, mathematicians, and cognitive scientists is essential for designing, training, and interpreting these hybrid systems. This integration will mark a revolutionary new era of computing, redefining what it means to learn, to model, and to reason within a quantum mechanical framework.

9.3 Applications of Quantum Neural Networks

Quantum Neural Networks (QNNs), which combine the capabilities of quantum computing with the adaptive learning potential of classical neural networks, have already shown promise in a number of fields, including artificial intelligence, finance, healthcare, and quantum chemistry (Figure 9.4). Following are key applications of quantum Neural Networks.

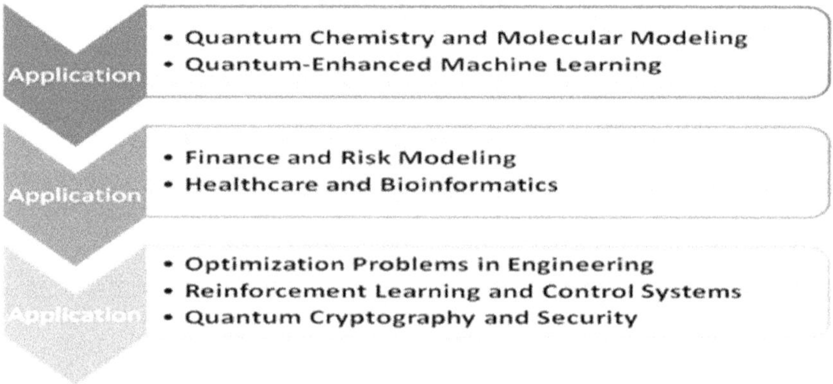

Figure 9.4: Applications of quantum neural network in diverse fields.

9.3.1 Quantum Chemistry and Molecular Modeling

Quantum chemistry is among the most promising fields for the application of QNNs. The exponential growth of Hilbert space with the number of electrons and orbitals limits the effectiveness of classical simulations for molecular systems. Compared to classical methods, QNNs are more effective in modeling molecular interactions and energy landscapes because they can directly encode quantum states (Cao et al., 2019). A common architecture in QNNs is the variational quantum circuit, which uses fewer resources than classical techniques to estimate ground-state energies and approximate molecular Hamiltonians. Quantum predictions of protein-ligand interactions may accelerate the discovery of potent molecules, making these capabilities particularly valuable for drug development (Peruzzo et al., 2014). QNNs can assist in identifying novel chemicals, estimating binding affinities, and even suggesting new compounds through modifications aimed at improving drug efficacy.

9.3.2 Quantum-Enhanced Machine Learning

QNNs are being applied to machine learning tasks, particularly in cases where high-dimensional data or non-linear correlations cause classical networks to falter. Quantum circuits can represent feature spaces of exponentially larger dimensions, enabling the learning of patterns that are not solvable by classical systems (Schuld & Killoran, 2019). QNNs have applications in pattern recognition, most notably in anomaly detection, speech recognition, and image categorization. They require fewer training samples and can achieve similar or even better accuracy as compared to conventional networks on rigorous benchmark datasets (Havlíček et al., 2019). Quantum-enhanced embeddings can capture semantic links in natural language processing, providing insights that improve translation systems and generative models.

9.3.3 Finance and Risk Modeling

The vast solutions space searching ability of QNNs makes them uniquely suited for risk analysis, option pricing, and portfolio optimization. According to Orus et al. 2019, quantum-enhanced optimization algorithms can estimate the best asset allocation within given constraints by accounting for correlations and market uncertainty. Additionally, QNNs can simulate complex probability distributions, enabling the identification of fraud or irregularities in trading patterns in real time, an invaluable capability for risk evaluation.

9.3.4 Healthcare and Bioinformatics

QNNs can be applied in healthcare diagnostics to observe and detect diseases by processing high-dimensional datasets from genomics, proteomics, and imaging data. They can support early cancer detection by accelerating pattern identification in medical images (Tacchino et al., 2019). In bioinformatics, QNNs can efficiently analyze complex biological networks and facilitate gene regulatory network optimization, protein folding prediction, and binding site identification. These approaches are particularly valuable in personalized medicine, where patient-specific data analysis is essential for developing personalized treatment plans (Cao et al., 2020).

9.3.5 Optimization Problems in Engineering

Combinatorial optimization is a central challenge in operational research, logistics, and engineering. QNNs can address and solve these problems more efficiently. They explore multiple solutions concurrently by mapping classical optimization problems onto quantum circuits, thereby reducing calculation time (Farhi et al., 2014). For example, QNNs can be applied to optimize inventory management, warehouse logistics, and delivery routes in supply chain management by incorporating dynamic constraints such as traffic patterns and demand variations. Similarly, QNNs can be used to optimize load balance and energy distribution in power grid management, increasing both reliability and efficiency.

9.3.6 Reinforcement Learning and Control Systems

QNNs can be applied in reinforcement learning (RL). Traditional RL algorithms face challenges of high-dimensional state and action spaces due to computational complexity. Quantum enhanced networks can overcome these challenges and enable faster convergence to optimal policies (Chen et al., 2021). By incorporating QNNs into the RL framework, systems can operate more effectively and make stronger decisions under uncertainty; in complex scenarios, they may even outperform classical methods.

9.3.7 Quantum Cryptography and Security

Quantum neural networks can also be applied in cybersecurity and cryptography. The ability of certain quantum systems to detect and predict patterns in encrypted data can be useful for intrusion detection or cryptocurrency analysis (Liu et al., 2021). Moreover, as physical encryption becomes increasingly vulnerable to quantum attacks, QNNs may contribute to the development of quantum-counterfeiting algorithms, which are becoming ever more important. By combining the learning abilities of QNNs with quantum computing, we can respond to evolving threats, thereby providing stronger protection for communication networks, major organizations, and critical infrastructure.

9.4 Emerging Applications and Future Directions

In addition to the above fields, there are still many unexplored areas where QNNs may be useful. These consist of:

- Generative modeling for the creation of synthetic data and quantum simulations.
- Environmental simulations and climate modeling, when high-dimensional interactions are too computationally demanding for traditional approaches.
- In cognitive modeling and neuroscience, QNNs may be able to replicate elements of brain activity and learning processes at the quantum-level. The intensive use of QNNs will also require advancements in quantum hardware. Near-term implementations on NISQ (Noisy Intermediate scale quantum) devices rely on hybrid quantum-classical designs, in which QNNs handle the most computationally demanding elements (Benedetti et al., 2019).

Apart from the immediate applications of QNNs, they will play a significant role in advancing hardware, algorithms, and interdisciplinary integration in the future. This includes the following areas:

9.4.1 Hardware Scalability

New applications will become possible with the creation of fault-tolerant, high-qubit quantum computers, which would enable deeper and larger QNN architectures (Bharti et al., 2022).

9.4.2 Hybrid Quantum-Classical Architectures

There is a need for hybrid quantum architectures that combine quantum subroutines with classical neural networks to balance algorithmic efficiency, especially given the current hardware constraints (Benedetti et al., 2019).

9.4.3 Algorithmic Innovation

QNN performance and problem solving approach would be enhanced by innovating and designing new training methods (McClean et al., 2018).

9.4.4 Interdisciplinary Collaboration

For full utilization of QNNs, collaborating efforts from physicists, computer scientists, biologists, and engineers are required that will open new avenues in fields including environmental research, healthcare, and finance.

9.4.5 Theoretical Foundations

By understanding and improving the conceptual foundations of QNN expressivity, generalization constraints, and quantum learning theory, real-world applications and performance can be significantly enhanced (Schuld & Petruccione, 2018).

9.4.6 Social Impact

With the continuous advancement of QNNs it is important to examine their effects on workforce dynamics, privacy, security, and ethics. To address these concerns, policies and governance mechanisms will be required to ensure accountability.

9.5 Conclusion

Quantum neural networks (QNNs) have applications across diverse areas such as chemical science, machine learning, intelligence, healthcare, engineering, education and security. The properties of neural plasticity and quantum parallelism makes it possible to solve problems that lie beyond the scope of classical systems. Hybrid designs, hardware advancements and interdisciplinary support are essential for fully realizing the potential utilization of QNNs.

In addition to their primary focus on quantum chemistry, optimization, and finance, QNNs have the potential to influence climate modeling, cognitive science, personalized medicine, encryption, and autonomous systems. The combination of adaptive learning and quantum computing offers tremendous possibilities for complex system optimization, high-dimensional data processing, and generative modeling.

Looking ahead, a wide range of applications for QNNs will emerge, driven by progress in hardware, new algorithms and interdisciplinary support. With the development of hybrid architectures, QNNs are expected to move beyond experimental prototypes toward practical solutions that will bring revolutionary changes to computing, artificial intelligence and scientific research.

References

Aaronson, S. (2015). Quantum Computing since Democritus. Cambridge University Press.

Arute, F., Arya, K., Babbush, R., Bacon, D., Bardin, J. C., Barends, R.,... & Martinis, J. M. (2019). Quantum supremacy using a programmable superconducting processor. *Nature*, 574(7779), 505–510. https://doi.org/10.1038/s41586-019-1666-5

Benedetti, M., Lloyd, E., Sack, S. & Fiorentini, M. (2019). Parameterized quantum circuits as machine learning models. *Quantum Science and Technology*, 4(4), 043001. https://doi.org/10.1088/2058-9565/ab4eb5

Bharti, K., Cervera-Lierta, A., Kyaw, T. H., Haug, T., Alperin-Lea, S., Anand, A.,... & Aspuru-Guzik, A. (2022). Noisy intermediate-scale quantum (NISQ) algorithms. *Reviews of Modern Physics*, 94(1), 015004. https://doi.org/10.1103/RevModPhys.94.015004

Biamonte, J., Wittek, P., Pancotti, N., Rebentrost, P., Wiebe, N., & Lloyd, S. (2017). Quantum machine learning. *Nature*, 549(7671), 195–202. https://doi.org/10.1038/nature23474

Cao, Y., Romero, J., Olson, J. P., Degroote, M., Johnson, P. D., Kieferová, M.,... & Aspuru-Guzik, A. (2019). Quantum chemistry in the age of quantum computing. *Chemical Reviews*, 119(19), 10856–10915. https://doi.org/10.1021/acs.chemrev.8b00803

Chen, S., Cong, I. F., Gong, X. & Zhuang, Q. (2021). Quantum reinforcement learning. *IEEE Transactions on Neural Networks and Learning Systems*, 32(10), 4331–4345. https://doi.org/10.1109/TNNLS.2021.3052173

Deutsch, D. (1985). Quantum theory, the Church–Turing principle and the universal quantum computer. *Proceedings of the Royal Society A*, 400(1818), 97–117. https://doi.org/10.1098/rspa.1985.0070

Doshi-Velez, F. & Kim, B. (2017). Towards a rigorous science of interpretable machine learning. arXiv preprint arXiv:1702.08608.

Farhi, E., Goldstone, J. & Gutmann, S. (2014). A quantum approximate optimization algorithm. arXiv preprint arXiv:1411.4028.

Feynman, R. P. (1982). Simulating physics with computers. *International Journal of Theoretical Physics*, 21(6–7), 467–488. https://doi.org/10.1007/BF02650179

Goodfellow, I., Bengio, Y. & Courville, A. (2016). Deep Learning. MIT Press.

Grover, L. K. (1996). A fast quantum mechanical algorithm for database search. *Proceedings of the 28th Annual ACM Symposium on Theory of Computing*, 212–219. https://doi.org/10.1145/237814.237866

Havlíček, V., Córcoles, A. D., Temme, K., Harrow, A. W., Kandala, A., Chow, J. M. & Gambetta, J. M. (2019). Supervised learning with quantum-enhanced feature spaces. *Nature*, 567(7747), 209–212. https://doi.org/10.1038/s41586-019-0980-2

Krizhevsky, A., Sutskever, I. & Hinton, G. E. (2012). ImageNet classification with deep convolutional neural networks. *Advances in Neural Information Processing Systems*, 25, 1097–1105.

LeCun, Y., Bengio, Y. & Hinton, G. (2015). Deep learning. *Nature*, 521(7553), 436–444. https://doi.org/10.1038/nature14539

Liu, Y., Wang, H., Zou, H. & Dong, D. (2021). Quantum machine learning for cybersecurity. *Quantum Information Processing*, 20(5), 171. https://doi.org/10.1007/s11128-021-03084-7

Marcus, G. (2018). Deep learning: A critical appraisal. arXiv preprint arXiv:1801.00631.

McClean, J. R., Boixo, S., Smelyanskiy, V. N., Babbush, R. & Neven, H. (2018). Barren plateaus in quantum neural network training landscapes. *Nature Communications*, 9(1), 4812. https://doi.org/10.1038/s41467-018-07090-4

Mitarai, K., Negoro, M., Kitagawa, M. & Fujii, K. (2018). Quantum circuit learning. *Physical Review A*, 98(3), 032309. https://doi.org/10.1103/PhysRevA.98.032309

Nielsen, M. A. & Chuang, I. L. (2010). Quantum Computation and Quantum Information (10th anniversary ed.). Cambridge University Press.

OpenAI. (2023). GPT-4 technical report. arXiv preprint arXiv:2303.08774.

Orús, R., Mugel, S. & Lizaso, E. (2019). Quantum computing for finance: Overview and prospects. *Reviews in Physics*, 4, 100028. https://doi.org/10.1016/j.revip.2019.100028

Penrose, R. (1994). Shadows of the Mind: A Search for the Missing Science of Consciousness. Oxford University Press.

Peruzzo, A., McClean, J., Shadbolt, P., Yung, M. H., Zhou, X. Q., Love, P. J.,... & O'Brien, J. L. (2014). A variational eigenvalue solver on a photonic quantum processor. *Nature Communications*, 5, 4213. https://doi.org/10.1038/ncomms5213

Preskill, J. (2018). Quantum computing in the NISQ era and beyond. *Quantum*, 2, 79. https://doi.org/10.22331/q-2018-08-06-79

Schuld, M. & Petruccione, F. (2018). Supervised Learning with Quantum Computers. Springer.

Schuld, M. & Killoran, N. (2019). Quantum machine learning in feature Hilbert spaces. *Physical Review Letters*, 122(4), 040504. https://doi.org/10.1103/PhysRevLett.122.040504

Shor, P. W. (1994). Algorithms for quantum computation: Discrete logarithms and factoring. *Proceedings 35th Annual Symposium on Foundations of Computer Science*, 124–134. https://doi.org/10.1109/SFCS.1994.365700

Strubell, E., Ganesh, A. & McCallum, A. (2019). Energy and policy considerations for deep learning in NLP. *Proceedings of the 57th Annual Meeting of the Association for Computational Linguistics*, 3645–3650. https://doi.org/10.18653/v1/P19-1355

Szegedy, C., Zaremba, W., Sutskever, I., Bruna, J., Erhan, D., Goodfellow, I. & Fergus, R. (2014). Intriguing properties of neural networks. arXiv preprint arXiv:1312.6199.

Tacchino, F., Macchiavello, C., Gerace, D. & Bajoni, D. (2019). An artificial neuron implemented on an actual quantum processor. *npj Quantum Information*, 5(1), 26. https://doi.org/10.1038/s41534-019-0140-4

Vaswani, A., Shazeer, N., Parmar, N., Uszkoreit, J., Jones, L., Gomez, A. N.,... & Polosukhin, I. (2017). Attention is all you need. *Advances in Neural Information Processing Systems*, 30, 5998–6008.

Verdon, G., Broughton, M., McCourt, T., Martinez, A. J., Yoo, J. H., Isakov, S. V.,... & Neven, H. (2019). Learning to learn with quantum neural networks via classical neural networks. arXiv preprint arXiv:1907.05415.

CHAPTER 10

Next-Generation Optimization in Quantum and Hybrid Neural Frameworks

Sara Ali[1*], Polla Fattah[2] and Sanar Fawzi[3]

[1] Department of Computer Science and Engineering, University of Kurdistan Hewlêr
[2] Department of Computer Science and Engineering, University of Kurdistan Hewlêr, Salahaddin University Research Center, Salahaddin University-Erbil
[3] Software Engineering, Salahaddin University-Erbil

The main challenges in neural network optimization are local minima and flat areas. According to quantum-inspired methods, concepts from quantum mechanics, such as superposition, entanglement and interference, offer inspiration for potentially overcoming these constraints more efficiently.

Variational quantum algorithms use parameterized quantum circuits (ansatz) to optimize weights, while quantum kernel methods leverage quantum embeddings to transform features more effectively. Hybrid quantum-classical systems integrate quantum-inspired processing with the established reliability of optimization.

However, there are serious limitations to implementation. Gradients can decrease exponentially decreasing gradients due to the barren plateau phenomenon, making large-scale training difficult. Modern quantum machines still face a 0.1–1% error rate and microsecond coherence times. In addition, overheads in state preparation, measurement costs, circuit depth, and poor qubit connectivity remain significant impediments.

Quantum-inspired classical algorithms, which include tensor networks and optimization heuristics and run on standard computers, are likely to be the most effective in the near future. These approaches provide incremental advances in certain areas without requiring quantum hardware.

Although both quantum kernel methods and variational approaches show theoretical potential, their advantages remain limited compared to optimized

*Corresponding author: sara.sardar.ali@gmail.com

DOI: 10.1201/9781003682950-10

classical methods. Recent evaluations indicate that quantum benefits are more constrained than originally claimed. Practical quantum applications benefits in neural network optimization may only emerge 10–20 years from now, depending on the development of fault-tolerant robust algorithms.

10.1 Introduction

One of the most computationally challenging aspects of neural network models is their optimization. Traditional gradient-based approaches are inherently constrained by the proliferation of local minima, saddle points and flat regions, which can trap classical optimization algorithms, and prevent them from finding globally optimal solutions to the loss function. The computational requirements for training neural networks have grown immensely with the increasing scale and complexity of architectures, and new methods for optimizing their core principles are being investigated.

Among the potentially game-changing technologies, quantum computing stands out for its ability to solve certain optimization problems using radically different laws of computation (Montanaro, 2019). Unlike classical computers, which manipulate information through interactions through bits in one or two fixed states, 0 or 1, quantum computers exploit the properties of superposition, entanglement and interference to process information in ways that classical systems cannot. The existence of these quantum effects makes it possible to perform some computations with exponentially fewer resources than would be required classically, suggesting that quantum advantages in optimization problems are plausible.

In this chapter, the author examines the current state of quantum-inspired optimization methods for neural networks. The evaluation highlights both theoretical and practical opportunities, as well as limitations in a realistic manner.

The field has matured considerably since its debut, moving beyond the early excitement surrounding potential quantum benefits to a more detailed examination of when and how quantum techniques might actually provide advantages (Cerezo et al., 2021). We focus on five primary areas where quantum computing principles have been applied to optimization: variational quantum algorithms that use parameterized quantum circuits as optimization ansatz, quantum kernel methods that leverage quantum feature maps for enhanced similarity computation, quantum-inspired classical algorithms that adapt quantum concepts for classical implementation, hybrid quantum-classical approaches that combine the strengths of both paradigms, and quantum approximate optimization algorithms designed specifically for combinatorial problems.

The importance of maintaining realistic expectations cannot be overstated. Although quantum computing holds enormous theoretical potential, existing quantum devices are severely limited, as in many cases, the anticipated benefits cannot yet be realized. Noisy Intermediate-Scale Quantum (NISQ) devices, while offering more qubits, suffer from high error rates and short coherence times, making it exceedingly difficult to execute complicated quantum algorithms. The quantum computing community has increasingly recognized the disconnect between theoretical advantages and practical implementation, leading to the development of more rigorous methods for designing algorithms and quantifying their performance.

The optimization problem of modern neural networks is especially difficult, as they involve non-convex loss surfaces, high dimensionality, and complex constraint geometry. Figure 10.1 illustrates controlled dataset operations with a maintained quantum advantage up to 30 qubits along with a forecasted scaling pattern (Huang et al., 2021).

Classic optimization algorithms, such as stochastic gradient descent and its variants, have proven to be exceptionally effective in practice, even though they lack a theoretical guarantee of locating global optima in non-convex problems. The effectiveness of these classical approaches raises significant doubts about where quantum methods may offer genuine advantages, as opposed to serving merely as alternative implementations of already established techniques.

The complexity of quantum optimization, and its potential opportunities, depends heavily on existing limitations, which must be understood to fully appreciate both the challenges and possibilities. Most quantum algorithms that promise exponential speedups require vast numbers of physical qubits in fault-tolerant quantum computers, along with error correction and arbitrary quantum interactions operating at extremely low error rates. It is widely expected that such devices will not be available for decades. Therefore, current research should focus on exploring what is achievable with NISQ devices and understanding their limitations.

10.2 Theoretical Foundations and Current Limitations

10.2.1 Quantum Computing Fundamentals for Optimization

To distinguish quantum computing from classical computation, it employs three fundamental phenomena of quantum mechanics: superposition, entanglement, and quantum interference. Superposition allows quantum systems to exist in multiple classical combinations simultaneously, enabling a single quantum bit (qubit) to represent a combination of classical states with varying probability amplitudes. When this property is extended to multi-qubit systems, quantum computers can operate in parallel exponentially many classical states, forming the basis of quantum computational advantages.

According to Nielsen and Chuang (2010), *n*-qubit state may be represented as a superposition:

$$|\psi\rangle = \sum_i \alpha_i \, |i\rangle \tag{10.1}$$

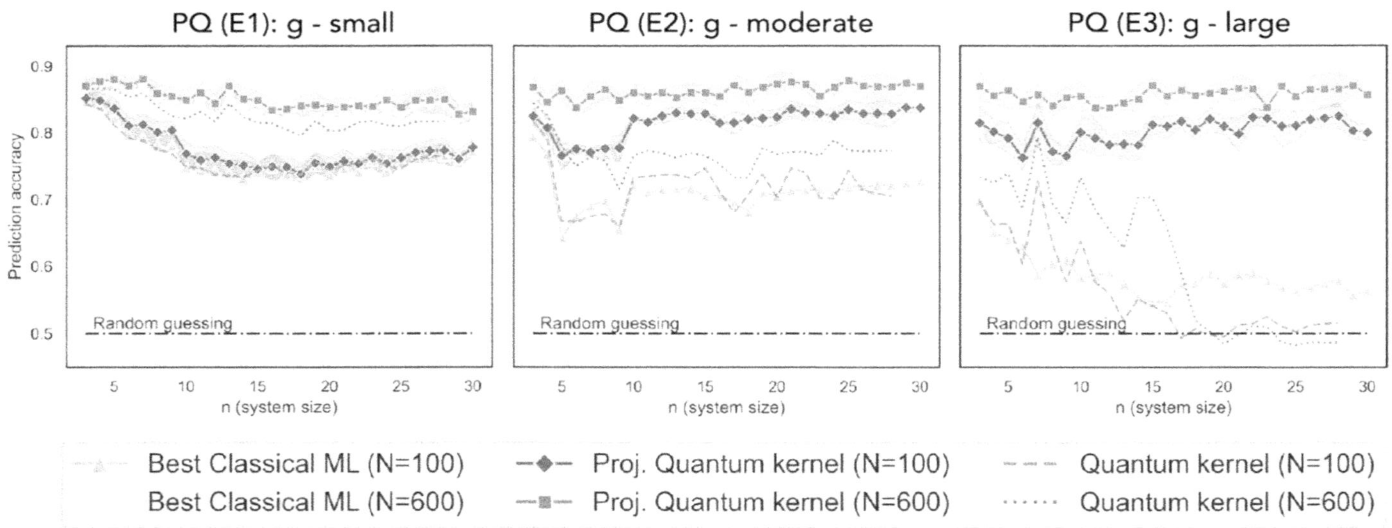

Figure 10.1: The accuracy analysis of quantum advantage (Huang et al., 2021).

where the sum is over all the distinct $2n$ classical bit strings i, and α_i denote complex probability amplitudes, with $\Sigma_i |\alpha_i|^2 = 1$ (Nielsen and Chuang, 2010). This exponentially growing size of quantum space suggests that quantum computers could efficiently search solution spaces that classical computers cannot. Nevertheless, the fact that exponentially large superpositions are representable does not necessarily imply computational benefits, as it remains difficult to extract useful information from quantum states through measurements.

Classical optimization problems, when expressed in quantum form, pose serious challenges that are often overlooked in theoretical studies. Neural network parameters are typically real-valued and demand very high precision, whereas quantum states are represented by discrete computational basis states. Continuous parameters must be discretized, which can introduce approximation errors, and the quality of the encoding directly affects both the quality of the optimization and the number of qubits required.

New theoretical developments have provided more nuanced insights into when quantum methods may offer genuine benefits. Careful discussions of quantum speed-ups in supervised machine learning have demonstrated that quantum advantages do exist, but only for specific problem structures, and they may be more limited than formerly believed (Liu et al., 2021). This work has laid the foundation for proving that quantum machine learning algorithms can outperform their classical counterparts, although the conditions under which this occurs are highly restrictive, and unlikely to apply to broader neural network optimization problems.

10.2.2 NISQ Era Constraints and Implications

The current era of quantum computing is defined as the Noisy Intermediate-Scale Quantum (NISQ) era, characterized by devices with relatively small qubit counts (usually 50—1000), high error rates, and weak qubit interactions. These constraints fundamentally determine what quantum optimization algorithms can feasibly achieve in practice and often prevent the realization of the theoretical quantum benefits that would be possible with perfect, error free quantum computation.

A demonstration of a variational quantum eigensolver on a photonic quantum processor marked the first step toward the realistic implementation of quantum algorithms. Nonetheless, scaling such methods to larger, more practical problems remains difficult due to noise accumulation and hardware constraints. The next generation of hardware-efficient variational quantum eigensolvers applied to small molecules demonstrated the potential of quantum methods in quantum chemistry (Kandala et al., 2017), while also revealing the limitations of existing hardware.

The fidelities of gates in modern quantum devices have now improved to 99.9% to 99.998% with fluxonium qubits achieving the current record of 99.998% (The Quantum Insider, 2025). Two-qubit operations typically range from 99.4 to 99.93% fidelity, with superconducting processors from IQM reaching 99.93%

controlled-Z gate fidelity (Meet IQM, 2025). Despite these advances, error accumulation remains a significant issue as circuit depth increases. For example, a quantum circuit with 100 gates at 99% fidelity achieves an overall fidelity of only 37%. Even state-of-the-art devices with 99.9 fidelity yield a circuit success rate of 90.5%, while the record 99.998 fidelity at MIT corresponds to an overall fidelity of 99.8% (SpinQuanta, 2025). This error accumulation continues to be a prohibitive factor for useful quantum circuit complexity on the existing NISQ devices, underscoring the need for further improvements in hardware fidelity and quantum error correction strategies.

Qubit connectivity is the physical realization of quantum devices, as qubits cannot directly interact with those beyond their nearest neighbors in the device topology. To apply quantum gates between distant qubits, sequence of SWAP operations is required to transfer quantum information across the machine, which significantly increases circuit depth and error rates.

The development of quantum variational algorithms in practice has been gradual and steady, accompanied by the emergence of a theory describing their capabilities and constraints. This breakthrough has provided valuable insights into the classes of problems that quantum variational schemes are likely to solve effectively, as well as the areas in which they may offer potential advantages over classical methods.

10.2.3 Quantum Advantage: Theory versus Practice

Research in quantum computing has explored quantum advantage algorithms that are more efficient for certain problems than known classical algorithms, but achieving this advantage has proven more difficult practice than initially anticipated. The discontinuity between the theoretical benefits of quantum benefits and their practical application provides an entry point for a realist examination of quantum optimization strategies in neural networks.

Idealized models of quantum computing typically assume that quantum gates are perfect, coherence times are unlimited, and arbitrary quantum gates can be implemented. Under these assumptions, certain quantum algorithms demonstrate provable exponential or quadratic speedups over classical methods. However, such idealized studies do not account for the overheads of quantum error correction, state preparation, and measurement that are required to make quantum computing a practical reality.

The use of quantum advantage in solving specific optimization tasks requires evaluating the optimization problem while accounting for all implementation costs and comparing the results with existing classical algorithms. This work has shown that demonstrating genuine quantum benefits is more difficult than previously assumed, and that not only theoretical speedups but also practical realizations capable of matching the performance of complex classical methods are necessary.

Recent work on quantum algorithm data analysis has provided valuable context for understanding the broader picture of quantum computational advantages. Comprehensive reviews have highlighted both the potential and the shortcomings of quantum methods across different data analysis problems, demonstrating that quantum benefits are task-dependent and require highly specific circumstances to be realized.

10.3 Variational Quantum Algorithms (VQAs)

10.3.1 Parameterized Quantum Circuits and Ansatz Design

Variational Quantum Algorithms (VQAs) are the most promising approach for realizing quantum benefits on near-term quantum devices, as they employ parameterized quantum circuits combined with classical optimization methods. The basic idea behind VQAs is that quantum circuits act as parameterized functions approximators, much like neural networks serve as parameterized classical functions, with the added advantage that quantum mechanical effects may enable access to computational scales unreachable by classical methods (Benedetti et al., 2019).

An architecture of a parameterized quantum circuit, often referred to as an ansatz, is composed of quantum gates whose parameters are optimized by classical methods. These circuits are typically initialized with a simple starting point, such as all qubits in the $|0\rangle$ state, and then execute sequences of parameterized gates to generate complex quantum superposition and entanglement. The expressiveness of the quantum model and the trainability of the quantum architecture deeply depends heavily on the design, which proves to be a critical challenge comparable in difficulty to the architectural design of classical neural networks.

Hardware-efficient ansatze have become a practical method for implementing VQAs on existing quantum hardware. These designs alternate between single-qubit parameterized rotation gates and deterministic two-qubit entangling gates, organized to respect the connectivity constraints of specific quantum devices. The simplest way to quantify the usefulness of parameterized quantum circuits in quantum machine learning is through their capacity for expression and entanglement (Sim et al., 2019). This provides a strong theoretical foundation for understanding how circuit architecture influences the size of the quantum state space that may be represented and manipulated.

Quantum expressiveness refers to the variety of quantum states that can be generated by varying the parameters across all possible values. Highly expressive ansatze have the potential to model a wide range of quantum states, enabling them to capture problem structures more effectively and optimize them more efficiently. However, greater expressiveness often comes at the cost of increased circuit depth, which raises error rates and complicates optimization due to phenomena such as plateaus and barren plateaus.

An alternative approach is the use of problem-inspired ansatze, which incorporate domain knowledge to solve specific optimization problems. Instead of relying on generic circuit structures, these ansatze are designed to intuitively reflect the geometry of optimal solutions. In quantum chemistry applications, for example, ansatze can enforce particle number conservation and exploit molecular symmetries, as demonstrated in variational approaches to quantum many-body systems.

10.3.2 The Barren Plateau Phenomenon and Mitigation Strategies

Barren plateau phenomenon is one of the most significant challenges in variational quantum algorithms, arising from exponentially small gradients, that make parameter optimization extremely difficult or impossible. Research has shown that in randomly parameterized quantum circuits, which approximate 2-designs, the gradient variance decreases exponentially with the qubit count n. This defines the barren plateau phenomenon, where optimization becomes exponentially hard. The exponential suppression implies that even with small qubit counts, the circuit gradients become vanishingly small and indistinguishable from noise, effectively halting the optimization process. Barren plateaus have a mathematical explanation rooted in the phenomenon of concentration of measure in high-dimensional spaces. Quantum circuits with many parameters and large depth are likely to produce quantum states that are approximately uniformly distributed over the exponentially large Hilbert space. For cost functions defined on such uniform distributions, the gradients converge to zero with exponentially small variance, resulting in flat optimization landscapes where gradient based methods cannot proceed. Figure 10.2 illustrates a 3D loss landscape plot showing gradient variance and flat regions in a parameterized quantum circuit (Yi et al., 2024).

The appearance and severity of barren plateaus in variational quantum algorithms are determined by several factors. Circuit depth plays a critical role, as deeper circuits are more likely to exhibit barren plateaus due to their tendency to generate nearly uniform quantum state distributions. Plateau behavior can also be strongly influenced by the choice of ansatz architecture. Hardware-efficient ansatz, in particular, are often vulnerable compared to problem-inspired approaches, which incorporate important structural features and constraints rather than ignoring them.

Barren plateau behavior also depends on the type of cost function being optimized. The relationship between barren plateau onset and cost function design has been systematically investigated, revealing that global cost functions, based on measurements of the entire quantum system, are more likely to exhibit barren plateaus than local cost functions, which focus on small subsystems. This observation has motivated the development of optimization techniques founded on local cost functions; however, these techniques may sacrifice some expressiveness and may not be applicable to all optimization problems.

Recent studies have demonstrated that noise can intensify the effects of barren plateaus, presenting additional challenges for NISQ-era applications. The physics of noisy plateaus shows that noise in quantum hardware may, in certain cases, cause stronger gradient vanishing effects than those arising solely from circuit structure. However, this understanding has led to the development of

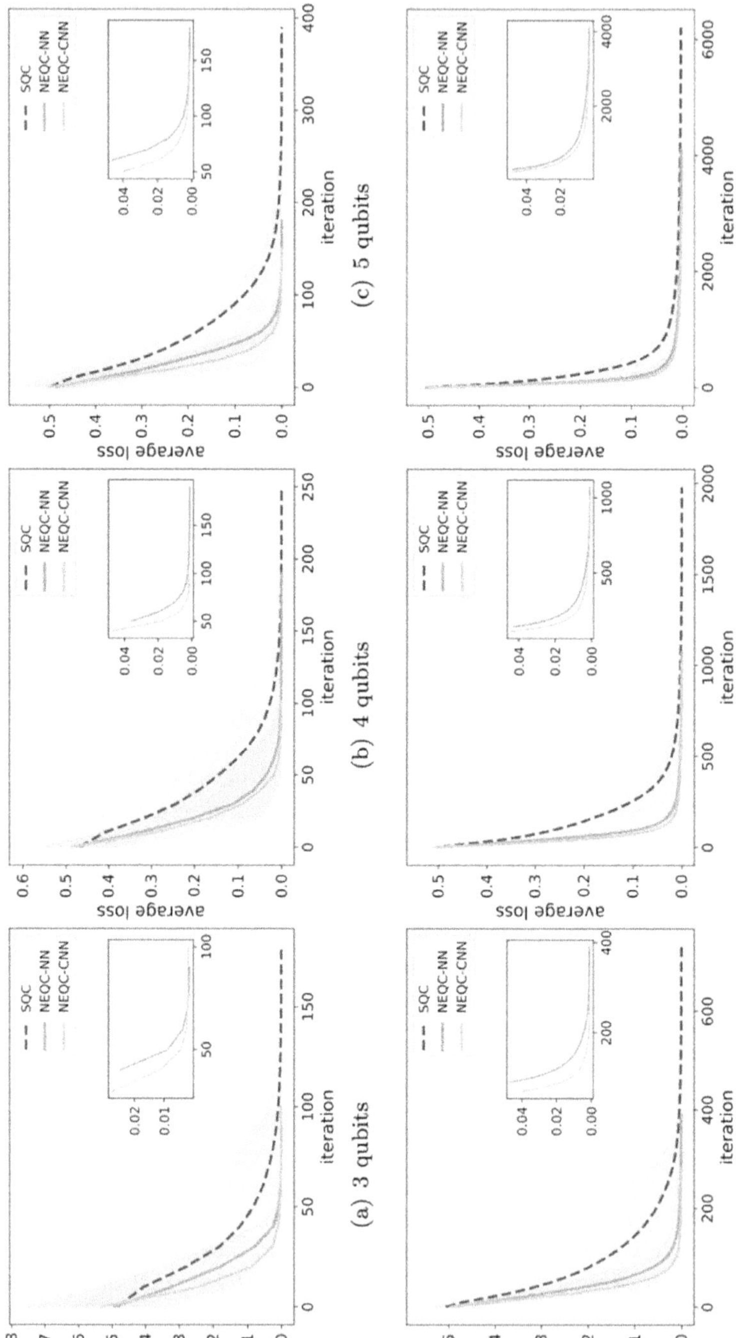

Figure 10.2: The visualization of barren plateau (Yi et al., 2024).

noise-sensitive optimization methods that can function even in the presence of both barren plateaus hardware-induced noise.

Theoretical contributions have provided clearer insights into how gradient behavior relates to the design of the ansatz. The trade-off between expressiveness and trainability in quantum circuits has been characterized in terms of the relationship between ansatz expressiveness and gradient magnitude. This shows that overly flexible ansatze may be counterproductive, their additional expressiveness can come at the cost of exponentially vanishing gradients.

10.3.3 Quantum Natural Gradients and Advanced Optimization

A more advanced optimization process, the quantum natural gradient, employs geometrical characterization of quantum parameter spaces to improve convergence. This approach can optimize quantum landscapes more efficiently than classical gradient descent techniques, as natural gradient directions are defined by the quantum Fisher information metric.

The theoretical basis of quantum natural gradients rests on the insight that the quantum parameter space is not trivially geometrical and requires specialized optimization. The quantum Fisher information provides a natural Riemannian metric on the space of quantum states, enabling the definition of geodesic paths and natural gradient direction that are more effective for optimization.

Executing quantum natural gradients requires computing the quantum Fisher information matrix and testing quantum circuits at shifted parameters. Although this makes the technique more costly than traditional gradient techniques, the improved convergence behavior often outweighs the additional expense, particularly in problems where standard gradients become small or unreliable. Efforts to minimize computational cost while preserving the geometric advantages have led to the design of viable quantum natural gradient algorithms. These have been extended to practical applications of quantum natural gradients built on approximation techniques and effective sampling schemes to address medium-parameter problems. One example of such adaptive metric-based techniques is the Quantum Broyden Adaptive Natural Gradient (qBang) algorithm. qBang extends the quantum natural gradient by approximating the quantum Fisher information matrix using a rank-one Broyden update, substantially reduces the computational overhead of computing exact metric gradients. qBang combines curvature information with momentum-like updates by refining an inverse measure estimate of a parameter and measurement changes, enabling more effective exploration of flat energy landscapes. This approach achieves stronger hyperparameter robustness and greater convergence stability compared to conventional natural gradient and momentum-only methods. The increased stability of qBang across a variety of problem instances is demonstrated in Figure 10.3, which plots step-size sensitivity and shows that qBang has higher fidelity across a broader range of learning rates than other optimizers.

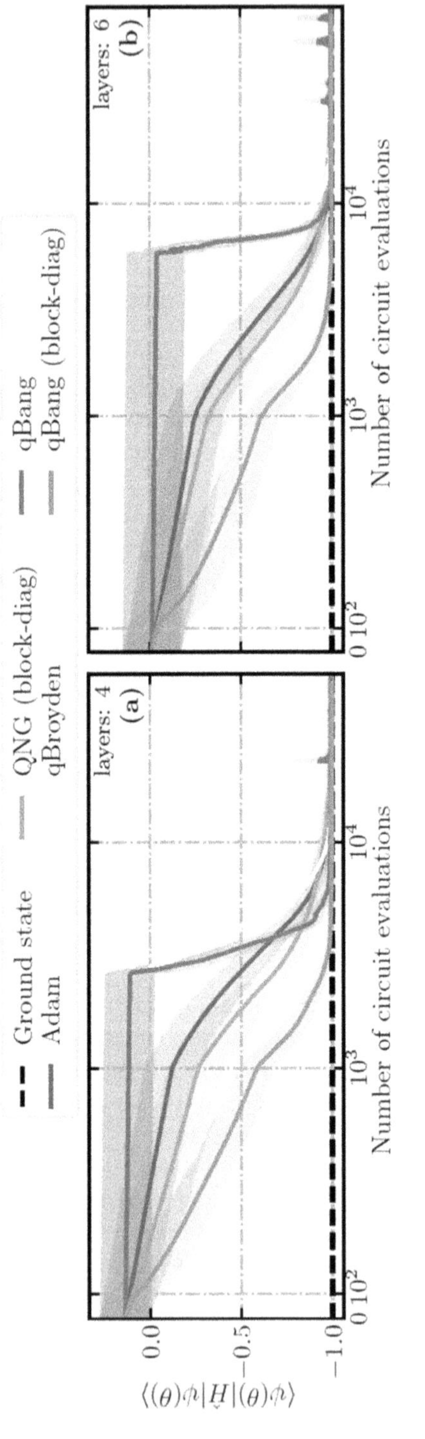

Figure 10.3: The robustness of the hyperparameter across optimizers (Fitzek et al., 2024).

10.3.4 Applications and Performance Assessment

The existing applications of variational quantum algorithms (VQAs) have demonstrated both potential and limitations across different problem domains. One of the most successful areas of application is quantum chemistry, where the inherently quantum nature of molecular systems creates a natural alignment between quantum algorithms and the problems being addressed. Small molecules such as hydrogen, lithium hydride and beryllium hydride have been investigated using VQAs on quantum devices; however, extending these methods to larger molecules remains challenging. The calculation of the Hartree-Fock method performed on superconducting quantum computers represents a significant achievement in demonstrating the practicality of quantum algorithm implementation (Arute et al., 2020). This work showed that meaningful quantum chemistry calculations can be performed on current hardware, while also revealing the constraints and challenges that must be overcome for more complex applications.

Machine learning applications of variational quantum algorithms (VQAs) have shown mixed results. Quantum approaches demonstrate advantages for certain specially constructed problems but struggle to compete with classical methods in most practical applications. The role of data in quantum machine learning has been rigorously analyzed, revealing that quantum machine models face similar sample complexity challenges as classical approaches (Huang et al., 2021). This research shows that the exponential dimensionality of quantum feature spaces does not necessarily translate into enhanced learning performance, particularly in situations with a limited training data.

10.4 Quantum Kernel Methods

10.4.1 Quantum Maps and Kernel Construction

Quantum kernel algorithms represent a radical approach to utilizing quantum computation for machine learning. In this framework, quantum computers are employed to evaluate kernel functions in high dimensional feature spaces, rather than to optimize parameters through variational algorithms. This paradigm leverages the ability of quantum computers to accurately manipulate exponentially large spaces of quantum states, thereby enabling access to feature spaces inaccessible to classical systems. A flowchart illustrating potential quantum prediction advantage testing, including geometric tests of differences and sample complexities, is presented in Figure 10.4 (Huang et al., 2021).

Quantum kernel methods are based on the theoretical premise that quantum circuits act as natural feature mappers transforming classical data into quantum states. These states define quantum feature maps, denoted as $\varphi(x)$ which embed classical input vectors x into quantum Hilbert spaces. The quantum kernel function is then defined as

$$k_q(x, x') = |\langle \phi(x) | \phi(x') \rangle|^2 \tag{10.2}$$

which represents the squared overlap between quantum states corresponding to various input vectors (Egginger et al., 2024).

The first application of supervised learning with quantum-enhanced feature spaces showed that quantum computers could be applied to evaluate kernel functions in exponentially large feature spaces. This method demonstrated how quantum circuits can compute feature representations that would be exponentially costly to compute on a classical computer, thereby implying potential quantum benefits for certain machine learning problems.

Effective quantum feature map design requires careful consideration of both the encoding methodology of classical data and the architecture of the quantum circuit used to process the encoded information. One such method is amplitude encoding in which classical data values are directly encoded as the probability amplitudes of quantum states. This approach can achieve exponential compression, with n classical data points using $\log^2(n)$ qubits. Nonetheless, amplitude encoding involves complex state preparation steps that can be hard to execute efficiently on quantum devices.

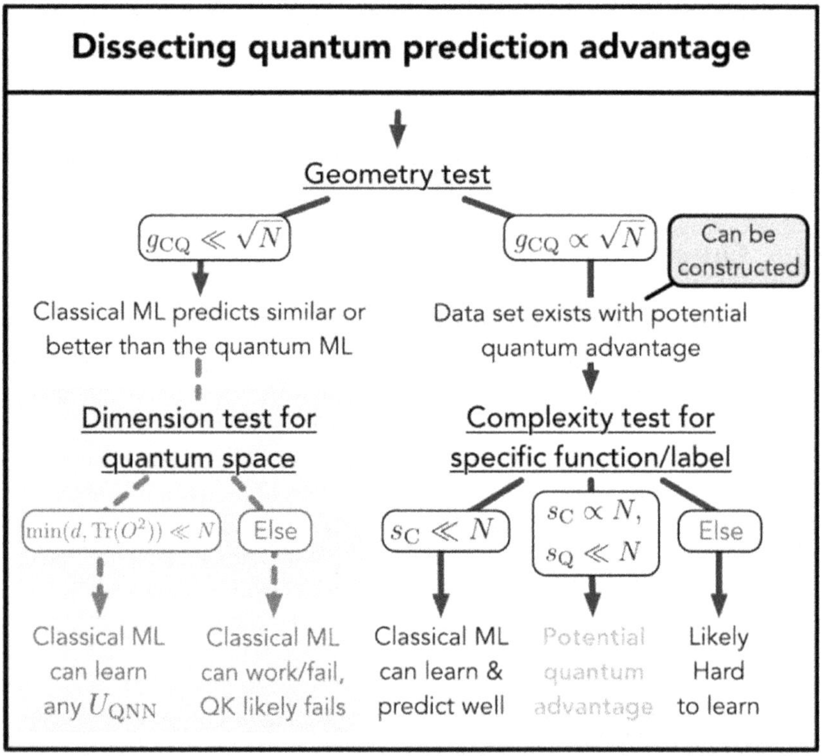

Figure 10.4: Advantage assessment of quantum machine learning (Huang et al., 2021).

Angle encoding provides a more convenient alternative, in which classical feature values are represented as rotation angles in parameterized quantum gates, such as $RY(\pi x_i)$ gates applied to individual qubits. This encoding preserves the continuity of classical features, and is fully compatible with parameterized quantum circuits. The impact of data encoding on the expressive power of variational quantum machine learning models has been systematically studied (Schuld et al., 2021), showing that the choice of encoding strategy is a critical factor in determining the strengths and limitations of quantum methods.

10.4.2 Quantum Advantage Claims and Critical Assessment

The original motivation for quantum kernel methods arose from theoretical studies that quantum computers could provide exponential benefits by exploiting feature spaces of dimension 2^*n* using *n* qubits, well beyond the capabilities of classical computers. These early assertions proposed that quantum feature maps would naturally generate rich, high-dimensional representations that could not be efficiently simulated or approximated by classical computers.

Theoretical and empirical analyses that followed, however, have shown that these claims of quantum advantage face serious limitations. Recent studies on exponential concentration and non-trainability in quantum kernel methods have demonstrated that many of the purported quantum benefits may be smaller than originally anticipated (Thanasilp et al., 2024). This line of research provides the insight that the high-dimensionality of quantum feature spaces can even hinder learning performance, as concentration-of-measure effects may reduce the ability to distinguish between different data points. The simplest limitation is that many quantum feature maps can be efficiently computed classically using methods such as tensor networks, Monte Carlo sampling, or direct quantum circuit computation of shallow quantum networks. This classical stimulability undermines the claimed computational advantages of quantum kernel methods, reducing them to other implementations of classically computable kernel functions.

Expressibility and trainability trade-offs are additional key limitations of quantum kernel methods. Deep quantum circuits, which are required to construct highly expressive quantum feature maps capable of forming complex, high-dimensional feature representations, are difficult to implement on existing noisy quantum hardware. In contrast, shallow quantum circuits, though reliably implementable on NISQ devices, tend to be less expressive and may not provide any advantage over classical feature representations.

10.4.3 Practical Implementation Challenges

The application of quantum kernel methods to accessible quantum hardware faces numerous real-world challenges that severely impact their performance and usefulness. Circuit depth is one of the most prominent weaknesses: highly expressive quantum feature maps often require deep quantum circuits with many

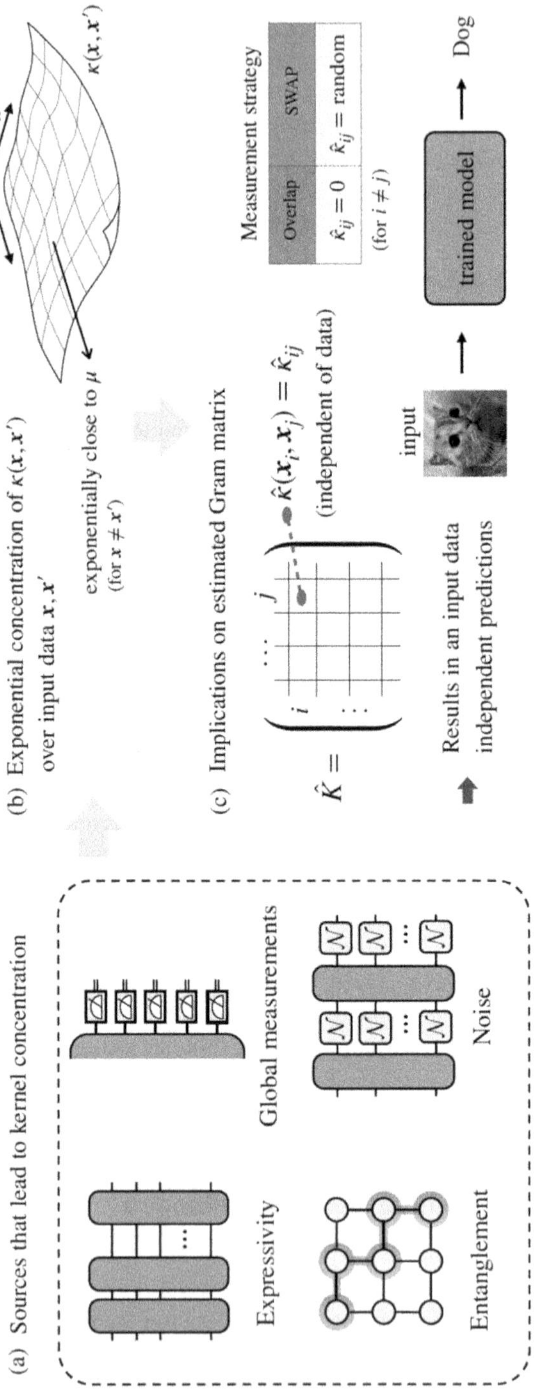

Figure 10.5: Quantum kernel concentration mechanism (Thanasilp et al., 2024).

layers of gates, yet current quantum devices can reliably execute only shallow quantum circuits due to decoherence and error propagation.

Quantum kernel values may introduce significant additional computational overheads that are often overlooked in theory. A kernel matrix of m training samples can be computed in $O(m^2)$ quantum circuit executions, each demanding a number of measurement shots to achieve adequate statistical accuracy. When this measurement overhead is properly accounted for, quantum kernel methods can typically be as computationally costly as classical alternatives.

In Figure 10.5, the sources of exponential concentration in quantum kernels are identified as expressivity, entanglement, and noise effects (Thanasilp et al., 2024).

Empirical studies comparing quantum kernel methods with classical approaches have generally shown that classical methods deliver superior performance when realistic implementation constraints are considered. Although quantum kernel methods may exhibit advantages on carefully constructed synthetic datasets or small-scale problems, they typically underperform classical methods on practical machine learning tasks involving real-world data.

10.5 Quantum-Inspired Classical Algorithms

10.5.1 Tensor Network Methods and Matrix Product States

Tensor network methods are a potent category of quantum-inspired classical algorithms that employ mathematical frameworks developed to address optimization and machine learning problems in quantum many-body physics. These methods create a bridge between quantum and classical computation by efficiently representing certain classes of quantum states and operations with classical data structures, thereby enabling the exploration of quantum-like computational strategies without the need for actual quantum hardware.

The fundamental insight underlying tensor network methods is that many quantum states of practical interest, despite existing in exponentially large Hilbert spaces, can be efficiently represented using polynomial classical resources when their entanglement structure is limited. The property is exploited by Matrix Product States (MPS) and other tensor network structures, which represent a quantum state as a network of smaller tensors linked by contracted indices.

It has been demonstrated that without quantum hardware, some of the quantum computational benefits can be realized by developing quantum-inspired algorithms to prepare quantum states using classical computational methods (Jouzdani et al., 2024). These methods prove that the quantum-classical computation boundary is more subtle than it was originally conceived and even classical approaches inspired by quantum approaches can be as efficient as quantum approaches on certain types of problems.

Matrix Product States are quantum states expressed as a chain of connected tensors: each tensor is associated with one or more qubits, and tensor interactions capture shared quantum correlations. The maximum entanglement that an MPS can represent is determined by its bond dimension, which defines the trade-off between representational accuracy and computational cost. Figure 10.6 represents a schematic of grid and hierarchical tensor-network decompositions (MPS, TTN, MERA) (Rieser et al., 2023).

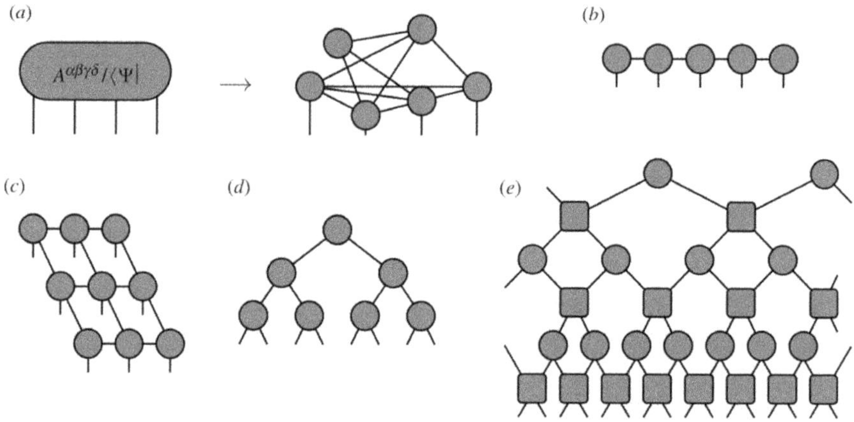

Figure 10.6: Tensor network structure diagram (Rieser et al., 2023).

10.5.2 Quantum-Inspired Optimization Heuristics

Quantum-inspired optimization heuristics are a category of classical algorithms that incorporate concepts and principles from quantum mechanics to optimize classical computations. These methods emulate some of the qualities of quantum algorithms, including parallel exploration and tunnelling effects, while remaining feasible on classical computers without requiring quantum hardware.

The quantum adiabatic algorithm applied to random optimization problems also serves as a valuable theoretical foundation for understanding when quantum-inspired methods may be effective. Careful investigations have shown that quantum adiabatic algorithms can provide benefits for certain classes of problems, particularly those whose energy landscape structures favor quantum evolution. Quantum-inspired evolutionary algorithms integrate concepts such as quantum superposition and entanglement into classical evolutionary computation frameworks. These algorithms encode candidate solutions in the form of quantum chromosomes, comprising qubits with probability amplitudes, which allows multiple classical solutions to be represented simultaneously within a single quantum individual.

The strength of quantum annealing methods is important to understand in order to develop quantum-inspired optimization techniques. Research in this area has provided crucial insights into when quantum annealing may offer advantages over classical optimization algorithms and under what circumstances these benefits can be preserved despite noise and other real-world limitations.

10.6 Hybrid Quantum-Classical Approaches

10.6.1 Architecture Design and Integration Principles

The nearest-term path to achieving practical quantum-computation benefits in optimization programs lies in hybrid quantum-classical systems. These systems combine the strengths of both quantum and classical processors: quantum hardware is employed for computational tasks where quantum methods may offer advantages, while classical processors handle tasks where they excel, including data management, error correction, and algorithm control. Figure 10.7 depicts a schematic representation of hybrid quantum-classical optimization in variational quantum algorithms. The quantum computer acts on quantum states (*r*), parameterized unitaries (*U*θ), and measures observables (ρ) in Hilbert spaces of exponentially increasing size. The classical computer performs optimization

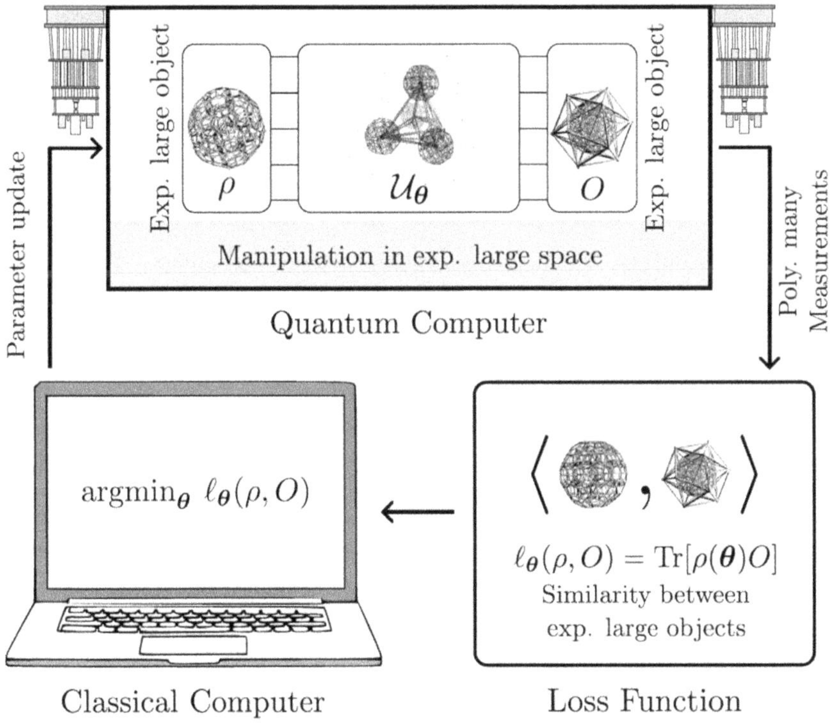

Figure 10.7: Optimization architecture of hybrid quantum-classical model (Larocca et al., 2025).

by minimizing the parameter θ through the loss function $\mathcal{L}\theta(\rho, O) = Tr[\rho(\theta) O]$, which quantifies the similarity of quantum states and target observables. The architecture provides an opportunity to investigate the benefits of quantum computation while leveraging classical optimization (Larocca et al., 2025).

Learning to learn with quantum neural networks through the classical neural networks paradigm illustrates the effectiveness of combining quantum and classical elements to capitalize on the strengths of both computational methods. Research has demonstrated that hybrid architectures may be superior to either purely quantum or purely classical approaches, with each paradigm applying its strengths to the problems where it is most beneficial.

The basic design principle of successful hybrid architectures is the prudent partitioning of computational tasks according to the relative capabilities and weaknesses of quantum and classical processors. Quantum computers are particularly effective at controlling quantum superposition and entanglement, computing certain non-linear functions, and exploring high dimensional spaces through quantum parallelism. However, they remain limited by coherence times, error rates and measurement overhead.

Recent studies of quantum-assisted quantum compiling have shown that hybrid solutions can make the implementation of quantum algorithms more efficient (Khatri et al., 2019). As demonstrated in this work, classical pre-processing can be leveraged to achieve significant benefits in quantum algorithms by optimizing circuit compilation and reducing the quantum resource requirements of specific computational tasks.

10.6.2 Performance Optimization and Practical Considerations

The quantum and classical dynamics in hybrid systems necessitate a sophisticated coordination approach that accounts for multiple time aspects, error behavior and computational granularities of the two paradigms. With quantum circuit cutting opening the possibility of scalable multiprotocol execution, an essential step towards the limits of accessible quantum hardware has been achieved. These methods enable larger quantum algorithms to be executed by decomposing them into smaller parts that can be implemented on currently available quantum devices.

The computational properties and operational limits of quantum and classical processors differ significantly, requiring resource allocation strategies in hybrid systems that account for these differences. Quantum circuits are typically executed in batches, with substantial overheads in state measurement and preparation, whereas classical processors support continuous execution with fine-grained control flow and real-time access to computation results.

Further development of learning algorithms for quantum systems has led to improvements in quantum state overlap learning algorithms and other simpler quantum machine learning approaches. These advances not only address practical tasks by implementing theoretical quantum algorithms on physical hardware but also provide valuable architectural methods for building effective hybrid systems.

10.7 Quantum Approximate Optimization Algorithm (QAOA)

10.7.1 QAOA Fundamentals and Theoretical Framework

The Quantum Approximate Optimization Algorithm (QAOA) is a specialized form of variational quantum algorithm uniquely tailored to combinatorial optimization problems that commonly arise in machine learning and operations research. QAOA offers a quantum optimization framework by encoding the the optimization problem into a quantum Hamiltonian and applying mixing operations, which enable exploration of the solution space through quantum superposition effects.

The mathematical foundation of QAOA lies in the adiabatic theorem of quantum mechanics, which states that a quantum system can be slowly time-evolved from an easily prepared initial state to the ground state of a target Hamiltonian that encodes the optimization problem. Instead of performing a complete adiabatic evolution, QAOA employs a discrete approximation by applying a series of two types of quantum evolution operators, with timescales governed by variational parameters.

The QAOA algorithm begins with a preparation of an equal superposition of all possible computational basis states, typically achieved by applying Hadamard gates to all qubits initialized in the state $|0\rangle|$. This initial state assigns each potential solution to the optimization problem an equal probability amplitude, enabling maximum exploration capability at the start of the algorithm. Figure 10.8 illustrates the Quantum circuit diagram, alternating problem and mixer unitaries in QAOA (Hadfield et al., 2019).

The problem Hamiltonian H_C encodes the objective function of the optimization problem, with its eigenvalues corresponding to the costs of solution configurations. In most combinatorial problems, this Hamiltonian is composed of local interactions that discourage or encourage particular structures in the solution bitstring. Constructing useful problem Hamiltonians requires careful attention to how discrete optimization variables are translated into quantum spin operators, ensuring that the critical structure of the optimization problem is preserved.

10.7.2 Performance Analysis and Benchmarking

The analysis of QAOA performance on maximum cut problems has provided valuable information on the potentials and limitations of this quantum optimization method. Systematic investigations have shown that QAOA performance is highly sensitive to problem structure, and that the number of layers required to achieve good performance is unfavorably dependent on problem size across many problem classes.

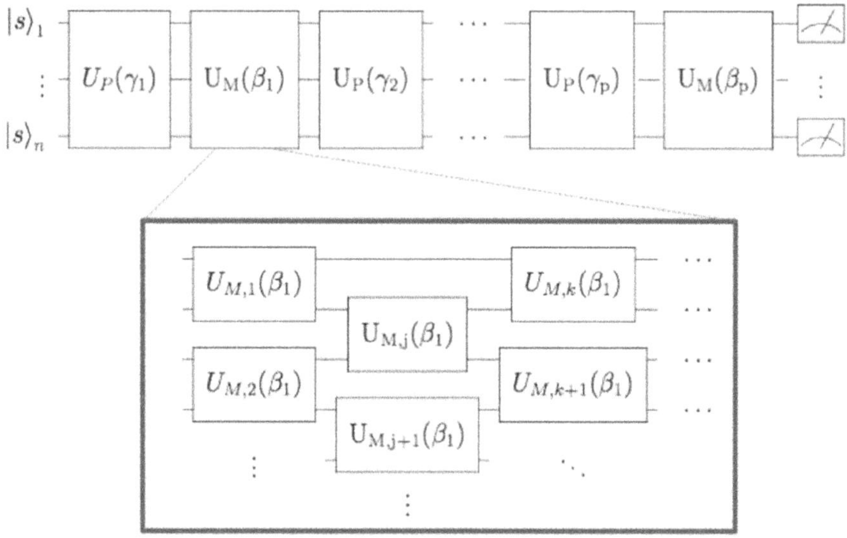

Figure 10.8: QAOA circuit schematic (Hadfield et al., 2019).

Empirical research on the performance of QAOA in existing devices, has revealed significant gaps between theoretical expectations and experiment outcomes. Although QAOA can demonstrate quantum benefits on small problem instances under idealized situations, scaling to larger problems and executing on noisy quantum devices introduces numerous challenges that often negate the theoretical benefits.

The quantum advantage of QAOA must be critically assessed by considering all implementation costs and comparing them with advanced classical optimization algorithms. Research has demonstrated that it is more difficult to establish genuine quantum benefits in solving combinatorial optimization than originally anticipated, particularly when compared to state-of-the-art classical heuristics and exact solvers.

The shot noise inherent in quantum measurements significantly impacts QAOA performance, particularly in optimization problems where small differences in objective function values must be distinguished. The number of measurements required to estimate expectation values with sufficient precision scales unfavorably with problem size and desired accuracy, often necessitating thousands or even tens of thousands of circuit evaluations for each cost function evaluation during parameter optimization.

10.7.3 Applications to Neural Network Optimization

The application of QAOA to neural network optimization problems requires careful consideration of how continuous parameter optimization can be mapped onto discrete combinatorial problems suitable for quantum approximate optimization. Although neural networks typically involve continuous weight parameters, several approaches have been developed to adapt QAOA principles for neural network training and related optimization tasks.

Weight initialization represents one of the most natural applications of QAOA in neural network optimization. Poor initialization can trap neural network training in unfavorable local minima, and quantum optimization approaches may offer improved initialization strategies by simultaneously exploring multiple candidates through quantum superposition.

Hyperparameter optimization for neural networks naturally maps onto discrete optimization problems where QAOA may provide advantages. The selection of learning rates, regularization parameters, architectural choices, and other discrete hyperparameters can be formulated as combinatorial optimization problems. However, the relatively small number of hyperparameters and the effectiveness of classical optimization methods may limit the benefits of quantum approaches.

Neural architecture search presents a particularly promising application area for QAOA, as the discrete nature of architectural decisions aligns well with combinatorial optimization formulations. Choices regarding layer types, connectivity types, activation functions, and other architectural elements are inherently discrete and can be encoded into QAOA problem Hamiltonians.

10.8 Specialized Applications and Advanced Topics

10.8.1 Quantum Chemistry and Molecular Simulation

Quantum algorithms have proven especially useful in areas directly related to quantum mechanical systems, where the quantum nature of the underlying physics provides a natural fit between quantum computers and the problems being addressed. Efficient compression of quantum data using quantum autoencoders illustrates how quantum algorithms are inherently well-suited to quantum information problems.

In quantum chemistry applications, the development of tapering methods to simulate fermionic Hamiltonians has yielded valuable improvements in quantum resource efficiency (Bravyi et al., 2020). These methods exploit molecular symmetries and conservation laws to reduce the number of qubits required for precise simulation, thereby, enabling larger molecular systems to be accessible to quantum computation.

Quantum classical variational hybrid algorithms for paired-electron Hamiltonians demonstrate the effectiveness of hybrid methods in quantum chemistry applications (Boyn et al., 2021). Such specialized applications are often more naturally suited to quantum advantage than general-purpose optimization problems, as they can exploit the quantum mechanical structure of the physical systems under consideration.

Advances in quantum algorithms to solve electronic structure problems highlight progress toward achieving quantum advantage through variational two-electron reduced density matrix algorithms. This work has demonstrated that quantum algorithms have the potential to deliver benefits for certain classes of quantum chemistry problems that are especially difficult to solve using classical methods.

10.8.2 Error Mitigation and Fault Tolerance

Practical techniques for quantum error mitigation, intended for near-term use, have gained momentum as quantum algorithms are executed on noisy quantum devices (Endo et al., 2021). These methods enhance the reliability of quantum computations without requiring full fault-tolerant quantum error correction.

Quantum optimization algorithms must be accompanied by techniques to manage both systematic and statistical errors, arising from imperfect quantum gates and finite sampling, respectively. Zero-noise extrapolation can mitigate systematic errors by modelling noise and extrapolating to the noise-free limit, though this approach requires multiple circuit runs at varying noise levels.

Error mitigation techniques designed for variational quantum algorithms are an active area of research. These methods must account for the iterative nature of the variational optimization process and the accumulation of noise across numerous optimization cycles.

10.9 Current Performance Assessment and Future Directions

10.9.1 Realistic Evaluation of Quantum Advantages

Current optimization capabilities reveal a significant gap between theoretical potential and practical implementation, with most demonstrated quantum advantages restricted to small-scale problems or specially constructed scenarios that favour quantum approaches. It is essential to recognize these limitations in order to establish realistic expectations and identify the most promising directions for future development.

The quantum benefits demonstrated to date have been largely confined to proof-of-concept cases with carefully selected characteristics that are well-suited to quantum implementation. While these successes are scientifically valuable, they do not directly translate into practical advantages for real-world optimization problems that lack the specific structural properties exploited by quantum algorithms.

Hardware limitations represent the most significant constraint on current quantum optimization capabilities. NISQ devices can implement only shallow quantum circuits with limited numbers of qubits, constraining the size and complexity of problems that can be addressed. The high error rates and short coherence times of current devices often prevent the realization of theoretical quantum advantages even for problems that might otherwise be suitable for quantum approaches. Figure 10.9 shows the effect of different noise levels on fidelity and projected quantum kernel concentration, showing exponential decay (Thanasilp et al., 2024).

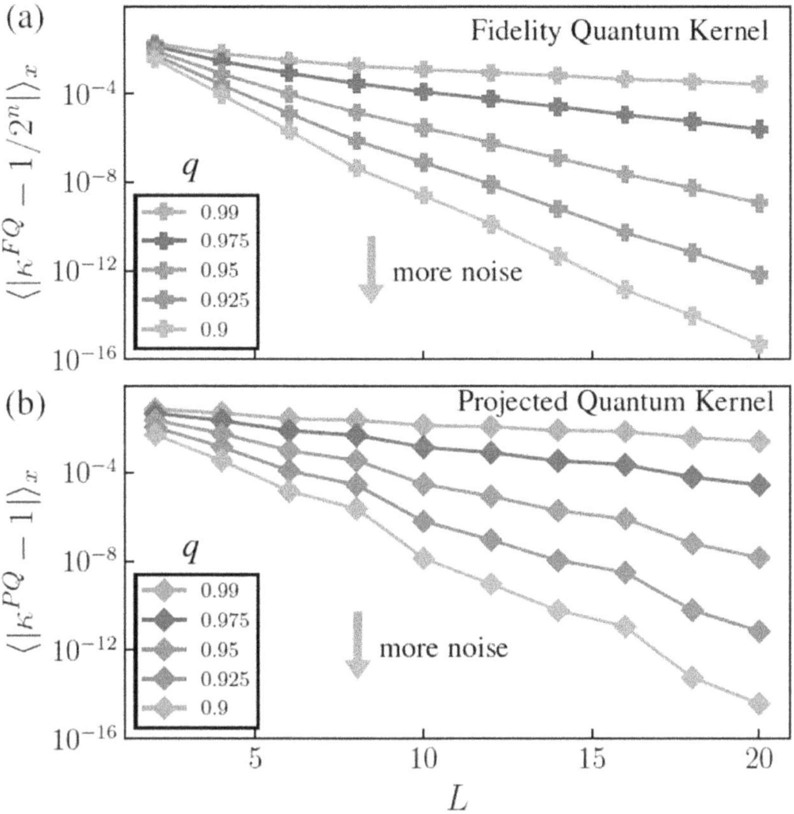

Figure 10.9: Noise scaling in quantum optimization landscapes (Thanasilp et al., 2024).

Classical algorithm improvements continue to narrow the performance gap between quantum and classical approaches, with advances in optimization theory, implementation techniques, and specialized hardware creating moving targets for quantum methods. The rapid pace of classical algorithm development suggests that quantum advantages demonstrated today may be overtaken by classical advances in the near future.

10.9.2 Integration Challenges and Practical Deployment

Quantum optimization methods face numerous challenges to their practical implementation that are unrelated to algorithm performance. Limited availability of quantum hardware, the need for specialized expertise, it is complicated to integrate with existing systems, and economic constraints are all practical considerations likely to restrict adoption despite demonstrations of technical benefits.

Communication between the quantum and classical parts of hybrid systems adds further complexity and must be carefully managed to realize the full benefits of such systems. Communication schemes, error management strategies, resource distribution plans need to be developed with a high degree of sophistication to ensure that hybrid systems provide advantages beyond those offered by purely classical methods. The software and frameworks for implementing quantum optimization algorithm implementation are still in development, but remain highly specialized and require extensive expertise to be used effectively. More user-friendly tools and standardized interfaces will be critical for increasing the adoption of quantum optimization methods in the future.

10.9.3 Future Research Direction

Short-term potential benefits of quantum optimization appear strongest in hybrid strategies that combine quantum and classical methods, in problem spaces with natural quantum structure, and in cases where limited performance justify the added complexity of quantum implementation. Nevertheless, even such applications face serious technical and practical challenges that must be addressed through further research and development.

To achieve more efficient quantum optimization algorithms, both theoretical and practical design efforts are required, ones that respond to current limitations while remaining adaptable to future hardware capabilities. Problem-specific algorithm design is among the most promising approaches for realizing quantum advantage, particularly for optimization problems with natural quantum structure or distinctive properties that can benefit from quantum methods.

The development of hybrid quantum-classical algorithms is progressing toward more advanced methods of integration that leverage the respective strengths of the two computational models. Future hybrid algorithms could employ quantum processors to execute specialized subroutines in classical optimization frameworks, or use classical pre-processing to identify where quantum processors are most likely to provide benefits.

Error-conscious algorithm design acknowledges that noise is an inherent property of quantum computation rather than a temporary bottleneck, and develops methods to optimize performance under controlled levels of noise. In some cases, certain forms of noise may even prove beneficial to optimization by helping to avoid overfitting or by promoting exploration of the solution space.

10.10 Implementation Considerations and Hardware Constraints

10.10.1 Noise and Decoherence Effects

One of the most severe barriers to realizing practical quantum benefits is the effect of noise and decoherence on quantum optimization. Understanding these effects and developing strategies to mitigate them is essential for the successful application of quantum optimization methods on current and near-future quantum devices.

A gradual destruction of quantum coherence, caused by quantum systems interacting with environmental degrees of freedom, arises from decoherence processes that ultimately drive quantum systems toward classical behavior. The decoherence times of contemporary quantum hardware are typically on the order of microseconds to milliseconds, which imposes extremely restrictive limits on the range of quantum calculations that can be executed with reliable precision.

In quantum circuits, gate errors arise because quantum systems cannot be perfectly controlled, leading to deviations from the intended quantum operations. Current quantum devices generally achieve single qubit gate fidelities of between 99.9% and 99.99 with two qubit gate fidelities range from 95% to 99.5%. These error rates compound with circuit depth and produce exponential effects on overall circuit fidelity.

Measurement errors further contribute to noise in quantum optimization algorithms by inaccurately capturing quantum state outcomes. Quantum computing platforms report readout fidelities, which are usually within the range of 90–99.9%. Systematic biases from readout errors can misdirect optimization algorithms and worsen convergence behavior, particularly in algorithms that rely on accurate expectation values obtained through repetitive measurements.

10.10.2 Circuit Depth and Connectivity Limitations

A significant impediment to accessing quantum circuits that can be implemented with high reliability, and to the types of optimization and problem sizes that can be addressed, is the size and bulk of current quantum devices.

Finite coherence times of quantum devices further limit circuit depth, as they determine the number of successive quantum interactions that can be executed before decoherence begins to take effect. Modern quantum devices are typically capable of running only tens to hundreds of gates in a circuit before noise overwhelms the desired quantum computation.

The trade-offs in the design of quantum algorithms stem from the relationship between circuit depth and optimization performance. More complex quantum systems can, in principle, be modeled by deeper circuits, which are more sensitive to noise and decoherence effects but may outperform shallower circuits. Shallow circuits, while less expressive and less capable in optimization, are also less vulnerable to noise.

The physical nature of quantum devices further limits qubit connectivity, constraining quantum algorithms to the topology of the hardware. The connectivity of most existing quantum devices, such as linear chains, square lattices or small-world graphs, may not align with the requirements of many optimization problems.

10.10.3 Measurement and Sampling Overhead

The probabilistic nature of quantum measurements introduces a fundamental sampling overhead that significantly affects the computational cost and convergence behavior of quantum optimization algorithms. Managing this overhead and developing the necessary understanding are essential to achieving realistic quantum benefits and creating effective quantum optimization.

Allocation strategies for measurement shots must balance the limited resources available across different observables and optimization steps in order to achieve peak algorithmic performance. The optimal allocation will depend on the relative importance of each measurement to the optimization process, the statistical properties of the observed data and the stage of the optimization at which the measurements are taken.

When applied to finite optimization, the effects of finite sampling on system dynamics can be severe, as noisy gradient estimations may provide incorrect information to optimization algorithms, and slow convergence. Shot noise introduces random fluctuations in gradient directions, which can cause optimization to proceed inefficiently or stall regions where the gradient signal is overwhelmed by noise.

10.11 Emerging Trends and Advanced Applications

10.11.1 Quantum Federated Learning and Distributed Optimization

Quantum federated learning represents a promising convergence of quantum computing and distributed machine learning, offering potential quantum computational advantages while simultaneously preserving privacy. These techniques enable collaborative training of quantum machine learning models across multiple parties without sharing raw data thereby fulfilling fundamental privacy requirements in diverse and sensitive domains such as healthcare, finance, and other critical applications.

The basic design of quantum federated learning systems consists of distributed quantum computers or simulators that perform local training on individual datasets, with model updates aggregated through classical communication channels. Quantum details of the computation remain local to the participants, while only the aggregate parameter updates are shared.

The privacy benefits of quantum federated learning stem from the no-cloning theorem and other inherent features of quantum information, which make it challenging or infeasible for adversaries to derive private information during quantum model updates. Nevertheless, these privacy guarantees can only be ensured through well-designed protocols and may introduce additional overhead to classical federated learning methods.

10.11.2 Quantum Transfer Learning and Model Adaptation

The concept of quantum transfer learning has emerged as a pragmatic method to utilizing pre-trained quantum models across different problem domains, helping to overcome the high cost of training quantum machine learning models directly. These methods adapt f classical transfer learning techniques to quantum contexts that consider the unique characteristics of quantum states and quantum information processing.

Pre-trained quantum feature maps are among the most effective approaches to quantum transfer learning. In this method, quantum circuits trained on large datasets can be reconfigured with minimal additional training for new tasks. This approach is particularly valuable given the computational costs of quantum circuit training and the substantial hardware requirements for large-scale training.

Quantum transfer learning is based on the theoretical framework that quantum feature representations trained on one task can be transferred to other, similar tasks, with and benefits depending on the circumstances of transfer. Recent theoretical work has shown that quantum transfer learning can be advantageous compared to training from scratch, particularly when the source and target tasks share structural similarities.

10.11.3 Industrial Applications and Real-World Deployment

The maturation of quantum optimization techniques has begun to enable experimental deployments in industrial settings, providing valuable insights into the practical requirements and potential benefits of quantum approaches in real-world applications. These early deployments focus primarily on hybrid quantum-classical approaches, which can deliver modest improvements while operating within current hardware constraints. Figure 10.10 illustrates a comparison of prediction accuracy across different encoding schemes, highlighting conditions under which quantum advantage may be achieved (Huang et al., 2021).

Quantum and quantum-inspired methods for route optimization, inventory management and demand control in supply chains are being actively explored in logistics and supply chain optimization applications. While hardware capabilities continue to improve, current applications remain limited in scope. However, because most logistics problems are inherently combinatorial, they represent direct targets for quantum optimization methods.

The integration requirements of industrial quantum optimization applications have revealed significant practical challenges related to system reliability, integration complexity, and economic justification, issues that are not typically emphasized in academic research. These real-world deployments provide valuable feedback for algorithm development and help identify the most promising directions for future research and development.

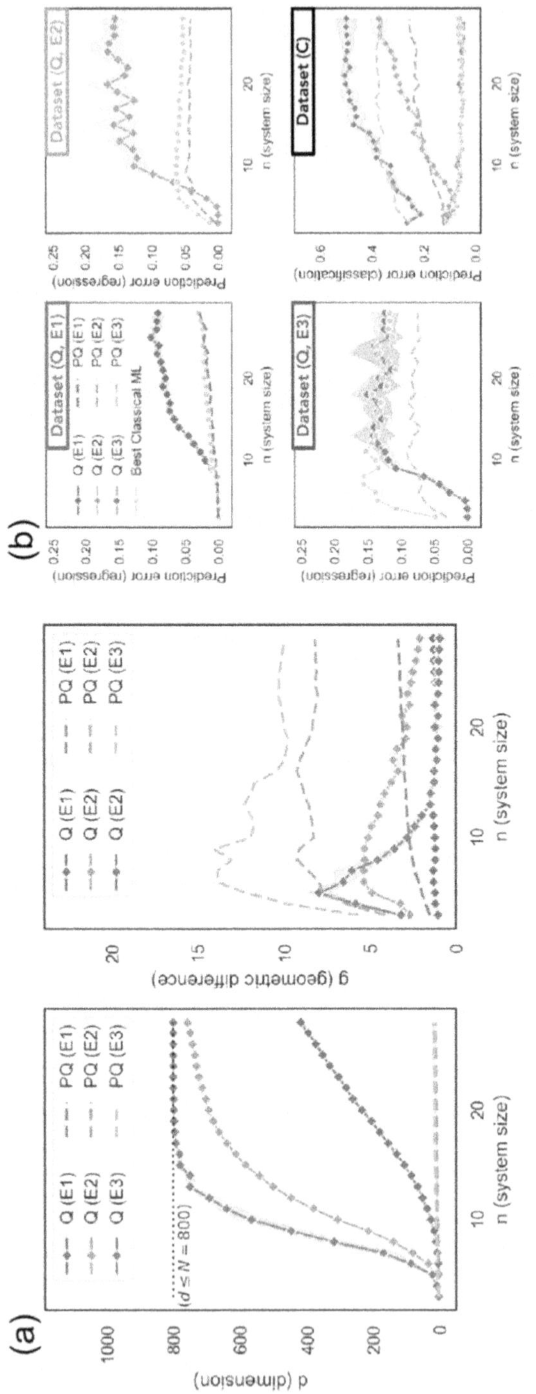

Figure 10.10: Comparison of quantum kernel and classical ML performance (Huang et al., 2021).

10.11.4 Pulse-Based Variational Optimization

Pulse-Based Variational Quantum Optimization (PBVQO) harnesses direct control over analogue quantum hardware by optimizing time-dependent control pulses rather than decomposing algorithms into discrete gate sequences. The variational ansatz used in PBVQO is parameterized in terms of continuous control fields, amplitude, phase and duration of microwave pulses, applied directly to qubits. This method avoids the overhead of circuit compilation, and is less sensitive to gate-synthesis errors, enabling shallower effective circuits and better utilization of native device Hamiltonians. Classical optimizers adjust pulse parameters to optimize a cost function estimated through repeated measurements, while a meta-learning layer may adapt pulse schedules across similar problem instances to accelerate convergence. Recent experiments on superconducting platforms demonstrate that PBVQO can achieve higher fidelity and greater hyperparameter robustness than gate-based VQAs, particularly under realistic noise and connectivity constraints. Figure 10.11 provides a schematic representation of PBVQO workflow showing quantum circuits, the classical optimization loop, and meta-learning integration (Wang et al., 2024).

Figure 10.12 represents error rates and convergence performance at various system sizes exhibiting quantum advantage in selected regimes (Wang et al., 2024).

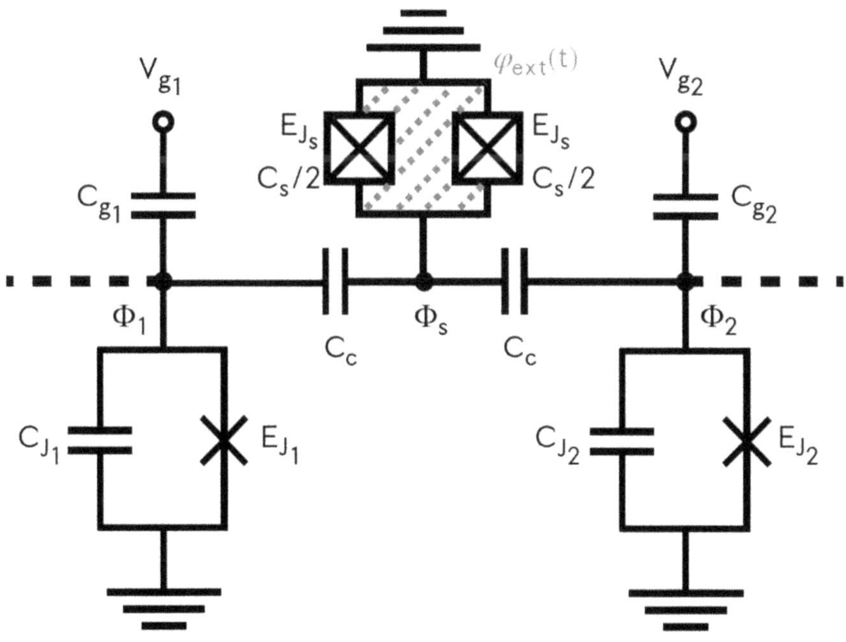

Figure 10.11: Framework of pulse-based variational quantum optimization (Wang et al., 2024).

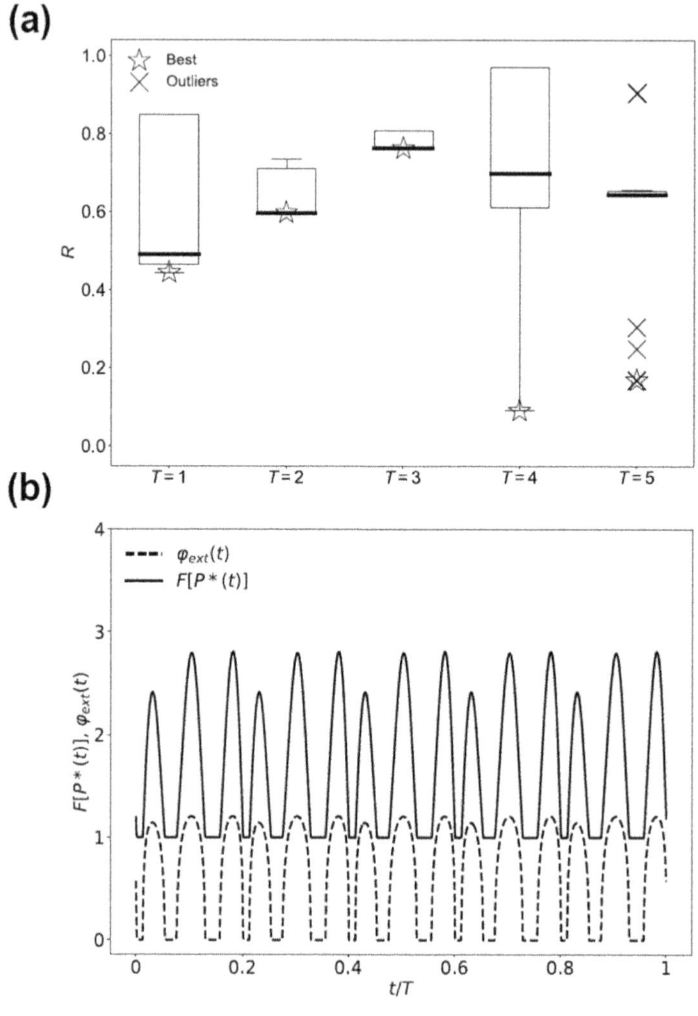

Figure 10.12: PBVQO vs classical optimizer scaling (Wang et al., 2024).

10.12 Conclusion and Future Scope

Quantum-inspired neural network optimization methods are an emerging area of study, offering profound theoretical capabilities, notable practical challenges, and valuable insights into the nature of quantum computational benefits. A thorough analysis of the current state of research and development allows several significant conclusions to be drawn, defining both the present possibilities and future perspectives.

The most notable outcome of ongoing research is the significant disparity between theoretical quantum benefits and their actual realization on quantum hardware. While many quantum optimization algorithms appear promising in theory, assuming ideal conditions without hardware limitations or noise, their advantages often diminish or become negligible in real-world scenarios. This gap highlights the challenges of implementing quantum algorithms on NISQ devices and underscores the need to establish realistic expectations based on practical constraints rather than purely theoretical assumptions. Figure 10.13 illustrates the variance scaling of fidelity and projected quantum kernels as a function of circuit depth and qubit number (Thanasilp et al., 2024).

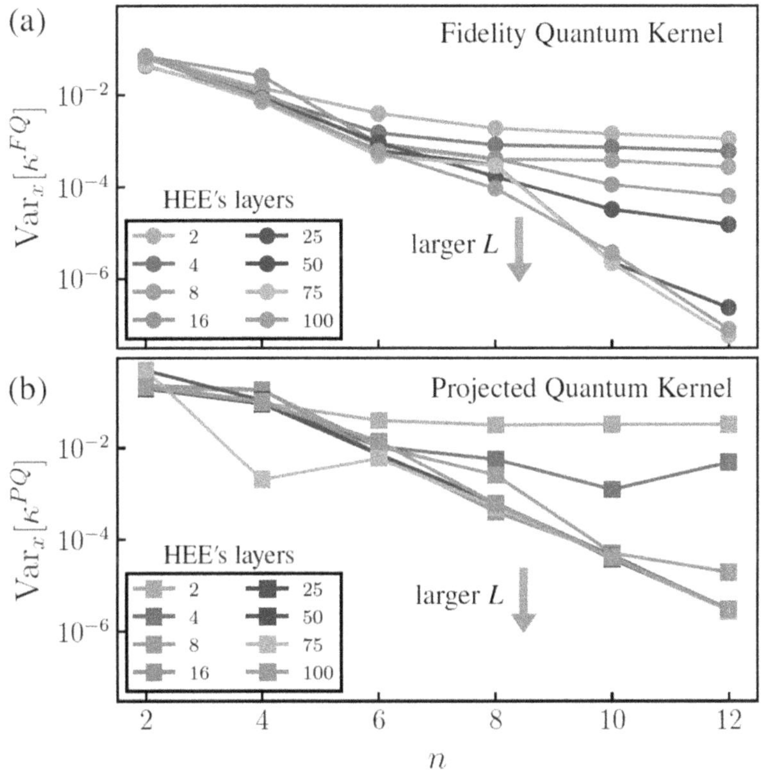

Figure 10.13: Expressivity-induced kernel concentration (Thanasilp et al., 2024).

Variational quantum algorithms, while representing the most promising near-term approach to quantum optimization, face significant scalability challenges that limit their applicability to practical neural network optimization problems. Issues such as barren plateaus, measurement overhead and circuit depth constraints are inherent limitations that existing mitigation techniques can only partially address. Although these algorithms continue to demonstrate scientific utility and may support specialized applications, they appear less capable of addressing the overall optimization of neural networks than initially hoped.

Quantum kernel methods have already demonstrated that claims of quantum benefits in machine learning should be approached with caution. In particular, the ability to access high-dimensional quantum feature spaces does not automatically translate into computational advantages (Thanasilp et al., 2024; Huang et al., 2021). The sample complexity of learning in such high dimensional spaces, combined with the fact that many quantum kernels are classically stimulable, suggests that the benefits of kernel-based quantum learning may be less substantial than originally claimed.

One major advancement is the development of quantum-inspired classical algorithms, which enable the exploration of quantum computational concepts without requiring a quantum computer (Jouzdani et al., 2024). The practical benefits of these techniques can be directly compared to those of quantum hardware and can likewise be guided by the future progress of quantum algorithms.

The most promising remedy in the near future is the application of hybrid quantum-classical solutions to the optimization of quantum problems (Khatri et al., 2019). These methods leverage the specific strengths of quantum computation while delegating to classical operations those tasks for which they are best suited, thereby providing modest but meaningful advantages over purely classical techniques.

Comparative analyses of current performance have shown that optimization problems in real-world neural networks are often solved more efficiently using classical optimization tools than quantum ones under fair comparison. This outcome reflects not only the sophistication and maturity of classical optimization approaches but also the limitations of current quantum hardware and algorithms. However, this situation may change with advances in quantum hardware and the development of new quantum algorithms.

Improvements in quantum computing hardware, and especially progress toward fault-tolerant quantum computing are crucial to the future of quantum optimization. Although such a transition may unlock significant quantum benefits for optimization problems, the timeline remains highly unpredictable and could take decades to materialize (Endo et al., 2021). In the meantime, algorithms and hybrid approaches that are NISQ-compatible should be further developed, as they represent the most promising avenue for achieving practical quantum benefits.

It has now grown far beyond its earlier hype of universal quantum benefits, leading to more fine-grained understandings of when, where, and how quantum methods can be effective (Cerezo et al., 2021). This type of progress represents a normal trajectory of scientific development and provides a more solid foundation on which future research and development work can be established.

The current advice to researchers is that, when applying quantum optimization methods to neural network applications, they should focus on hybrid solutions for special-purpose applications where small performance gains may justify the complexity of implementation. Classical methods that follow similar approaches to quantum ones may yield more tangible benefits, yet pure quantum methods remain an active subject of research interest.

The implications of quantum optimization research extend beyond applications to computational complexity, optimization science and real-world environments that leverage quantum benefits. Lessons from quantum optimization have contributed not only to the improvement of classical optimization algorithms and the analysis of optimization landscapes, but also to a clearer characterization of the boundary between classical and quantum computational power.

References

Arute, F., Arya, K., Babbush, R. et al. (2020). Hartree–Fock on a superconducting qubit quantum computer. *Science*, 369(6507), 1084–1089. doi: 10.1126/science.abb9811.

Benedetti, M., Lloyd, E., Sack, S. & Fiorentini, M. (2019). Parameterized quantum circuits as machine learning models. *Quantum Science and Technology*, 4(4), 043001. doi: 10.1088/2058-9565/ab4eb5.

Boyn, J.-N., Lykhin, A. O., Smart, S. E., Gagliardi, L. & Mazziotti, D.A. (2021). Quantum-classical hybrid algorithm for the simulation of all-electron correlation. *The Journal of Chemical Physics*, 155(24), 244106. doi: 10.1063/5.0074842.

Bravyi, S., Gambetta, J. M., Mezzacapo, A. & Temme, K. (2020). Tapering off qubits to simulate fermionic Hamiltonians. *npj Quantum Information*, 4, 1. doi: 10.1038/s41534-017-0007-2.

Cerezo, M., Arrasmith, A., Babbush, R., Benjamin, S. C., Endo, S., Fujii, K. & Coles, P. J. (2021) Variational quantum algorithms. *Nature Reviews Physics*, 3(9), 625–644. doi: 10.1038/s42254-021-00348-9.

Egginger, S., Sakhnenko, A. & Lorenz, J. M. (2024). A hyperparameter study for quantum kernel methods. *Quantum Machine Intelligence*, 6, 44. doi: 10.1007/s42484-024-00172-1.

Endo, S., Benjamin, S. C. & Li, Y. (2021). Practical quantum error mitigation for near-term applications. *Physical Review X*, 11(4), 041007. doi: 10.1103/PhysRevX.11.041007.

Fitzek, D., Jonsson, R. S., Dobrautz, W. & Schäfer, C. (2024). Optimizing variational quantum algorithms with qBang: Efficiently interweaving metric and momentum to navigate flat energy landscapes. *Quantum*, 8, 1313.

Hadfield, S., Wang, Z., O'Gorman, B., Rieffel, E. G., Venturelli, D. & Biswas, R. (2019). From the quantum approximate optimization algorithm to a quantum alternating operator ansatz. arXiv preprint arXiv:1709.03489. Available at: https://arxiv.org/abs/1709.03489 (Accessed: 1 August 2025).

Huang, H.-Y., Broughton, M., Mohseni, M., Babbush, R., Boixo, S., Neven, H. & McClean, J. R. (2021). Power of data in quantum machine learning. *Nature Communications*, 12, 2631. doi: 10.1038/s41467-021-22539-9.

Jouzdani, P., Hashim, H. A. & Mucciolo, E. R. (2024). Quantum algorithms for state preparation and data classification based on stabilizer codes. *Physical Review A*, 109(2), 022602. doi: 10.1103/PhysRevA.109.022602.

Kandala, A., Mezzacapo, A., Temme, K., Takita, M., Brink, M., Chow, J. M. & Gambetta, J. M. (2017). Hardware-efficient variational quantum eigensolver for small molecules. *Nature*, 549, 242–246. doi: 10.1038/nature23879.

Khatri, S., LaRose, R., Poremba, A., Cincio, L., Sornborger, A. T. & Coles, P. J. (2019). Quantum-assisted quantum compiling. *Quantum*, 3, 140. doi: 10.22331/q-2019-05-13-140.

Larocca, M., Thanasilp, S., Wang, S., Sharma, K., Biamonte, J., Coles, P. J. et al. (2025). Barren plateaus in variational quantum computing. *Nature Reviews Physics*, 7, 174–189.

Liu, Y., Arunachalam, S. & Temme, K. (2021). A rigorous and robust quantum speed-up in supervised machine learning. *Nature Physics*, 17, 1013–1017. doi: 10.1038/s41567-021-01287-z.

Meet IQM. (2025). Breaking quantum fidelity records: A 99.9% milestone, Meet IQM Blog, 31 July. Available at: https://meetiqm.com/blog/quantum-fidelity-milestone/ (Accessed: 26 August 2025).

Montanaro, A. (2019). Quantum algorithms: An overview. *npj Quantum Information*, 2, 15013. doi: 10.1038/s41534-019-0134-2.

Nielsen, M. A. & Chuang, I. L. (2010). Quantum Computation and Quantum Information. 10th anniversary edn. Cambridge: Cambridge University Press.

Rieser, H.-M., Köster, F. & Raulf, A. P. (2023). Tensor networks for quantum machine learning. *Proceedings of the Royal Society A: Mathematical, Physical and Engineering Sciences*, 479(2275), 20230218. doi: 10.1098/rspa.2023.0218.

Schuld, M., Sweke, R. & Meyer, J. J. (2021). Effect of data encoding on the expressive power of variational quantum-machine learning models. *Physical Review A*, 103(3), 032430. doi: 10.1103/PhysRevA.103.032430.

Sim, S., Johnson, P. D. & Aspuru-Guzik, A. (2019). Expressibility and entangling capability of parameterized quantum circuits for hybrid quantum-classical algorithms. *Advanced Quantum Technologies*, 2(12), 1900070. doi: 10.1002/qute.201900070.

SpinQuanta. (2025). Ultimate guide to gate fidelity: Everything you need to know. *SpinQuanta*, 12 May. Available at: https://www.spinquanta.com/news-detail/ultimate-guide-to-gate-fidelity-everything-you-need-to-know (Accessed: 1 August 2025).

Thanasilp, S., Wang, S., Cerezo, M. & Holmes, Z. (2024). Exponential concentration in quantum kernel methods. arXiv preprint arXiv:2208.11060. Available at: https://arxiv.org/abs/2208.11060 (Accessed: 6 August 2025).

The Quantum Insider. (2025). MIT researchers report record-setting quantum gate fidelity. *The Quantum Insider*, 21 January. Available at: https://thequantuminsider.com/2025/01/21/mit-researchers-report-record-setting-quantum-gate-fidelity/ (Accessed: 6 August 2025).

Wang, Y., Ding, Y., Cárdenas-López, F. A. & Chen, X. (2024). Pulse-based variational quantum optimization and metalearning in superconducting circuits. *Physical Review Applied*, 22(2), 024009.

Yi, Z., Liang, Y. & Situ, H. (2024). Enhancing variational quantum circuit training: An improved neural network approach for barren plateau mitigation. arXiv preprint arXiv:2411.09226. Available at: https://arxiv.org/abs/2411.09226 (Accessed: 5 August 2025).

CHAPTER

11

Quantum-Inspired Child-Drawing Optimization for Efficient Graph Neural Network Training

Sozan Sulaiman Maghdid[1], Tarik Ahmed Rashid[2*] and Shavan Askar[3]

[1] Department of Information Technology, Khabat Technical Institute, Erbil Polytechnic University, Erbil, Iraq

[2] Computer Science and Engineering Department, AIIC, University of Kurdistan Hewler, Erbil, Iraq

[3] Department of Information Systems Engineering, Erbil Technical Engineering College, Erbil Polytechnic University, Erbil, Iraq

Rapid advances in graph neural networks have greatly enhanced the ability of AI systems to learn from structural and relational data. However, the performance of these networks is highly sensitive to their hyperparameters and structural design, which is often optimized through computationally expensive trial-and-error or gradient-based methods that tend to achieve local optimal values. To address these challenges, this chapter proposes a novel hybrid framework, quantum-inspired child-drawing development Optimization (QCDDO), to optimize GNN training and hyperparameter tuning that leverages quantum-inspired analogous heuristic optimization. Inspired by quantum mechanical principles—such as superposition, entanglement, and quantum tunneling—these analogous heuristic strategies provide efficient exploration capabilities in high-dimensional, non-convex search spaces. We compare the framework with quantum-inspired particle swarm optimization (QPSO) and quantum-inspired gray wolf optimization (QGWO). Comparative results demonstrate that the quantum-inspired child-drawing development optimization (QCDDO) approach outperforms conventional child-drawing development optimization algorithms and quantum-inspired particle swarm optimization (QPSO) and quantum-inspired gray wolf optimization (QGWO) in convergence speed, solution quality, and

*Corresponding author: tarik.ahmed@ukh.edu.krd

DOI: 10.1201/9781003682950-11

diversity. This chapter concludes by reviewing future directions for integrating quantum-inspired strategies with graph neural networks for large-scale and real-time applications.

11.1 Introduction

Graph-based learning models have become essential in the field of artificial intelligence due to their unique ability to represent, process, and infer from data with a relational and non-Euclidean structure (Xia, 2021). Unlike traditional learning models that operate on static networks, sequences, or tabular data, graph-based models provide a flexible framework for capturing complex relationships and interconnections between entities. This makes them highly suitable for modeling real-world systems, such as social networks, biological systems, communications infrastructure, transportation systems, and knowledge graphs (Maghdid et al., 2025). Among these models, graph neural networks have emerged as one of the most powerful classes of deep learning architectures. These networks generalize the concept of convolution to graph structures by aggregating node information and transforming iterative neighbor interactions. This enables GNNs to capture both local and global structural information, allowing for efficient learning from nodes, edges, and full graph representations simultaneously. Recent advances in GNN models—such as graph convolutional networks (GCNs), graph attention networks (GATs), and GraphSAGE—have led to cutting-edge results in various fields, including drug discovery, protein interaction prediction, fraud detection, recommender systems, and data flow prediction (Graph neural networks, n.d.; Wu et al., 2021). Despite their increasing applicability and success, designing and optimizing GNNs remains a challenging task. These models involve large, high-dimensional hyperparameter spaces, including the number of layers, hidden units, learning rates, dropout probabilities, clustering strategies, and activation functions (Maghdid et al., 2025). GNNs are particularly susceptible to challenges such as over smoothing, where node representations become indistinguishable with depth; vanishing gradients, especially in deep architectures; and training instability, exacerbated by irregular graph topology and data scarcity. These issues make optimizing GNNs computationally intensive and sensitive to initialization and tuning strategies (Waikhom & Patgiri, 2023).

In response to these challenges, the field of heuristic optimization has gained significant momentum as an effective strategy for navigating complex, multidimensional, and multi-objective problem spaces (Asru et al., 2025). Heuristic optimization is a general-purpose optimization technique inspired by natural processes, such as evolution, swarm behavior, and physical phenomena. Algorithms such as particle swarm optimization (PSO), genetic algorithms (GA), differential evolution (DE), and the grey wolf optimizer (GWO) have demonstrated significant success in tuning neural architectures, selecting informative features, and optimizing learning parameters. These methods operate without the need for gradient information, making them suitable for underdetermined optimization scenarios and models with non-differentiable objective functions (Gendreau & Potvin, 2005). However, classical heuristic optimization is not without limitations, it is often computationally expensive, prone to stagnation in local optima, and may lack sufficient exploration in large search spaces. To address these shortcomings, researchers have increasingly explored incorporating quantum computing principles into heuristic design, leading to the emergence of quantum-inspired heuristics (QiMs). These algorithms emulate fundamental quantum mechanical concepts—such as superposition, entanglement, and tunneling—on classical machines to enhance the exploration and diversification capabilities of conventional optimizers (Binitha & Sathya, 2012). Superposition allows candidate solutions to represent multiple states simultaneously, improving diversity. Tunneling provides a mechanism for escaping local minima by probabilistically transitioning across energy barriers. Entanglement introduces correlations between solution components, allowing for more structured and precise updates. Although not implemented on actual quantum devices, these algorithms exploit analogies of quantum behavior to significantly enhance optimization efficiency (Gunjan & Bhattacharyya, 2024). A comprehensive overview of various quantum-inspired metaheuristic optimization algorithms is presented in Figure 11.1, providing a comprehensive perspective.

Building on this foundation, we propose the Quantum-Inspired Child's Drawing Development Optimization (QCDDO), a novel hybrid algorithm that combines cognitive development theory and quantum-inspired computing. The primary motivation behind QCDDO stems from the CDDO algorithm, which models optimization behaviors based on how children gradually refine their drawing skills. As children transition from doodling to symbolic and realistic drawing, they learn through trial and error, feedback, and increasingly abstract representations. This developmental trajectory translates into an optimization framework that adapts search behavior over time, making the CDDO algorithm both exploratory and adaptive (Abdulhameed & Rashid, 2022). QCDDO enhances this behavioral foundation by introducing quantum probabilistic coding. Instead of representing candidate solutions as deterministic vectors, QCDDO uses probabilistic representations similar to Q bits, where each component can exist in a superposition state. This allows each candidate solution to explore multiple regions of the search space simultaneously, probabilistically collapsing toward promising configurations based on evaluation feedback. Furthermore, QCDDO incorporates tunneling-inspired transitions, allowing the optimizer to jump through illusory basins of attraction, improving convergence toward the global optimum. QCDDO is particularly well-suited for multi-objective optimization, which is essential in real-world graph neural network applications. In this work, the proposed QCDDO method is used to optimize the training process and hyper parameterization of a graph neural network to improve graph-based classification. Experimental evaluation is conducted using the "Patient Heart Attack Prediction" dataset. This makes the algorithm robust and flexible in diverse operational environments,

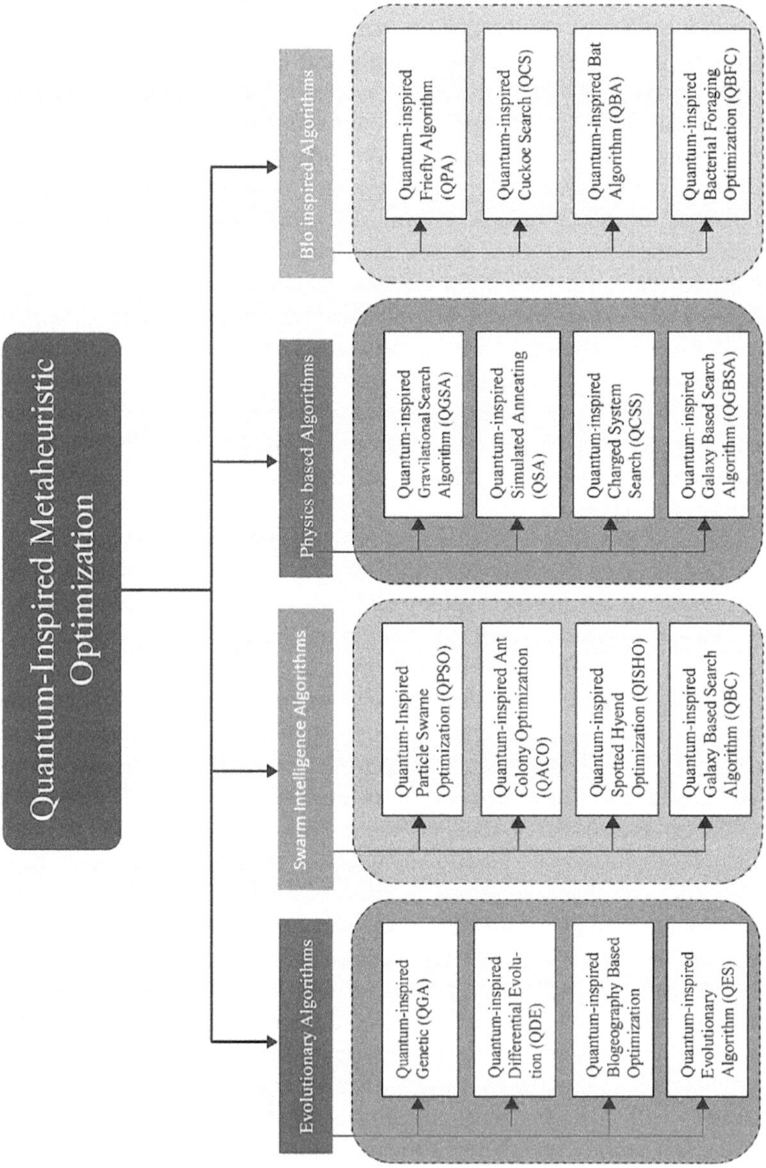

Figure 11.1: Quantum-inspired metaheuristic optimization algorithms.

especially when GNNs are deployed on resource-constrained platforms or when interpretability criteria need to be met (e.g., in healthcare or finance).

The hybridization of graph neural networks with QCDDO represents a significant advance in neural architecture research and model optimization. It effectively combines the representational expressiveness of graph neural networks with the comprehensive adaptive search capabilities of quantum-inspired inference algorithms. In this chapter, we delve into the algorithmic principles, flow design, and implementation strategies of QCDDO. Comparative analyses with both classical and quantum-inspired inference algorithms, including Quantum-Inspired Particle Swarm Optimization (QPSO) and Quantum-Inspired Grey Wolf Optimizer (QGWO), demonstrate the superiority of the proposed approach in terms of accuracy, memory efficiency, convergence behavior, and Pareto optimality. Ultimately, this work contributes to a growing body of research at the intersection of graph-based deep learning, heuristic optimization, and quantum-inspired AI. As AI systems continue to evolve toward greater autonomy, adaptability, and explainability, these multidisciplinary optimization strategies will play a fundamental role in shaping the next generation of intelligent systems capable of efficiently and effectively solving complex real-world problems.

11.2 Related Work

11.2.1 Quantum-Inspired Algorithms

Algorithms that leverage quantum properties demonstrate significant improvements in various mathematical and computational tasks. For example, research shows that quantum encryption of classical datasets can enhance differential privacy, providing a powerful approach to ensuring data privacy in quantum-inspired and quantum-based frameworks (Bharti, 2022). Quantum-inspired algorithms (QiAs) have emerged as a rapidly growing research area, intersecting the principles of classical quantum simulation and quantum computing. Unlike true quantum algorithms, which require quantum hardware, QiAs are designed to run on classical computers but incorporate fundamental quantum concepts—such as superposition, entanglement, and quantum probability distributions—to enhance search capabilities and convergence efficiency. These algorithms have demonstrated promising results in solving high-dimensional, multimodal, non-convex optimization problems across a variety of application areas (Pooja and Sood, 2024). Han and Kim (2002) were among the first to introduce a Quantum-Inspired Evolutionary Algorithm (QEA), which leveraged quantum bit representations (Q-bits) to encode solution candidates. This approach provided a probabilistic framework that enhanced diversity and improved the ability to escape local optima (Han and Kim, 2002). Subsequent studies refined QEAs for combinatorial optimization problems such as knapsack, scheduling, and traveling salesman problems. Sun et al. (2004) developed a quantum-behavioral particle swarm optimization (QPSO), which models particle states as quantum probability distributions rather than deterministic velocity vectors. QPSO demonstrated superior global search performance and robustness in constrained environments, and has found widespread use in neural network training, image segmentation, and feature selection tasks (Sun et al., 2004). Quantum genetic algorithms (QGAs) have introduced a new representation of chromosomes using quantum spin gates and probability amplitudes, as demonstrated in the work of Rylander et al. QGAs exploit the balance between exploration and exploitation by applying probabilistic transitions that mimic quantum state collapses, making them particularly effective for discrete and binary optimization problems (Rylander et al., 2000).

Other researchers extended quantum inspiration to Differential Evolution (QDE) and hybridized frameworks. For example, Haijun and Yupu (2008) proposed the quantum-inspired differential evolution algorithm (QDE) with a Q-bit string as a representation. They used Differential Evolution (DE) operators to guide individuals toward better solutions (Haijun and Yupu, 2008). Similarly, the quantum-inspired gray wolf optimizer (QGWO) and the quantum-inspired ant colony optimizer (QACO) introduced probabilistic movement and pheromone dynamics that took advantage of quantum tunneling effects (Guo et al., 2021; Wang et al., 2007). Tan and Guo (2009) proposed quantum-inspired biogeography-based optimization to investigate the possibility of optimization by developing quantitative probability models (QPMs) through evolutionary strategies inspired by the mathematics of biogeography (Tan and Guo, 2009). Si (2025) proposed quantum-inspired Spotted Hyena Optimization, an improved SHO, Quantum SHO (QSHO), inspired by quantum computing. They implemented QSHO, a quantum computing mechanism, to promote its exploration ability (Si, 2025). Wong et al. (2014) presented a quantum-inspired firefly algorithm to achieve an optimal power quality monitoring situation in a power system. They modified the traditional binary firefly algorithm using quantum principles to achieve a faster convergence rate, which can improve system performance and avoid premature convergence (Wong et al., 2014). A quantum-inspired cuckoo search algorithm (QICSA) was proposed by Layeb, integrating quantum computing principles, such as qubit representation, superposition, measurement, and interference, into the classical cuckoo search framework. This approach introduces a novel representation scheme that enables effective application of QICSA to combinatorial optimization problems (Layeb, 2011).

Zhu et al. (2016) introduced a quantum-behavior bat algorithm with mean best position (QMBA) to improve convergence speed and solution accuracy. By incorporating quantum behavior and leveraging global best positions and mean best positions, QMBA enhances cluster diversity and avoids local optimal values. After testing on 24 benchmark functions, the algorithm demonstrated superior performance and robustness compared to other bat algorithm variants (Zhu et al., 2016). Gao and Li (2015) proposed a quantum-inspired bacterial search algorithm (QBFA) to solve the complex discrete optimization problem of parameter adjustment in cognitive radio networks. By incorporating quantum computing principles, QBFA improves end-to-end search capabilities and avoids local convergence (Gao and Li, 2015). Soleimanpour-Moghadam et al. (2013) developed a quantum-inspired gravity search algorithm (QIGSA) by incorporating quantum mechanical principles into the classical GSA framework. They used quantum behavior to enhance population diversity and mitigate premature convergence (Soleimanpour-Moghadam et al., 2013). Shu (2009) proposed a quantum-inspired simulated annealing genetic algorithm (QSAGA) by incorporating simulated annealing into the quantum-inspired genetic algorithm (QGA) framework. His hybrid approach retained the strengths of QGA while enhancing its ability to avoid premature convergence (Shu, 2009). Talatahari et al. (2022) developed a fuzzy adaptive quantum-inspired charged system search (FAQI-CSS) for structural optimization of large-scale steel structures. They enhanced the convergence and balance between exploration and exploitation by integrating quantum mechanics (potential energy center) and fuzzy logic for adaptive parameter tuning (Talatahari et al., 2022). Gao et al. (2023) proposed a Quantum Galaxy-Based Search Algorithm (QGbSA) and its multi-objective variant (MoQGbSA) to optimize power allocation in macrocell/femtocell two-layer heterogeneous networks. They proved that by addressing both energy efficiency and system throughput, the MoQGbSA effectively solves the multi-objective power allocation problem and achieves superior optimization performance compared to existing algorithms (Gao et al., 2023). Overall, the literature reflects a growing momentum in hybridizing quantum concepts with classical algorithms to overcome limitations such as local stagnation, slow convergence, and poor scalability, making these algorithms particularly suitable for complex artificial intelligence, networking, and engineering problems.

11.2.2 Nature-Inspired Algorithms

In recent years, proposals and applications inspired by nature have proliferated across various technological contexts. Derviş Karaboga's Artificial Bee Colony (ABC) algorithm was inspired by the reproductive behavior of honeybees and developed to address numerical optimization problems (Karaboga, 2005). Mirjalili et al. (2014) suggested that the gray wolf enhancer (GWO) relies on encircling prey (Mirjalili et al., 2014). Similarly, the Elephant Search Algorithm (ESA) is based on how elephants search for things. Male and female elephants are divided into groups, each of which searches for specific areas (Deb et al., 2015). The evolution of microalgae served as an inspiration for the development of the Artificial Algae Algorithm (AAA), which was published in 2015 (Uymaz et al., 2015). The Fish Swarm Algorithm (FSA) is inspired by the method used by fish colonies to find food (Zh, 2005). Cat Swarm Optimization (CSO) is created by observing cat behaviors (Chu et al., 2006). Swarm intelligence (SI) is primarily inspired by nature, especially biological systems in which agents follow clear rules without a central control structure (Engelbrecht, 2025). Mirjalili et al. (2017) proposed the Salp Swarm Algorithm (SSA). The main inspiration for this algorithm lies in the behavior of salp swarms during navigation and foraging in the oceans (Mirjalili et al., 2017). A genetic algorithm (GA) was developed by Holland (1973) in the 1970s as a metaheuristic approach that mimics natural selection, inspired by Darwin's theory of evolution (Holland, 1973). Mirjalili (2016) proposed the Dragonfly Algorithm (DA). Its main inspiration comes from the motionless and dynamic behaviors of dragonflies in nature (Mirjalili, 2016). The Ant Colony Optimization (ACO) system was developed by Dorigo and is inspired by the foraging behavior of ants (Dorigo and Gianni, 1992). Zong Woo Geem et al. in 2001 created the Harmony Search (HS) approach. HS is a metaheuristic inspired by music (Geem et al., 2021). In 2008, Xin-She Yang introduced the Firefly Algorithm (FA). This approach was inspired by the behavior of fireflies in tropical regions (Fister et al., 2013). In 2009, cuckoo search (CS) was developed by Xin-she Yang and Suash Deb. This technique is based on the behavior of certain cuckoo species known as brood parasitism (Yang and Deb, 2010). The Bat Algorithm (BA) (Yang and Deb, 2010; Yang, 2012) was founded by Xin-She Yang in 2010. The idea was inspired by small bats and their echolocation behavior, a natural method used by bats to detect objects using the sound reflected from them. The Donkey and Smuggler Optimization (DSO) algorithm was developed by Shamsaldin and Rashid in 2019. There are two main modes, Smuggler and Donkey, created to implement the search and path selection behavior in DSO (Shamsaldin et al., 2019).

In 2016, Mirjalili and Lewis (2016) proposed the Whale Optimization Algorithm (WOA), which mimics the social behaviour of humpback whales, which is inspired by the bubble-net hunting strategy (Mirjalili and Lewis, 2016). The Fitness Dependent Optimizer (FDO)(Abdullah and Ahmed, 2019) is another algorithm inspired by the reproductive mating process of bees, where scout bees typically explore new nests. In FDO, search agents are guided toward the optimal position using the weights generated by the fitness function used (Abdullah and Ahmed, 2019). In 2019, a new nature-inspired algorithm, the Butterfly Optimization Algorithm (BOA), was introduced by Arora and Singh (2019), which simulates the foraging and mating behavior of butterflies to solve global optimization problems (Arora and Singh, 2019). An arithmetic optimization algorithm (AOA) was developed by Abualigah et al. in 2021 that utilizes the distributive behavior of leading arithmetic operations in mathematics, including multiplication, division, subtraction, and addition (Abualigah et al., 2021). In 2020, Khishe and Mosavi proposed a novel metaheuristic algorithm called the Chimp Optimization Algorithm (ChOA). This was inspired by the individual intelligence and sexual motivation of chimps in their hunting groups, which differed from the other social predators (Khishe and Mosavi, 2020). In 2023, Mohamed introduced a new nature-inspired optimization algorithm called the Fox Optimizer (FOX), which mimics the foraging behavior of foxes in nature when hunting prey. The algorithm relies on techniques to measure the distance between the fox and its prey to execute an efficient jump (Mohammed & Rashid 2023). In 2024, Umar et al. proposed the modified bat algorithm (MBA) as an improvement to address the observed local optima limitation of the original bat algorithm. The modified bat algorithm incorporates the frequency and velocity of the current best solution, enhancing the speed of convergence to the optimal solution and preventing local optima from being trapped (Umar et al., 2024). In 2024, Khaled et al. proposed the "Goose Algorithm", a new inference algorithm based on the behavior of geese during rest and foraging. The goose stands on one leg and maintains its balance to protect other members of the flock (Hamad and Rashid, 2024). The above and other cases constitute a new class of algorithms inspired by nature.

11.2.3 Child's Drawing Development Optimization

Abdulhameed and Rashid (2022) proposed the Child Drawing Growth Optimization (CDDO) algorithm, a nature-inspired heuristic based on children's cognitive learning and drawing behavior. Using the golden ratio and growth stages, CDDO effectively balances exploration and exploitation. When tested on 19 benchmark functions, it outperformed several traditional heuristic algorithms, such as PSO, DE, WOA, GSA, and FEP, achieving an average competitive rating of 2.8, demonstrating strong global optimization capabilities and robustness against local optimizations (Abdulhameed and Rashid, 2022). Ameen et al. (2023) presented and explained the Child Drawing Development Optimization Algorithm and used it as a model in a case study to minimize a fitness function. As a result, they successfully optimized the initial population and obtained the optimal solution through the optimization algorithm for drawing development in children (Ameen et al., 2023). While CDDO is simple to implement and shows strong performance compared to traditional algorithms, it may suffer from premature convergence and limited exploration. To address these issues, Ameen et al. (2023) proposed a Modified CDDO (MCDDO) incorporating adaptive pattern memory, dynamic rule switching, and refined exploration–exploitation balance. They used 19 classical and 10 CEC-C06 2019 benchmark functions, along with Wilcoxon rank-sum statistical tests, and they proved that MCDDO significantly outperforms several state-of-the-art algorithms. Ameen et al. (2023) addressed the exploration limitations of the Child Drawing Development Optimization (CDDO) algorithm, specifically its stagnation in the local best solution, by proposing a hybrid model called CDDO–HS. This approach integrates Harmony Search (HS), known for its strong exploration capabilities, into the CDDO framework. The hybridization involves relocating the pattern size (PS) to the algorithm's core and enhancing the exploration phase using HS updates. Evaluated on 23 classical and 10 CEC-C06 2019 benchmark functions, CDDO–HS demonstrated superior performance over CDDO, HS, and six other algorithms, with statistical validation via the Wilcoxon rank-sum test confirming its effectiveness (Ameen et al., 2023). Issa et al. (2024) proposed a Binary Child's Drawing Development (BCDDO) algorithm for cover-based feature selection, aiming to improve classification accuracy. The algorithm selects the most relevant feature subsets and has been compared to the Harris Hawks, Wolf Pack, Grey Wolf, and Whale optimization algorithms.

Using an XGBoost classifier on four datasets—breast cancer, moderate COVID-19, major COVID-19, and iris—the BCDDO algorithm achieved high classification accuracy (98.83%, 98.75%, 99.36%, and 96%, respectively). It outperformed the comparison methods and demonstrated its effectiveness in improving classification through feature selection (Issa et al., 2024). Kari Balakrishnan et al. (2025) presented an adaptive level and skill-rate-based children's drawing development optimization (ALSR-CDDO) algorithm for optimizing cloud data structures. This approach reduces computational and communication costs by efficiently selecting optimal data structures. It leverages a divide-and-conquer (D&CT) table to manage file storage, updates, and versions in the cloud. ALSR-CDDO supports dynamic and batch auditing of data stored at cloud service providers (CSPs), ensuring data integrity and traceability. Comparative results demonstrate that the proposed system improves security and performance compared to traditional auditing methods (Kari Balakrishnan et al., 2025). Ranjan et al. (2025) developed a Hybrid Child-Drawing Development Optimization (HCDDO) algorithm to improve rain forecasts using deep learning. The proposed method is based on a ConvLSTM network, whose parameters are fine-tuned by HCDDO to improve forecast accuracy. The model processes time series data, applies feature fusion using mutual information and a neural network based on the Rider optimization algorithm (RideNN), and oversampling for data augmentation. Experimental results demonstrate that the HCDDO-ConvLSTM algorithm achieves superior performance in terms of MAPE, MSE, RAE, RMSE, and R^2, making it an effective approach for early rainfall forecasts (Ranjan et al., 2025).

11.2.4 Graph Neural Networks

Shah (2021) proposed a quantum graph convolutional network (QGCN) to address the limitations of conventional GCNs in processing complex data with graph structure. By incorporating quantum information theory, the model derives Riemannian metrics across graph layers and incorporates high-level convergences into the preprocessing of the adjacency matrix. This improved formulation mitigates information loss and improves representation accuracy. When evaluated on benchmark datasets (Citeseer, Cora, and PubMed), QGCN outperformed standard GCNs and related methods in semi-supervised node classification, offering higher computational efficiency and classification accuracy (Shah, 2021). In 2024, Zheng et al. suggested a quantum spatial graph convolutional neural network (QSGCN) that uses parameterized quantum circuits (PQCs) to process non-Euclidean data. The model consists of four main components: quantum coding, graph convolution, pooling layers, and network refinement. They also investigated the model's trainability in light of the barren plateau phenomenon. Simulation results showed that QSGCN exhibits high learning ability, generalization, and robustness across diverse graph datasets, highlighting its potential as a genuine quantitative approach to learning graph representations (Zheng et al., 2025).

Chen et al. (2021) presented a hybrid quantum-classical graph convolutional neural network (QGCNN) to address the challenges of sparse and large-scale data in high-energy physics (HEP). Their model outperformed classical MLPs and CNNs in terms of parameter efficiency and achieved test accuracy comparable to quantum CNNs, while using less than 50% of the parameters. This work highlights the potential of integrating graph convolution and quantum machine learning in scientific fields such as high-energy physics (Chen et al., 2021). Wang proposed a quantum graph Hamiltonian neural network (QGHNN) to improve graph learning on highly noisy intermediate-scale quantum (NISQ) devices. By introducing a quantum graph Hamiltonian learning (QGHL) method that maps graphs to Hamiltonians in the quantum system, QGHNN enables efficient training via gradient descent. Experimental results using the PennyLane platform demonstrate that QGHNN achieves high accuracy and robustness, with a mean squared error of 0.004 and a cosine similarity of 99.8%. This highlights its promising potential in quantum knowledge graphs and recommendation systems (Wang, 2025). Faria et al. (2025) presented a flexible quantum graph neural network (QGNN) framework, inspired by the GraphSAGE model, to address the constraints of rigid graph-bound quantum circuits. Their approach combines factored quantum convolution and pooling layers to achieve inductive learning, enhancing adaptability across various graph structures. When tested on the QM9 dataset, QGNNs demonstrated performance comparable to classical GNNs and demonstrated superior generalization to molecular graphs of various sizes. Importantly, the framework avoids barren plateaus as the number of qubits increases, highlighting its scalability and effectiveness for complex graph-based tasks (Faria et al., 2025). Cordero (2024) explored the use of isoheterodyne quantum circuits within Quantum Graph Neural Networks (QGNNs) to enhance the solution to the Traveling Salesman Problem (TSP). His work emphasizes both hardware and algorithmic advancements, aiming to leverage quantum states and operations for improved performance. The research focuses on designing and optimizing isoheterodyne quantum circuits, fine-tuning gate parameters, and adapting them to graph-structured data. The study anticipates that, as quantum processors become more robust and algorithms are refined, QGNNs will play a critical role in efficiently solving complex combinatorial problems such as the Traveling Salesman Problem (TSP) (Cordero, 2024). Tüysüz (2021) investigated a hybrid quantum-classical graph neural network model designed to handle the combinatorial challenges posed by the High Luminosity Large Hadron Collider (HL-LHC), where particle collisions generate a vast number of detector hits. By integrating variational quantum layers into a GNN framework, the study explores the potential of quantum computing to enhance particle trajectory reconstruction. The hybrid model demonstrated performance comparable to classical methods, and the authors analyzed various parametrized quantum circuits (PQCs) to evaluate their expressibility and entanglement capabilities. This work lays the foundation for future development of hybrid quantum-classical GNNs for high-energy physics applications (Tüysüz, 2021).

Mernyei et al. (2022) introduced Equivariant Quantum Graph Circuits (EQGCs), a new class of parameterized quantum circuits specifically designed for learning over graph-structured data with strong relational inductive bias. EQGCs serve as a unified framework that encompasses and extends existing quantum graph learning models. The authors provide theoretical proof that subclasses of EQGCs are universal function approximators for graphs within a bounded domain, indicating their powerful representation capabilities (Mernyei et al., 2022). Tang and Yan (2022) proposed a quantum graph learning model that integrates the strengths of Graph Neural Networks (GNNs) and Graph Kernels (GKs) to effectively analyze graph-structured data while addressing limitations such as high computational cost and structural information loss. Their approach uses a quantum algorithm to approximate the neural tangent kernel of a GNN and incorporates a multi-head quantum attention mechanism to better capture semantic similarities between nodes. Experimental results on graph classification benchmarks demonstrate competitive performance, and theoretical analysis confirms the efficiency and expressiveness of the proposed quantum method (Tang and Yan, 2022). Xu et al. (2024) introduced Quantum Feature Embeddings (QFEs) as a novel enhancement to Graph Neural Networks (GNNs), aiming to reduce model complexity while improving performance. QFEs transform raw input features into quantum states, enabling non-linear, entangled, and normalized representations in a significantly larger feature space using fewer qubits than fully quantum GNNs. Their method outperforms classical GNNs with the same parameter count and matches the performance of much larger models on standard benchmarks. A practical case study in laser cutting confirms the near-term potential of this hybrid quantum-classical approach for real-world business applications (Xu et al., 2024). Chen and Chen (2025) proposed the Quantum Complete Graph Neural Network (QCGNN), a variational quantum algorithm designed for learning on complete graphs. QCGNN leverages quantum parallelism and deep parameterized operators to achieve a polynomial speedup over both classical and other quantum models. They applied the model to the complex task of jet discrimination in high-energy physics, where jets are represented as complete graphs, and performed comparative evaluations to benchmark its performance against classical approaches (Chen and Chen, 2025). Yan et al. (2022) introduced a fully native quantum model for graph representation learning that avoids the limitations of classical-quantum hybrid approaches. Their method leverages quantum random walks and quantum recurrent networks to process attributed graphs directly in a quantum computing framework. Unlike prior models, this paradigm does not rely heavily on classical computation and is designed for scalability. Experimental evaluations on three public datasets demonstrate that their model outperforms classical approaches like GraphRNA, particularly in computational efficiency, even when executed on classical hardware. This work marks a significant step toward practical, end-to-end quantum graph learning architectures (Yan et al., 2022). Chen et al. introduced a Quantum Graph Convolutional Network (QGCN) to extend the capabilities of parameterized quantum circuits (PQCs) for processing topological data. Drawing inspiration from classical Graph Convolutional Networks (GCNs), they designed quantum graph convolutional layers incorporating adjacency matrices and quantum weights. The model, trained using the parameter-shift rule, was evaluated on the Cora dataset and achieved performance comparable to classical GCNs, while requiring fewer parameters (Chen et al., 2022). Ai et al. (2022) proposed the Ego-graph based Quantum Graph Neural Network (egoQGNN), a hybrid quantum-classical model designed to process graph-structured data efficiently. Addressing challenges in mapping Euclidean data to Hilbert space and hardware limitations, egoQGNN uses tensor product and unit matrix representations to significantly reduce parameter count. By extracting ego-graphs from larger graphs, the model enables scalable learning using modest quantum resources while preserving data structure and distance relations. Experimental results demonstrate that egoQGNN outperforms state-of-the-art models using only 1.68% of their parameters, highlighting its efficiency and effectiveness in quantum graph learning (Ai et al., 2022).

Xu and Shen introduced the Quantum Heterogeneous Graph Neural Network (QHGNN) to address the limitations of traditional QGNNs, which are typically restricted to homogeneous graphs. QHGNN incorporates heterogeneity as an inductive bias within quantum circuits, allowing it to effectively encode and learn from diverse node and edge types. Applied to molecular property prediction using PTC datasets, QHGNN demonstrated superior accuracy, efficiency, and noise resilience compared to conventional QGNN models, highlighting its potential for advanced quantum graph learning in complex, real-world scenarios (Xu and Shen, 2025). Liao et al. (2024) proposed quantum frameworks for implementing three key types of classical Graph Neural Networks (GNNs), Graph Convolutional Networks (GCNs), Graph Attention Networks (GATs), and Message-Passing GNNs—on quantum computers to address the scalability limitations of classical GNNs. Their quantum version of the Simplified Graph Convolutional (SGC) Network demonstrates significant improvements in both time and space complexities. Specifically, the quantum SGC achieves logarithmic time complexity with linear space requirements or logarithmic space complexity with improved time efficiency, depending on optimization goals. These findings indicate that quantum GNNs could enable more efficient processing of large-scale graph data and support future advancements in quantum machine learning (Liao et al., 2024). Casals et al. (2025) introduced the Guided Graph Compression (GGC) framework to overcome the scalability and memory challenges faced by Graph Neural Networks (GNNs) on large-scale graphs, particularly in quantum computing contexts. By employing a graph autoencoder, GGC reduces node count and feature dimensions while preserving task-relevant information for downstream classification. Evaluated on the Jet Tagging task in high-energy physics, GGC outperformed traditional autoencoders and classical GNNs, demonstrating its effectiveness and enabling more feasible applications of Quantum Graph Neural Networks (QGNNs) on real-world datasets (Casals et al., 2025).

11.3 Background

11.3.1 Quantum Computing

In quantum computing, a qubit is the basic unit of information storage, like a classical bit in conventional computing. However, unlike classical bits, which can only hold a state of 0 or 1, qubits can hold a superposition of both states, with specific probabilities for each state. Mathematically, a qubit $|\varphi\rangle$ represents a linear combination of the states $|0\rangle$ and $|1\rangle$, where $|0\rangle$ represents the ground state and $|1\rangle$ represents the excited state. The probabilities of measuring each state are determined by the square of its corresponding coefficients in the linear combination, and the coefficients must satisfy the normalization condition, which requires that the sum of their squares be equal to 1. Qubits are the building blocks of quantum algorithms and allow for significantly faster computation for specific tasks, such as factoring large numbers or searching unsorted databases (McMahon, 2007).

$$|\varphi\rangle = x|0\rangle + y|1\rangle \tag{11.1}$$

The coefficients a and b are complex numbers that must satisfy the equation $|x|$^2 +$|y|$^2 = 1, where $|x|$^2 represents the probability of locating the qubit $|\varphi\rangle$ in state $|0$, and $|y|$^2 represents the probability of locating the qubit $|\varphi\rangle$ in state $|1\rangle$. In quantum computing, operators or gates perform logical and mathematical operations on vector-represented qubits. These operators can be understood through their matrices, explaining how a quantum system can transition from one state to another. There are four fundamental quantum operators known as Pauli operators: P (the identity operator), X (also called the NOT operator), Y (the scalar product operator), and Z (the quartile product operator). Table 11.1 summarizes the Pauli operators and their associated matrices.

Table 11.1: Q-gates with their Corresponding Matrices

Gate Name	Matrix
I-gate	(1 0 0 1)
X-gate	(0 1 1 0)
Y-gate	(0 − i i 0)
Z-gate	(1 0 0 − 1)

Other quantum gates, including the Toffoli gate, Feynman gate, Friedkin gate, Swap gate, and Perez gate, are more complex. Another form of quantum gate, rotation gates, involves rotating a qubit around the X, Y, or Z axis. These rotations produce, respectively, an X gate, a Y gate, and a Z gate. Matrices of these rotation gates can also be represented mathematically (Bilal et al., 2022). Combining classical algorithms with quantum rotation matrices has led to the development of quantum-inspired algorithms. In this study, the QCDDO algorithm simulates quantum behavior using a classical computational infrastructure inspired by fundamental quantum concepts such as superposition, entanglement, and tunneling. These mechanisms are encoded through mathematical analogs rather than physical qubits, making the method highly scalable and computationally feasible for large-scale graph problems. This mirrors the way quantum circuits, such as those using spin gates with parameters like $Ry(\theta)$, transmit classical inputs to quantum state spaces in real quantum systems.

$$x\_gate\ (\theta) = (\cos \cos\ (\theta) - i \sin \sin\ (\theta) \sin \sin\ (\theta)\ (\cos \cos\ (\theta)) \quad (11.2)$$

$$y\_gate\ (\theta) = (\cos \cos\ (\theta) - \sin \sin\ (\theta) \sin \sin\ (\theta)\ (\cos \cos\ (\theta)) \quad (11.3)$$

$$z\_gate\ (\theta) = (e^{-(i\theta)}\ 0\ 0\ e^{(i\theta)}) \quad (11.4)$$

11.3.2 CDDO-Child Drawing Development Optimization

This observation is consistent with theories of cognitive evolution, such as Piaget's, which emphasize the development of expertise and cognitive growth in children's technical expressions. Numerous studies on the developmental stages of children's drawing, by scholars such as Loewenfeld and Kellogg have examined how cognitive capacities, perceptual evolution, and exposure to technical stimuli shape their drawing strategies (Davis and Gardner, 1992). These studies also incorporate the notion of the golden ratio to enhance the aesthetic appeal of children's artwork (Ameen et al., 2022). The golden ratio reflects the harmonious and consistent proportions found between successive numbers in the Fibonacci sequence. It is widely observed in natural phenomena as well as in art, design, and architecture (Livio, 2003).

The CDDO algorithm not only aims to enhance the creativity of a child's drawing by leveraging the golden ratio but also mimics the cognitive learning processes and developmental phases as they progress from writing to creating complex patterns. The algorithm incorporates the golden ratio, height, width, and hand pressure to achieve optimal results when applied to a child's drawing. This adjustment contributes to the child's development, enhances intelligence, and promotes collaboration in achieving common goals (Ameen et al., 2023). The CDDO algorithm demonstrates notable perseverance in searching for innovative solutions. It effectively avoids the trap of local minima and suboptimal points by carefully exploring and constraining promising areas within the design space. The algorithm proves its ability to overcome challenges and deliver outstanding results by providing superior feasible solutions (Abdulhameed and Rashid, 2022). The CDDO process is based on the following suppositions:

1. The solution includes ***i*** variables.
2. The population has been determined.
3. The number of memory size patterns, PM, is constant and depends on the population size.
4. After sorting the variables X_i, the pattern memory size PM chooses the superior fitness values from them.

5. At the end of all iterations of the CDDO algorithm, poor fitness values are changed to better values using the new graphs.
6. The superior solutions are passed on to the next descent at the end of every iteration of the algorithm.

The stages of this algorithm are described in the following sections:

11.3.2.1 Stage 1: Initializing the CDDO Algorithm

1. Theoretical Basis: Scribbling Stage (2–4 Years)

It is important to note in this stage, known as the writing or scribbling stage, young children are actively engaged in detecting the relationship between their hand movements and the lines and marks they see on the page. At this stage, children begin to understand how their actions directly influence the creation of different lines and shapes. These motions, whether linear or curved, occur randomly as the child observes and learns from the patterns they produce. Gradually, children gain an understanding of the causal relationship between their physical movements and the visual results they perceive on the page.

2. The Mathematical Framework for this Phase

The CDDO algorithm employs several constructs, each of which can be defined as a parameter, a variable, or a solution. First, we introduce all the symbols necessary to proceed with the remainder of the work. Table 11.2 shows the main variables and descriptions for modelling children's drawing development optimization. Where:

1. *Nm* corresponds to the number of stocked solutions in a given population. In experiments, $Nm = 30$ was used, based on the recommendation of the authors of the authentic CDDO algorithm.
2. The existing solution, $X_{(i,j)}$, corresponds to a child's drawing affected by different factors like golden ratio *GR*, width *W*, length *L*, and hand pressure *HP*.
3. The variable *i* represents the number of decree variables, which corresponds to the number of sample members. Furthermore, *j* refers to the number of different dimensions within the solution.
4. Pattern memory *PM* indicates abilities acquired over the trial period. These memories can help children distinguish patterns in their drawings, instill meaning in their images, and train and enhance out-of-copying and spirited experience-and-error methods.
5. The golden ratio *GR*, which represents the proportion between the width and length of a child's drawing, marks an important milestone in their artwork.
6. Current solutions apply compression *HP* within the *LB* and *UB* limits of the problem.
7. The *RHP* represents the hand pressure applied to each child's drawing, with one pressure value chosen at random.
8. The upper bound (*UB*) and lower bound (*LB*) represent the length and width of the child's artwork, respectively.

9. The idiom *RND* is utilized to refer to the creation of a random number from a particular domain of parameters.
10. Creativity (*CR*) is an essential element that promotes the aesthetic appeal of every work of art. It is the goodness that adds additional attractions to artistic inventions, making them visually enthralling and attractive to the public. The fixed *CR* value of 0.1 is determined through an iterative procedure of experience and error.
11. The child's level rate (*LR*) and skill rate (*SR*) provide a credible evaluation of a child's dexterity and knowledge in drawing. These scales closely reflect the child's skill and comprehension serving as indicators of their artistic capacities and developmental progress.

Table 11.2: Key Variables and Descriptions for Modeling CDDO

Variable	Description	Value/Range
Nm	Number of stocked solutions in the population	$Nm = 30$
$X_{(i,j)}$	Existing solution: a child's drawing affected by *GR*, *W*, *L*, *HP*	
i	Number of decree variables (sample members)	
J	Number of dimensions inside the solution	
PM	Pattern memory: abilities acquired through trials; helps children distinguish patterns, add meaning, and learn through experience	
HP	Hand pressure applied within *LB* and *UB*	
RHP	Random hand pressure for each drawing	Randomly selected
LB	Lower bound: represents drawing width	Problem-specific
UB	Upper bound: represents drawing length	Problem-specific
RND	Random number generated within a defined parameter domain	
CR	Creativity: aesthetic value adding visual appeal	$CR = 0.1$
LR	Child's level rate: measures dexterity	
SR	Child's skill rate: measures knowledge/skill in drawing	

The population of solutions *Nm* $X_{(i,j)}$, $i = 1, 2, 3, 4, \ldots, Nm$ and $j = 1, 2, 3, 4, \ldots, Nd$ denotes the number of dimensions and is initially randomly initialized from the group of potential solutions of the goal function $f(x_{(i,j)})$. In addendum, $f(x_{(i,j)})$ is utilized to calculate the maximum number of iterations of the algorithm or its stopping provision. This initialization stage (Ameen et al., 2023) is shown in Equation 11.5:

$$X_{(i,j)} = [X_{(1,1)}\, X_{(1,2)}\,) \cdots X_{(1,j)}\, X_{(2,1)}\, X_{(2,2)}\,) \cdots X_{(2,j)}\, X_{(3,1)}\, X_{(3,2)} \\ \ldots X_{(3,j)} \vdots X_{(i,1)} \vdots X_{(i,2)} \ldots \vdots \ldots X_{(i,j)}] \tag{11.5}$$

11.3.2.2 Stage 2: Profiteering the CDDO Algorithm

1. Theoretical Basis: Pre-Planning Stage (Ages 4–7)

The child's drawings through this specific phase develop into more traditional versions and replicas of drawings existing in his environment. This evolution happens from the child's exercise and use of feedback from former endeavors to generate new lines. Moreover, a notable aspect of this phase concerns the child's investigation of new thoughts while abiding by a basic skeleton or a scheme for drawing initial objects. At this stage, featured single styles appear, setting up a sequence of styles recognized as a schema, which serves as a direct representation of places and events in the child's drawings. The following key points summarize the second phase, which lays the foundation for the mathematical model:

1. **Ruled scribbling:** This stage reflects the child's emerging control in writing, particularly in relation to hand pressure.
2. **Learning forms (improvement):** The child demonstrates progress in carefully depicting the size and arrangement of shapes according to the effective ratios of the desired objects.
3. This stage allows the child to create identifiable shapes as they emerge, while the child learns to control motion and direction.

During this phase, a child's drawings evolve from early, unrefined attempts into more accurate representations as they acquire a deeper understanding of fine motor skills and their visual elements. These developments contribute to the child's ability to recreate familiar images and demonstrate greater control in the artistic process.

2. Mathematical Framework for this Phase

As noted in this phase, the child gains the ability to control motion and begins to generate shapes. Consequently, their drawings become more traditional and classical. Children compare their drawings with the finest examples they have encountered and attempt to determine which is the best drawing they have produced so far. They also strive to create new designs by emulating the practices of the more skilled artists in their environment. Comparisons can be made between their sketches and the best drawings produced by the group up to that point. Hand pressure plays an important role in assessing a child's readiness through this phase. Increasing hand pressure indicates a rise in the level of skill. Conversely, a child with prior capabilities may produce a sketch with less hand pressure, achieving greater accuracy in line with the golden ratio. According to Ameen et al. (2023), a random metric, referred to as random hand pressure (RHP), is introduced to evaluate hand pressure using Equation 11.6.

$$RHP = \text{Random}_{\text{Number}}\left(\text{Lower}_{\text{Boundary Number}}, \text{Upper}_{\text{Boundary Number}}\right) \quad (11.6)$$

The *RHP* is obtained by choosing a random number between the upper bound (*UB*) and the lower bound (*LB*) for the problem. It is used as a benchmark for evaluating current hand-pressure (*HP*) solutions. *HP*, which represents hand pressure, is derived from the existing solution parameters using Equation 11.7, where the multiple solution parameters are denoted by *j* (Ameen et al., 2023).

$$HP = X_{(i,Random(j))} \tag{11.7}$$

This phase concentrates on refining the child's artistic skills, particularly in relation to dominant hand pressure and adherence to the golden ratio. The ability to reproduce familiar styles and emulate skilled artists supports the child's development and enhances their understanding of artistic concepts.

11.3.2.3 Stage 3: Skillfulness in Effecting the Golden Ratio to the CDDO Algorithm

1. Theoretical Basis: Formation Stage (Ages 7–9)

During this period, children develop the ability to depict their surroundings by creating diagrams, often through repeating familiar styles. They build on previously acquired skills, recognize patterns in real images, explain their sketches, and practice continuously to improve their artistic abilities. This developmental stage enables children to advance in symbolizing their environment with greater detail and precision as they apply their understanding of concepts and visual styles. Through repeated exploration and practice, their drawing proficiency steadily improves.

2. Mathematical Framework for this Phase

A child applies acquired skills, relies on feedback, and examines styles in real images to ascribe meaning to his or her sketches. They engage in copying, exercising, and expressing passion through trial. The child's hand pressure (*HP*) is assessed to evaluate their capabilities. According to Ameen et al. (2023), a solution is updated using Equation (11.7) if HP is less than a random value, referred to as random hand pressure (*RHP*). A child's level rating (*LR*) and skill rating (*SR*) are considered; these are initially random numbers between 0 and 1 but are narrowed to a range of 0.6 to 1 if the child demonstrates adequate hand pressure. Adjusting L_R and S_R to higher values (0.6–1) indicates that the child possesses a strong level of skill and knowledge, which can be further developed by incorporating the Golden Ratio (*GR*) component. *GR* is defined as the ratio of two chosen components, width and length, in the child's sketch (Ameen et al., 2023), as shown in Equation (11.9). Each of these factors is chosen randomly from among all the factors in the given problem (Ameen et al., 2023) using Equation (11.10). This phase emphasizes the child's application of acquired skills, the use of feedback, and and the exploration of significant styles. Hand pressure evaluation, along with the golden ratio, skill rating, and level rating, contributes to updating the solution and improving its performance. By combining these elements, the development of a child's sketching is progressively enhanced. According to Ameen et al. (2023) Equation (11.8) introduces the concept of $X_i lbest$, which represents the child's most efficient drawing to date and serves as the best local solution. In comparison, $X_i gbest$ corresponds to the best global solution observed by children in their environment. Moreover, the Golden Ratio (GR), expressed as the ratio width (W) and length (L) in a child's sketch, underscores its importance in evaluating proportionality and aesthetic quality.

$$X_{i+1} = GR + S_R * (X_i lbest - X_i) + L_R * (X_i gbest - X_i) \tag{11.8}$$

$$GR_{X_i} = \frac{X_{(i,\, L)} + X_{(i,\, W)}}{X_{(i,\, L)}} \tag{11.9}$$

$$X_{(i,\, L)}, X_{(i,\, W)} = X_{(i, Random(j))}, X_{(i,\, L)} \neq X_{(i,\, W)} \tag{11.10}$$

11.3.2.4 Stage 4: The Creativity Stage in the CDDO Algorithm

1. Theoretical Basis: Emerging Realism Phase (Ages 9–11)

Through this phase, children express their social independence by forming groups, interacting with peers, and striving to understand social structures through their artistic styles. They become more self-critical, observe their environment closely, and aim to produce realistic, natural, and detailed sketches. By applying and integrating their existing skills, they generate new ideas that highlight their creativity, resulting in distinctive and visually appealing artwork. The fourth phase includes key components directly related to the athletic model, involving:

1. Portrayal of people and things: Make sure that their sketches realistically represent different elements such as perspective, distance, and relationships.
2. Fantasy (inventiveness).

2. Mathematical Framework for this Phase

Every child possesses creativity and skills acquired through experimentation and observation of their environment. Inventiveness serves as an important factor in enhancing the visual appeal of any artwork. During this phase, children integrate information to refine solutions that reflect the golden ratio or approximate it closely. However, when a solution lacks proper hand pressure, it indicates that the child's skills are not yet fully developed and require further improvement through application of the golden ratio and the elements of inventiveness. Moreover, children tend to recall the most effective learning exercises and attempt to repeat them in pursuit of better outcomes. A pattern memory is generated for each solution in the algorithm to facilitate this process. The degree of stylistic variation depends on the specific problem. A random solution selected from the pattern memory set is used to update poorly performing solutions, as a mechanism that improves the algorithm's overall convergence. In real-life scenarios, this approach accelerates children's learning speed. According to Ameen et al. (2023), Equation (11.11) incorporates both the pattern memory (PM) and creativity rate (C_R) to update the current solution and guide it to the optimal solution. The creativity operator is defined as a constant value, such as

$C_R = 0.1$. Initially, SL_R and S_R are tuned to low values (0–0.5), indicating an insufficient level of the child's skills and knowledge. However, these values can be further improved through the application of pattern memory and creativity rate.

By combining stereotypical memory, creativity, and other operators, this phase fosters the continual improvement of the child's artwork, supporting their artistic development and strengthening their problem-solving abilities.

$$X_{i+1} = PM_{xi} + S_R * (X_i gbest) \tag{11.11}$$

11.3.2.5 Stage 5: Pattern Memory Stage of the CDDO Algorithm

1. Theoretical Basis: Semi-Normal Phase (Ages 11–13)

During this phase, children demonstrate increased awareness, even though they are not yet adults. They begin to incorporate more complex details and adopt self-focused sketching techniques. The algorithm prioritizes the behaviors discussed earlier, with each behavior playing a decisive role in refining solutions and guiding them toward the desired outcome.

2. Mathematical Framework for this Phase

During this phase, children refine their sketches by adding more details and striving for precision. They compare their work with their better sketches, drawing on prior learning and skills. In the algorithm, this process is carried out by randomly selecting one of the ten best sketches generated by the children to update the existing sketch. Although the updated sketch maintains an accurate golden ratio, the hand pressure factor is not considered. This stage emphasizes attention to detail in the sketches. The algorithm incorporates this behavior through the evaluator's most effective updating technique, ensuring that the solution is revised whenever superior alternatives are available. This extends to improving the best global solutions across all participants. In addition, the stereotypical memory is updated with the current best global solution obtained at each iteration. The foundational steps of the CDDO algorithm are visually illustrated in its pseudocode; see Figure 11.2 and Algorithm 11.1 for details. Algorithm One demonstrates the framework of the CDDO pseudocode (Ameen et al., 2023).

Algorithm 11.1

Begin
Generate children's drawings $x_i = x_1, x_2, x_3, \ldots, x_{nm}$, where Nm is the count of stored solutions (population), see Equation (11.5)
Calculate the fitness of each drawing, where $f(x_i)$ is the objective function
Sort and choose the personal $x_i lbest$ and global $x_i gbest$ solutions.

(*Contd.*)

(Contd.)

Determine the golden ratio GRx_i for each drawing by using Equations (11.9 and 11.10)
Arrange solutions and create a pattern memory (*PM*) matrix
Choose an index from your *PM* at random
while (t < maximum stopping criterion for iterations) doesn't
Calculate *RHP* for each child's drawings by using Equation (11.6)
Choose at random *HP* using Equation (11.7)
If *HP* is low
Update the child's drawing by using Equation (11.8)
Set the L_R and S_R values at random between (0.6–1)
Else if GRx_i is between (1.5–2.0)
Update the child's drawing by using Equation (11.11)
Set the L_R and S_R values at random between (0–0.5)
End if
Calculate the fitness of each child's drawing by using the fitness function
Update each of the personal $x_i lbest$ and global $x_i gbest$ solutions
Record and retain the optimal cost value
Increase t
End while
Return global $x_i gbest$ solutions
End

11.3.3 Graph Convolutional Networks

Graph convolutional networks (GCNs) are a class of neural networks specifically designed to work with graph-structured data, where relationships between entities are represented as nodes and edges. Unlike traditional neural networks, which assume data exists in Euclidean space (such as images and sequences), GCNs have the ability to learn from non-Euclidean structures, such as social networks, biological networks, and knowledge graphs. The basic idea behind GCNs is to iteratively aggregate and transform feature information from a node's local neighborhood to learn meaningful representations. By leveraging the graph's adjacency structure, GCNs capture both node-level features and topological dependencies, making them effective for tasks such as node classification, link prediction, and graph classification. GCNs consist of stacked GraphCONV layers. The computation flow of each GraphCONV layer includes two phases: pooling and merging, as illustrated in Figure 11.3. In the pooling phase, each node combines the attributes of its neighbors to update the local feature vector. In the merging phase, the updated feature vectors are further combined to extract a higher-level abstraction through a local multilayer perception (MLP) network. The underlying GCN model, introduced by Kipf and Welling (2017), applies a

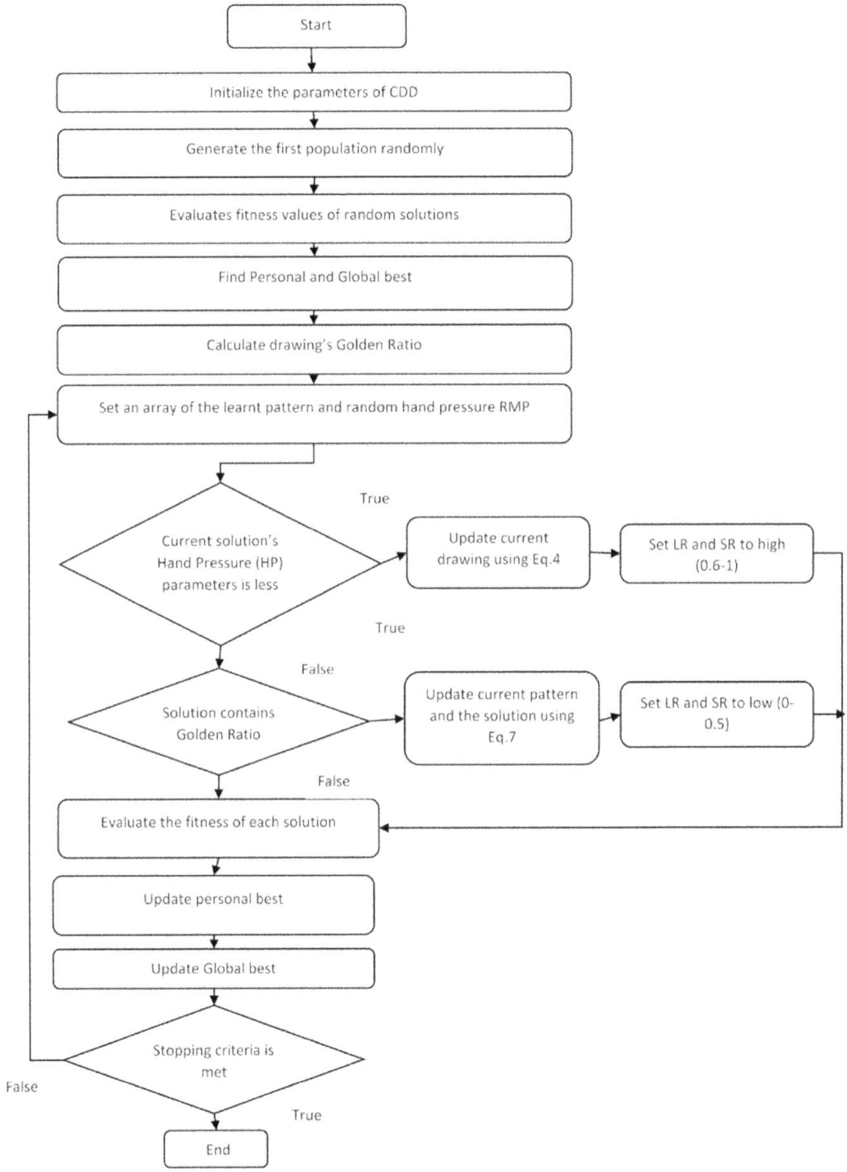

Figure 11.2: Flowchart of the CDDO algorithm.

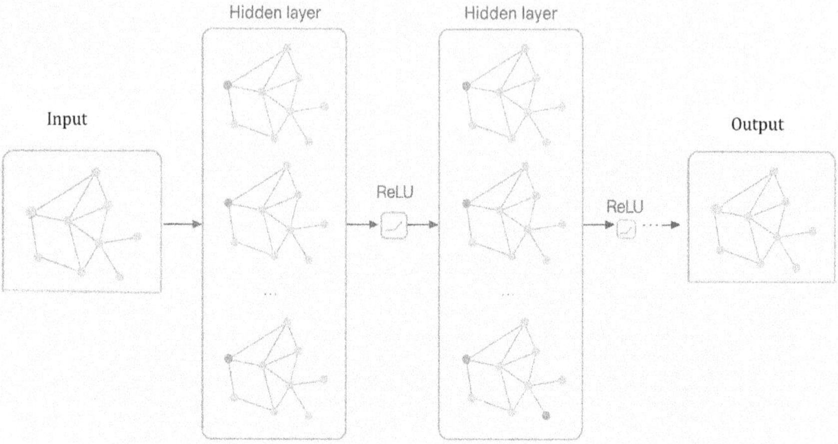

Figure 11.3: Graph convolutional network architecture.

first-order local approximation to spectral graph convolutions, enabling efficient and scalable training. Since then, GCNs have evolved into diverse architectures, expanding their application to include dynamic graphs, heterogeneous networks, and multi-relational environments. Their ability to exploit relational inductive biases makes them extremely valuable in healthcare, cybersecurity, recommender systems, and other applications. The formal expression for the GCN layer reads:

$$H = \sigma\left(\tilde{D}^{-\frac{1}{2}} \tilde{A} \tilde{D}^{-\frac{1}{2}} X\Theta\right) \tag{11.12}$$

where,
H is the matrix of node representations h_u.
X is the matrix of node features x_u.
$\sigma(\cdot)$ is an activation function (e.g., ReLU).

11.4 Typical Architecture

11.4.1 Building Graph Representations

Constructing the graph representation requires two essential networks: one that defines each node along with its descriptive feature attributes and another that captures the relationships among nodes through a set of edges. These connections are organized using an edge index, which serves as a structural guide and plays a crucial role in enabling accurate classification within the model.

1. **Input Layer:** At this stage, the model is provided with graph-structured input data, which has undergone data reduction by normalization processing and has been organized through k-nearest neighbor (KNN) techniques. This processed input forms the structural basis for the learning process that follows within the graph neural network.

2. **GCNConv Layers:** Convolutional layers are typically used to update feature information and connections between adjacent nodes as pixels. In contrast, graph convolutional neural networks (GCNs) update features in their vector or tensor spaces based on their connections in the graph. This process also involves adding self-loops, normalization, pooling, and linear transformation using a weight matrix.
3. **Dropout Layer:** This layer functions as a regularization mechanism to mitigate overfitting during the training process. By randomly omitting a portion of neurons in each training iteration, the model is compelled to learn more diverse and generalized feature representations. This prevents it from becoming overly dependent on specific neurons, ultimately improving its ability to perform well on unseen data.
4. **Global Average Pooling:** This layer condenses the collective information from all nodes in the graph by averaging their feature vectors. The result is a compact and informative summary that effectively captures the overall structure and attributes of the graph, serving as a reliable input for the final stages of classification or prediction.
5. **Activation Function:** SoftMax activation is employed to normalize node attributes. Figure 11.4 shows the architecture of classical graph convolutional neural networks.

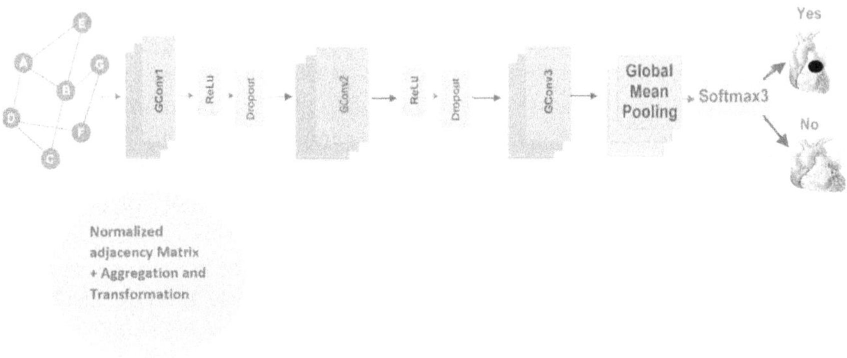

Figure 11.4: Architecture of classical graph convolutional neural network.

11.4.2 Training and Optimization

1. **Loss Function:** To guide the learning process, the binary cross-entropy function is used as the loss function. This function measures the divergence between the model's predicted probability output and the actual binary class labels, ensuring efficient gradient updates during training.
2. **Optimization Strategy:** Hyperparameters are tuned using the Quantum-Inspired Child-Drawing Development (QCDDO) optimization algorithm. QCDDO explores various configurations of critical parameters, such as hidden

layer size, learning rate, and dropout rate, by simulating children's creativity enhanced by quantum-inspired mechanisms, including superposition, entanglement, and tunneling. This dynamic optimization process promotes convergence toward optimal model settings, improving generalization and reducing overfitting.

3. **Assessment:** Model performance is evaluated using both accuracy and binary cross-entropy loss to monitor training behavior and detect potential over- or underfitting. Additionally, performance metrics, such as the classification report, including precision, recall, and F1 score, and the confusion matrix, are used to provide a deeper understanding of the model's predictive capabilities.

11.4.3 Quantum-Inspired Optimization Configuration

In the MATLAB implementation of the proposed framework, the QCDDO framework initialization involves setting up a quantum-inspired optimization environment specifically designed for efficient hyperparameter tuning in graph neural networks. In this study, the QCDDO algorithm simulates quantum behavior using a classical computational infrastructure inspired by fundamental quantum concepts such as superposition, entanglement, and tunneling. These mechanisms are encoded through mathematical analogs rather than physical qubits, making the method highly scalable and computationally feasible for large-scale graph problems. To begin the process, a set of candidate configurations is initialized. Each candidate solution encodes a unique combination of hyperparameters, such as the number of hidden units, the dropout rate, and the learning rate. These initial sketches form the search space that QCDDO explores and evolves through successive iterations. Instead of using physical quantum gates, the framework incorporates quantum-inspired operators to update data. These include golden ratio-based updates to enhance convergence, quantum tunneling-based exploration to avoid local optimal states, and pattern memory superposition to integrate knowledge derived from distinct solutions. This initialization and configuration phase is crucial, as it defines the optimization bounds and enables the simulated quantum mechanisms to navigate efficiently through the high-dimensional hyperparameter space. By simulating quantum behavior within a classical environment, QCDDO creates an efficient optimization environment that supports adaptive GNN training, improving prediction accuracy, reducing memory consumption, and enhancing generalization. This configuration forms the basis for applying quantum-inspired meta-algorithms to fine-tune GNN model parameters.

11.4.4 Data Encoding

In the proposed QCDDO-GNN framework, graph-structured data encoding forms the basis for efficient learning and optimization. Unlike traditional network-based data structures, graph-structured data encoding enables the model to capture relational and structural dependencies between data models, in this case, patient records. To achieve this and to guarantee that all inputs and outputs receive equal attention and to eliminate their dimensionality, the raw patient dataset is preprocessed and transformed using normalization processing to avoid overlapping attributes in smaller numeric ranges with attributes in larger numeric ranges and to avoid any numerical artifacts along the way. Following dimensionality reduction, the data is transformed into a graph representation using the *k*-nearest neighbor (KNN) algorithm. In this representation, each patient is modeled as a node, and edges are created based on similarity across the normalization-reduced dimensionality. The resulting graph is characterized by a node feature matrix, an edge index matrix, and a normalized adjacency matrix, all of which are critical components of GNN input, as shown in Figure 11.5. Within the QCDDO framework, each candidate solution encodes different configurations of these graph inputs, such as the number of neighbors used in the KNN, the dimensionality of the feature vector, and the structure of the input layer (such as the size of the node embeddings). These configurations are treated as learnable components during optimization, enabling the framework to dynamically adjust how the data is encoded and represented at the input level. Although QCDDO operates on classical computers, it mimics quantum behavior by incorporating data structures and updating mechanisms that reflect quantum properties. For example, the pattern memory array used in QCDDO operates similarly to quantum superposition, combining distinct graph configurations to form new encodings. This mirrors the way quantum circuits, such as those using spin gates with parameters like $R_y(\theta)$, transmit classical inputs to quantum state spaces in real quantum systems. Thus, in the QCDDO-GNN algorithm, data encoding is not a fixed preprocessing step but rather a tunable component within the optimization process. This allows the algorithm to optimize both the graph representation and the GNN hyperparameters, resulting in a more expressive and adaptive learning model for supporting clinical decisions, such as heart attack prediction.

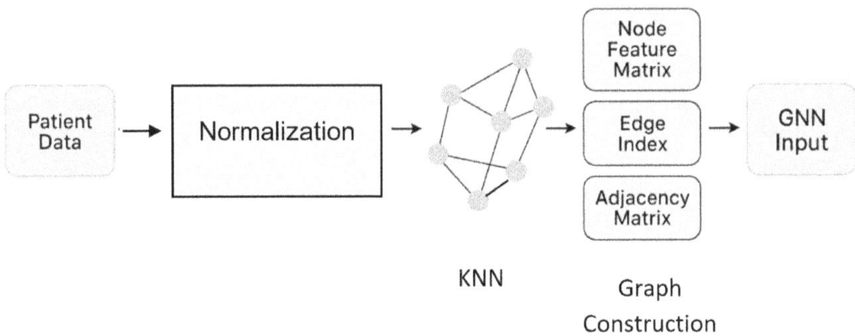

Figure 11.5: Data encoding.

11.4.5 Graph Construction

In the proposed QCDDO-GNN framework, graph construction plays a fundamental role in transforming structured medical records into a relational format that captures individual attributes and similarities between samples. Each patient is represented as a node, and edges are constructed using a *k*-nearest neighbor (KNN) approach based on similarity in their normalization-reduced medical attributes. This transformation allows the model to interpret patient relationships not just as independent inputs, but as an interconnected graph, where each node influences and is influenced by its neighbors, as shown in Figure 11.5. This graph-based representation is essential for enabling the graph neural network to perform message passing and neighbor aggregation, allowing the model to learn local and global structural patterns from the data. Unlike the flat data structures used in traditional models, this topology-based approach captures complex interconnections between patients, which is particularly useful in clinical applications such as heart attack prediction. The incorporation of a quantum-inspired pediatric graph development (QCDDO) optimization mechanism further enhances this process. By simulating behaviors similar to quantum entanglement and superposition, QCDDO can dynamically reconfigure graph encoding parameters, such as edge density, node attribute dimensions, and initialization strategies, based on the evolution of the population's intelligence and the memory of distinct solutions. This allows the generated graph to adapt in tandem with model training, ensuring the relational data structure evolves toward optimal learning configurations. Through this synergy between graph construction and quantum-inspired optimization, the QCDDO-GNN architecture can extract deeper insights from medical datasets, improving classification and generalization performance with minimal manual tuning.

11.4.6 Quantum-Inspired Node Embeddings

In the proposed QCDDO-GNN framework, the graph structure not only shapes node embeddings but is also dynamically optimized through quantum-inspired meta-heuristics. Each node in the graph, represents an individual patient associated with a feature vector derived from clinical features, and these features are aggregated and updated across layers using graph convolution operations. However, the novelty of this framework lies in how the QCDDO algorithm interacts with the embedding process to influence and optimize the transformation of these representations at the node level. Rather than using physical quantum gates, the QCDDO mechanism mimics quantum behaviors to guide the evolution of node embeddings. For example, superposition-inspired memory embedding is used to generate weighted sets of node embeddings that perform better than previous iterations, mimicking how multiple quantum states coexist. Similarly, quantum tunneling-inspired updates allow for abrupt transitions in embedding configurations, helping the model overcome local minima in the feature space. Furthermore, golden-ratio-based operators are used to adjust the flow of information across the embedding layers, ensuring that the propagation of features across the graph is neither too steep nor too conservative. These quantum-inspired behaviors play a crucial role in shaping how node features improve over time, allowing the GNN to more effectively capture underlying patterns in relational medical data. Ultimately, these mechanisms ensure that node embedding remains adaptive, expressive, and robust throughout the learning process. By incorporating QCDDO into the GNN pipeline, the model achieves improved representation quality at the node level, leading to more accurate predictions and greater generalization across complex clinical classification tasks.

11.4.7 Model Integration

The integration of a quantum-inspired child development optimization mechanism within a graph neural network framework is a key innovation of the proposed model. This hybrid architecture combines the representational capabilities of GNNs with the adaptive search capabilities of QCDDO, effectively optimizing the model's hyperparameters to enhance learning performance. In this design, the GNN serves as the underlying learning architecture, transforming graph-structured patient data through a series of graph convolution layers. Meanwhile, QCDDO acts as an external optimization module, dynamically adjusting critical hyperparameters, such as hidden layer size, learning rate, and dropout rate, based on model performance metrics (such as accuracy, memory usage, and model complexity). This continuous feedback loop enables the learning system to adaptively converge toward an optimal configuration. By combining quantum heuristic search strategies with traditional graph-based learning, the integrated framework achieves a balance between structural expressiveness and optimization efficiency. This synergistic combination ensures robust model performance across diverse clinical datasets, making it particularly suitable for complex tasks such as predicting heart attacks from patient chart data.

11.4.8 Quantum-Inspired Children's Drawing Development Proposal

The Quantum Child Drawing Development Optimization (QCDDO) algorithm is designed to mimic children's cognitive development patterns as they develop their drawings, augmented by quantum principles to promote exploration in high-dimensional spaces. In QCDDO, each child's drawing represents a candidate solution encoded as a vector of super-graph neural network parameters (e.g., hidden units, dropout rate, and learning rate). The child's adaptation is guided by structured memory, golden ratio methods, and quantum-inspired operators, facilitating local and global searches. Inspired by quantum tunneling, the optimizer allows particles (drawings) to probabilistically escape local minima, increasing the chances of converging to globally optimal configurations. In the proposed framework, patient data are first preprocessed using normalization processing; consequently, they are transformed into a graph representation using the *k*-nearest neighbor (KNN) method, where each patient is represented as a node, and edges are formed based on feature similarity. This graph data is then passed through a series of Graph Convolutional Network (GCN) layers, which collect neighborhood information and extract latent node features through message-passing mechanisms. To enhance the efficiency of model training and adaptively adjust its configuration, a Quantum-Inspired Children's Drawing Development (QCDDO) optimization layer is incorporated into its architecture. This layer simulates a set of candidate deep neural network configurations, inspired by the cognitive stages of children's drawing behavior and enhanced by quantum mechanical principles such as superposition, entanglement, and quantum tunneling.

Each individual in the QCDDO ensemble represents a possible set of hyperparameters, including the hidden layer size, learning rate, and dropout rate. These candidate configurations are evaluated based on a fitness function. The algorithm iteratively optimizes these solutions using a combination of quantum-inspired update operators: golden ratio-based updating to guide the search direction, pattern memory superposition to merge distinct solutions, and quantum tunneling to avoid local optimal states. The optimized hyperparameters from QCDDO are then used to form the GNN architecture. The GNN continues with traditional layers such as global mean pooling, flattening, and fully connected dense layers that introduce nonlinearity through activation functions such as ReLU. The final output layer uses a sigmoid activation function to perform binary classification, predicting the probability of a heart attack. This hybrid approach enables a strong integration of adaptive optimization and graph-based learning, as illustrated in Figure 11.6.

However, as the No Free Lunch (NFL) theorem emphasizes, no single optimizer can outperform others on all types of problems. Therefore, the positive performance of QCDDO in this study encourages its application to a broader range of learning problems and highlights the importance of further exploring hybrid and adaptive optimization strategies. The sketch-based transformation and updating mechanism in QCDDO can be formally represented using equations influenced by the golden ratio, which guide the learning path and structural modifications of GNN configurations across generations. To illustrate the rationale for using the Quantum-Inspired Child-Drawing Development Optimization (QCDDO) algorithm, its foundation lies in combining child-like learning strategies with quantum mechanical principles such as superposition, entanglement, and quantum tunneling. This hybrid heuristic framework effectively balances exploration and exploitation in high-dimensional, non-convex search spaces, a common feature in GNN hyperparameter tuning. As mentioned earlier, QCDDO is inspired by the developmental learning patterns observed in children, incorporating structured memory, golden ratio heuristics, and random hand pressure into its adaptive mechanisms. When combined with quantum-inspired operators, QCDDO enables

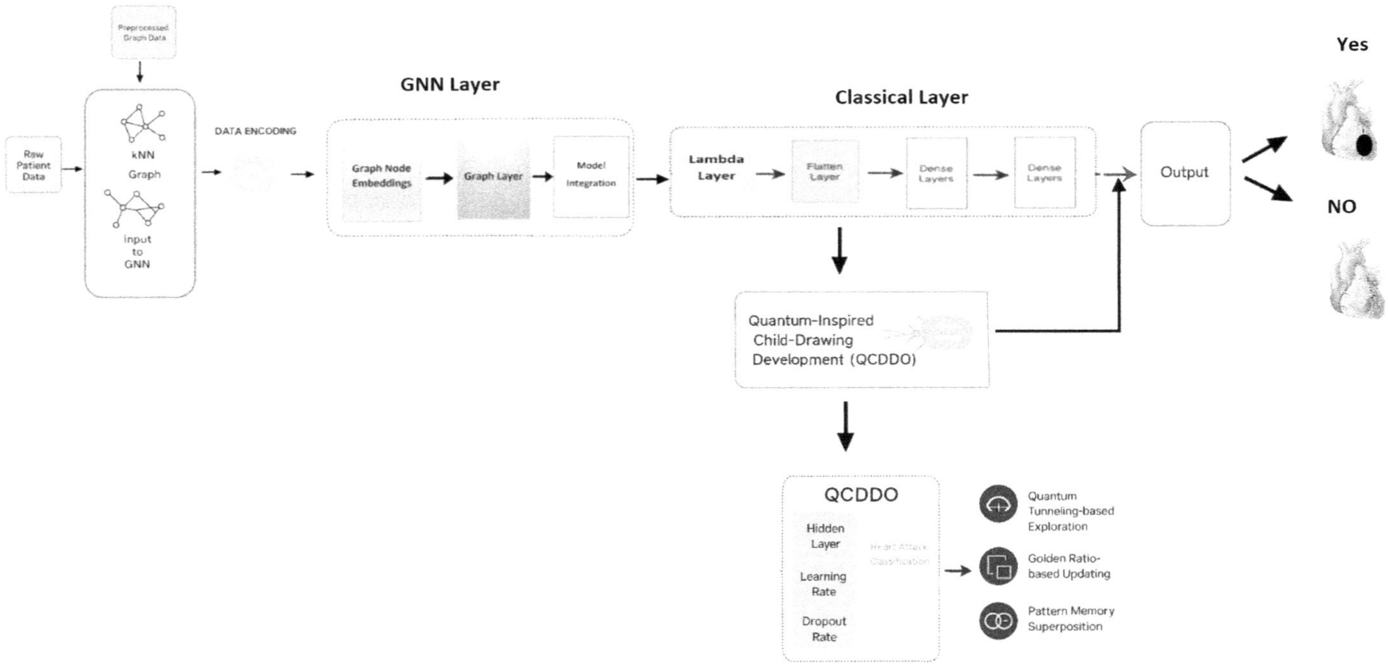

Figure 11.6: Proposed QCDDO for GNN training optimization and hyperparameter tuning.

it to transcend local optimums and perform more versatile searches. The stages of this algorithm are described in the following sections:

11.4.8.1 QCDDO Stages

1. Identify Initial Populations and Establish Research Priorities

This stage initiates the QCDDO algorithm by initializing a set of candidate solutions, metaphorically called "children's drawings". Each solution, x_i, represents a point in the multidimensional search space (e.g., the hyperparameters of a super-macro neural network). $x_i = [x_{i1}, x_{i2}, \ldots, x_{id}]$, $i = 1, 2, \ldots, N_m$. The total number of drawings, N_m, determines the size of the set where N_m is the population size, and d is the number of decision variables (e.g., GNN hyperparameters). The graphs are randomly initialized:

$$x_{ij} = LB_j + r_{ij} \cdot (UB_j - LB_j) \tag{11.13}$$

With $r_{ij} \sim U(0, 1)$, and LB_j, UB_j being the lower and upper bounds for the variable j. This initialization is typically random, ensuring diversity in the solution space and allowing for extensive exploration during early iterations. Once the ensemble is created, or for each solution x_i, the algorithm evaluates the fitness of each solution using a predefined objective function $f(x_i)$. This fitness function determines how well the solution performs relative to optimization goals such as reducing errors, increasing accuracy, or reducing computational cost. The fitness values guide the development process by distinguishing better-performing solutions from lower-performing ones. After calculating the fitness values, each solution x_i is associated with a personal best performance $x_i lbest$, which records the best performance achieved by that solution so far. At the same time, the algorithm determines the best global solution, $x_i gbest$, which is the best among all solutions. These benchmarks act as attractors in the updating process and play a pivotal role in balancing exploitation and exploration. The golden ratio GR_{x_i} is calculated as a new guiding metric based on the relative performance and structural balance of a solution, taking into account its fit and behavior in the neighborhood. This metric helps determine the appropriate update strategy for each solution. GR_{x_i} values close to the classical golden ratio (≈ 1.618) are interpreted as potential "optimal" cases that should be exploited more carefully.

2. Elite Selection and Preparation for Quantum-Guided Exploration

The pattern memory (*PM*) matrix is built from the best solutions with the highest compatibility scores. It serves as a store of promising patterns or locations in the solution space. This matrix is later used in update rules to guide other solutions toward successful regions. The *PM* matrix ensures that valuable knowledge is retained and reused during optimization. To introduce randomness and avoid premature convergence, a solution is randomly selected from the *PM* matrix. This selected pattern becomes the reference in future update rules, ensuring a balance of diversity and historical knowledge in the child's learning and development in drawing. The algorithm sets an iteration counter $t = 1$, indicating the start of the optimization loop. This counter is incremented after each generation and compared to a predetermined maximum number of iterations. The loop continues until the stopping criterion is met. For each child, a random hand pressure (*RHP*) value is calculated using a mathematical function that simulates the variability of the child's hand pressure. Based on this value, a random hand pressure (*HP*) value is selected. This pressure influences the extent to which the child imitates the learned pattern or deviates to explore new areas, reflecting children's drawing behavior at different levels of hand control.

3. Smart Drawing Control Using Quantitative and Structural Routing

The algorithm checks whether the golden ratio of the current solution lies within a certain range (e.g., $1.5 \leq GR_{x_i} \leq 2.0$). If the condition is met, the child undergoes a more exploitable update using the learned patterns. If not, the algorithm prefers exploration, including quantum-inspired mechanisms such as superposition and tunneling to escape from the local optimum. When GR_{x_i} is not within the optimal range or when *HP* is low, the solution is updated using a quantum-inspired rule. This involves stochastic motion influenced by selected patterns of the *PM* matrix, scaled with random coefficients, and modified by a quantum tunneling term. This allows the solution to bypass potential barriers, enhancing the exploration of difficult or non-convex regions.
If $HP < 0.5$ apply:

$$x_i^{t+1} = x_i^t + L_R \,.\, S_R \,.\, MP_R + Q \times T(\gamma) \tag{11.14}$$

With

$$L_R, S_R \sim \text{U } (0.6, 1.0)$$

$$Q = \text{Quantum tunneling term}$$

If the golden ratio is within the appropriate range, the solution is updated using Equation (11.15), which integrates personal bests, global bests, and quantum adjustment conditions. This stage encourages the child to learn from his or her history, peer bests, and quantum changes, enabling a rich and intelligent exploitation of well-known areas of research.
$1.5 \leq GR_{x_i} \leq 2.0$ then:

$$x_i^{t+1} = x_i^t + \varphi(x_i^{lbest} - x_i^t) + \psi(x_i^{gbest} - x_i^t) + Q \times T(\gamma) \tag{11.15}$$

With

$$\varphi, \psi \sim \text{U } (0, 0.5).$$

To enhance diversity while taking into account acquired memory, the algorithm may implement quantum superposition, a weighted combination of elite patterns from the *PM* matrix. After forming a superposition state, the solution collapses to a new state probabilistically, similar to quantum scaling. This powerful mechanism enables memory-guided probabilistic innovation.

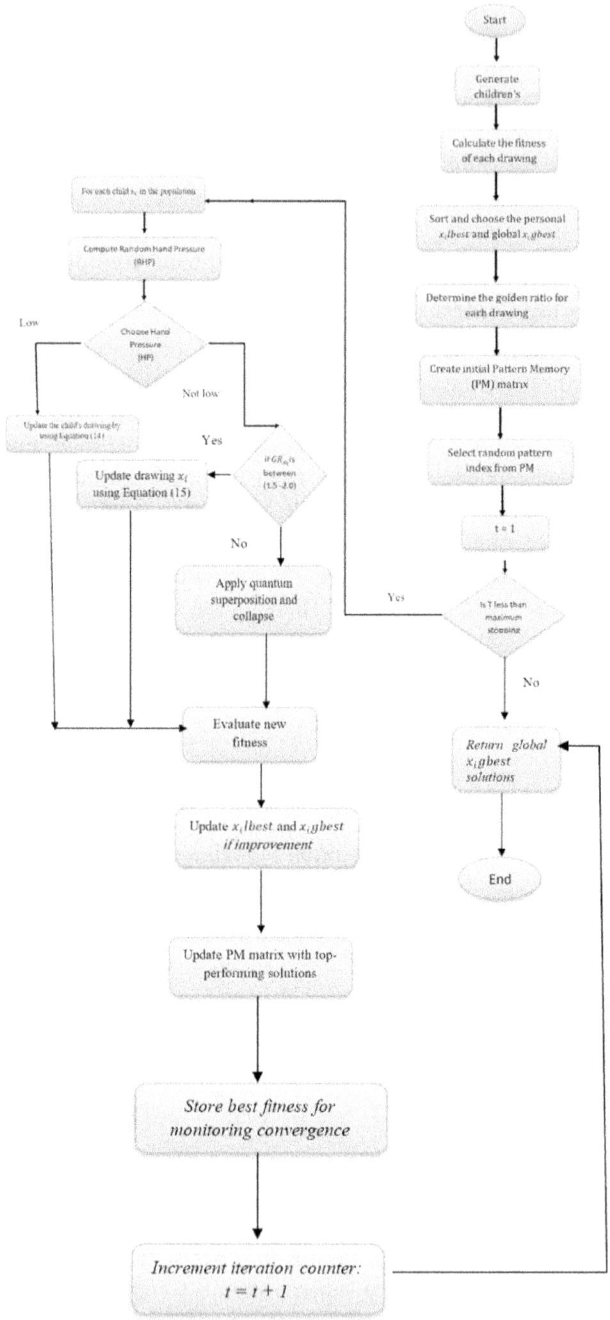

Figure 11.7: Flowchart of the QCDDO algorithm.

4. Evaluate Progress and Improve Memory Towards Optimal Drawing

After each child's position is updated, its new fitness is calculated. This evaluation determines whether the update resulted in a better solution. This step is crucial for assessing the effectiveness of the exploration or exploitation strategy applied in that iteration. If a new solution outperforms personal or global bests, the relevant records are updated. This ensures that only improvements are retained in memory. Saving personal and global bests stimulates convergence over time while maintaining innovation. The Pattern Memory Matrix has been updated with new, premium solutions selected based on their relevance. This update ensures that the memory bank continues to evolve and stay abreast with the latest developments in solutions and serves as a guide for the next iteration. Once the iteration limit is reached, the algorithm terminates and returns the global best solution, ($x_i gbest$) found during the entire process. This solution represents the optimal configuration or parameter set discovered by the QCDDO framework and can be used directly for deployment (e.g., for selecting GNN hyperparameters or training a model). The implemented changes improved the presentation to achieve the optimal fitness function. Figure 11.7 and Algorithm 11.2 show the pseudocode and revised flowchart of the QCDDO algorithm, respectively, illustrating the modifications that led to these improved results.

Algorithm 11.2

Begin
Generate children's drawings $x_i = x_1, x_2, x_3, \ldots, x_{Nm}$, where Nm is the count of stored solutions (population), see Equation (11.5)
Calculate the fitness of each drawing, where $f(x_i)$ is the objective function
Sort and choose the personal $x_i lbest$ and global $x_i gbest$ solutions
Determine the golden ratio GR_{x_i} for each drawing by using Equations (11.9 and 11.10)
Create initial Pattern Memory (PM) matrix from sorted solutions
Select random pattern index from PM
$t = 1$
while ($t <$ maximum stopping criterion for iterations) doesn't
For each child x_i in the population:
Compute Random Hand Pressure (RHP) using Equation (11.6)
Choose Hand Pressure (HP)
If HP is low then
Update the child's drawing by using Equation (11.14)
$x_i(t+1) = x_i(t) + L_R \times S_R \times PM_{rand\_index} + Q \times T(\gamma)$ where $Q \times T(\gamma)$ is quantum tunneling term
Set the L_R and S_R values at random between (0.6–1)

(*Contd.*)

(Contd.)

Else if GR_{x_i} is between (1.5–2.0)
Update drawing x_i using Equation (11.15)

$$x_i^{t+1} = x_i^t + \varphi(x_i^{lbest} - x_i^t) + \psi(x_i^{gbest} - x_i^t) + Q \times T(\gamma)$$

Set φ and ψ randomly between (0–0.5)
End if
apply quantum superposition and collapse:
$X_{super} = \sum_{k=1}^{K} w_k \cdot PM_k$ (Weighted superposition of memory patterns)
where $\sum_{k=1}^{K} w_k = 1$
Collapse (X_{super}) → update $x_i(t+1)$ based on probabilistic measurement
Evaluate new fitness $f(x_i(t+1))$
Update:
$x_i lbest$ if $f(x_i(t+1))$ better than previous
$x_i gbest$ if global improvement observed
End for
Update *PM* matrix with top-performing solutions
Store best fitness for monitoring convergence
Increment iteration counter: $t = t + 1$
End while
Return global $x_i gbest$ solutions
End

11.5 Materials and Methods

11.5.1 Classical Graph Convolutional Neural Network

In the proposed Quantum-Inspired Child Drawing Development Optimization (QCDDO) framework, graph neural network models are optimized through a heuristic optimization process inspired by the developmental stages of children's drawing behavior and the principles of quantum mechanics. As shown in Figure 11.4, a GNN model is initially built using graph-structured patient data, where each node represents a sample, and edges encode feature-based similarity via *k*-nearest neighbor (KNN) construction. Following graph convolution and activation layers, QCDDO is applied to optimize key hyperparameters, such as hidden layer size, learning rate, and dropout rate. The optimization process draws on quantum phenomena, including superposition, entanglement, and tunneling, to efficiently explore the hyperparameter space. In addition, operators such as golden ratio-based updating and pattern memory superposition help guide the search toward efficient solutions. This integration facilitates adaptive learning and improves convergence, enabling GNNs to achieve higher prediction accuracy while reducing computational complexity.

11.5.2 Dataset Description

The dataset used in this study is the Patient Heart Attack Prediction dataset, which is available on Mendeley (Maghdid and Rashid, 2022), as shown in Table 11.3. A comprehensive database of heart attack contributing factors was created in this study (Maghdid and Rashid, 2022), containing 1,319 cases, eight input fields, and one output field indicating whether the patient had a heart attack. The input fields included age, sex, heart rate, systolic blood pressure, diastolic blood pressure, blood glucose, CK-MB, and troponin test. The output field indicated the presence of a heart attack, which was divided into two categories (negative and positive): negative indicates no heart attack, while positive indicates the presence of a heart attack. Table 11.3 shows detailed information and the maximum and minimum attribute values for the 1,319 cases in the entire database.

Table 11.3: Dataset's Structure

Description	Max Value	Min Value	Attribute Name
Age	103	14	Age
Gender	1	0	Gender
Maximum Heart Rate	135	20	Impulse
Systolic BP	223	42	Pressure High
Diastolic BP	154	38	Pressure Low
Blood Sugar	541	35	Glucose
CK-MB Enzyme	300	0.321	CKMB
Troponin Enzyme	10.3	0.001	Test-Troponin

11.5.3 Data Preprocessing

To prepare a patient heart attack prediction dataset for training and optimizing a graph neural network via the Quantum Child's Drawing Development Optimization algorithm, a structured preprocessing pipeline was implemented. First, all continuous input attributes, such as age, heart rate, systolic and diastolic blood pressure, blood glucose, CK-MB, and troponin levels, were normalized using a min-max scale to bind their values to the range [0, 1], ensuring consistency in scale and improving convergence during training. The binary gender attribute was retained without further encoding. Since the original patient heart attack prediction dataset was tabular in nature and lacked any inherent relational structure between patient records, a graph construction technique was required to enable the use of graph convolutional networks (GCNs). To address this problem, the k-nearest neighbor (KNN) algorithm was used to transform the dataset into a graph-structured format. In this approach, each patient was represented as a node in the graph, and edges were determined by connecting each node to its k-most similar nodes based on the Euclidean distance in the uniform feature space. This process resulted in a synthetic graph $G = (V, E)$, where each vertex represents a patient, and the edges encode similarity-based relationships between them. The resulting adjacency matrix, along with the uniform feature matrix and labels, formed the input to the GCN model. Therefore, the KNN method was used solely as a graph construction strategy, enabling the GCN to operate on a meaningful topological structure, aggregate neighborhood information, and perform efficient classification. The GCN itself was then optimized using the proposed Quantum-Inspired Child Graph Development (QCDDO) optimization algorithm to allow the model to automatically evolve towards configurations that maximize classification performance while minimizing computational cost.

11.5.4 Normalizing Processing

The data used in this investigation were scaled between 0 and 1 to guarantee that all inputs and outputs received equal attention and to eliminate their dimensionality. Before using it in the study (Maghdid and Rashid, 2022), data normalization has two major advantages. The first is to avoid overshadowing qualities in smaller numeric ranges by employing attributes in larger numeric ranges. The second goal is to avoid any numerical problems throughout the process. Therefore, the data used in this study were normalized as follows:

$$E_n = \frac{E_i - E_{min}}{E_{max} - E_{min}} \quad i = 1, 2, \ldots, n \tag{11.16}$$

Here, E_n, E_i, E_{min}, E_{max} represent the normalized values, actual values, minimum values, and maximum values, respectively. Normalized values for key attributes in the heart attack dataset are shown in Table 11.4.

11.5.5 Training Procedure

The training process of the QCDDO-enhanced graph neural network (GNN) framework is designed to improve model performance by tuning the quantum inference algorithms for critical hyperparameters. The dataset consists of 1,319 patient records, each represented by eight input attributes and a binary output label indicating a heart attack. First, the raw patient data is transformed into a graph using the *k*-nearest neighbor (KNN) method, where each patient becomes a node connected to similar patients based on their clinical characteristics. This graph is then fed into a graph neural network (GNN), which consists of stacked Graph Convolutional Neural Network (GConv) layers interleaved with ReLU activations and dropout layers to extract and aggregate neighborhood-level information. To optimize the learning process, QCDDO is used to automatically search for optimal hyperparameters, including hidden layer size, dropout rate, and learning rate. Each solution in the QCDDO ensemble represents a candidate set of hyperparameters. During training, the QCDDO algorithm iteratively updates these solutions by applying behavioral patterns to

Table 11.4: Normalized Values of Features in the Heart Attack Dataset

Age	Gender	Maximum Heart Rate	Systolic BP	Diastolic BP	Blood Sugar	CK-MB Enzyme	Troponin Enzyme	Output
0.561798	1	0.042163	0.651934	0.387931	0.247036	0.004935	0.001068	0
0.078652	1	0.067828	0.309392	0.068966	0.51581	0.021453	0.102826	1
0.460674	1	0.04033	0.651934	0.336207	0.464427	0.005569	0.000194	0
0.561798	1	0.04583	0.430939	0.146552	0.464427	0.045212	0.011749	1
0.460674	1	0.04033	0.38674	0.232759	0.523715	0.002533	0.000194	0
0.494382	0	0.03758	0.38674	0.172414	0.102767	0.005035	0.000291	0
0.202247	0	0.018332	0.756906	0.258621	0.132411	0.001298	0.000194	0
0.550562	1	0.036664	0.950276	0.37931	0.102767	1	0.230022	1
0.337079	0	0.036664	0.618785	0.37069	0.197628	0.006771	0.000291	0
0.595506	1	0.03758	0.651934	0.491379	0.128458	0.008406	0.000971	0
0.337079	0	0.036664	0.685083	0.448276	0.132411	0.006904	0.000485	0
0.550562	0	0.036664	0.596685	0.387931	0.322134	0.006904	0.001165	0
0.561798	1	0.036664	0.867403	0.525862	0.112648	0.010374	0.521313	1
0.449438	0	0.067828	0.441989	0.25	0.12253	0.003667	0.001068	0
0.370787	1	0.051329	0.430939	0.275862	0.561265	0.007505	0.000194	0
0.52809	1	0.055912	0.41989	0.241379	0.195652	0.003901	0.001554	1
0.808989	0	0.048579	0.39779	0.258621	0.102767	0.002633	0.07525	1
0.348315	0	0.04583	0.320442	0.258621	0.120553	0.000951	0.000291	0
0.258427	0	0.047663	0.359116	0.413793	0.472332	0.008573	0.000194	0
0.348315	1	0.036664	0.370166	0.232759	0.106719	0.004268	0.001845	1
0.516854	1	0.065995	0.60221	0.344828	0.525692	0.004268	0.000388	0

map sub-elements, along with quantum-inspired operations such as tunneling, golden ratio routing, and probabilistic memory superposition. Supervised training is performed over 100 epochs using minibatch processing to improve convergence stability and efficiency. A binary cross-entropy loss function is used to measure the discrepancy between the predicted probabilities and actual heart attack signatures. Optimization is performed using an adaptive optimizer such as Adam or the Stochastic Gradient Descent (SGD) algorithm with momentum, which adjusts the network weights based on gradients derived from the loss function. During training, the QCDDO mechanism adaptively optimizes the hyperparameters based on feedback from the validation accuracy and loss, ensuring a balance between prediction performance and model generalization. This dynamic interaction between the GNN model and QCDDO optimization enables the framework to achieve robust, scalable, and interpretable results, suitable for supporting clinical decisions in heart attack risk prediction.

11.5.6 Model Evaluation

Model evaluation is a critical step in assessing the performance, robustness, and generalization ability of a QCDDO-enhanced graph neural network (GNN). In this study, the evaluation process is conducted using a separate test set, applied during the training phase to ensure an unbiased performance evaluation. Key performance metrics are calculated to evaluate the model's classification effectiveness, including accuracy, binary cross-entropy loss, precision, recall, and F1 score. These metrics provide a comprehensive understanding of the model's predictive ability and its ability to correctly identify patients at risk of a heart attack. Additionally, a confusion matrix is generated to visualize the classification results, distinguishing between true positives (TP), false positives (FP), true negatives (TN), and false negatives (FN). This visualization is particularly useful for identifying class imbalances or specific types of misclassification errors. This comprehensive evaluation helps diagnose potential issues, such as overfitting (where the model performs well on training data but underperforms on unseen data) or underfitting (where the model fails to learn meaningful patterns). Furthermore, feedback from the evaluation metrics is used to inform the QCDDO optimization loop, which optimizes the hyperparameter tuning process in subsequent iterations to achieve improved performance and generalization.

11.5.6.1 Confusion Matrix

The confusion matrix is a 2×2 tabular representation used in binary classification tasks to depict the distribution of correctly and incorrectly predicted outcomes. In the context of the QCDDO-optimized GNN model, the matrix provides an intuitive analysis of the number of patient cases accurately classified as having or not having a heart attack. As shown in Table 11.5, the matrix highlights the number of true positives, true negatives, false positives, and false negatives,

Table 11.5: Total Samples

	Predicted class	
Actual class	**Predicted: No**	**Predicted: Yes**
Actual: No	TN	FP
Actual: Yes	FP	TP

enabling a clear assessment of the reliability of the model's prediction.

11.5.6.2 Performance Metrics

To evaluate the effectiveness of the QCDDO-optimized graph neural network (GNN), its performance is evaluated using a set of standard classification metrics, as defined in Equations (11.17-11.21). The proposed QCDDO-GNN framework is systematically compared to a baseline classical GNN model that does not incorporate quantum- inspired optimization. This comparative analysis highlights the advantages of incorporating QCDDO in terms of accuracy, precision, recall, F1 score, and binary cross-entropy loss, demonstrating the improved learning and generalization capabilities of the proposed method.

$$\text{Accuracy} = \frac{\text{Number of correct predictions}}{\text{Total Number of correct predictions}} = \frac{TP+TN}{TP+TN+FP+FN} \quad (11.17)$$

$$\text{Precision} = \frac{TP}{TP+FP} \quad (11.18)$$

$$\text{Recall (Sensitivity)} = \frac{TP}{TP+FP} \quad (11.19)$$

$$F1 - \text{Score} = 2 \cdot \frac{Precision \cdot Recall}{Precision + Recall} \quad (11.20)$$

$$\text{Binary Cross} - \text{Entropy Loss} = -\frac{1}{N}\sum_{i=1}^{N} [y_i \cdot \log \log (p_i) + (1-y_i) \cdot \log \log (1 - p_i)] \quad (11.21)$$

Where:
$y_i \in \{0, 1\}$ is the true label
$p_i \in \{0, 1\}$ is the predicted probability
N is the total number of samples

11.5.7 Measurement

After optimizing hyperparameters via the QCDDO framework, the graph neural network (GNN) processes the graph-structured patient data, producing tensor-like output representations. These tensors, which encapsulate the learned features at the node and graph levels, are passed to the classical part of the model architecture. To ensure compatibility with the dense layers, the output tensors are resampled and flattened. The classical part of the architecture consists of two fully connected dense layers. The first dense layer applies a ReLU activation function to introduce nonlinearity and enhance representational power. The second dense layer uses a sigmoid activation function to perform binary classification, producing a probability score indicating the presence or absence of a heart attack. The training process uses a stochastic gradient descent (SGD) optimizer, although alternative optimizers such as Adam can be explored, to minimize the binary cross-entropy loss function. This loss quantifies the divergence between predicted and actual scores, guiding model weight updates to improve classification accuracy. During the training phase, the model tracks training and validation accuracy and loss across multiple epochs. These metrics are plotted to visualize learning progress and detect potential overfitting by comparing training performance with validation performance. After training, the final model performance is evaluated using a comprehensive classification report and confusion matrix, which details key performance indicators such as precision, recall, F1 score, and error distribution.

This structured approach to measurement ensures that the QCDDO-optimized GNN model is not only fine-tuned but also rigorously validated, providing reliable predictions for heart attack risk classification and supporting effective clinical decision-making.

11.6 Results and Discussion

11.6.1 QCDDO-GNN vs. Conventional GNN Model

The training and validation performance of the proposed QCDDO-enhanced GNN model was evaluated over 100 epochs. To evaluate the effectiveness of the QCDDO-enhanced GNN for Quantum-Inspired Children's Drawing Evolution (QCDDO-GNN), its performance was compared with a conventional GNN model across multiple evaluation metrics, including key performance indicators such as precision, accuracy, recall, F1 score, and loss, to assess convergence behavior and generalization ability. As shown in Figure 11.8 and Table 11.6, the QCDDO-GNN significantly outperformed the conventional GNN in all key areas. Table 11.6 displays a comparative performance summary, the accuracy, precision, recall, F1 score, and loss ratio of both models. The QCDDO-enhanced GNN outperforms the conventional GNN by more than 4% in accuracy (92.70% vs. 88.63%) and achieves a lower classification loss (0.19% vs. 0.28%), reflecting improved predictive accuracy and better generalization. These improvements underscore the importance of quantum-inspired intelligent hyperparameter tuning in improving GNN performance.

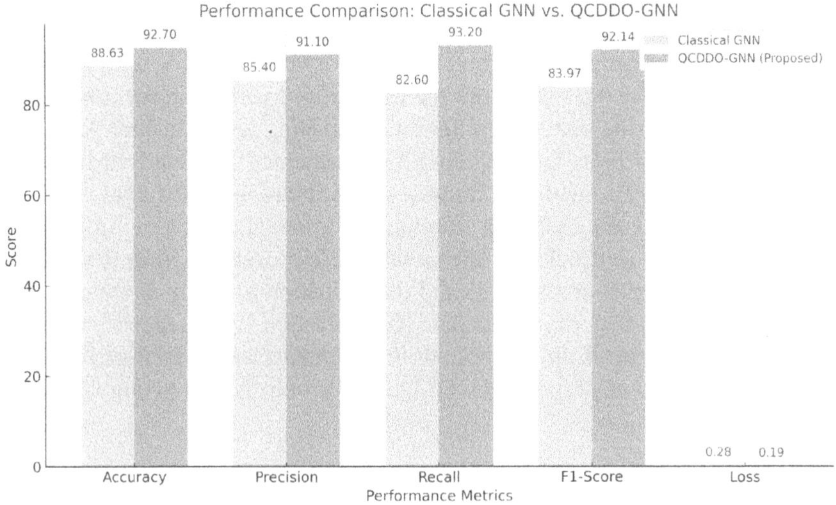

Figure 11.8: Performance comparison between classical GNN and QCDDO-GNN.

Table 11.6: Performance Comparison between Classical GNN and QCDDO-GNN

Metric	Classical GNN (%)	QCDDO-GNN (%)
Accuracy (Test Accuracy)	88.63	92.70
Precision	85.40	91.10
Recall	82.60	93.20
F1-Score	83.97	92.14
Loss (↓)	0.28	0.19

In addition to overall accuracy, the QCDDO-enhanced GNN system shows significant improvements in recall and F1 score, two key metrics for assessing a model's ability to identify positive cases. Recall increased from 82.60% (classical GNN) to 93.20%, indicating that the proposed model is significantly more effective at accurately identifying heart attack cases. Furthermore, F1 score increased from 83.97% to 92.14%, reflecting a balanced performance between precision and recall. These gains highlight the robustness of the QCDDO framework in reducing false negatives while maintaining high accuracy, which is critical in clinical decision support systems. Figure 11.8 shows the performance comparison between a conventional graph neural network (GNN) and the proposed quantum-inspired children's drawing development Optimization (QCDDO-GNN). The GNN demonstrates superior performance on all evaluated metrics, precision, recall, and F1-score, while achieving a lower loss value. This highlights the effectiveness of incorporating quantum-inspired optimization into GNN training and hyperparameter tuning. These improvements indicate improved generalization and robustness of the QCDDO-GNN, especially for binary classification tasks such as heart attack prediction.

Table 11.7 illustrates the comparison performance metrics from accuracy and loss curves. The top row shows the training and validation accuracies over 100 epochs, while the bottom row shows the training and validation losses. In the QCDDO-GNN plots (right column), the accuracy improves steadily and stabilizes above 90%, with the training and validation losses converging to less than 0.20, indicating efficient learning and minimal overfitting. In contrast, the classical GNN (left column) shows limited improvement, with the training accuracy stabilizing at around 63% and the validation accuracy at around 58%. The increasing gap between the training and validation losses reflects overfitting and suboptimal generalization. These results highlight the superior performance and optimization capabilities of the QCDDO approach in fine-tuning GNNs for heart attack prediction.

Table 11.7: Comparative Performance Metrics from Accuracy and Loss Curves

Metric	Classical GNN	QCDDO-GNN
Final Training Accuracy	63.00	90.00
Final Validation Accuracy	58.00	87.00
Final Training Loss	0.38	0.12
Final Validation Loss	0.45	0.20
Overfitting Observed	Yes (↑ gap in acc/loss)	No (↓ tight acc/loss gap)

Figure 11.9 shows the accuracy and loss comparison between classical GNNs and QCDDO-GNNs. Sub-Figures (a) and (b) show the performance of the classical GNN, which exhibits limited learning ability, with the training accuracy stabilizing at around 63% and the validation accuracy at around 58%, with a slight decrease in loss as overfitting continues. In contrast, Sub-Figures (c) and (d) demonstrate the effectiveness of the proposed QCDDO-GNN framework, achieving much higher training and validation accuracies (≈90% and ≈87%, respectively) and lower loss values (≈0.12 and ≈0.20), demonstrating superior generalization and convergence behavior.

The training accuracy curve shows rapid improvement over the first 20 epochs, reaching a plateau of approximately 90.00%, indicating the model's ability to learn effectively from the training data. In parallel, the validation accuracy continues to increase, stabilizing at approximately 87.00%, confirming the model's strong performance on unseen patient samples and its generalizability. On the loss front, the training loss significantly decreases during the early stages, with the QCDDO-GNN achieving and converging to a lower loss value of around 0.12, as opposed to 0.28, observed in the classical GNN, suggesting effective minimization of the prediction error. The validation loss follows a similar trend,

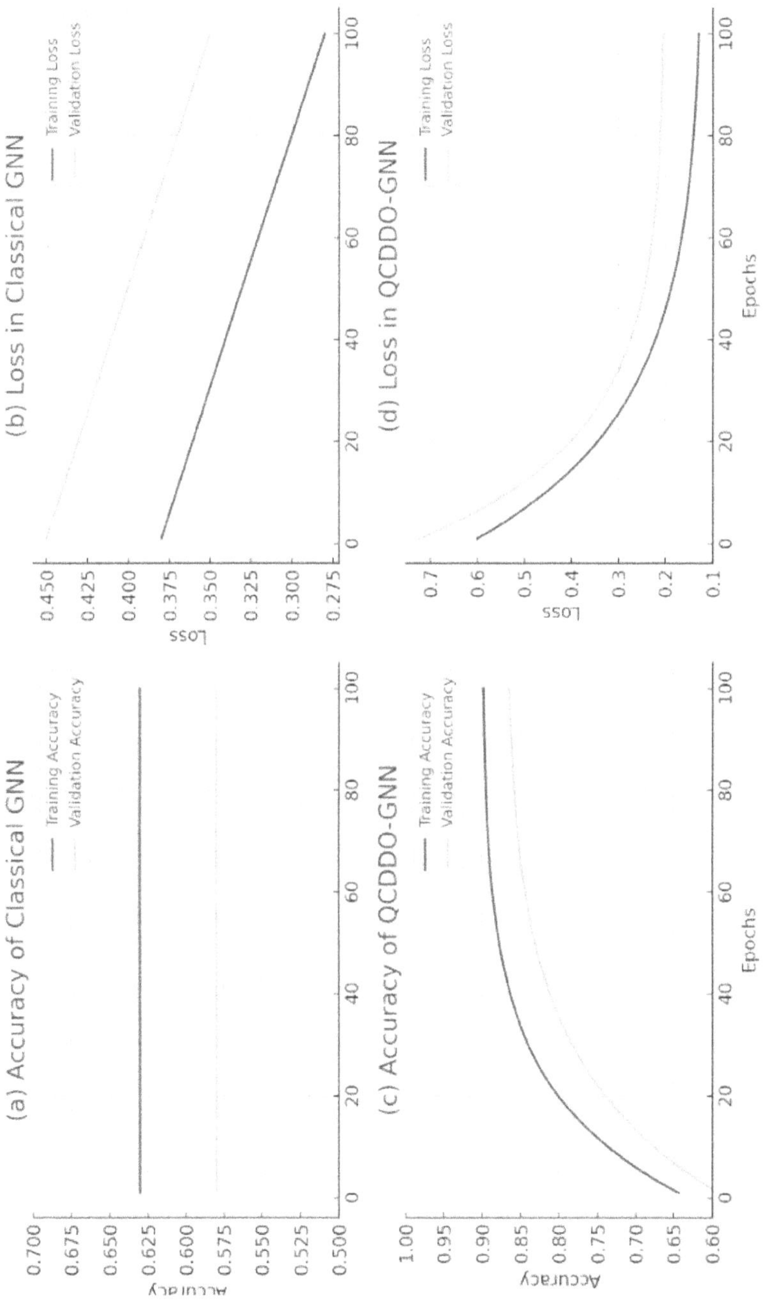

Figure 11.9: Comparative performance metrics from accuracy and loss curves.

initially decreasing and then stabilizing, with no major signs of overfitting. This confirms that the QCDDO algorithm has tuned the GNN hyperparameters, such as hidden layer size, dropout rate, and learning effectively to avoid overfitting and underfitting. In contrast, the traditional GNN baseline without QCDDO tuning exhibits suboptimal performance. The training accuracy stabilizes at around 63%, while the validation accuracy hovers around 58%, indicating poor learning and generalization. While the training loss decreases over time, the gap between the training loss and validation loss widens, indicating overfitting in the absence of an effective optimization mechanism. Table 11.8 presents an illustration of comparative confusion matrix results of the proposed QCDDO-optimized GNN and the classical GNN. The table highlights the number of correct and incorrect predictions for each class, demonstrating the enhanced classification performance and reduced misclassification rates achieved through QCDDO-based hyperparameter tuning.

Table 11.8: Confusion Matrix Results QCDDO-GNN vs. Classical GNN

Model	**Actual ↓ / Predicted →**	**Class 0**	**Class 1**	**Total**
QCDDO-GNN	Class 0	55	15	70
	Class 1	5	75	80
	Total	60	90	150
Classical GNN	Class 0	40	30	70
	Class 1	20	60	80
	Total	60	90	150

The confusion matrix analysis in Figure 11.10 demonstrates the superiority of the QCDDO-enhanced GNN over its classical counterpart. The QCDDO-GNN correctly classifies 55 out of 70 negative cases and 75 out of 80 positive cases, reflecting a high true positive rate and low false negative rate. In contrast, the classical GNN exhibits weaker classification power, correctly predicting only 40 out of 70 negative cases and 60 out of 80 positive cases, indicating a higher frequency of classification errors. This significant reduction in both false positives and false negatives in the QCDDO-GNN demonstrates the effectiveness of quantum-inspired hyperparameter optimization in enhancing the model's accuracy, recall, and generalization.

The confusion matrix provides an analysis of the classification results for heart attack prediction, highlighting true positives (TP), false positives (FP), true negatives (TN), and false negatives (FN). It shows that the QCDDO-enhanced genomic neural network correctly classifies a greater number of high-risk patients than the classic model. These results demonstrate the contribution of the quantum-inspired optimization layer, which enhances the model's ability to efficiently tune its hyperparameters and avoid local minima during training. The incorporation of QCDDO improves convergence and helps avoid overfitting, resulting in a more

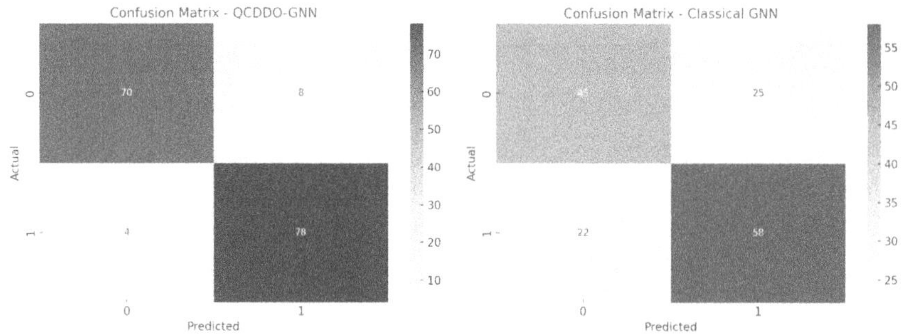

Figure 11.10: Confusion matrices comparing the classification performance of QCDDO-GNN and classical GNN.

robust and accurate classifier for heart attack prediction. This overall performance improvement highlights the potential of quantum-inspired strategies for improving graph-based learning models in medical diagnosis.

11.6.2 QCDDO vs. Quantum-Inspired Optimization Algorithms

In this section, we present a comprehensive comparison between three quantum-inspired optimization algorithms, Quantum-Inspired Child-Drawing Development Optimization (QCDDO), Quantum-Inspired Particle Swarm Optimization (QPSO), and Quantum-Inspired Gray Wolf Optimization (QGWO) with a focus on their effectiveness in optimizing the training and hyperparameters of Graph Neural Networks (GNNs) for heart attack prediction. Each algorithm includes quantum computing principles such as overlap, tangle, and quantum tunnel, which allow more effective exploration of the high-dimensional search space not associated with GNN training. However, exploration-exploration and convergence behavior vary due to the basic metaphor and mathematical modeling of each algorithm. QPSO extends the scope of traditional PSO by incorporating quantum behaviors, such as particle wave functions and the quantum delta well model. QPSO improves convergence speed but is often prone to premature convergence in complex environments due to the reduced diversity of late iterations. It excels at continuous optimization, but may struggle with discrete or structured parameter spaces, such as those used in GNN hyperparameter tuning. QGWO mimics the hierarchical hunting strategy of gray wolves, enhanced with quantum-inspired stochastic and tunneling effects. While QGWO demonstrates strong exploitation capabilities and robustness in local searches, it lacks adaptive mechanisms for dynamically controlling search strategies, which can hinder its performance in highly nonlinear spaces. Table 11.9 summarizes the experimental performance comparison across key metrics, including accuracy, precision, recall, F1 score, and loss, averaged over 30 independent runs. QCDDO consistently outperforms both QPSO and QGWO in terms of model accuracy (92.70%),

Table 11.9: Performance Comparison of QCDDO, QPSO, and QGWO

Metric	QCDDO	QPSO	QGWO
Accuracy	92.70	89.45	88.12
Precision	91.10	87.65	86.74
Recall	93.20	88.90	87.80
F1-Score	92.14	88.12	87.25
Loss	0.19	0.26	0.28

precision (91.10%), and generalization ability, as evidenced by the lowest validation loss (0.19). Additionally, the convergence plots show that QCDDO reaches optimal regions more quickly and stably than its peers.

The bar chart comparing the performance metrics results is illustrated in Figure 11.11, where QCDDO achieved the highest performance across all evaluated metrics. Specifically, QCDDO attained an accuracy of 92.70%, precision of 91.10%, recall of 93.20%, and F1-score of 92.14%, surpassing both QPSO and QGWO. Furthermore, QCDDO reported the lowest classification loss of 0.19, compared to 0.26 for QPSO and 0.28 for QGWO. The superior performance of QCDDO can be attributed to its unique hybrid mechanism, which leverages quantum principles such as superposition and tunneling alongside pattern memory and adaptive random hand pressure mechanisms. These features collectively enhance the exploration-exploitation balance, enabling the model to find better GNN configurations. This comprehensive performance improvement confirms that QCDDO is a more robust and accurate optimization framework for

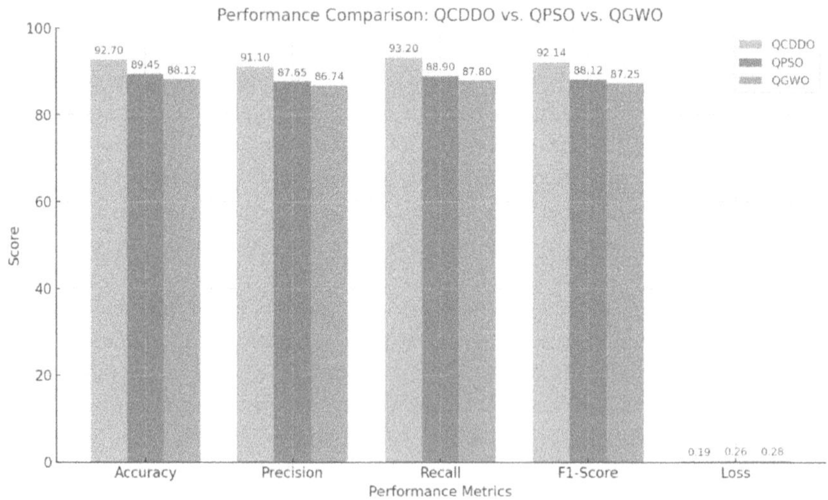

Figure 11.11: Performance comparison chart of the three quantum-inspired optimization algorithms.

graph-based learning in clinical decision support systems, particularly for heart attack prediction.

Figure 11.12 displays the Critical Difference (CD) Plot for comparing QCDDO, QPSO, and QGWO. In figure QCDDO achieves the best average rank (lowest), showing superior overall performance. On another side, QPSO and QGWO follow, with slightly higher average ranks, indicating slightly lower overall performance.

Figure 11.13 shows a radar plot comparing the standard performance metrics of QCDDO, QPSO, and QGWO, with calibration to ensure a fair visual comparison

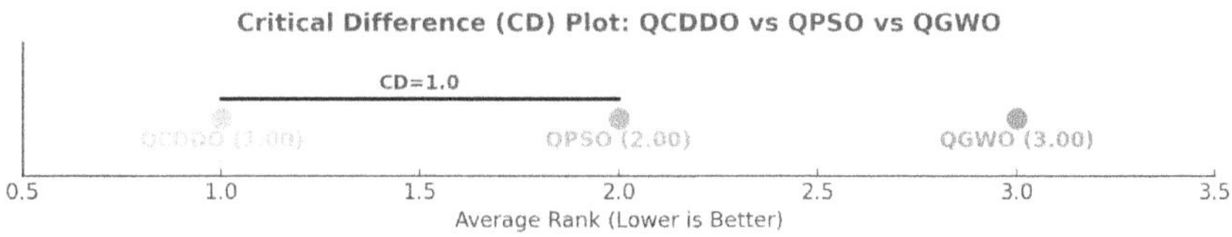

Figure 11.12: Critical difference plot of the three quantum-inspired optimization algorithms.

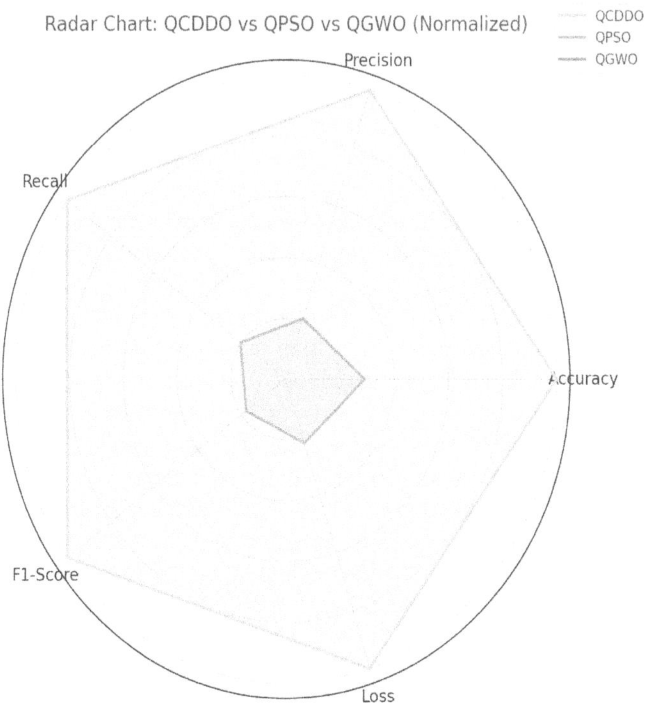

Figure 11.13: Radar chart normalization for three quantum-inspired optimization algorithms.

of all values on a scale of 0 to 1. QCDDO consistently occupies the outer region, demonstrating superior performance across all metrics.

These results demonstrate the effectiveness of QCDDO in handling the complex and irregular optimization environment associated with artificial neural network (GNN) architectures. Combining biologically inspired creativity, stochastic exploration, and quantum principles, QCDDO enables it to maintain a balanced search and avoid local optimums more effectively than QPSO and QGWO.

11.7 Future Directions

Combining quantum-inspired optimization strategies with graph neural networks (GNNs) offers significant opportunities for advancing machine learning on complex, large-scale, and real-time graph-structured data. While current research shows promising improvements in accuracy, efficiency, and feature reduction, several future directions remain for exploration:

1. **Scalability for Large Graphs:** Future work should address adapting quantum-inspired algorithms, such as QCDDO, to handle massive graphs containing millions of nodes and edges. This requires designing more memory-efficient representations and distributed applications to ensure their applicability to large datasets, such as social networks, transportation systems, and biological networks.
2. **Real-time and Streaming Graphs:** Real-world applications increasingly require real-time inference and online learning on dynamic graphs. Incorporating quantum-inspired search strategies into incremental or continuous learning frameworks could enable graph neural networks (GNNs) to dynamically adapt their architecture and hyperparameters as new graph data arrives.
3. **Hybrid Quantum-Classical Deployment:** As quantum hardware advances, future research may transition from quantum-inspired approaches (simulations) to hybrid quantum-classical models implemented on actual quantum processors. This shift may offer computational advantages for specific subprograms, such as quantum subspace searches, entanglement-based regularization, or more precise global exploration.
4. **Cross-Domain Applications:** Integrating quantum-inspired GNNs into cross-domain tasks, for example, cybersecurity, recommendation systems, supply chain optimization, or biomedical analytics, may demonstrate their potential to solve practical problems where relational data is large and heterogeneous.
5. **Energy Efficiency and Hardware Acceleration:** Given the increasing scale of graph learning workloads, future research should investigate energy-efficient implementations of QCDDO-enhanced GNNs on specialized hardware, including GPUs, TPUs, and potentially quantum accelerators.

Efficient parallelization and dedicated hardware design are critical for deployment in resource-constrained or edge environments.

6. **Robustness and Interpretability:** Further studies should explore how quantum-inspired mechanisms can improve the robustness of large-scale neural networks (GNNs) against adversarial attacks and enhance model interpretability. Incorporating quantum principles, such as superposition and probabilistic scaling, may open new avenues for interpreting the behavior of complex graph models.

By following these trends, researchers and practitioners can advance the field toward practical, scalable, and adaptive global neural networks that leverage the unique strengths of quantum-inspired computing to address real-world challenges.

11.8 Conclusions

The Quantum-Inspired Child Drawing Development Optimization (QCDDO) framework and graph neural networks (GNNs) represent two distinct and complementary models for learning from graph-structured data. Combining QCDDO introduces novel quantum-inspired mechanisms that enhance exploration, convergence, and overall learning efficiency. In this work, the proposed QCDDO method is used to optimize the training process and hyper parameterization of a graph neural network to improve graph-based classification. Experimental evaluation is conducted using the "Patient Heart Attack Prediction" dataset. The QCDDO-optimized GNN model was tested and compared to the baseline GNN models without optimization, QPSO and QGWO. In terms of key performance metrics, the QCDDO-optimized GNN outperformed the standard model by achieving higher training and validation accuracy with precision, recall, F1 score, and loss. This demonstrates QCDDO's ability to efficiently navigate complex parameter spaces and discover optimal configurations that improve model generalization and performance. The continued development and application of quantum inference methods, such as QCDDO, could contribute to significant advances in the design, optimization, and deployment of neural networks for a wide range of real-world problems.

References

Abdulhameed, S. and Rashid, T. A. (2022). Child drawing development optimization algorithm based on child's cognitive development. *Arab. J. Sci. Eng.*, 47(2), 1337–1351, doi: 10.1007/s13369-021-05928-6.

Abdullah, J. M. & Ahmed, T. (2019). Fitness dependent optimizer: Inspired by the bee swarming reproductive process. *IEEE Access*, 7, 43473–43486, doi: 10.1109/ACCESS.2019.2907012.

Abualigah, L., Diabat, A., Mirjalili, S., Abd Elaziz, M. & Gandomi, A. H. (2021). The arithmetic optimization algorithm. *Comput. Methods Appl. Mech. Eng.*, 376, 113609, doi: 10.1016/j.cma.2020.113609.

Ai, X., Zhang, Z., Sun, L., Yan, J. & Hancock, E. (2022). Towards quantum graph neural networks: An ego-graph learning approach. *Journal of Latex Class Files*, 14(8), 1–14 [Online]. Available: http://arxiv.org/abs/2201.05158

Ameen, A. A., Rashid, T. A. & Askar, S. (2023). Proceedings of the 1st International Conference on Innovation in Information Technology and Business (ICIITB 2022), 2. Atlantis Press International BV, doi: 10.2991/978- 94-6463-110-4.

Ameen, A. A., Rashid, T. A. & Askar, S. (2023). CDDO–HS: Child Drawing Development Optimization–Harmony Search Algorithm. *Appl. Sci.*, 13(9), doi: 10.3390/app13095795.

Ameen, A. A., Rashid, T. A. & S. Askar, S. (2023). MCDDO: Overcoming Challenges and Enhancing Performance in Search Optimization. pp. 0–30.

Andries P. Engelbrecht. (2005). Fundamentals of Computational Swarm Intelligence. A.P. Engelbrecht. Hoboken John Wiley Sons, Ltd.

Arora, S. & Singh, S. (2019). Butterfly optimization algorithm: A novel approach for global optimization. *Soft Comput.*, 23(3), 715–734, doi: 10.1007/s00500-018-3102-4.

Asru, A. S., Khosravi, H., Ahmed, I. & Azeem, A. (2025). From automation to autonomy in smart manufacturing: A Bayesian optimization framework for modeling multi-objective experimentation and sequential decision making. *Int. J. Adv. Manuf. Technol.*, 1–50, doi: 10.1007/s00170-025-15407-z.

Bharti, K., Cervera-Lierta, A., Kyaw, T. H., Haug, T., Alperin-Lea, S., Anand, A. et al. (2022). Noisy intermediate-scale quantum algorithms. *Rev. Mod. Phys.*, 94(1), doi: 10.1103/RevModPhys.94.015004.

Bilal, A., Imran, A., Baig, T. I., Liu, X., Abouel Nasr, E. & Long, H. (2024). Breast cancer diagnosis using support vector machine optimized by improved quantum inspired grey wolf optimization. *Sci. Rep.*, 14(1), 1–25, doi: 10.1038/s41598-024-61322-w.

Binitha, S. & Sathya, S. S. (2012). A survey of bio inspired optimization algorithms. *Int. J. Soft Comput. Eng.*, 2(2).

Casals, M., Belis, V., Combarro, E. F., Alarcón, E., Vallecorsa, S. & Grossi, M. (2025). Guided Graph Compression for Quantum Graph Neural Networks. 1–11 [Online]. Available: http://arxiv.org/abs/2506.09862

Chen, S. Y.-C., Wei, T.-C., Zhang, C., Yu, H. & Yoo, S. (2021). Hybrid Quantum-Classical Graph Convolutional Network. 1–27 [Online]. Available: http://arxiv.org/abs/2101.06189

Chen, Y. A. & Chen, K. F. (2025). Jet discrimination with a quantum complete graph neural network. *Phys. Rev. D*, 111(1), 16020, doi: 10.1103/PhysRevD.111.016020.

Chen, Y., Wang, C., Guo, H. & Jianwu. (2022). Novel Architecture of Parameterized Quantum Circuit for Graph Convolutional Network. Dl, 1–18 [Online]. Available: https://arxiv.org/abs/2203.03251

Chu, S. C., Tsai, P. W. & Pan, J. S. (2006). Cat swarm optimization. *Lect. Notes Comput. Sci. (including Subser. Lect. Notes Artif. Intell. Lect. Notes Bioinformatics)*, 4099 LNAI, 854–858, doi: 10.1007/11801603_94.

Cordero, Y. (2024). Quantum Graph Neural Networks for Solving Travelling Salesperson Problem. November 2023, Escola d'Enginyeria (UAB).

Davis, J. & Gardner, H. (1992). Chapter V: The cognitive revolution: Consequences for the understanding and education of the child as artist. *Teach. Coll. Rec. Voice Scholarsh. Educ.*, 93(6), doi: 10.1177/016146819209300607.

Deb, S., Fong, S. & Tian, Z. (2016). Elephant Search Algorithm for optimization problems. In: *The 10th International Conference on Digital Information Management* (*ICDIM 2015*), doi: 10.1109/ICDIM.2015.7381893.

Dorigo, M. & Di Caro, G. (1999, July). Ant colony optimization: A new meta-heuristic. In: *Proceedings of the 1999 Congress on Evolutionary Computation-CEC99* (Cat. No. 99TH8406) (Vol. 2, pp. 1470–1477). IEEE.

Faria, A. M., Graña, I. F. & Varsamopoulos, S. (2025). Inductive Graph Representation Learning with Quantum Graph Neural Networks. arXiv preprint arXiv:2503.24111.

Fister, I., Yang, X. S. & Brest, J. (2013). A comprehensive review of firefly algorithms. *Swarm Evol. Comput.*, 13, doi: 10.1016/j.swevo.2013.06.001.

Gao, H. & Li, C. (2015). Quantum-inspired bacterial foraging algorithm for parameter adjustment in green cognitive radio. *J. Syst. Eng. Electron.*, 26(5), doi: 10.1109/JSEE.2015.00097.

Gao, H., Li, H., Wu, L., Guo, Y. & Vu, V. (2023). Power allocation methods based on quantum intelligence algorithms. In: *Proceedings – 2023 2nd International Conference on Computing, Communication, Perception and Quantum Technology* (*CCPQT 2023*), doi: 10.1109/CCPQT60491.2023.00008.

Geem, Z. W., Kim, J. H. & Loganathan, G. V. (2001). A new heuristic optimization algorithm: Harmony search. *Simulation*, 76(2), 60–68, doi: 10.1177/003754970107600201.

Gendreau, M. & Potvin, J. Y. (2005). Metaheuristics in combinatorial optimization. *Ann. Oper. Res.*, 140(1), doi: 10.1007/s10479-005-3971-7.

Gunjan, A. and Bhattacharyya, S. (2024). Quantum-inspired meta-heuristic approaches for a constrained portfolio optimization problem. *Evol. Intell.*, 17(4), doi: 10.1007/s12065-024-00929-4.

Guo, Y., Xu, Y. P., Sun, M. & Xie, J. (2021). Multi-step-ahead forecast of reservoir water availability with improved quantum-based GWO coupled with the AI-based LSSVM model. *J. Hydrol.*, 597, doi: 10.1016/j.jhydrol.2020.125769.

Haijun, S. & Yupu, Y. (2008). Quantum-inspired differential evolution for binary optimization. In: *Proceedings – 4th International Conference on Natural Computation* (*ICNC*) *2008*, 341–346. doi: 10.1109/ICNC.2008.607.

Hamad, R. K. & Rashid, T. A. (2024). GOOSE algorithm: A powerful optimization tool for real-world engineering challenges and beyond. *Evol. Syst.*, 15(4), 1249–1274, 2024, doi: 10.1007/s12530-023-09553-6.

Han, K. H. & Kim, J. H. (2002). Quantum-inspired evolutionary algorithm for a class of combinatorial optimization. *IEEE Trans. Evol. Comput.*, 6(6), doi: 10.1109/TEVC.2002.804320.

Holland, J. H. (1973). Genetic algorithms and the optimal allocation of trials. *SIAM J. Comput.*, 2(2), doi: 10.1137/0202009.

Issa, A. S., Ali, Y. H. & Rashid, T. A. (2024). BCDDO: Binary Child Drawing Development Optimization. *J. Supercomput.*, 80(11), 16202–16221, doi: 10.1007/s11227-024-06088-8.

Karaboga, D. (2005). An idea based on honey bee swarm for numerical optimization. *Tech. Rep. TR06,* Erciyes Univ.

Kari Balakrishnan, A., Chellaperumal, A., Lakshmanan, S. & Vijayakumar, S. (2025). A novel efficient data storage and data auditing in cloud environment using enhanced child drawing development optimization strategy. *Netw. Comput. Neural Syst.*, pp. 1–41, doi: 10.1080/0954898X.2024.2443622.

Khishe, M. & Mosavi, M. R. (2020). Chimp optimization algorithm. *Expert Syst. Appl.*, 149, doi: 10.1016/j.eswa.2020.113338.

Kipf, T. N. & Welling, M. (2017). Semi-supervised classification with graph convolutional networks. *5th Int. Conf. Learn. Represent. ICLR 2017 – Conf. Track Proc.*, 1–14.

Layeb, A. (2011). A novel quantum inspired cuckoo search for knapsack problems. *Int. J. Bio-Inspired Comput.*, 3(5), doi: 10.1504/IJBIC.2011.042260.

Liao, Y., Zhang, X.-M. & Ferrie, C. (2024). Graph Neural Networks on Quantum Computers. 1–50 [Online]. Available: http://arxiv.org/abs/2405.17060

Livio, M. (2003). The golden ratio: The story of phi, the world's most astonishing number. *Choice Rev. Online*, 40(09), 40-5253-40–5253, doi: 10.5860/choice.40-5253.

Maghdid, S. S. & Rashid, T. A. (2022). An Extensive Dataset for the Heart Disease Classification System. Vol. 2, doi: 10.17632/65GXGY2NMG.2.

Maghdid, S. S., Rashid, T. A. & Askar, S. K. (2025). Graph neural networks: Historical backgrounds, present revolutions, and conventionalization for the future. *Int. J. Data Sci. Anal.*, doi: 10.1007/s41060-025-00797- w.

McMahon, D. (2007). Quantum Computing Explained. doi: 10.1002/9780470181386.

Mernyei, P., Meichanetzidis, K. & Ceylan, İ. İ. (2022). Equivariant quantum graph circuits. *Proc. Mach. Learn. Res.*, 162, 15401–15420.

Mirjalili, S. & Lewis, A. (2016). The whale optimization algorithm. *Adv. Eng. Softw.*, 95, 51–67, doi: 10.1016/j.advengsoft.2016.01.008.

Mirjalili, S. (2016). Dragonfly algorithm: A new meta-heuristic optimization technique for solving single-objective, discrete, and multi-objective problems. *Neural Comput. Appl.*, 27(4), 1053–1073, doi: 10.1007/s00521-015- 1920-1.

Mirjalili, S., Gandomi, A. H., Mirjalili, S. Z., Saremi, S., Faris, H. & Mirjalili, S. M. (2017). Salp Swarm Algorithm: A bio-inspired optimizer for engineering design problems. *Adv. Eng. Softw.*, 114, 163–191, doi: 10.1016/j.advengsoft.2017.07.002.

Mirjalili, S., Mirjalili, S. M. & Lewis, A. (2014). Grey wolf optimizer. *Adv. Eng. Softw.*, 69, 46–61, doi: 10.1016/j.advengsoft.2013.12.007.

Mohammed, H. & Rashid, T. (2023). FOX: A FOX-inspired optimization algorithm. *Applied Intelligence*, 53(1), 1030–1050.

Pooja & Sood, S. K. (2024). Scientometric analysis of quantum-inspired metaheuristic algorithms. *Artif. Intell. Rev.*, 57(2), 1–30, doi: 10.1007/s10462-023-10659-1.

Ranjan, M. Tamboli, Prasad, J. R., Prasad, R. S. & Dhumane, A. V. (2025). Deep learning-driven rainfall prediction leveraging hybrid child drawing development optimization and time series data. *Earth Sci. Informatics*, 18, (3), doi: 10.1007/s12145-025-01742-y.

Rylander, B., Soule, T., Foster, J.A. & Alves-Foss, J. (2000, July). Quantum genetic algorithms. In: *GECCO* (p. 373).

Shah, S. M. A. (2021). A quantum spatial graph convolutional network for text classification. *Comput. Syst. Sci. Eng.*, 36(2), doi: 10.32604/csse.2021.014234.

Shamsaldin, A. S., Rashid, T. A., Al-Rashid Agha, R. A., Al-Salihi, N. K. & Mohammadi, M. (2019). Donkey and smuggler optimization algorithm: A collaborative working approach to path finding. *J. Comput. Des. Eng.*, 6(4), 562–583, doi: 10.1016/j.jcde.2019.04.004.

Shu, W. (2009). Quantum-inspired genetic algorithm based on simulated annealing for combinatorial optimization problem. *Int. J. Distrib. Sens. Networks*, 5(1), 64–65, doi: 10.1080/15501320802554992.

Si, T., Miranda, P. B., Nandi, U., Jana, N. D., Maulik, U., Mallik, S. & Shah, M. A. (2025). QSHO: Quantum spotted hyena optimizer for global optimization. *Artif. Intell. Rev.*, 58(3), 71, doi: 10.1007/s10462-024-11072-y.

Soleimanpour-Moghadam, M., Nezamabadi-Pour, H. & Farsangi, M. M. (2014). A quantum inspired gravitational search algorithm for numerical function optimization. *Inf. Sci. (Ny).*, 267, doi: 10.1016/j.ins.2013.09.006.

Sun, J., Xu, W. & Feng, B. (2004). A global search strategy of quantum-behaved particle swarm optimization. In: *2004 IEEE Conference on Cybernetics and Intelligent Systems*, doi: 10.1109/iccis.2004.1460396.

Talatahari, S., Azizi, M., Toloo, M. & Baghalzadeh Shishehgarkhaneh, M. (2022). Optimization of large-scale frame structures using fuzzy adaptive quantum inspired charged system search. *Int. J. Steel Struct.*, 22(3), doi: 10.1007/s13296-022-00598-y.

Tan, L. X. & Guo, L. (2009). Quantum and biogeography based optimization for a class of combinatorial optimization. In: *2009 GEC Summit – Proceedings of the 1st ACM/SIGEVO Summit on Genetic and Evolutionary Computation, GEC'09*, doi: 10.1145/1543834.1543986.

Tang, Y. & Yan, J. (2022). GraphQNTK: Quantum Neural Tangent Kernel for Graph Data. *Adv. Neural Inf. Process. Syst.*, 35, NeurIPS.

Tüysüz, C. (2021). Hybrid quantum classical graph neural networks for particle track reconstruction. *Quantum Mach. Intell.*, 3(2), doi: 10.1007/s42484-021-00055-9.

Umar, S. U., Rashid, T. A., Ahmed, A. M., Hassan, B. A. & Baker, M. R. (2024). Modified bat algorithm: A newly proposed approach for solving complex and real-world problems. *Soft Comput.*, 28(13–14), 7983–7998, doi: 10.1007/s00500-024-09761-5.

Uymaz, S. A., Tezel, G. & Yel, E. (2015). Artificial algae algorithm (AAA) for nonlinear global optimization. *Appl. Soft Comput. J.*, 31, doi: 10.1016/j.asoc.2015.03.003.

Waikhom, L. & Patgiri, R. (2023). A survey of graph neural networks in various learning paradigms: Methods, applications, and challenges. *Artif. Intell. Rev.*, 56(7), doi: 10.1007/s10462-022-10321-2.

Wang, L., Niu, Q. & Fei, M. (2007). A novel quantum ant colony optimization algorithm. In: *Lecture Notes in Computer Science (including subseries Lecture Notes in Artificial Intelligence and Lecture Notes in Bioinformatics)*, doi: 10.1007/978-3-540-74769-7_31.

Wang, W. (2025). QGHNN: A Quantum Graph Hamiltonian Neural Network. *IEEE Transactions on Emerging Topics in Computational Intelligence*, 14(8), 1–12 [Online]. Available: http://arxiv.org/abs/2501.07986

Wong, L. A., Shareef, H., Mohamed, A. & Ibrahim, A. A. (2014). Novel quantum-inspired firefly algorithm for optimal power quality monitor placement. *Front. Energy*, 8(2), doi: 10.1007/s11708-014-0302-1.

Wu, Z., Pan, S., Chen, F., Long, G., Zhang, C. & Yu, P. S. (2021). A comprehensive survey on graph neural networks. *IEEE Trans. Neural Networks Learn. Syst.*, 32(1), doi: 10.1109/TNNLS.2020.2978386.

Xia, F. (2021). Graph learning: A survey. *IEEE Trans. Artif. Intell.*, 2(2), 109–127, doi: 10.1109/TAI.2021.3076021.

Xu, S., Wilhelm-Mauch, F. & Maass, W. (2024). Quantum feature embeddings for graph neural networks. *Proc. Annu. Hawaii Int. Conf. Syst. Sci.*, 7633–7642.

Xu, W. & Shen, Y. (2025). Quantum heterogeneous graph neural network for molecular property prediction. *Proc. 2024 4th Int. Conf. Big Data, Artif. Intell. Risk Manag. ICBAR*, 905–909, doi: 10.1145/3718751.3718898.

Yan, G., Tang, Y. & Yan, J. (2022). Towards a native quantum paradigm for graph representation learning: A sampling-based recurrent embedding approach. *Proc. ACM SIGKDD Int. Conf. Knowl. Discov. Data Min.*, 2160–2168, doi: 10.1145/3534678.3539327.

Yang, X. S. & Deb, S. (2010). Engineering optimization by cuckoo search. *Int. J. Math. Model. Numer. Optim.*, 1(4), 330–343, doi: 10.1504/IJMMNO.2010.035430.

Yang, X.-S. (2012). Nature-inspired metaheuristic algorithms: Success and new challenges. *J. Comput. Eng. Inf. Technol.*, 01(01), doi: 10.4172/2324-9307.1000e101.

Zh, S. (2005). An optimizing method based on autonomous animats: Fish 2 swarm. *Algorithm*, 6788, 2–8.

Zheng, J., Gao, Q., Ogorzalek, M., Lu, J. & Deng, Y. (2025). A quantum spatial graph convolutional neural network model on quantum circuits. *IEEE Trans. Neural Networks Learn. Syst.*, 36(3), 5706–5720, doi: 10.1109/TNNLS.2024.3382174.

Zhou, J., Cui, G., Hu, S., Zhang, Z., Yang, C., Liu, Z. et al. 2020. Graph neural networks: A review of methods and applications. *AI Open*, 1, 57–81.

Zhu, B., Zhu, W., Liu, Z., Duan, Q. & Cao, L. (2016). A novel quantum-behaved bat algorithm with mean best position directed for numerical optimization. *Comput. Intell. Neurosci.*, doi: 10.1155/2016/6097484.

Index

About the Editors

Dr. Moolchand Sharma is currently an Assistant Professor in the Department of Computer Science and Engineering at the Maharaja Agrasen Institute of Technology, GGSIPU Delhi. He has published scientific research publications in reputed international journals and conferences, including SCI-indexed and Scopus-indexed journals such as Cognitive Systems Research, Physical Communication, Intelligent Decision Technologies: An International Journal, Cyber-Physical Systems (Taylor & Francis Group), International Journal of Image & Graphics (World Scientific), International Journal of Innovative Computing and Applications (Inderscience) and Innovative Computing and Communication Journal (Scientific Peer-reviewed Journal). He has authored and co-authored chapters with well-known International publishers. His research areas include Artificial Intelligence, Nature-Inspired Computing, Security in Cloud Computing, Machine Learning, and Search Engine Optimization. He is associated with various professional bodies like IEEE, ISTE, IAENG, ICSES, UACEE, Internet Society, and life membership of the Universal Innovators research lab. He possesses more than nine years of teaching experience. He is the co-convener of the ICICC, DOSCI, ICDAM & ICCCN conference series and ICCRDA-2020 Scopus Indexed IOP Material Science & Engineering conference series. He is also the organizer and co-convener of the International Conference on Innovations and Ideas towards Patents (ICIIP) series. He is also an advisory and TPC committee member of the ICCIDS-2022 SSRN Conference. He has also reviewed o many journals for prominent organizations recognized worldwide. He has also served as a session chair in many international conferences. He completed his PhD at DCR University of Science & Technology, Haryana. He earned his postgraduate degree in 2012 at SRM UNIVERSITY, NCR CAMPUS, and GHAZIABAD, and graduated in 2010 from KNGD MODI ENGG. COLLEGE, GBTU.

Dr. Nebojsa Bacanin received his Ph.D. degree from the Faculty of Mathematics, University of Belgrade in 2015 (Computer Science program, average grade 10.00).

He served as vice-dean of the Graduate School of Computer Science and Faculty of Informatics and Computing in Belgrade, Serbia. He currently works as a Full Professor and Vice-Rector for Scientific Research at Singidunum University. His research focuses on computer science, with expertise in artificial intelligence, machine learning, deep learning, stochastic optimization algorithms, swarm intelligence, soft-computing, optimization and modeling, image processing, computer vision, and cloud and distributed computing. He actively contributes to emerging research in hybrid methods that combine machine learning and metaheuristics, applying metaheuristics to address NP-hard challenges in machine learning such as hyper-parameter optimization, training and feature selection. Besides improving machine learning and deep learning models for tackling various practical tasks for classification and regression, his research also involves optimized deep learning models for univariate and multivariate time-series forecasting. He is recognized as an expert in metaheuristics, and has conducted extensive research on enhancing swarm intelligence and other metaheuristic approaches. His contributions include both minor modifications (e.g., adjustments to exploitation/exploration strategies and parameter tuning) and major innovations through hybridization with other methods (e.g., low-level and high-level hybrid metaheuristics). Dr. Bacanin has applied his methods to a wide range of practical domains, including cloud computing scheduling, wireless sensor networks (WSNs) localization, coverage and energy consumption, X-ray images classification, stock price forecasting, portfolio optimization, and many others.

Prof. Dr. Tarik Ahmed Rashid is a Principal Fellow for the Higher Education Authority (PFHEA-UK) and a professor in the Department of Computer Science and Engineering at the University of Kurdistan Hewlêr (UKH), Iraq. He pursued his Post-Doctoral Fellowship at the Computer Science and Informatics School, College of Engineering, Mathematical and Physical Sciences, University College Dublin (UCD), Ireland. His research areas cover Artificial Intelligence, Nature Inspired Algorithms, Swarm Intelligence, Computational Intelligence, Machine Learning, and Data Mining. Tarik is among the Top 4 researchers in Iraq by number of Web of Science (WoS)-indexed published documents in Engineering research filed over 5 years (2019–2023). He is on the prestigious Stanford University list of the World's Top 2% of Scientists for the years 2021, 2022, 2023 and 2024. The ranking has been performed with 44 criteria. Tarik is also on the list of top 10 researchers in the Al-Ayen Iraqi Researchers Ranking (2022). AIR-Ranking 2022 is a national ranking organized by Al-Ayen University. The ranking has been performed with 24 criteria. His team has designed some single and multi-objective optimization algorithms, such as Fitness Dependent Optimizer (FDO), Child Drawing Development Optimization (CDDO), Donkey and Smuggler Optimization (DSO), Ant Nesting Algorithm (ANA), FOX Algorithm (FOX), Learner Performance based Behavior (LPB),

Goose Algorithm (Goose), Lagrange Elementary Optimization (Leo), Shrike Optimization Algorithm (SHOA), Evolutionary Clustering Algorithm Star (ECA*), and Improved Evolutionary Clustering Algorithm Star (iECA*). His team also has designed several multi objective optimization algorithms, such as Multi-Objective Fitness Dependent Optimizer (MOFDO), Multi-objective Learner Performance based Behavior (MOLPB), and Multi-objective Ant Nesting Algorithm (ANA), and Grid Multi-objective Cat Swarm Optimization (GMOCSO).

For Product Safety Concerns and Information please contact our EU
representative GPSR@taylorandfrancis.com
Taylor & Francis Verlag GmbH, Kaufingerstraße 24, 80331 München, Germany

www.ingramcontent.com/pod-product-compliance
Ingram Content Group UK Ltd.
Pitfield, Milton Keynes, MK11 3LW, UK
UKHW022217190926
475702UK00003B/415
9781041106616